Academic Motivation and the Culture of School in Childhood and Adolescence

Academic Motivation and the Culture of School in Childhood and Adolescence ⠶

Cynthia Hudley

University of California, Santa Barbara

Adele Eskeles Gottfried

California State University, Northridge

OXFORD
UNIVERSITY PRESS

2008

OXFORD

UNIVERSITY PRESS

Oxford University Press, Inc., publishes works that further
Oxford University's objective of excellence
in research, scholarship, and education.

Oxford New York
Auckland Cape Town Dar es Salaam Hong Kong Karachi
Kuala Lumpur Madrid Melbourne Mexico City Nairobi
New Delhi Shanghai Taipei Toronto

With offices in
Argentina Austria Brazil Chile Czech Republic France Greece
Guatemala Hungary Italy Japan Poland Portugal Singapore
South Korea Switzerland Thailand Turkey Ukraine Vietnam

Published by Oxford University Press, Inc.
198 Madison Avenue, New York, New York 10016
www.oup.com

Oxford is a registered trademark of Oxford University Press

Library of Congress Cataloging-in-Publication Data
Hudley, Cynthia.
Academic motivation and the culture of school in childhood and adolescence /
Cynthia Hudley, Adele Eskeles Gottfried.
p. cm.—(Child development in cultural context)
Includes bibliographical references and index.
ISBN 978–0–19–532681–9
1. Motivation in education.
2. School environment.
I. Gottfried, Adele Eskeles.
II. Title.
LB1065.H77 2008
370.15'4—dc22   2007044013

9 8 7 6 5 4 3 2 1

Printed in the United States of America
on acid-free paper

This book is dedicated to my husband, James Robert Cook; without his unflagging support and understanding of late hours at work this book would have never been completed.

Cynthia Hudley

This book is dedicated to my husband and colleague, Allen, and to our children Michael and Jeff. They have all helped me to reflect on the significance of academic motivation and its role in learning and performance.

Adele Eskeles Gottfried

PREFACE ⠸

This volume came into being thanks to a long-standing friendship between two women who have shared an enduring interest in children and their motivation to succeed in school and achieve to their full capacity. Our mutual participation at our universities and at convention presentations, as well as an intimate knowledge and respect for each other's research, led us to recognize the need for research on academic motivation to be elaborated to attend to the cultural context of schooling. Our many conversations about motivation, culture, and schooling that have occurred over the years of our friendship, collegiality, and collaboration have led directly to this volume. We are delighted that, with teamwork, we have assembled this substantial contribution to the literature on academic motivation.

We have studied academic achievement motivation in children over several decades, although in different settings. I, Cynthia Hudley, began thinking about and examining achievement motivation as a middle school teacher several decades ago in a public opportunity school for children who were unable to adjust in the regular school setting. The students I encountered there were often academically competent and sometimes excellent but too frequently academically disengaged. A great deal of my time was spent simply getting students to participate in class and complete their work.

Initially, responses such as "I don't want to right now"; "I hate this"; "This is too easy" were difficult to connect to the learning activities in the classroom. Thus, one of my first tasks was to understand the "why" of interactions in the classroom as well as in the school. This need for understanding led me to graduate school and to the literature on achievement motivation long before I became an academic and a contributor to that literature. My interest in the effects of school culture is undoubtedly the result of the contrast between the unique school culture in which I began teaching and the comprehensive, suburban high school that was the final setting for my career teaching in K-12 schools. I was able to see from day to day interactions in settings in which I worked that every school has both a unique character and amazingly similar characteristics that reflect the larger society in which the school is embedded. Most important for this volume, I saw within my first five years of teaching that student behavior and attitudes are reflections of the conditions of the larger society, of students' personal life circumstances, and of the culture of the school. These complex relationships between societal, organizational, and individual factors remain at the forefront of my thinking and my work in academia, keeping me ever mindful of the young people whose life experiences started me down this path.

I, Adele Eskeles Gottfried, became involved in studying academic intrinsic motivation shortly after completing my Ph.D. dissertation in a classic area of children's learning, incidental learning paradigms as related to paired-associate memory. After completing the doctoral research, I was approached by the superintendent of instruction of the school district in which the dissertation study had been completed and asked whether I would like to participate in the district's effort to help their underachieving students. Thus was born my interest in academic intrinsic motivation. I could think of no other factor that would be more important than intrinsic motivation in searching for explanations of underachievement. After reading everything I could about intrinsic motivation over a single summer, I realized that there was no instrument to measure academic intrinsic motivation across subject areas and school in general. Right then I began the development of the Children's Academic Intrinsic Motivation Inventory. After the psychometrics of the instrument were established, it became the grounding for a major research program to understand the motivational foundations of children's learning and performance. Over several decades I have worked with many wonderful colleagues in advancing knowledge on academic intrinsic motivation as related to performance and achievement. It is easy to see how this became my life's work, and this book brings me full circle to the role of intrinsic motivation in academic underachievement, the issue that I originally pondered.

We would like to thank the editors at Oxford for their careful review of this project and for their comments, which helped frame the integrative nature of this volume. Additionally, we thank all the contributors who carefully presented their own research and also addressed the ways their scholarship informs the field of academic motivation in the culture of schooling. We are grateful to them for their time and attention to helping make this volume a reality. We also greatly appreciate the support provided by our respective universities over the years that have enabled us to pursue our scholarship. Finally, we hope that these contributions will stimulate others to further pursue this topic to create educational opportunity and equity to all.

Cynthia Hudley
University of California, Santa Barbara
Adele Eskeles Gottfried
California State University, Northridge

Contents ❖

Contributors ⚞

Elizabeth Cambray-Engstrom
College of Education
University of Illinois at Chicago
1040 West Harrison Street
Chicago, Il 60607-7133
ecambr2@uic.edu

Clayton R. Cook
Graduate School of Education
University of California, Riverside
Riverside, CA 92521
cook2142@yahoo.com

Annette M. Daoud
College of Education
California State University,
    San Marcos
San Marcos, CA 92096
adaoud@csusm.edu

Collette P. Eccleston
Department of Psychology
Syracuse University
Syracuse, New York 13244
cpeccles@syr.edu

John W. Fantuzzo
Graduate School of Education
University of Pennsylvania
3700 Walnut Street—314
Philadelphia, PA 19104
johnf@gse.upenn.edu

Marika Ginsburg-Block
School of Education
University of Delaware
206B Willard Hall Education
    Building
Newark, DE 19716
marika@udel.edu

Courtney J. Golant
College of Education
University of Illinois at
    Chicago
1040 West Harrison Street
Chicago, IL 60607-7133
cgolan2@uic.edu

Adele Eskeles Gottfried
Department of Educational
    Psychology
Center for Teaching and Learning
California State University,
    Northridge
Northridge, CA 91330
adele.gottfried@csun.edu

Allen W. Gottfried
Department of Psychology
California State University,
    Fullerton
Fullerton, CA 92834
agottfried@fullerton.edu

Cynthia Hudley
Gevirtz Graduate School of
    Education
University of California,
    Santa Barbara
Santa Barbara, CA 93106-9490
hudley@education.ucsb.edu

Miles Anthony Irving
Educational Psychology and
    Special Education
Georgia State University
P.O. Box 3979
Atlanta, GA 30303
iam@gsu.edu

Claudia Kouyoumdjian
Gevirtz Graduate School of
    Education
University of California,
    Santa Barbara
Santa Barbara, CA 93106-9490
ckouyoum@education.ucsb.edu

Nancy Lavigne
School of Education
University of Delaware
206C Willard Hall Education
    Building
Newark, DE 19716
nlavigne@udel.edu

Marguerita Lightfoot
Department of Psychiatry
UCLA
10920 Wilshire Boulevard
    Ste. 350
Los Angeles, CA 90024
mal@ucla.edu

Brenda Major
Department of Psychology
University of California,
    Santa Barbara
Santa Barbara, CA 93106-9660
major@psych.ucsb.edu

Phillip E. Morris
Department of Psychology
University of California,
    Davis
Davis, CA 95616
pemorris@ucdavis.edu

Cynthia Rohrbeck
Department of Psychology
George Washington University
2125 G Street NW
Washington DC 20052
Email: rohrbeck@gwu.edu

Laura F. Romo
Gevirtz Graduate School of
    Education
University of California,
    Santa Barbara
Santa Barbara, CA 93106-9490
lromo@education.ucsb.edu

Heather L. Rouse
Graduate School of Education
University of Pennsylvania
3700 Walnut Street
Philadelphia, PA 19104
rouseh@gse.upenn.edu

Theresa A. Thorkildsen
College of Education
University of Illinois at Chicago
1040 West Harrison Street
Chicago, IL, 60607-7133
thork@uic.edu

Kristen Bogner Warzon
Department of Psychology
University of Notre Dame
204 Haggar Hall
Notre Dame, IN 46556
kwarzon@nd.edu

Olga M. Welch
School of Education
Duquesne University
600 Forbes Avenue
Pittsburgh, PA 15282

Kathryn R. Wentzel
Department of Human
    Development
College of Education
University of Maryland
College Park, MD 20742
wentzel@umd.edu

1 ❖

Introduction

Cynthia Hudley and Adele Eskeles Gottfried

Academic motivation and school success in childhood and adolescence are most often realized in organized and regulated social settings (i.e., schools) that have demonstrable social networks and hierarchies of groups. Several decades of research have established important connections among school contexts, social relationships, and academic motivation and achievement (e.g., Juvonen & Wentzel, 1996). However, the overall organizational context and social relations in complex settings such as schools are to some degree the product of norms and expectations that are constructed in the local setting. Taken together, the axiomatic beliefs, norms, and expectations that govern programs, organization, and behavior make up a school's culture. As well, local school culture is also a reflection of the larger society in which a school is embedded. Most important for our discussion, school culture often crystallizes shared understandings of the meaning of learning and therefore influences student motivation and achievement in powerful ways.

The prevailing norms and expectations of a school's culture that are typically evident in the broader cultural milieu as well have often been left invisible in motivational analyses. Rather, motivational research for too many years equated culture with ethnic minority and placed the axiomatic assumptions that framed the study of motivation outside the purview of culture. Motivational research from the mid-twentieth century (e.g., McClelland, 1961; White, 1959), which has had a consequential impact on the succeeding motivational literature, provides an excellent example. This foundational work typically foregrounded individual striving for some particular goal, a model that is clearly based in cultural assumptions about the primacy of individualism and individual achievement. Although McClelland's work acknowledged the influence of cultural beliefs "derived from a particular historical sequence of events in Western Europe" (p. 63), he firmly believed that the construct of individualized success was universal, applicable in any culture at any time or place. Yet today motivational research has clearly demonstrated that the belief in individual achievement is driven by cultural assumptions and expectations that are not shared across all cultures or all subcultures in a pluralistic society (Markus & Kitayama, 1991).

⠃⠃ School Culture and Academic Motivation

Motivational research will be significantly advanced by moving beyond cultural influences at the individual level to produce a richer literature base that attends to the culture of the school and the relationship of school culture to the larger societal culture. American schools (like schools in all countries) are grounded in a variety of culturally bound beliefs and values. Some American values and beliefs that shape our understanding of success, including school success, include individualism, competition, cultural stereotypes of certain student groups, and extrinsically controlled rewards. Further, the cultural assumptions present in schools have powerful yet largely unexamined implications for all children's motivation and adjustment in school, irrespective of a child's individual characteristics. Questions of social contexts, motivation, and achievement have been pursued among a variety of previously understudied groups including ethnic minority children and adolescents, children with special needs, and gifted children. Yet the puzzle of academic underachievement remains insidious and largely unsolved for too many of our students. Understanding the extent to which student motivation accounts for achievement may assist in the solution of that puzzle. Illuminating the role of school culture and the larger cultural milieu in students' motivational processes may be an important step toward that solution.

Research in the past two decades has begun to examine how the complex organizational setting of a school as well as the interpersonal relationships and individual perceptions that transpire within that setting are shaped by often invisible expectations, understandings, and values that are the products of the cultural milieu that surrounds the school (e.g., Salili & Hoosain, 2007). The chapters we have gathered in this edited volume will extend an already substantial understanding of academic motivation by moving beyond important and well-studied cultural, relational, and personal variables to a direct examination of school culture and academic motivation. We consider student motivation across a variety of understudied groups with particular attention to the role of the culture of school in shaping academic motivation. In examining motivation with students of various ethnicities, languages, ages, achievement levels, special needs, and social classes, these chapters explicitly attend to the often invisible workings of cultural processes in American schools for all students.

∷ Organization of the Book

This book is intended to be more than simply an interesting collection of individual chapters. While each chapter will address a particular topic relevant to academic motivation, all of the chapters are expressly included to create a more comprehensive perspective on the multiple dimensions of school culture in the United States. Each of the contributors specifically attends to the culture of the school by examining how and why school culture influences the findings presented in his or her chapter. Further, three clearly defined conceptual questions organize the topical contents of this volume.

Contributors in the first section address change in academic motivation for specific groups of students over time. How do various students adapt to the demands of schooling, and how do students' motivational processes and achievement outcomes change over time and across ages? To answer that question, the chapter authors look longitudinally at students as they transition through school and beyond. This section will attempt to make visible and disentangle the influences on academic motivation that can be attributed to characteristics of the group, to the culture of the school, and to developmental change. Taken together, chapters in this section provide a discussion of changes in motivational processes and achievement outcomes from preschool to adulthood.

The Rouse and Fantuzzo chapter begins our discussion most appropriately in early childhood, when children are just beginning to participate in relatively more formal school structures. The authors present research from a brief longitudinal study of the relationships between competence motivation, socioemotional adjustment, and early literacy and mathematics abilities for a population of urban Head Start children.

Findings focus on concurrent and predictive relationships between preschool competence motivation and multiple developmental competencies with attention to the context of the preschool culture as well as the home culture, which may differ substantially. Further, motivation is examined in concert with other learning constructs to determine its unique contribution to the success of children across the transition to kindergarten, where they must adjust to a substantially different school culture.

Gottfried and colleagues examine motivation from school entry through early adulthood (ages 6 through 24) as they articulate the concept of motivational risk. Students who are motivationally at risk are significantly and consistently disengaged in school from early childhood through adulthood, but the etiology of their disengagement cannot be located in already familiar and empirically defined causes such as economic disadvantage, racial and ethnic discrimination, or inadequate schools. Rather, this chapter presents data on a sample of middle-class, predominantly Anglo children, a population not typically considered to be at risk for school failure. The chapter considers early identification and interventions to maintain academic intrinsic motivation in the context of an extrinsically oriented school culture. As well, the authors discuss possibilities for structuring school culture to increase academic intrinsic motivation and thus decrease motivational risk.

Chapters in the next section address student perceptions of the school and of themselves by considering how students' social cognition influences their motivational processes and outcomes in school. Again, we know that self-perceptions, perceived expectations, perceived opportunities, and perceived peer influences are but some of the social perceptions that can have a profound influence on students' academic motivation. These chapters expand on extant literature as they incorporate the ways in which students' perceptions of the cultural assumptions that surround schooling impact their motivational processes and outcomes. How do students perceive the demands and expectations of the traditional culture of schooling, of home, and of peers, and how do those perceptions shape their academic motivation? Many who study academic motivation or multicultural education have explored the cultural disconnect between home and school; the chapters in this section are unique in explicitly drawing connections to the culture of school. Where appropriate, comparisons are drawn between and within groups to explain how students' perceptions of school culture influence their motivation.

The chapter by Thorkildsen and colleagues examines the structure of one large urban school and the community in which it is situated to understand the influence of perceived school culture on Latino adolescents' motivation. The chapter uses an interdisciplinary notion of culture to ground a discussion of a unique form of school engagement that the authors refer to as moral engagement. The research examines the importance of moral engagement in the context of school by exploring adolescents' beliefs about an ideal school, their life goals, and their participation in academic activities. By drawing together and comparing sociocultural contexts of school, students' cultural belief systems, and students' individual systems of meaning, the authors are able to clearly delineate the intersection of school culture and student motivation and to draw inferences about ways in which the school culture can be constructed to enhance Latino students' motivation and strengthen student retention.

Continuation schools, also referred to as alternative schools, serve our most vulnerable adolescent students but are severely underrepresented in the literature on academic motivation. Students are placed in alternative schools based on failing grades, lack of credits, truancy, severe behavioral problems, and in the case of adolescent girls, pregnancy. Unfortunately, aggregating youth with varying types of academic and behavioral difficulties in alternative schools can adversely affect their academic motivation and school-appropriate behavior because of a concept known as negative "peer contagion" or iatrogenic effects. Romo and colleagues examine peer contagion effects on adolescent girls that result from the unique influences of the alternative high school culture. Their chapter explores the influence of perceived peer attitudes concerning childbearing on adolescents' educational goals and childbearing attitudes to explore how educational aspirations might motivate girls to avoid pregnancy. The data examining the educational goals of low-achieving girls attending an alternative school also include perceived parental attitudes toward early childbearing, allowing the authors to investigate the intersection of the alternative school culture and the home culture on adolescent childbearing attitudes and academic motivation.

A long tradition of research on cultural continuity between home and school has more recently turned to the study of disparities between these socializing contexts as predictors of students' motivation. Much of the research in this relatively new field, which is focused on students from diverse ethnic and socioeconomic backgrounds, has been theoretical or qualitative in nature. Warzon and Ginsburg-Block discuss results and implications from a recent descriptive study of continuity between home and school for culturally based, educationally relevant values and behaviors (e.g., achievement values, motivation orientations, communication preferences, behavioral norms, management styles). They are specifically interested in how the values and norms present in the culture of school are consistent or inconsistent with the values and norms present in the child's home culture and whether continuity in cultural values makes a unique contribution to student motivation. Their research describes the areas of continuity between home and school cultures that are most important in the relationship between family and teacher and students' motivational outcomes.

A positive attitude toward educational success coupled with poor school performance has been described elsewhere as an achievement paradox among African Americans. The Irving chapter discusses this achievement paradox for African American males by exploring the relationship between student attitudes toward the culture of school, academic motivation, and academic achievement. Although students may value educational success, their understanding of racism and racial inequity in schools and communities may cause them to believe that the life benefits of education (i.e., a good job, financial success) will be denied them due to racial discrimination. This lack of trust in the dominant culture, referred to in the literature as cultural mistrust, posits that African Americans' extensive experiences with racism create skepticism toward institutions that reflect the values of the dominant culture. The Irving chapter presents and discusses data that examine the relationship between academic outcome expectations, academic outcome value, and cultural mistrust among African American male high school students.

Eccleston and Major discuss school culture as a contributor to stigmatizing students. Stigmatized individuals are believed to possess characteristics that convey a social identity that is devalued in a particular social context. Within the academic context, many ethnic minority groups and those of low socioeconomic status are stigmatized as having less academic ability than members of other groups. These negative group stereotypes are so widely present in academic settings as to create a culture of schooling that is hostile to the motivation and consequently the achievement of students who belong to these stigmatized groups. Drawing from expectancy/value theories of motivation, the authors first review theoretical and empirical evidence demonstrating that membership in a stigmatized group affects expectations and valuing of success and then explore how these theories and findings apply to academic motivation in particular. The authors then turn to a discussion of factors in the school culture that can support motivation among members of groups stigmatized by the larger cultural milieu. A school culture can construct social and organizational cues demonstrating that stigmatized individuals may succeed despite generally unfavorable larger cultural stereotypes. More important, even subtle cues can influence the behavior of stigmatized individuals in ways that may not only enhance individual motivation but also produce reciprocal changes in the academic culture.

The Hudley and Daoud chapter discusses two features of school culture that relate to student engagement: perceived teacher support and cultural compatibility. How students engage or participate in school has a great deal to do with their school experiences and outcomes, and the institutional culture of school is one important determinant of student engagement. Thus student engagement and school culture are in a continuing transactional relationship. We examine ethnic differences in the relationship between perceived school culture and engagement, given the troubling reality that teachers' views of students differ according to student ethnicity. American cultural values (individualism, competition, materialism, personal achievement) that typically guide the culture of schooling dictate specific desirable qualities for students, but such qualities may not always be compatible with students' cultural understandings. Students who do not fit a socially constructed ideal may perceive bias in the reactions they experience at school, and perceived bias may reciprocally influence student engagement. The chapter reviews literature on engagement and student perceptions of school climate, presents empirical data pertaining to students' perceptions of school climate and student engagement, and concludes with implications of these findings for school organization and teacher preparation.

Chapters in the next section describe what has been done to enhance academic motivation. Authors present empirically validated intervention programs that have been shown to improve academic motivation in students from elementary school through high school. Although there is a relative wealth of research on motivational processes and the consequences of particular motivational profiles, there is a relative paucity of empirical work on intervention programs for students at risk for poor school outcomes due to motivational problems. What are the relevant motivators for students; how does the culture of school deploy or constrain those motivators; and how can intervention programs consciously transmit culturally scripted strategies for academic success? The chapters in this section answer these and other questions in the context of describing intervention programs that have served students who are not succeeding to the full extent of their potential. Although academic intervention programs have proliferated over the years and several have rigorously documented gains in achievement, little research on these programs addresses their motivational consequences. The chapters in this section make a substantial contribution to a sparse literature.

Welch discusses a nine-year longitudinal study designed to explore how educationally disadvantaged African American adolescents with the potential to attend college began to define themselves as "scholars." The study examined Project EXCEL (Encouraging Excellence in Children Extends Learning), an intervention that served juniors (first cohort) and sophomores (second and third cohorts) who self-identified and were identified by teachers and guidance counselors as college bound. The program served students in inner-city schools with a culture that tended to promote athletic accomplishments (e.g., perennial successes of football and/or boys' basketball teams) rather than academic excellence. The intervention was grounded in the premise that a scholar identity required more than an academically enriched curriculum to assist marginalized students achieve to their full capacity. In addition, the EXCEL program helped students address prevailing cultural stereotypes by developing a critical understanding of the culture of the school and of the larger society. The research presented here examines both the development of the scholar identity and the effect of that identity on students' motivation to achieve academically.

Our second intervention study explores the influence of culture on academic motivation through an examination of peer-assisted learning (PAL). Socialization experiences with peers have a powerful influence on student academic achievement and motivation. When peer interactions, such as those encouraged by PAL strategies, provide students with positive messages about academic accomplishments, students may be more likely to accept the values of the school and pursue academic tasks and goals. Peer socialization for achievement is particularly important for high-risk children who may be receiving conflicting messages from home, school, and peers about the value of schooling. In addition to creating social motivation for achievement, the success of PAL methods has also been attributed to the continuity that PAL creates between the culture of the school and the child's home culture. Ginsburg-Block and colleagues review the theoretical and empirical evidence on PAL's effectiveness in socializing students into the culture and values of the school and enhancing motivation among youth from diverse racial, ethnic, and social class backgrounds. The review will examine research linking the properties typical of PAL that also reflect the unique values of American schools, such as opportunities for autonomy and self-regulated learning, to student achievement and motivation outcomes. The authors also include the results of a meta-analysis of experimental studies examining the effects of PAL interventions on motivation among elementary school students and discuss implications for intervention and future research.

The final section of this volume presents three unique perspectives on this work. Each of the co-editors has contributed a chapter of synthesis, analysis, and reflection that represents her individual thinking on the contents of this volume. Hudley's chapter concentrates on the themes that emerge across chapters, beginning with an examination of the individual sections of the volume and moving to a consideration of the themes that characterize the volume as a whole. Gottfried turns her attention to an examination of the common threads visible in the findings presented in this volume. Her perspective cuts across sections to examine convergence in results and conclusions both among chapters and across the entire volume. Both chapters conclude with discussions of future directions in research and intervention strategies relevant to the culture of schooling that might build on the findings from this volume and ultimately inform both theory and practice. Finally, we present a commentary chapter by Wentzel, a noted scholar in the field of academic motivation. This commentary assesses the relevance of the work presented to the extant body of research literature on achievement motivation.

In conclusion, rather than presenting a cross-national approach all of the chapters pay explicit attention to the influence of school culture on student academic motivation in U.S. populations. Each chapter explores within-group variability as opposed to making comparisons among ethnically or nationally defined groups of students. This focus will advance research and theory on academic motivation by clarifying the ways in which an often invisible school culture can impact student motivation and achievement.

⁜ References

Juvonen, J., & Wentzel, K. (Eds.). (1996). *Social motivation: Understanding children's school adjustment.* New York: Cambridge University Press.

Markus, H., & Kitayama, S. (1991). Culture and the self: Implications for cognition, emotion, and motivation. *Psychological Review, 98,* 224–253.

McClelland, D. (1961). *The achieving society.* Oxford, England: Van Nostrand.

Salili, F., & Hoosain, R. (Eds.). (2007). *Culture, motivation and learning: A multicultural perspective.* New York: Information Age.

White, R. (1959). Motivation reconsidered: The concept of competence. *Psychological Review, 66,* 297–333.

PART 1 ⠿

Examining Motivation Over Time

2 ▪▪

Competence Motivation in Head Start

An Early Childhood Link to Learning

Heather L. Rouse and John W. Fantuzzo

Significant achievement gaps for minority and low-income students have shown little change over the past two decades despite considerable increases in spending for public education (National Center for Education Statistics [NCES], 2007; Stipek & Hakuta, 2007). National recognition of these persistent achievement gaps has resulted in federally mandated improvements in public education. No Child Left Behind (NCLB) represents major federal legislation to ensure that public school systems are accountable for children's meeting minimal reading proficiency standards by third grade (U.S. Department of Education, 2002). This legislation also calls for public school systems to use scientifically based evidence to inform classroom intervention. With proficiency targets set at third grade and evidence-based methods required, NCLB underscores the significance of early childhood research to support the development of critical school readiness competencies especially for young, low-income, minority children who are disproportionately at risk for academic failure.

Early childhood educators and researchers have criticized NCLB legislation for its exclusive emphasis on reading achievement (Hodgkinson, 2003; Kafer, 2004). They have raised concerns about the developmental appropriateness of focusing assessment and instruction on only one skill at the expense of other important early childhood competencies (Stipek, 2005). Developmental science has identified school readiness as a rich multidimensional concept that includes diverse cognitive, social, and physical skills sets related to academic success

(Pianta, Cox, & Snow, 2007; National Association for the Education of Young Children [NAEYC], 1996). Critics of NCLB fear that mandated accountability standards for reading will restrict preschool education to an undue emphasis on reading that neglects other essential components of school readiness (Raver & Zigler, 2004). This tension between mandates and developmental science enhances the need for rigorous, applied developmental research that demonstrates the relationship between multiple sets of classroom competencies and later school success (Knitzer 2003; Raver & Knitzer, 2002).

A developmental-ecological model provides a useful theoretical framework in which to examine early childhood research. Person, context, process, and time are the major defining properties of this model for understanding child development (Bronfenbrenner, 2005; Cicchetti & Toth, 1997). *Person* comprises child competencies in multiple areas of functioning (social, emotional, physical, language, and cognitive) that a child requires for mastering challenges at each stage of development. *Context* refers to the multiple systems in the child's environment that influence the development of these multiple competencies. The early childhood classroom is an important proximal system designed to foster competence in both academic motivation and academic achievement. This context intentionally requires children to use all their abilities across domains of functioning to acquire skills that are necessary for early school success. *Process* is defined by the transactions between a child's current competencies and multiple contextual demands. These transactions over *time* influence the course of a child's development (Cicchetti & Toth, 1997). Children with successful experiences in the preschool classroom develop stronger sets of competencies that facilitate their successful transition into the primary grades. Because the classroom demands increase as the child transitions from preschool to elementary school, students are required to build on current competencies to develop more complex sets of skills (Pianta, Kraft-Sayre, Rimm-Kaufman, Gercke, & Higgins, 2001). Research that identifies these important preschool competencies can inform strategic interventions to improve student achievement.

The National Education Goals Panel 2000 identified five key sets of child competencies for school success that correspond to developmental-ecological theory: cognitive, language and literacy, social-emotional, physical, and approaches to learning (Kagan, Moore, & Bredekamp, 1995). The construct of approaches to learning has been recognized as the most important, yet least researched child competence that is important for early school success (Barnett, Bauer, Ehrhardt, Lentz, & Stollar, 1996; Bredekamp & Copple, 1997). A variety of research focuses have been associated with learning-related concepts, including effectiveness motivation (Stott & Albin, 1975), achievement goals (Ames & Archer, 1988), attributional styles (Bandura, 1989; Wentzel, 1991), and temperament or disposition (Thomas & Chess, 1977). It is accepted that approaches to learning represent a complex multidimensional construct, but there has been scant empirical work focused on multidimensionality. Much of the existing research has focused on individual aspects of approaches to learning and their individual relations to academic achievement. A multidimensional approach may better serve to advance our understanding of the distinctiveness of learning-related concepts and the overlap among the different concepts within the larger approaches to learning construct.

Further, many of these unidimensional concepts are not readily observable in the preschool classroom and therefore are not as easy to target in classroom-based interventions for young children. Unobservable concepts (e.g., cognitive style, goal orientation, effectiveness motivation) are typically derived from observer inferences about children's internal, psychological processes (McDermott, 1999). Intrinsic motivation, for example, has been studied through child self-report or teacher inferences about children's internal preferences and motivational states (Gottfried, 1990; Harter, 1981). Other techniques for assessing these concepts include extensive individually administered assessments or experimental procedures that are not readily applied outside of a controlled research context (Barrett & Depinet, 1991) and may not be appropriate for early childhood. We also lack consistent evidence of the mutability of these concepts in early childhood and the degree to which they could be addressed in preschool curricula. To implement change in early childhood education classrooms, applied research must comprehensively identify observable and mutable classroom-based competencies that are related to academic achievement.

McDermott and colleagues have intentionally conducted programmatic research on approaches to learning for application within the regular elementary school classroom (McDermott, Green, Francis, & Stott, 1999). Nationally representative studies with school-age children have found four distinct, observable dimensions of approaches to learning behaviors: competence motivation, attention/persistence, strategy/flexibility, and attitude toward learning (McDermott, Leigh, & Perry, 2002). *Competence motivation* reflects behaviors indicating children's curiosity, initiative, and motivation to understand and succeed in learning activities. *Attention/persistence* refers to a child's ability to attend to relevant stimuli and persevere with difficult tasks. *Strategy/flexibility* represents the way a child approaches tasks and solves problems that arise within the learning context. *Attitude toward learning* characterizes a child's general demeanor in learning activities and the quality of the interactions with peers and adults during those learning activities.

Programmatic research with these dimensions has tested the unique contribution of each learning behavior to academic achievement for school-age students. Findings indicated that these dimensions of approaches to learning were empirically distinct from general intelligence (McDermott, 1984). A second set of findings documented the predictive validity of learning behavior dimensions for ethnic minority and low-income groups (Schafer, 1996). This research found strong reliability and predictive power for these dimensions and no socioeconomic or ethnic bias (Schaefer & McDermott, 1999; Worrell, Vandiver, & Watkins, 2001). Finally, epidemiological studies have demonstrated that adequate learning behaviors provide a substantial buffer for elementary and secondary school students who are at risk for academic failure and social maladjustment, and this buffering effect is greater than that afforded by higher levels of cognitive ability (Grim, Tighe, & McDermott, 2001; McDermott & Beitman, 1984).

Researchers at the University of Pennsylvania have extended this multidimensional work with school-age children with a programmatic line of research to examine approaches to learning behaviors for young children in preschool environments. This chapter focuses on findings from a series of studies that have explored competence motivation, one dimension of learning behaviors. We explore the significance of this construct to inform school readiness interventions for low-income, urban preschool children. Three sets of studies are reviewed that investigate the (1) construct validity of competence motivation in preschool, (2) associations between competence motivation and social-emotional and cognitive school readiness competencies, (3) relationship of competence motivation to school readiness indicators in the context of other constructs of preschool competence, and (4) longitudinal contribution of preschool competence motivation to reading and mathematics achievement at kindergarten and first grade entry.

∷ Competence Motivation Within the Multidimensional Construct of Approaches to Learning

Our research initially took the observable, classroom behaviors representing competence motivation, attention/persistence, and attitude toward learning for school-age children and adapted them for preschool classrooms. Master early childhood teachers worked with our research team to identify observable behaviors that were typical for routine, preschool classroom situations (e.g., large and small group, hands-on and free choice activities) and reflected our constructs of interest. These efforts resulted in a preschool classroom teacher rating scale of observable learning behaviors (Preschool Learning Behaviors Scale [PLBS]; McDermott, Green, Francis, & Stott, 2000).

We next conducted a national validation study of this teacher rating scale with a stratified, random sample of preschool-age children (McDermott, Leigh, & Perry, 2002). Common factor analyses revealed three reliable and valid dimensions of learning behaviors for preschool children: competence motivation, attention/persistence, and attitude toward learning. *Competence motivation* represented attitudes and behaviors that connect children to classroom learning opportunities. These included initiation of activities, eagerness to try new activities, actively seeking answers and solutions to problems, and confidence in approaching difficult activities. The *attention/persistence* dimension was related to sustained attention to instruction and perseverance with difficult tasks. *Attitude toward learning* comprised preschool children's general demeanor in learning activities, emotional responses to support and correction, and the quality of interactions with peers and adults during those learning activities. Together, these three preschool learning behavior dimensions explained a significant amount of unique variance that is distinct from cognitive ability. Empirical tests of this overlapping variance revealed that only 10.2% of learning behavior variability was shared by cognitive ability, indicating a substantial amount of variance that was not directly attributable to general cognitive ability (McDermott, Leigh, & Perry, 2002).

A second validation study investigated the fit of these empirically defined dimensions for low-income, preschool children in a large, urban public school context (Fantuzzo, Perry, & McDermott, 2004). Exploratory common factor analyses replicated the same three dimensions of learning behavior found in the national validation study. Competence motivation, attention/persistence, and attitude toward learning dimensions were further affirmed through cross-validation and confirmatory analyses. These constructs were congruent across gender and ethnic groups. Relative to the other dimensions, competence motivation represented the largest amount of unique variance contributing to the overall, multivariate construct of approaches to learning behavior as well as the least amount of error variance. The variability shared across all three dimensions was 49%. The unique variability for competence motivation was found to be 42%, compared to 18% for attention and 35% for attitude toward learning dimensions. Error variance, on the other hand, was found to be 15% for competence motivation, followed by 17% for attention and 25% for attitude toward learning.

▓ Competence Motivation and Concurrent School Readiness Competencies

Four comprehensive studies with low-income preschool children examined the unique relationships between competence motivation and other school readiness competencies in the context of other learning behavior dimensions. Competence motivation was related to specific sets of social-emotional and cognitive competencies when controlling for other preschool learning behaviors.

Social-Emotional Competencies

The first group of research findings highlights the concurrent relationships between competence motivation and social-emotional skills in the preschool classroom. Two studies demonstrated an inverse relationship between competence motivation and disengaged, disconnected classroom peer play interactions (Coolahan, Fantuzzo, Mendez, & McDermott, 2000; Fantuzzo et al., 2004). Coolahan and colleagues (2000) found that compared to the other learning behaviors, children evidencing low competence motivation were hesitant to join peer activities, took less initiative in play activities, and were less likely to participate in cooperative, interactive peer play activities in the classroom. In a subsequent study that confirmed these findings with low-income, minority preschool children, Fantuzzo et al. (2004) demonstrated that classroom competence motivation was related to disconnected, disengaged peer play behaviors in the classroom as well as in the home-neighborhood contexts.

A second finding from this collection of research indicated that competence motivation was significantly related to verbal assertiveness in prosocial peer interactions in the preschool classroom (McDermott, Leigh, & Perry, 2002). Teacher observations indicated that children demonstrating competence motivation behaviors in the classroom were more likely to initiate verbal interactions with peers and adults and verbally assert their ideas, interests, and concerns across multiple experiences. On the other hand, attention and attitude toward learning dimensions were more strongly related to self-control but more weakly related to verbal assertiveness.

A third concurrent relationship was found between preschool competence motivation and classroom observations of self-directed behavior for low-income, urban children (Fantuzzo et al., 2004). An observational measure of classroom self-regulation was used to capture two constructs: emotion regulation and autonomy (California Child Q-Set; CCQ; Block & Block, 1980). Autonomy was characterized by initiative, agency, choice, and self-determination whereas emotion regulation was defined by reactivity, flexibility, and modulation of emotions. These constructs were used to investigate the canonical relationships with competence motivation, attention/persistence, and attitude toward learning. Compared to the other dimensions of learning, competence motivation had the strongest relationship to observed classroom autonomy. As well, bi-multivariate analyses revealed two distinct sets of behaviors defined as *independent learner* and *attentive regulated*. Competence motivation and autonomy were the significant contributors to the independent learner set of behaviors. attention/persistence, attitude, and emotion regulation comprised the attentive regulated set of behaviors. Competence motivation was uniquely related to creative, generative, engaged, and initiative behaviors that serve to connect the child with learning opportunities. Attitude toward learning and attention/persistence were related to regulatory behaviors that modulate emotional responses to classroom activities, inhibit impulsive actions, and minimize interpersonal conflict with peers and adults in the preschool classroom. These findings provide support for the distinction between the three dimensions of approaches to learning behaviors.

Cognitive Competencies

The unique, concurrent relationship between competence motivation and school readiness skills in the context of other learning behaviors has been examined in three empirical studies. The first study demonstrated that competence motivation was most related to a measure of spatial/nonverbal cognitive ability relative to the other learning behavior dimensions (McDermott, Leigh, & Perry, 2002). Characteristics of this indicator of cognitive ability included executive functioning, spatial reasoning, and general problem-solving capabilities.

Rouse and Fantuzzo (2004) conducted a concurrent multivariate examination of competence motivation in the context of other learning behaviors and nationally standardized measures of mathematics and reading achievement for low-income, urban preschool children. Hierarchical regression analyses were used to determine the relations between competence motivation and preschool achievement outcomes, controlling for other dimensions of learning behavior. Competence motivation and mathematics achievement demonstrated a stronger relationship than the relationship between competence motivation and reading achievement. This study was the first to demonstrate that competence motivation evidenced the strongest relationships with achievement outcomes when compared to attention and attitude dimensions. Subsequently, another large, representative study of Head Start learning behaviors demonstrated concurrent relationships between competence motivation and mathematics, alphabetic knowledge, vocabulary, and listening comprehension (Axelrod, Fantuzzo, & Warley, 2007). Competence motivation again showed the strongest relationships with all four outcomes.

∷ Competence Motivation and Other Multivariate Competencies Related to School Readiness

The next set of studies examined relationships between school readiness and competence motivation in the context of other learning behaviors, social-emotional competencies, and cognitive abilities. This research used higher order investigations to determine whether there were latent structures of competence within the multidimensional set that included learning behaviors, social-emotional characteristics, and cognitive skills. The primary criterion variable selected for these studies was a standardized measure of school readiness, the ESI-K (Meisels, Marsden, Wiske, & Henderson, 1997). This indicator measured child competence across major developmental areas including speech, language, cognition, perception, and fine and gross motor coordination. Predictive validity studies have demonstrated that children classified at risk for poor school achievement by this measure are most likely to experience early school failure in the absence of appropriate early intervention (Meisels et al., 1997).

The first higher order study demonstrated the distinctiveness of preschool competence motivation and other learning behaviors when considered simultaneously with a large set of cognitive and social-emotional competencies for low-income, preschool children (McWayne, Fantuzzo, & McDermott, 2004). Higher order factor analysis revealed three latent dimensions of competence: general classroom competency (GCC), interpersonal behavior problems (IBP), and specific approaches to learning (SAL). General classroom competency comprised skills associated with cognitive ability, social engagement and peer interaction, and movement/coordination in regular preschool classroom situations. Interpersonal behavior problems included negative attitude, play disruption, and play disconnection behaviors. Specific approaches to learning was uniquely comprised of each of the three learning behavior dimensions: competence motivation, attention, and attitude. General classroom competency and specific approaches to learning were significantly related to our measure of school readiness at the end of preschool (Meisels et al., 1997). However, specific approaches to learning explained a greater amount of the variance in this outcome than general classroom competency. This study documented the unique contribution of specific approaches to learning, including competence motivation, to school readiness. Controlling for general classroom competency and behavior problems, specific approaches to learning demonstrated the strongest relationships to our measure of school readiness.

The second higher order investigation documented two psychologically meaningful latent dimensions among approaches to learning and classroom emotional and behavioral problems: academically disengaged behavior and regulated behavior (Fantuzzo et al., 2007). Low competence motivation contributed the most variance to the academically disengaged behavior dimension, followed by withdrawn and socially reticent behaviors. Regulated behavior included difficulties with attention and attitude, and aggressive and inattentive-hyperactive behavioral problems. This finding highlights the unique characteristic of competence motivation, as it was the only learning behavior dimension that related to academic disengagement. Further analyses revealed that compared to regulated behavior, academically disengaged behavior was consistently associated with all readiness outcomes measured and explained a greater amount of variance than regulated behavior across these outcomes. Children who were at least 1.5 standard deviations above the mean on academically disengaged behavior were nearly 10 times more likely to be classified at risk for poor outcomes according to the ESI-K. Academically disengaged behavior was also related to mathematics achievement, general cognitive skills, movement/coordination skills, and social engagement at the end of preschool.

⁚ Preschool Competence Motivation and the Transition to Elementary School

It is evident from these concurrent findings that specific approaches to learning behaviors, including competence motivation, are consistently related to indicators of school readiness for low-income preschool children. It is also clear from the developmental literature that the transition between preschool and kindergarten is a critical time, particularly for vulnerable children who are at risk for early academic difficulties (Pianta, Cox, & Snow, 2007). Person-centered empirical approaches are increasingly being used in conjunction with variable-centered methods to provide a different perspective for understanding child competencies across the preschool-to-kindergarten transition (Konold, Glutting, McDermott, Kush, & Watkins, 1999). Person-centered approaches capture the within-child variation in behavior patterns by determining competency profiles across multiple sets of skills within the child (Stattin & Magnusson, 1996). A profile comprises variations in high and low ability across different behaviors within the set. Variable-centered analyses complement this profile approach by providing the kinds of construct-specific data that were presented above in the concurrent findings. Together, these approaches to analysis provide a comprehensive picture of the multidimensional relationships between competencies within the child and between groups of children.

These two approaches were used in two longitudinal studies to examine the relationships between preschool competence motivation and later school success. Angelo (2006) used a person-centered approach to examine profiles of children's learning behaviors at the beginning of Head Start. The resulting profiles were then examined to determine how different patterns of competency related to overall proficiency gains across one year of preschool. Competence motivation, attention/persistence, and attitude toward learning were used to statistically group children displaying similar patterns of behavior. Six unique profiles were found, varying in competency levels across these three dimensions. The profile distinguished by high competence motivation was related to the greatest increases in overall school readiness from the beginning to the end of preschool. Competence motivation early in the preschool year was found to predict greater gains in general cognitive skills associated with early literacy, math concepts, and fine and gross motor skills by the end of the year.

Another longitudinal investigation of competence motivation within the multidimensional learning behavior context used variable-centered analyses to examine these multivariate relationships. Rouse and Fantuzzo (2004) used a representative sample of preschool children attending Head Start in a large, urban center to examine the relationships between preschool learning behaviors and school success at kindergarten and entry into first grade. Preschool competence motivation was related to nationally standardized reading and mathematics achievement scores at kindergarten and first grade entry. Assessments of alphabetic awareness, reading conventions, reading comprehension, and mathematics ability were also used at two time points to determine the relative magnitude of preschool competence motivation associations with achievement across this critical transition. Competence motivation was the only dimension to demonstrate significance across all outcomes. Hierarchical multiple regression analyses also revealed that preschool learning behaviors, including competence motivation, predicted more of the variance in outcomes at first grade entry than variance in the same outcomes at kindergarten entry. This finding underscores the developmental importance of competence motivation by highlighting an increase in the magnitude of variance explained between kindergarten and first grade. Children who demonstrated strong competence motivation in early childhood had greater achievement across one year of preschool and continued to surpass their peers with lower competence motivation in reading and math achievement in both kindergarten and first grade. This study provided the first empirical, multivariate examination of these longitudinal relationships for this population. It further provided the first examination of preschool learning behaviors related to the two most critical policy relevant outcomes in kindergarten and first grade, that is, reading and mathematics achievement.

:: Discussion

Research findings presented in this chapter demonstrate how competence motivation, in the context of other learning behaviors, is related
to other school readiness competencies and predicts later academic
achievement. Competence motivation emerged empirically as a distinct
dimension of approaches to learning behaviors, along with attention/
persistence and attitude toward learning dimensions. Children with
high scores on classroom competence motivation initiated more independent learning, excelled at problem solving, were more actively engaged in productive classroom activities with peers and teachers, and
evidenced greater reading and mathematics achievement. This chapter
provides evidence for the relative strength of competence motivation as
it relates specifically to academic achievement.

The relationship between competence motivation and academic
achievement outcomes was also demonstrated to have a progressive impact over time. Longitudinal studies found that preschool competence
motivation was related to greater reading and mathematics achievement in kindergarten and first grade. Children with higher levels of
competence motivation evidenced achievement benefits in preschool,
and these benefits continued to improve academic achievement in elementary school. These findings suggest that competence motivation
skills become progressively more important as the classroom demands
increase throughout elementary school. This programmatic line of research with preschool competence motivation has demonstrated its
importance for academic achievement, and its potential for intervention. Children with higher scores on attention/persistence and attitude
toward learning dimensions, on the other hand, demonstrated greater
self-regulation behaviors that facilitated their management of social
situations and regulation of emotional frustration with difficult activities. These dimensions appear more related to the prevention of
social-emotional and behavior problems in the classroom, compared to
competence motivation.

Theoretical Relevance of Classroom Culture

Using a developmental-ecological framework, this research underscores
the importance of identifying age-salient competencies and examining
their interaction with the classroom context over time. These findings
concur with previous research demonstrating that preschool children

who exhibit self-initiated learning behaviors also evidence greater independence, higher expectations, and better achievement outcomes than children without such behaviors (Stipek, 1996). This line of research also supports developmental theories that characterize the preschool period as a time of child-initiated discovery (see Erikson, 1984; Piaget, 1969; Vygotsky, 1990). As such, they call attention to the need to provide preschool children with diverse opportunities to explore and manipulate their environment with peers.

The culture of early childhood education reflects these theoretical preferences for independence and autonomy in preschool by endorsing initiation and exploration through classroom activities. Preschool classrooms judged to be of high quality are designed intentionally to provide opportunities for the development of independent learning skills such as choice, initiation, and problem solving, often by providing multiple activity centers that encourage children to interact in new and creative ways. Children who actively initiate and engage in these activities with others increasingly develop multiple competencies that equip them for success in the prevailing culture of kindergarten through 12th grade (K-12) schooling that also endorses independence and autonomy. Children who are not able to fully adjust to the typical American preschool classroom culture will be less prepared to meet similar expectations in elementary school, where the academic demands also increase substantially.

Transactions between competence motivation and school contexts over time are reflected in the finding that preschool competence motivation increases in importance to academic achievement as children transition to elementary school. Our research demonstrates that children who effectively meet culturally determined classroom demands to develop competence motivation in preschool demonstrate greater achievement outcomes in kindergarten and first grade. Previous research supports this progressive theory of preschool motivation and academic achievement in elementary school. Wentzel (1999), for example, emphasizes the relationship between classroom-based goals for social acceptance and task mastery as they influence achievement motivation. Preschool children's motivation to engage and succeed in the preschool culture is influenced by prior experiences of self-initiation and sustained collaboration activities with peers. These successful experiences lead to increased motivation for participation and success with classroom activities, and child motivation, in turn, impacts future academic success (Wentzel & Watkins, 2002). Over time these interactions are mutually reinforcing, creating a progressive influence on academic achievement. Dweck and colleagues have also theorized a particular model of motivation by defining it as an orientation toward mastery with a focus on improvement over time (Grant & Dweck, 2003). This framework asserts that independent, mastery-oriented approaches that emphasize self-improvement are related to sustained motivation and higher achievement in the face of challenge (Molden & Dweck, 2006). Our research supports these theories by demonstrating the unique, progressive impact of preschool competence motivation on academic achievement in elementary school.

Practical Implications

Enhancing approaches to learning for young children is a national priority for public education (U.S. Department of Education, 2000). Findings presented in this chapter underscore the need for students to develop self-initiated learning competencies in preschool that equip them to succeed in the prevailing culture of schooling. Empirically based strategies must be developed to teach important behaviors to students who are not adequately adapting to the culture of the preschool classroom. Our findings can be used to inform the development of preschool curricula that integrate competence motivation instruction into existing academic-based instructional practices for reading and mathematics. Competence motivation behaviors such as initiation, risk taking, and strategic problem solving that are significantly related to subsequent cognitive and achievement outcomes can be reliably observed, supported, and encouraged in the preschool classroom.

Research with school-age children has provided a model for intentionally incorporating learning behaviors into educational curriculum (Glutting, 1986; McDermott & Watkins, 1987; Stott, 1978). First, large populations of children were sampled to collect teacher observations of student learning behavior across the empirically validated dimensions. Second, advanced statistical techniques were used to identify subsets of behaviors within each dimension to inform the scope of the curriculum. Third, master teachers were recruited to expand the list of behaviors within each set. This expanded set was used to develop a hierarchy of behaviors based on levels of difficulty. This hierarchy was then used to create specific curricular objectives for each developmental level (McDermott & Watkins, 1987). In a final step, these behavioral objectives were used to create intentional, classroom learning experiences.

Curriculum was designed to fit the multiple levels in the behavioral hierarchy. Research based on this curriculum has demonstrated that competence motivation, and other approaches to learning behaviors, can be altered by creating intentional classroom learning experiences focusing on a developmental progression of behavioral objectives (Barnett et al., 1996; Engelmann, Granzin, & Severson, 1979; Stott, 1978).

Research is currently under way using this model to develop a scope and sequence for a preschool learning behavior curriculum. The U.S. Department of Health and Human Services sponsored a large-scale longitudinal project to provide empirical evidence for this scope and sequence (McDermott & Fantuzzo, 2000). Following the steps used in the model with school-age children, this project has identified nine distinct behavioral sets across competence motivation, attention/persistence, and attitude toward learning dimensions (McDermott, Menaker, Steinberg, & Angelo, 2002). These behavioral sets are organized into two categories of curriculum modules: *Competence motivation* and *learning strategies*. Competence motivation modules included expression of interest/choice, curiosity/exploration, and control of attention. Learning strategies included trial-and-error approaches to difficult new tasks (multiple trials and multiple approaches), adaptive responses to frustration, giving and receiving help, and cooperative group learning with peers.

The next step in this inquiry process involved working with master preschool teachers to determine a developmental hierarchy of behaviors within each curriculum module. This work has informed the development of a scope and sequence for preschool curriculum, *Learning Links*, that is currently under investigation through another large, nationally funded project (Fantuzzo, Gadsden, & McDermott, 2003). This project is testing the efficacy of this curriculum and integrating behavioral objectives with reading and mathematics instruction for preschool children.

∷ Conclusions

National accountability mandates require early childhood educators to provide high-quality, evidence-based curricula to improve learning outcomes for vulnerable children (U.S. DOE, 2002). Applied developmental research findings from this chapter underscore the significance of identifying important preschool learning-related behaviors such as competence motivation to inform such curriculum. In collaboration with teachers and parents, our research team developed and validated a reporting mechanism to identify unique dimensions of learning behaviors (PLBS; McDermott et al., 2000). After documenting the construct validity of competence motivation for diverse populations of preschool children (McDermott et al., 2002), we empirically examined the relationships between competence motivation, other approaches to learning behaviors, and academic success across multiple years of schooling (Angelo, 2006; Fantuzzo et al., 2004; McWayne et al., 2004; Rouse & Fantuzzo, 2004). Current research incorporating competence motivation and learning strategies into preschool curriculum objectives will determine the validity of an empirically based instructional approach for low-income and minority children at risk for early academic achievement difficulties.

Classroom instruction to teach and reinforce learning behaviors for low-income children is an important component of a comprehensive system to promote educational well-being for all children. Programmatic research presented in this chapter reflects an applied developmental perspective that is focused on vulnerable populations to enhance educational outcomes. These findings inform current strategies for the developmentally appropriate implementation of No Child Left Behind legislation for preschool age children. Preschool competence motivation is an important set of behaviors that should be included in early childhood curriculum to improve academic achievement. We now face the challenge of using this evidence to enhance public education for diverse populations of low-income preschool children.

:: References

Ames, C., & Archer, J. (1988). Achievement goals in the classroom: Students' learning strategies and motivational processes. *Journal of Educational Psychology, 80,* 260–267.

Angelo, L. E. (2006). Child-centered examination of preschool learning behavior: A typological investigation (doctoral dissertation, University of Pennsylvania, 2006). *Dissertation Abstracts International, 67,* 2456.

Axelrod, C., Fantuzzo, J., & Warley, H. (2007). The value of learning to learn: The relationship between learning behaviors and academic achievement in urban Head Start children. Unpublished thesis, University of Pennsylvania, Philadelphia.

Bandura, A. (1989). Self-regulation of motivation and action through internal standards and goal systems. In L. A. Pervin (Ed.) *Goal concepts in personality and social psychology* (pp. 19–85). Hillsdale, NJ, England: Lawrence Erlbaum Associates Inc.

Barnett, D. W., Bauer, A. M., Ehrhardt, K. E., Lentz, F. E., & Stollar, S. A. (1996). Keystone targets for changes: Planning for widespread positive consequences. *School Psychology Quarterly, 11,* 95–117.

Barrett, G. V., & Depinet, R. L. (1991). A reconsideration of testing for competence rather than for intelligence. *American Psychologist, 46,* 1012–1024.

Bredekamp, S., & Copple, C. (Eds.) (1997). *Developmentally appropriate practice in early childhood programs.* Washington DC: National Association for the Education of Young Children.

Bronfenbrenner, U. (2005). *Making human beings human: Bioecological Perspectives on human development.* Thousand Oaks, CA: Sage.

Block, J. H., & Block, J. (1980). The California Child Q-Set. Palo Alto, Calif.: Consulting Psychologists.

Cicchetti, D., & Toth, S. L. (1997). Transactional ecological systems in developmental psychopathology. In S. S. Luthar, J. A. Burack, D. Cicchetti, & J. R. Weisz (Eds.), *Developmental psychopathology: Perspectives on adjustment, risk, and disorder* (pp. 317–349). New York, NY: Cambridge University Press.

Coolahan, K., Fantuzzo, J. W., Mendez, J., & McDermott, P. (2000). Preschool peer interactions and readiness to learn: Relationships between classroom peer play and learning behaviors and conduct. *Journal of Educational Psychology, 92,* 458–465.

Engelmann, S., Granzin, A., & Severson, H. (1979). Diagnosing instruction. *The Journal of Special Education, 13,* 355–363.

Erikson, E. H. (1984). Reflections on the last stage—and the first. *Psychoanalytic Study of the Child, 39,* 155–165.

Fantuzzo, J. W., Gadsden, V., & McDermott, P. A. (2003). *Evidence-based program for the integration of curricula: A comprehensive iInitiative for low-income preschool children* (#HD 046168). Philadelphia: Graduate School of Education, University of Pennsylvania.

Fantuzzo, J., Bulotsky-Shearer, R., McDermott, P. A., McWayne, C., Frye, D., & Perlman, S. (2007). Investigation of dimensions of social-emotional classroom behavior and school readiness for low-income urban preschool children. *School Psychology Review, 36,* 44–62.

Fantuzzo, J. W., Perry, M. A., & McDermott, P. A. (2004). Preschool approaches to learning and their relationship to other relevant classroom characteristics for low-income children. *School Psychology Quarterly, 19,* 212–230.

Glutting, J. J. (1986). The McDermott multidimensional assessment of children: applications to the classification of childhood exceptionality. *Journal of Learning Disabilities, 19,* 331–335.

Gottfried, A. E. (1990). Academic intrinsic motivation in young elementary school children. *Journal of Educational Psychology, 82,* 525–538.

Grant, H., & Dweck, C. S. (2003). Clarifying achievement goals and their impact. *Journal of Personality and Social Psychology, 85,* 541–553.

Grim, S. M., Tighe, E. A., & McDermott, P. A. (2001, April). *Risk and protective factors for school psychopathology.* Paper presented at the Annual Convention of the American Educational Research Association, Seattle, WA.

Harter, S. (1981). A new self-report scale of intrinsic versus extrinsic orientation in the classroom: Motivational and informational components. *Developmental Psychology, 17,* 300–312.

Hodgkinson, H. L. (2003). *Leaving too many children behind: A demographer's view on the neglect of America's youngest children.* Institute for Educational Leadership, Washington, D.C.

Kafer, K. (2004). No child left behind: Where do we go from here? *Backgrounder, #1775.* Washington, DC: Heritage Foundation.

Kagan, S. L., Moore, E., & Bredekamp, S. (Eds.). (1995). *Reconsidering children's early development and learning: Toward common views and vocabulary.* Washington, DC: National Education Goals Panel.

Knitzer, J. (2003, January). *Social and emotional development in young low-income children: What research tells us and why it matters for early school success.* Report presented at a meeting of the National Head Start Association, Washington, DC.

Konold, T. R., Glutting, J. J., McDermott, P. A., Kush, J. C., & Watkins, M. M. (1999). Structure and diagnostic benefits of a normative subtest taxonomy developed from the WISC-III standardization sample. *Journal of School Psychology, 37,* 29–48.

McDermott, P. A. (1984). Comparative functions of preschool learning style and IQ in predicting future academic performance. *Contemporary Educational Psychology, 9,* 38–47.

McDermott, P. A. (1999). National scales of differential learning behaviors among American children and adolescents. *School Psychology Review, 28,* 280–291.

McDermott, P. A., & Beitman, B. S. (1984). Standardization of a scale for the study of children's learning styles: Structure, stability, and criterion validity. *Psychology in the Schools, 21,* 5–13.

McDermott, P. A. & Fantuzzo, J. W. (2000). *Learning-in-time and teaching-to-learn: Study of the unique contributions of learning behaviors to school readiness* (Head Start-University Partnership Grant

No. 90-YD-0080). Washington, DC: U.S. Department of Health and Human Services, Administration on Children, Youth, and Families.

McDermott, P. A., Green, L. F., Francis, J. M., & Stott, D. H. (1999). Learning Behaviors Scale. Philadelphia: Edumetric and Clinical Science.

McDermott, P. A., Green, L. F., Francis, J. M., & Stott, D. H. (2000). Preschool Learning Behaviors Scale. Philadelphia: Edumetric and Clinical Science.

McDermott, P. A., Leigh, N. M., and Perry, M. A. (2002). Development and validation of the preschool learning behaviors scale. *Psychology in the Schools, 39,* 353–365.

McDermott, P. A., Menaker, M. R., Steinberg, C. M., and Angelo, L. (June, 2002). *Behavioral performance objectives for the Head Start Classroom.* Poster presented at the National Head Start Conference. Washington, DC.

McDermott, P. A., & Watkins, M. W. (1987). *Microcomputer systems manual for McDermott Multi-dimensional Assessment of Children* (IBM version). San Antonio, TX: Psychological Corporation.

McWayne, C. M., Fantuzzo, J. W., & McDermott, P. A. (2004). Preschool competency in context: An investigation of the unique contribution of child competencies to early academic success. *Developmental Psychology, 40*(4), 633–645.

Meisels, S. J., Marsden, D. B., Wiske, M. S., & Henderson, L. W. (1997). *The Early Screening Inventory* (rev. ed.). Ann Arbor, MI: Rebus.

Molden, D. C., and Dweck, C. S. (2006). Finding "meaning" in psychology: A lay theories approach to self-regulation, social perception, and social development. *American Psychologist, 61,* 192–203.

National Association for the Education of Young Children (NAEYC). (1996). *Developmentally appropriate practice in early childhood programs serving children birth through age 8.* A position statement of the National Association for the Education of Young Children.

National Center for Education Statistics. (2007). *The condition of education 2006,* NCES 2006-. Washington, DC: U.S. Government Printing Office.

Piaget, J. (1969). *Psychology of the child.* New York: Basic Books.

Pianta, R. C., Cox, M. J., & Snow, K. L. (2007). *School readiness and the transition to kindergarten in the era of accountability.* Baltimore, MD: Paul H. Brookes Publishing.

Pianta, R. C., Kraft-Sayre, M., Rimm-Kaufman, S., Gercke, N., & Higgins, T. (2001). Collaboration in building partnerships between families and schools: The National Center for Early Development and Learning's Kindergarten transition intervention. *Early Childhood Research Quarterly. Special issue, 16*(1), 117–132.

Raver, C. C., & Knitzer, J. (2002). *Ready to enter: What research tells policy-makers about strategies to promote social and emotional school readiness among three- and four-year-old children.* New York: National Center for Children in Poverty, Mailman School of Public Health, Columbia University.

Raver, C. C., & Zigler, E. F. (2004). Another step back? Assessing readiness in Head Start. *Beyond the journal: Young children on the Web,* 1–5. Retrieved from http://www. journal. naeyc. org/btj/200401/Raver. pdf.

Rouse, H. L., & Fantuzzo, J. F. (2004, October). *Approaches to learning in Head Start and success in kindergarten.* Paper presented at the Head Start Research Scholars Grantees Meeting, Washington, D.C.

Schaefer, B. A., & McDermott, P. A. (1999). Learning behavior and intelligence as explanations for children's scholastic achievement. *Journal of School Psychology, 37,* 299–313.

Stattin, H., & Magnusson, D. (1996). Antisocial development: A holistic approach. *Developmental Psychopathology, 8,* 617–645.

Stipek, D. (1996). Motivation and instruction. In D. C. Berliner, and Calfee, R. C. (Eds.), *Handbook of educational psychology* (pp. 85–113). New York: Macmillan Library.

Stipek, D. (2005, July/August). Early childhood education at a cross-roads: Access to preschool has come a long way, but critical choices lie ahead. *Harvard Education Letter.* Boston, MA: Harvard Education Publishing Group.

Stipek, D., & Hakuta, K. (2007). Strategies to ensure that no child starts from behind. In A. J. Lawrence, S. J. Bishop-Josef, S. M. Jones, K. T. McLearn, & D. A. Phillips (Eds.), *Child development and social policy: Knowledge for action* (pp. 129–145). Washington, DC: American Psychological Association.

Stott, D. H. (1978). The hard-to-teach child: A diagnostic-remedial approach. Baltimore: University Park Press.

Stott, D. H., & Albin, J. B. (1975). Confirmation of a general factor of effectiveness motivation by individual tests. *British Journal of Educational Psychology, 45,* 153–161.

Thomas, A., & Chess, S. (1977). *Temperament and development.* Oxford, England: Brunner/Mazel.

U.S. Department of Education. (2000). *Strategic plan, 2001–2005.* Washington, DC: Author.

U.S. Department of Education. (2002). *No Child Left Behind Act.* Washington, DC: Author.

Vygotsky, L. S. (1990). Imagination and creativity in childhood. *Soviet Psychology, 28,* 84–96.

Wentzel, K. R. (1991). Classroom competence may require more than intellectual ability: Reply to Jussim (1991). *Journal of Educational Psychology, 83,* 156–158.

Wentzel (1999). Social-motivational processes and interpersonal relationships: Implications for understanding motivation at school. *Journal of Educational Psychology, 91,* 76–97.

Wentzel, K. R., & Watkins, D. E. (2002). Peer relationships and collaborative learning as contexts for academic enablers. *School Psychology Review, 31,* 366–377.

Worrell, F. C., Vandiver, B. J., & Watkins, M. W. (2001). Construct validity of the Learning Behavior Scale with an independent sample of students. *Psychology in the Schools, 38,* 207–215.

3 ::

Low Academic Intrinsic Motivation as a Risk Factor for Adverse Educational Outcomes

A Longitudinal Study from Early Childhood Through Early Adulthood

Adele Eskeles Gottfried, Allen W. Gottfried,
Phillip E. Morris, and Clayton R. Cook

The purpose of this research and chapter is to advance the notion and provide evidence that low academic intrinsic motivation is a risk factor with regard to a broad array of academic outcomes over an extensive time period. A unique aspect of this research is that exceptionally low motivation is studied in a population not typically considered at risk, that is, in a wide range of middle-class children. We examine whether and to what extent having exceptionally low motivation places students at risk with regard to their academic attainment within a group not possessing other aspects of risk, such as low socioeconomic status or low birth weight.

Academic intrinsic motivation formed the basis of the identification of motivational risk status. This motivational construct is defined as enjoyment of school learning characterized by an orientation toward mastery; curiosity; persistence; task-endogeny; and the learning of challenging, difficult, and novel tasks (A. E. Gottfried, 1985, 1986a). Academic intrinsic motivation is positively related to school competency. Greater academic intrinsic motivation relates to higher academic achievement (standardized tests and teacher grades), classroom adaptation, self-concept, and lower academic anxiety. Students with high academic intrinsic motivation also engage in significantly more leadership positions within the academic as well as nonacademic realms during the high school years. Conversely, students with low academic intrinsic motivation have poorer academic outcomes across these academic and developmental outcomes. Moreover, academic intrinsic motivation contributes uniquely to academic achievement above and beyond intellectual performance. Therefore, academic intrinsic motivation provides an important contribution to successful school performance (A. Gottfried & Gottfried, 2007; A. E. Gottfried, 1985, 1990; A. E. Gottfried & Gottfried, 2004; A. E. Gottfried, A. W. Gottfried, Cook, & Morris, 2005; A. E. Gottfried, Marcoulides, Gottfried, Oliver, & Guerin, 2007).

Long-term developmental and educational aspects of extremely low academic intrinsic motivation from childhood through late adolescence have not been previously investigated. Whereas studies have examined motivation of individuals at risk demographically, such as being a member of a minority group or of low socioeconomic status (Anderson & Keith, 1997; Murdock, 1999), research has not examined motivation as a risk factor in and of itself. Dicintio and Gee (1999) used the term *motivationally disadvantaged* and found that students who were at risk for academic failure were unmotivated to learn. In a review of literature, Dai (2002) proposed that there are aspects of motivational disadvantage in gifted girls that create obstacles for their academic achievement. Whereas these articles put forth the notion of motivational disadvantage, there is a dearth of empirical data. Dicintio and Gee (1999) studied six students, and Dai (2002) reviewed literature on motivational differences pertaining to gender and giftedness. We prefer the term *motivationally at risk* to motivational disadvantage as it conveys the potential of a compromised academic future.

Low academic motivation has been found to be associated with a variety of adverse outcomes, such as lower achievement (e.g., Carr, Borkowski, & Maxwell, 1991; A. E. Gottfried, 1985, 1990; A. E. Gottfried, Fleming, & Gottfried, 1994; Pintrich & Schunk, 2003; Stipek, 2002; Wigfield, Eccles, Schiefele, Roeser, & Davis-Kean, 2006), school retention and dropout (e.g., Alexander, Entwisle, & Dauber, 2003; Christenson & Thurlow, 2004; Hardre & Reeve, 2003; Rumberger, 1987, 1995; Vallerand, Fortier, & Guay, 1997), and less school engagement (e.g., Fredericks, Blumenfeld, & Paris, 2004; Miserandino, 1996). Nevertheless, the present research is distinct by studying developmental and educational factors antecedent to, concurrent with, and subsequent to identification of extremely low academic intrinsic motivation in a long-term longitudinal study from childhood through adulthood. This research elaborates the concept of academic risk by investigating a specific type of motivation: academic intrinsic motivation. The theoretical and applied implications of the concept of motivational risk are considered as well as the relation of motivational risk status and the culture of schooling.

The Fullerton Longitudinal Study (FLS), a contemporary long-term study of development from infancy through adulthood, provided the database. Academic intrinsic motivation in the low extreme was systematically and comprehensively studied in relation to theoretically relevant variables throughout childhood, adolescence, and early adulthood. To accomplish this, an extreme group (subgroup) methodology was used. Use of extremes or subgroups in developmental research has precedence in other domains such as temperament, gifted intelligence, and gifted motivation (e.g., A. W. Gottfried et al., 1994; A. W. Gottfried et al., 2005; Guerin, A. W. Gottfried, Oliver, & Thomas, 2003; Kagan, Snidman, & Arcus, 1998; Radke-Yarrow, 1998; Wachs, 1991a, 1991b). For example, Guerin et al. (2003) examined the extremes of temperament from infancy on and found important developmental regularities associated with very high and low scores on various temperament dimensions. Kagan et al. (1998) advocated use of extreme groups that differ qualitatively from a population to study temperament longitudinally. Similarly, extreme group analyses have been advocated by Wachs (1991a) to study organism-environment interactions. Wachs (1991b) also stated that power may be increased when extreme group designs are used, either through an increase in variance or a more accurate classification of subjects or environments. In research on intellectual giftedness and gifted motivation, extreme group methodology was used and consistent differences were obtained between participants with gifted intelligence and gifted motivation, and their cohort comparison groups (A. W. Gottfried et al., 1994; A. W. Gottfried et al., 2005). In the present longitudinal research, this methodology was used to identify those with the lowest motivation and compare them to their peer cohort group. By being able to identify a group that is at the lowest end of the academic intrinsic motivation distribution, we were able to study developmental patterns that would not be detected when this group is merged with the broader population.

We hypothesized that individuals with consistently low academic intrinsic motivation would evidence significantly diminished developmental and academic outcomes including achievement, motivation, classroom functioning, intellectual performance, self-concept, and post-secondary educational accomplishments. Because academic intrinsic motivation increases in stability during adolescence (A. E. Gottfried, Fleming, & Gottfried, 2001), this age period was chosen to designate the motivationally at-risk subgroup. Because academic intrinsic motivation has been shown to be an independent contributor to achievement above and beyond IQ (Cool & Keith, 1991; A. E. Gottfried, 1985, 1990; A. E. Gottfried & Gottfried, 2004; Lehrer & Hieronymus, 1977; Lloyd & Barenblatt, 1984), we hypothesized that the construct of motivational risk would prove to be independent of intelligence as well.

∷ Method

Participants

The Fullerton Longitudinal Study (FLS) served as the database for the present study. The FLS is an ongoing investigation that was initiated in 1979 with 130 infants and their families. Beginning at age 1, children were assessed at 6-month intervals throughout infancy and the preschool years, and annually throughout school (age 5 to age 17). At each assessment through adolescence a comprehensive battery of standardized measures was administered to examine development across a broad variety of domains. At age 24, 104 participants were surveyed as to their current educational status. (We are currently in the process of surveying the participants at age 29). The retention rate of this sample was substantial with no less than 80% of the original sample returning at any assessment. There was no evidence of attrition bias throughout the course of the study (Guerin & A. W. Gottfried, 1994; Guerin et al., 2003).

The socioeconomic status of the sample represented a wide, middle-class range, from semiskilled workers through professionals, as determined by the Hollingshead Four-Factor Index of Social Status (Hollingshead, 1975; also see A. W. Gottfried, 1985; A. W. Gottfried, Gottfried, Bathurst, Guerin, & Parramore, 2003). The mean Hollingshead Social Status Index was 45.6 (standard deviation [SD] = 11.9) at the initiation of the FLS and 48.6 (SD = 11.4) at the 17-year assessment. At the initiation of the study, participants were predominantly European American (90%) with inclusion of other ethnic groups (Hispanic, East Indian, Hawaiian, Iranian). The percentages of males and females were 52 and 48, respectively. The criteria used in the selection process were that all infants were full-term, of normal birth weight, and free of visual and neurological abnormalities. All families spoke English. For further details concerning sample characteristics and study design, see A. W. Gottfried et al. (1994), A. W. Gottfried, Gottfried, and Guerin (2006), and Guerin et al. (2003).

Measures

Throughout the course of investigation, numerous standardized developmental, motivation, and academic instruments of established and substantial reliability and validity were administered. Information was also collected directly from the participants' school records and survey. Measures included the following.

Academic intrinsic motivation. Academic intrinsic motivation was measured with the Children's Academic Intrinsic Motivation Inventory (CAIMI), a reliable and valid instrument that provides measurement of motivation including four subject area subscales (reading, math, social studies, and science) as well as a subscale for school in general (A. E. Gottfried, 1986a). In the high school years, the subject designation of reading was referred to as English, and social studies as history to be consistent with subject areas in the secondary school years (see A. E. Gottfried et al., 2001). The CAIMI was administered at ages 9, 10, 13, 16, and 17 years. Because the school in general scale assesses overall pleasure inherent in school learning, it was deemed to be the most generalizable across the various outcomes in the present study and hence was chosen to designate the comparison groups in this research as well as to analyze previous motivation.

Achievement. Achievement was assessed with a number of measures across the years. At ages 7 through 10 years, the Woodcock-Johnson Psycho-Educational Battery (Woodcock & Johnson, 1977, 1989) was employed, and at ages 11 though 17 years the revised Woodcock-Johnson was used. Reading and math grade percentile scores were analyzed across the ages. The advantage of the grade percentile is that it furnishes a score correcting for grade level at a given age. Participants' school records provided high school grade point average (GPA), using a 4-point scale, from the freshman through senior years as well as the cumulative GPA at the end of high school. Scholastic Aptitude Test (SAT) scores were also obtained from the participants' school records. High school completion versus dropout status was assessed from self-report and high school records. Finally, at age 24, the participants were surveyed as to their highest level of postsecondary education attained, degree obtained, and attendance in graduate school.

Classroom functioning. Participants' classroom functioning was appraised with standardized ratings on the Teacher's Report Form of the Child Behavior Checklist (Achenbach & Rescorla, 2001) at ages 6, 7, 8, 9, 10, and 11. This comprised 4 items: how hard is the child working; how appropriately is the child behaving; how much is the child learning; and how happy is the child. Each rating involved a 7-point Likert-type scale on which the teacher compared the participant to other pupils of the same age with a rating of 1 designating much less, a rating of 7 designating much more, and a rating of 4 being the average. Inasmuch as children attended different schools, approximately 700 teachers completed the Child Behavior Checklist across these assessment periods.

Intellectual performance. Intellectual performance was measured with the Wechsler Intelligence Scale for Children—Revised (WISC-R; Wechsler, 1974) at ages 6, 7, 8, and 12; the Wechsler Intelligence Scale for Children—Third Edition (WISC-III; Wechsler, 1991) at age 15; and theWechsler Adult Intelligence Scale-Revised (WAIS-R; Wechsler, 1981) at age 17.

Test-taking behavior. Test-taking behavior was measured at ages 15 and 17 with the Guide to the Assessment of Test Session Behavior (GATSB, 1993), which was used with the administration of the Wechsler intelligence tests. Using this scale, the examiner rates the testee's behavior during the testing session on 29 items using a three-category rating including Doesn't apply, Sometimes applies, or Usually applies. Responses are then summed yielding four scale scores: Avoidance, Inattentiveness, Uncooperative Mood, and Total. Higher GATSB scores indicate less effective test-taking behaviors.

Self-appraisals. Self-concept was measured with the Self-Description Questionnaire II (Marsh, 1990). The General School and General Self measures were used when the participants were ages 12, 14, and 16. In the adolescent years, two self-appraisal measures—perception of academic competence and academic anxiety—were analyzed. Perception of competence was measured at ages 16 and 17 with the perception of competence inventory (A. E. Gottfried, 1985) consisting of five items that were summed providing a total score (I do well in English, math, history, science, and school in general), with higher scores representing greater perception of competence. Students' anxiety about performance in school was assessed at ages 13, 16, and 17 with the Children's Academic Anxiety Inventory (CAAI; A. E. Gottfried, 1982, 1985), which consists of 13 items yielding a total score measuring worry about school work and taking tests in reading (English at ages 16 and 17), math, social studies (history at ages 16 and 17), science, and for school in general. The scores were summed providing an overall anxiety score with higher scores representing higher anxiety.

Analytic Strategy for Group Designation

To identify the at-risk motivation group we applied a conceptualization and methodology that originated in our previous research on the intellectually gifted (A. W. Gottfried et al., 1994). In that work we selected the traditional and ubiquitous standard cutoff score of 130 IQ or above and designated those participants the gifted group. This resulted in 19% (20 of 107) of the children in our longitudinal study sample being designated as intellectually gifted at the age 8 assessment. These intellectually gifted children were then compared to their cohort peer comparison group (A. W. Gottfried et al., 1994).

In the next analysis of extreme groups, motivational giftedness was studied (A. E. Gottfried & Gottfried, in press; A. W. Gottfried et al., 2005, 2006). In the absence of a standardized cutoff score to designate gifted motivation, which does exist for gifted intelligence, we successfully applied a rationale to create the groups to be compared. We used the same rationale in the present study, which entailed the following methodology. Because academic intrinsic motivation increases in interindividual (i.e., rank order) stability during adolescence (A. E. Gottfried et al., 2001), this developmental period was selected to designate the comparison study groups. The school in general scale raw scores (henceforth referred to as the general score) of the CAIMI at ages 13, 16, and 17 were aggregated to provide an appraisal of the adolescents' overall pleasure inherent in learning in the academic setting. Aggregation was done to maximize reliability (Epstein, 1979; Rushton, Brainerd, & Pressley, 1983) by creating a composite of the most consistently and least motivated adolescents and at the same time maximizing the available sample size. At ages 13, 16, and 17 there were 108, 112, and 111 participants assessed, respectively. The aggregation resulted in 111 participants (only one subject was eliminated because of having only one score). Participants missing only one score, who would have been excluded due to missing data at a particular age, were included and their missing score was estimated using the ordinary least squares estimation procedure (OLS) recommended by Cohen, Cohen, West, and Aiken (2003, p. 445), albeit missing data were minimal, to ensure that missingness had no bearing on group membership. OLS utilizes a regression line based on nonmissing CAIMI general scores to estimate the missing values. Sensitivity analysis revealed that the groups formed prior and subsequent to the estimation of missing data remained constant, that is, no participant changed group status. Thus the original groups were preserved for subsequent analysis.

In the absence of a standard cutoff score to designate individuals with extremely low motivation, the lowest 19% of adolescents in academic intrinsic motivation were identified as having consistently low motivation in this study population. This percentage was chosen so as to be consistent with the percentage of the incidence of gifted intellect (A. W. Gottfried et al., 1994) and the identification of the gifted motivation group (A. W. Gottfried et al., 2005). Hence, 21 of the 111 participants emerged as having the lowest motivation scores at ages 13, 16, and 17, and these formed the at-risk motivation group. We recently corroborated the existence of these groups using latent transition analysis (Marcoulides, Gottfried, Gottfried, & Oliver, 2008).

:: Results

Data Analytic Strategy

Two dimensions were utilized to organize and guide the analyses: time frame and type of measure. Time frame consisted of three developmental periods that were defined relative to the designation of adolescent motivational group status: antecedent, which comprised ages 6 to 12; concurrent, which comprised ages 13 to 17; and subsequent, which comprised the early adulthood period of 24 years of age. Regarding type of measure, these included motivation, educational performance/achievement, classroom functioning, intellectual performance, test-taking behavior, and self-appraisals (self-concept, perception of competence, and academic anxiety). Statistical assumptions were assessed and transformations conducted when necessary to satisfy normality. Sensitivity analyses of the original and transformed data revealed no discrepancies; therefore, the original data will be presented and interpreted. All other remaining assumptions were met. The majority of analyses consisted of repeated measures ANOVAs and MANOVAs as appropriate. T-tests were performed between the at-risk motivation and their cohort comparison group when a single time point was involved. Regarding the repeated measure ANOVAs, only between-group results are reported because they are the only relevant differences with which this study is concerned.

The between-subjects factor was always motivational group status (i.e., at-risk motivation vs. cohort comparison); therefore, it was a fixed factor. We also examined the within-subjects effects (time) and these did not change any conclusions of the between-subjects effects. There were no reliable significant interactions obtained between motivational group status and time. In the few instances in which data on outcome variables were missing, list-wise deletion was utilized for each analysis, but each analysis was examined for missing cases on its own merit.

Chi-square statistics were also computed as pertinent. In the instances for which the expected frequencies were not met, the percentages are interpreted descriptively. As for gender, a few points are noteworthy regarding this study. Research on academic intrinsic motivation has consistently revealed no significant differences in gender (e.g., A. E. Gottfried et al., 2001); the proportion of males and females was not significantly different within the two motivational status groups and the number of boys and girls within the at-risk motivation group was too small to generate any reliable conclusions.

Across ANOVA, MANOVA, and t-test analyses, both p values and effect sizes were employed. The importance of effect size estimates is that they provide important information beyond the significance level regarding the magnitude and practical importance of the results. In this regard, two effect sizes are presented in Tables 3.1 and 3.2, eta-squared and r binomial effect size displays, or r_{BESD}. Eta-squared represents the magnitude of the overall effect, a more traditional approach. However, Rosenthal, Rosnow, and Rubin (2000) have suggested that labeling effect sizes as small, medium, or large can result in misleading interpretations of results. Therefore, the effect sizes for the analyses were transformed into the r_{BESD} and then into the binomial effect size display (BESD) which is readily interpretable and highlights the practical importance of an effect size. Specifically, the BESD addresses the question, What is the effect of group membership (at-risk motivation vs. cohort comparison) on the success/nonsuccess rates of a given outcome? In this research, the r_{BESD} reported represents the difference between the nonsuccess rates for the two groups (i.e., at-risk motivation vs. cohort comparison). In essence, the BESD is a 2 x 2 contingency table with the columns representing motivational group status (at-risk motivation vs. cohort comparison) and the rows representing success and nonsuccess rates, respectively. Nonsuccess rate is defined as the percentage of individuals expected to fall below the mean.[1] It should be noted that with unequal sample size, the r_{BESD} provides a conservative estimate of the true population effect size (Rosenthal et al., 2000). We have presented the r_{BESD} and the nonsuccess rates for the at-risk motivation and cohort comparison groups. Success rates are simply the reciprocal of the nonsuccess rate (i.e., 1 minus the nonsuccess rate), and hence, were not presented.

By providing success and nonsuccess rates for each group on outcomes, the magnitude and practical importance of the effect size may be interpreted based on knowledge of the subject at hand. For example, in Table 3.2, for cumulative GPA, the r_{BESD} of .49 is the effect size of the difference between the two groups, and the percentages presented beneath the r_{BESD} of .74 and .26 are the nonsuccess rates for the motivationally at-risk adolescents and the cohort comparison, respectively. This indicates that 74% of those adolescents with at-risk motivation do not achieve success with regard to GPA, that is, they fall below the overall group mean when compared to the cohort group, whereas only 26% of the cohort group would not achieve success, that is, they fall below the group mean, with regard to GPA, a substantially lower percentage of nonsuccess. Had both groups received a 50% success rate there would be no effect, which equates to a r_{BESD} of .00 both of which indicate no group differences. Hence, membership in the at-risk motivation group results in a substantially lower likelihood of being successful in terms of GPA. All other r_{BESD} and BESD effect sizes are to be interpreted likewise.

Motivation

A repeated measures ANOVA was conducted on the antecedent CAIMI general scores at ages 9 and 10. Results revealed that motivationally at-risk adolescents had significantly lower academic intrinsic motivation during the elementary school years. Results are reported in Table 3.1. The r_{BESD} effect size indicates a 35% difference between the two groups, with 67% of the adolescents with at-risk motivation having lower motivation during middle childhood compared to 33% for the cohort comparison group. Therefore, adolescents with low academic intrinsic motivation were significantly more likely to have lower academic intrinsic motivation compared to their cohorts prior to high school.

Academic Achievement Through High School

Woodcock-Johnson. Repeated measures ANOVAs were used to analyze the Woodcock-Johnson reading and math variables. Antecedent Woodcock-Johnson scores were grouped into two age periods

TABLE 3–1 Antecedent and Concurrent ANOVA Results for the Motivationally At Risk and Cohort Comparison Groups

MEASURE (AGES)	AT RISK MOTIVATION	MEANS (STANDARD DEVIATIONS) COHORT COMPARISON	F	df	η2	r_{BESD} (DISPLAY)[a]
MOTIVATION						
Children's academic Intrinsic motivation Inventory (9 and 10 years)	65.15 (8.47)	70.46 (8.30)	8.41**	1,100	.08	.35[b] (.67/.33)
ACADEMIC ACHIEVEMENT						
WOODCOCK JOHNSON						
Reading (7, 8, 9, and 10 years)	51.62 (27.15)	68.48 (24.45)	8.63**	1,98	.08	.35 (.67/.33)
Reading (11 and 12 years)	67.19 (28.97)	85.17 (18.96)	12.67***	1,101	.11	.40 (.70/.30)
Reading (13, 14, 15, 16, and 17 years)	67.13 (26.16)	83.38 (19.64)	13.24**	1,98	.12	.45 (.72/.28)
Math (7, 8, 9, and 10 years)	58.76 (26.07)	71.28 (24.93)	5.20*	1,98	.05	.28 (.64/.36)
Math (11 and 12 years)	78.07 (21.87)	89.34 (14.00)	10.65**	1,101	.10	.37 (.68/.32)

Math (13, 14, 15, 16, and 17 years)	56.57 (27.39)	76.63 (23.46)	13.90***	1,98	.12	.46 (.73 / .27)
Grade point average (Freshman to senior)	2.51 (.55)	3.22 (.77)	13.91***	1,96	.13	.47 (.73 / .27)

CLASSROOM FUNCTIONING

CHILD BEHAVIOR CHECKLIST TEACHER'S REPORT FORM

Hard working (6, 7, 8, 9, 10, and 11 years)	3.81 (1.15)	4.88 (1.16)	14.18***	1,103	.12	.42 (.71 / .29)
Behavior (6, 7, 8, 9, 10, and 11 years)	4.25 (1.33)	5.08 (1.23)	7.41**	1,103	.07	.32 (.66 / .34)
Learning (6, 7, 8, 9, 10, and 11 years)	4.22 (1.21)	5.21 (.99)	15.30***	1,103	.13	.43 (.71 / .29)
Happy (6, 7, 8, 9, 10, and 11 years)	4.51 (.99)	5.10 (.82)	7.92**	1,103	.07	.33 (.66 / .34)

INTELLECTUAL PERFORMANCE

Wechsler intelligence Scale for children (6, 7, 8, and 12 years)	107.49 (11.09)	117.36 (12.77)	13.12***	1,96	.12	.42 (.71 / .29)

TEST-TAKING BEHAVIOR

GUIDE TO THE ASSESSMENT OF TEST-TAKING BEHAVIOR

Avoidance (15 and 17 years)	63.81 (11.75)	52.84 (10.13)	25.29***	1,101	20	.55 (.77 / .23)

(continued)

	Mean (SD)	Mean (SD)	F	df	r	r_{BESD}[a] (success/nonsuccess)
SELF-APPRAISALS						
Inattentiveness (15 and 17 years)	54.14 (8.07)	48.94 (7.40)	16.04***	1,101	.14	.47 (.73/.27)
Uncooperative mood (15 and 17 years)	50.14 (8.23)	47.73 (5.50)	5.35*	1,101	.05	.29 (.64/.36)
Total (15 and 17 years)	57.32 (8.19)	49.98 (7.25)	26.58***	1,101	.21	.56 (.78/.22)
SELF-CONCEPT: SELF-DESCRIPTION QUESTIONNAIRE						
General school (14 and 16 years)	3.79 (.99)	4.87 (.86)	31.96***	1,103	.24	.58 (.79/.21)
General self (14 and 16 years)	4.65 (.69)	5.19 (.70)	11.44***	1,103	.10	.39 (.69/.31)
CHILDREN'S ACADEMIC SELF-PERCEPTIONS						
Anxiety (13, 16, and 17 years)	36.97 (10.54)	31.47 (8.86)	10.54**	1,100	.10	.66 (.83/.17)
Perception of competence (16 and 17 years)	14.73 (3.65)	19.89 (3.13)	45.87***	1,106	.30	.39 (.69/.31)

*p < .05. **p < .01. ***p < .001. *Note:* r_{BESD} represents the effect size correlation.

[a]Display represents the Binomial Effect Size Display (Rosenthal et al., 2000).

[b]For all r_{BESD}s with odd values, the numbers were rounded down to provide more conservative estimates of nonsuccess rates.

because when participants were 11 years the newly revised version was employed. Thus, for the antecedent measures, for both reading and math, repeated measures analyses were conducted across ages 7, 8, 9, and 10, and across ages 11 and 12. Results are organized by reading at both time periods and then by math at both time periods. The concurrent period of 13 through 17 years was also analyzed for reading and math using repeated measures ANOVA and presented separately. Results evidence pervasive significant mean differences in reading and math achievement throughout the antecedent and concurrent years (see Table 3.1). Adolescents with at-risk motivation evidenced lower reading and math achievement throughout their elementary, middle school, and high school years. Nonsuccess rates ranged from 64% to 73% for the at-risk motivation group compared to 27% to 36% for the cohort comparison across reading and math. These results indicate that students with at-risk motivation during the adolescent years have substantially lower achievement throughout all the school years from early childhood through adolescence when compared to the cohort comparison group.

GPA. Analyses were conducted with a repeated measures ANOVA across freshman, sophomore, junior, and senior GPA and also with a *t*-test comparing group differences on cumulative GPA. The repeated measures analysis revealed significant group differences between the GPAs of the motivationally at-risk adolescents and the cohort comparison (see Table 3.1). The *t*-test result for cumulative GPA was also significant (see Table 3.2). Nonsuccess rates were 73% and 74% for the at-risk motivation group, and 27% and 26% for the cohort comparison, respectively. These results demonstrate that adolescents with at-risk motivation were significantly more likely to obtain lower grades in high school than their cohort comparison group.

Dropout Rates. A cross-tabulation was conducted to examine the percentage of high school dropouts within the two comparison groups. In a 2 (Motivational Group Status) × 2 (Dropout Status) contingency table, results revealed that 2 (11.8%) of the motivationally at-risk students dropped out of high school while 3 (3.5%) of the cohort comparison group dropped out of high school. Although this analysis did not meet the desired expected frequency, and hence significance testing was not feasible, these percentages suggest that students with at-risk motivation are approximately 3 to 4 times more likely to drop out of high school than members of their cohort comparison group.

SAT. To compare the two groups as to whether they took the SAT, a 2 (Motivational Group Status) × 2 (Took SAT vs. Did not take SAT)

Table 3–2. Antecedent, Concurrent, and Subsequent T-Test Results for Motivationally At Risk and Cohort Comparison Groups

MEASURE (AGE)	MEANS (STANDARD DEVIATIONS) AT RISK MOTIVATION	COHORT COMPARISON	t	df	η^2	r_{BESD} (DISPLAY)[a]
ACADEMIC ACHIEVEMENT						
Grade point average (Cumulative) (24 years)	2.49 (.44)	3.21 (.68)	−4.04***	101	.09	.49[b] (.74/.26)
Total years of education completed	13.28 (1.60)	14.21 (1.78)	−2.06*	100	.04	.26 (.63/.37)
INTELLECTUAL PERFORMANCE						
Wechsler intelligence Scale for children — III (15 years)	99.75 (9.74)	109.90 (13.52)	−3.17***	105	.09	.37 (.68/.32)
Wechsler adult Intelligence scale (17 years)	104.28 (8.45)	111.63 (12.82)	−2.33*	106	.05	.29 (.64/.36)
SELF-APPRAISALS						
Self-concept: Self-description questionnaire						
General school (12 years)	4.25 (.86)	5.21 (.74)	−5.13***	98	.21	.54 (.77/.23)
General self (12 years)	4.62 (.87)	5.44 (.56)	−5.23***	98	.22	.54 (.77/.23)

*p < .05. **p < .01. ***p < .001. *Note:* r_{BESD} represents the effect size correlation.

[a]Display represents the Binomial Effect Size Display (Rosenthal et al., 2000).

[b]For all r_{BESD}s with odd values, the numbers were rounded down to provide more conservative estimates of nonsuccess rates.

chi-square analysis was conducted. The resulting chi-square analysis was significant, $\chi^2(1, N = 111) = 17.69$, $p < .001$, indicating that adolescents with at-risk motivation were significantly less likely to take the SAT than members of the cohort comparison group. Only 1 of the 21 (4.8%) in the at-risk motivation group took the SAT compared to 50 of the 90 (55.6%) of the cohort comparison. Odds ratio for the chi-square results indicated that motivationally at-risk adolescents were 25 times less likely to take the SAT when compared to their cohort. Inasmuch as the SAT is generally required for admission into a four-year college, these results imply that motivationally at-risk students are less interested in attending a four-year college than those in the comparison cohort (see postsecondary education analyses below).

Classroom Functioning. A MANOVA was conducted using the four items on the Teacher's Report Form of the Child Behavior Checklist. Across ages 6 through 11, each participant's scores were aggregated to form an averaged composite for each of the four individual items. These composite scores were used to prevent loss of an individual participant across the years if a teacher had not returned the form in a particular year. This procedure maximized sample size and power. A significant multivariate main effect for motivation group status was obtained, with both Pillai's Trace and Wilk's Lambda $F(4, 100) = 4.03$, $p < .01$. Step-down ANOVA analyses revealed that motivationally at-risk adolescents and their cohorts differed significantly on all four items (see Table 3.1). Nonsuccess rates ranged from 66% to 71% for the at-risk motivation group compared to 34% to 29% of the cohort group on the four subscales of classroom functioning. These results indicate that adolescents with at- risk motivation were viewed by their teachers as functioning less adequately in the classroom when compared to their cohorts across ages 6 through 11. Specifically, motivationally at-risk adolescents were observed to be working less hard, behaving less appropriately, learning less, and less happy in the classroom setting during the antecedent school years (ages 6 through 11) compared to the cohort comparison group.

Intellectual Performance

Group differences in IQ scores were analyzed with a repeated measure ANOVA for participants at ages 6, 7, 8, and 12 using the WISC-R Full Scale IQ score. T-tests were calculated to determine differences between the groups for the WISC-III at age 15 and the WAIS-R at age 17. Results for the repeated measures ANOVA and t-tests showed significant group differences (see Tables 3.1 and 3.2). These findings indicate that adolescents with at-risk motivation had significantly lower IQs compared to the cohort comparison group. Effect size percentages indicated the likelihood of the adolescents scoring below the mean IQ ranged from 64% to 71% for the at-risk motivation group compared to 36% to 29% of the cohort group. Although the at-risk motivation group had significantly lower intelligence test scores, their scores were, nevertheless, at or above the average of the general population.

To determine whether at-risk motivation and lower IQ were significantly overlapping constructs—that is, to determine whether the same adolescents identified as having at-risk motivation were significantly more likely to also be those with lower IQ scores—a 2 (Motivational Group Status) × 2 (Lower IQ vs. cohort) chi-square analysis was conducted. To conduct this analysis, we identified a lower IQ group by aggregating the IQ scores (ages 12, 15, and 17) that were assessed during a similar time period as the three CAIMI scores. To be consistent with the designation of the at-risk motivation group, the lowest 19% of this aggregate formed the lower IQ group, which was compared to the remainder in the cohort. The result was nonsignificant: $\chi^2 (1, N = 99) = 2.84, p = .092$. Hence, at-risk motivation and lower IQ were not significantly associated.

Test-taking Behavior

A repeated measure MANOVA was conducted on the subscales of the GATSB (Inattentiveness, Uncooperative Mood, and Avoidance), and an ANOVA conducted on the Total GATSB score, at ages 15 and 17. For the MANOVA, a significant multivariate main effect for motivational group status was obtained, with both Pillai's Trace and Wilk's Lambda $F (3, 99) = 11.01, p < .001$. Step-down ANOVA analyses revealed that motivationally at-risk adolescents and their cohorts significantly differed on all three subscales (see Table 3.1). Likewise, the ANOVA for the total GATSB score was significant (see Table 3.1). These findings indicate that adolescents with low motivation demonstrated more detrimental test-taking behaviors compared to their cohorts. They were more avoidant to the test administrator, displayed a more uncooperative mood, and were less attentive than the cohort comparison group.

From these analyses the question emerged as to whether test-taking behavior mediates the relationship between motivation and test outcome. Hence, a mediation model was tested examining whether, and if so, to what extent, the relationship between motivation and IQ was ac-

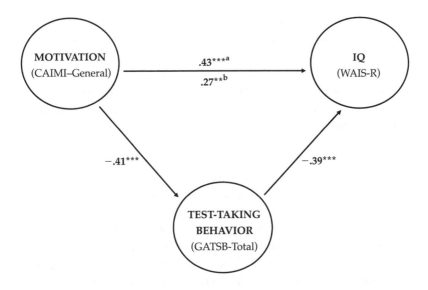

Figure 3–1. Partial mediation of motivation on IQ scores by test-taking behaviors at 17 years including significant beta weights.

**p < .01. ***p < .001.
Note: Larger GATSB Total scores indicate more test-taking problems.
[a]Path prior to inclusion of mediator.
[b]Path subsequent to inclusion of mediator.

counted for by test-taking behaviors. The 17-year assessment wave data provided a specific set of conditions with which to test the mediation model because IQ, motivation, and test-taking behaviors were concurrently appraised at this age. This model is presented in Figure 3.1.

Mediation

The method advanced by Baron and Kenny (1986) was used to test this mediation model. If the prediction of IQ from motivation proved to be significantly reduced when test-taking behaviors were added to the model, then it would be concluded that the effort and cooperation of the student during the testing session played a significant role in IQ performance and would hence be a mediator of motivation. On the other hand, if test-taking behavior did not significantly reduce the prediction of IQ by motivation, then motivation itself would account for prediction in the model depicted. This model was tested with the full-scale IQ score from the WAIS at age 17, the school in general scale score from the CAIMI at 17 years, and the total score from the GATSB at 17 years.

The predictive power of motivation on IQ was reduced from .43 to .27 when test-taking behaviors were entered into the model. To test the significance of the mediator, the Sobel test was conducted as recommended by Baron and Kenny (1986). Results revealed that there was a significant reduction in the beta weight of motivation on IQ subsequent to the addition of test-taking behaviors (Sobel = 2.40, p = .02). Although the path from motivation to IQ was reduced, it remained significant even after the addition of test-taking behaviors, indicating that test-taking behavior was a partial mediator and that motivation continued to play a unique role in the prediction of IQ. However, the fact that test-taking behaviors reduced the relationship between motivation and IQ suggests that students with at-risk motivation perform more poorly on intellectual tests because they are less effective in their approach to taking tests. Hence, they are not utilizing test-taking behaviors that would maximize their abilities.

Self-Appraisals

General School Self-Concept. General school self-concept was analyzed at the antecedent age of 12 and also at the concurrent ages of 14 and 16. The *t*-test performed on the antecedent age revealed a significant group difference, as did the concurrent repeated measures ANOVA. Students with at-risk motivation viewed themselves as significantly less academically competent at ages 12, 14, and 16 compared to their cohorts (see Tables 3.1 and 3.2). The effect size percentages indicated that 77% and 79% of the at-risk motivation group fell below the mean compared to 23% and 21% of the cohort group, showing that motivationally at-risk adolescents were considerably more likely to have lower school self-concept compared to the cohort group.

General Self-Concept. A *t*-test was conducted to assess group differences on the antecedent self-concept measure at age 12, and repeated measures ANOVA was conducted on the self-concept measure at ages 14 and 16. Results revealed significant differences between the general self-concepts of motivationally at-risk students and their cohorts (see Tables 3.1 and 3.2). The effect size percentages were 77% and 69% for the at-risk motivation group, and 23% and 31% for the cohort group indicating that adolescents with at-risk motivation were more likely to fall below the group mean on general self-concept at these ages. Adolescents with at-risk motivation had significantly poorer perceptions of themselves and lower percentages of favorable general self-concepts at both age periods compared to the comparison group.

Academic Anxiety and Perception of Competence. ANOVAs conducted on anxiety and perception of competence during adolescence revealed that the motivationally at-risk had significantly greater academic anxiety and significantly lower perception of their academic competence in adolescence (see Table 3.1). For academic anxiety, effect size percentages indicated that the likelihood of having higher anxiety was 83% for the at-risk motivation group, whereas only 17% of the cohort group had greater anxiety. Regarding perception of competence, 69% of the at-risk motivation group evidenced lower perception of competence compared with 31% of the cohort. Hence, these students are not only lower in their academic intrinsic motivation but they are also more anxious about their school performance and have more adverse views of their academic competence.

Postsecondary Education

Analyses were conducted on the 24-year data to provide a picture of the educational trajectories of the motivationally at-risk and cohort comparison groups during early adulthood. The variables included: college attendance versus no college attendance directly out of high school; type of college pursued directly out of high school (four-year university vs. community college or technical school); number of postsecondary education years attained; attainment versus nonattainment of an associate degree or equivalent; bachelor's degree awarded versus no bachelor's degree awarded; and pursuit or nonpursuit of graduate education. All but one of the variables were analyzed with 2 (Motivational Group Status) × 2 (outcome variable) chi-square. A *t*-test was performed to examine the mean difference between the adolescents with at-risk motivation and their cohort comparison on the number of years of postsecondary education attained.

Regarding college attendance analyses, results for college attendance versus no college attendance directly out of high school did not meet the minimum needed for expected cell frequencies to conduct a statistical test. However, the percentage of motivationally at-risk adolescents that did not go to college (22.2%, $n = 4$) was considerably larger than that of the cohort comparison (9.6%, $n = 8$). Regarding the analysis of the number of individuals who attended a four-year university directly out of high school, results were significant χ^2 $(1, N = 91) = 13.15, p < .001$. Only one (6.7%) of the motivationally at-risk adolescents attended a four-year university directly out of high school compared to 44 (57.9%) of the cohort comparison group. These findings are in accord with the previous findings on SATs—that is, adolescents with at-risk motivation have less desire to attend a four-year college.

Regarding types of degrees awarded, analysis of the number of individuals within each group that had attained an associate degree or equivalent did not meet the minimum needed for expected cell frequencies for us to conduct a statistical test, but it did show that seven (38.9%) of the adolescents with at-risk motivation had received an associate degree or equivalent by age 24 compared to 52 (61.9%) of the cohort comparison group. Regarding bachelor's degree versus no bachelor's degree awarded, results approached significance with χ^2 $(1, N = 102) = 3.02, p < .10$. Only three (16.7%) of the adolescents with at-risk motivation received their bachelor's degrees compared to 32 (38.1%) of the cohort comparison group.

Regarding education attained at age 24, a t-test on the mean number of years of education completed was significant (see Table 3.2). At 24 years, motivationally at-risk adolescents had attained significantly less postsecondary education, approximately 1 year less, compared to the cohort. To analyze the number of individuals in each motivational status group attending graduate school, the minimum needed for expected cell frequencies to conduct a statistical test was not met, but only one (5.8%) of the adolescents with at-risk motivation was attending a graduate program, whereas 12 (14.5%) of the cohort comparison group were attending graduate school. These findings regarding educational trajectories demonstrated that adolescents with at-risk motivation were lagging behind their cohort in postsecondary education.

∷ Discussion

The present research provides support regarding low academic intrinsic motivation as a risk factor for adverse educational outcomes. As predicted, results showed that adolescents with extremely low academic intrinsic motivation have a pervasive and long-term history of lower academic competence and performance across a multiplicity of educational indices including lower achievement, academic intrinsic motivation, classroom functioning, self-concept, perception of competence, higher academic anxiety, and diminished pursuit of higher education. Further, the findings show that being motivationally at-risk is a long-term phenomenon that places individuals at an educational disadvantage through compromised school competence and diminished lifelong educational performance from childhood through adulthood. The significance of these findings is augmented with evidence in the literature linking low educational achievement to poorer life success in general (Alexander et al., 2003). The breadth of these significant results across the entire spectrum of school years from early childhood through early adulthood increases their importance.

Being at risk with regard to academic intrinsic motivation may be considered problematic not only because of its association with a broad range of adverse educational outcomes, but it also bears on the quality of experience for the student. By definition, academic intrinsic motivation is the enjoyment of school learning characterized by an orientation toward mastery; curiosity; persistence; task-endogeny; and the learning of challenging, difficult, and novel tasks (A. E. Gottfried, 1985, 1986a). Therefore, those extremely low in academic intrinsic motivation do not find school learning enjoyable and evidence little curiosity, mastery striving, or orientation toward task-endogeny, challenge, difficulty, or novelty in learning. These students may be characterized as seeking easy tasks, avoiding academic challenge, and engaging as little as possible with schoolwork. Indeed, students at high risk motivationally may well be characterized as avoidant of academic endeavors.

This conclusion emerges from the convergence of analyses across domains. In the present research, students with at-risk academic intrinsic motivation were more anxious and less happy in school, had lower academic and general self-concepts as well as perception of competence, and were also more avoidant in the testing situation compared to those with higher motivation, which played a mediating role in intellectual performance. Teachers' ratings of children's classroom functioning showed that the children with lower motivation were compromised in other aspects of their classroom functioning aside from academic test achievement, including being significantly less hard working, behaving less appropriately, learning less, and being less happy.

These results have implications for understanding the processes underlying the compromised performance of children with at-risk academic intrinsic motivation. There appears to be a pattern of avoidance and withdrawal from the demands of school learning beginning in the early childhood years. The mediation model tested supports this explanation as well. In this model, lower engagement and greater avoidance in the testing situation played a significant role in mediating the relationship between academic intrinsic motivation and intellectual performance. The results of this mediation model further indicate that academic intrinsic motivation bears a direct and indirect relationship with intellectual performance, as it continued to be significantly related to IQ even after test-taking behaviors were taken into account. Hence, motivational risk has its own direct effect, as well as an indirect one, on intellectual performance.

These findings are consistent with inverse relationships between academic intrinsic motivation and anxiety that have previously been obtained supporting the view that those who withdraw from the threat of a challenging task have lower motivation and higher anxiety (A. E. Gottfried, 1982, 1985). This interpretation regarding academic avoidance is supported by Wolters (2004), who found that for junior high school students in math classes, procrastination, which can be considered a form of academic avoidance, was significantly and inversely predicted by their mastery orientation. Therefore, those with lower mastery orientation had significantly higher procrastination.

The use of extreme subgroup methodology provided a means to identify those who are motivationally at risk. This, combined with longitudinal methodology, allowed for consistency of results to be examined across measures and time. Moreover, this methodology contributed to understanding the concept of at-risk academic intrinsic motivation, which has potential educational applications—for example, identification of children with exceptionally low motivation at an early age and provision of appropriate motivational interventions. The current analyses further support the use of extreme groups with an underpinning rationale. Radke-Yarrow (1998) commented that "renewed attention to subgroups of children at the extremes in the samples for whom we assess central tendencies can bring a new level of insight into the nature of individual functioning."(p. 82) This helps to elucidate developmental data inasmuch as significant differences were obtained in a systematic fashion.

Motivational risk and lower IQ were found to be statistically independent. This is consistent with research cited above showing that motivation and IQ each contribute independently and uniquely to achievement. Moreover, the coefficient of alienation—that is, noncorrelation—between the motivation and IQ aggregate in the present longitudinal study is .87 (A. W. Gottfried et al., 2005) indicating that the overwhelming majority of variance in academic intrinsic motivation is not accounted for by intelligence. Hence, motivational risk can be considered as contributing to the depression in academic performance and persistence beyond and independent of intelligence. Motivational risk and lower IQ are not in one to one correspondence.

Motivational risk has implications for children's school trajectories beyond high school. Regarding postsecondary educational attainment, those motivationally at risk were not only unlikely to take the SAT, but by age 24 they had achieved significantly less educationally compared to their cohort, with a minimal number attaining college degrees, including two-year degrees. A case in point is illustrative. The one individual in the motivational risk group who did take the SAT scored 1530, yet did not attend a four-year college directly out of high school but rather went to a junior college for which the SAT scores were not needed. Had motivation been higher, perhaps this individual would have attended a higher level institution. It should also be noted that this student had the highest motivation score of the at-risk motivation group, had an IQ that approached giftedness at the time that giftedness was designated in this research, and had parental socioeconomic status that was above average in the study sample (A. W. Gottfried et al., 1994).

Students at risk regarding academic intrinsic motivation appear to encounter a double jeopardy. As previously found (A. E. Gottfried et al., 2001), there are two co-occurring continuity trends regarding academic intrinsic motivation from childhood to adolescence (see also Lerner et al., 1996; Roberts & DelVecchio, 2000, regarding continuity trends). One pertains to interindividual (rank order) continuity in which academic intrinsic motivation becomes more stable over time; the other continuity trend involves a concomitant decrease in the entire group's mean level of academic intrinsic motivation over time (A. E. Gottfried et al., 2001). Academic intrinsic motivation became more stable across adolescence compared to middle childhood and also showed significant mean declines. Additionally, using multivariate latent change modeling analyses, A. E. Gottfried et al. (2007) found that from ages 9 through 17, both math achievement and math intrinsic motivation of the entire sample evidenced significant developmental declines. Whereas initial math motivation and achievement were related to later declines in math motivation and achievement, for motivation the relationship was indirect (through achievement) whereas in the case of achievement it was direct. Therefore, math intrinsic motivation was indirectly related to its own developmental decline through its association with the decline in math achievement. Hence, when children begin schooling low in motivation, they are at risk for a continuation of low motivation as well as achievement throughout their schooling. The motivationally at risk are not only likely to be initially lower in their academic intrinsic motivation, but this motivation is also likely to decline over time and become more stable during adolescence. This should sound an alarm for developmentally oriented educators to incorporate academic intrinsic motivation in educational interventions and school programs as soon as possible.

Inasmuch as teachers' ratings of students' academic intrinsic motivation have been found to be significantly and positively correlated with students' own reports of motivation (A. E. Gottfried, 1985), it is apparent that teachers notice students' academic intrinsic motivation. This interpretation bolsters observations of the present effect size analyses. Indeed, Cohen (1988) argued that effect sizes of the magnitude obtained in the present study reach a level of distinction in the natural setting in which it becomes a noticeable phenomenon. In fact, in the present study, teachers' ratings on the Child Behavior Checklist (that had been provided by hundreds of teachers across a diversity of schools and locations [see Guerin, Gottfried, & Thomas, 1997]) showed that children who were identified as motivationally at risk were noticed to be working less hard, learning less, being more poorly behaved, and less happy than the cohort comparison group. It is noteworthy that teachers' ratings occurred independent of, and prior to, our designation of at-risk motivation. These were observations that teachers made on their own. Hence, discriminative and construct validity are provided regarding using the CAIMI to distinguish between the at-risk and cohort comparison groups. In the current study, the lowest 19% had a cutoff raw score of 62 on the aggregated CAIMI general scale. This may serve as a starting point by which researchers and educators can determine their own appropriate cutoff scores.

It should also be noted that the children in the present study were in the normal range of intelligence and not a clinical sample. Further, they attended different schools and hence did not reflect the environment of one school atmosphere in particular. Hence, the results are generalizable across different educational settings including public and private schools as well as in geographic diversity. Moreover, the families of the children in the FLS were of a broad range of the middle socioeconomic status, a demographic group that is not typically considered to be at risk or disadvantaged. Therefore, being motivationally at risk results in being at an educational disadvantage by having depressed academic strivings and success, regardless of being in a relatively more advantaged socioeconomic status. One can further speculate that being motivationally at risk would compound disadvantages for individuals who are also at risk because of socioeconomic disadvantage or by being a member of a culturally underrepresented group. Perhaps these aspects of disadvantage would have cumulative and interactive effects (see, for example, Bornstein & Bradley, 2003; Murdock, 1999).

With regard to relating motivational risk status to school culture, the nature of school and classroom environments are most relevant to this issue. A. E. Gottfried (1985, 1986b), has elaborated on dimensions of environment, both school and home, that facilitate the development of academic intrinsic motivation. These include cognitive discrepancy, competence/mastery, and attribution or overjustification theories of intrinsic motivation (A. E. Gottfried, 1986b). According to cognitive discrepancy theories, intrinsic motivation results from encountering stimuli that do not match existing cognitive structures, thereby creating motivation to reduce this discrepancy. Stimuli and learning materials that produce cognitive discrepancy produce intrinsic motivation as curiosity or exploration. Such stimuli would include those that are novel, complex, incongruous, and surprising, and provide a variety of experience (A. E. Gottfried, 2008).

Competence/mastery theories of intrinsic motivation concern children's experience of effectiveness in interaction with their environment. Children seek to interact effectively with their environment, and to the extent that they experience mastery, their intrinsic motivation is enhanced. Central to this theory is the child's sense of being in control—that is, being a causal agent or influencing the environment by producing successful and noticeable outcomes. Activities may be considered broadly, including play, interactions with toys, learning materials, or individuals including parents, peers, or teachers. Experiences that enhance competence/mastery intrinsic motivation include responsiveness of play materials and the social environment, parental provision of effectance feedback (i.e., competency information) to the child, and availability of materials and activities at an optimal level of challenge relative to the child's developmental abilities (A. E. Gottfried, 1986b; 2008).

The attribution/overjustification approach concerns the impact of extrinsic consequences for learning on intrinsic motivation. Provision of extrinsic consequences is external to the learning process and therefore not derived from learning per se. Such contingencies have important consequences for the development of intrinsic motivation because they affect children's perceptions of the reasons for their engagement in an activity. If children perceive the reason for being engaged in an activity as to receive an extrinsic consequence (e.g., money, toys), their focus of motivation is likely to shift from the process of learning to the receipt of the outcome. Hence, their sense of intrinsic motivation would be reduced. However, if the extrinsic consequence augments the child's sense of competence, then intrinsic motivation is not likely to be adversely affected. Therefore, a person's perception of intrinsic motivation is an outcome of the individual's interpretation of the extrinsic consequence—that is, whether the extrinsic consequence is viewed as the reason for learning or as an indication of the sense of competence. Research on this theoretical emphasis has concentrated on the role of extrinsic consequences for learning, including tangible rewards and praise (A. E. Gottfried, 1986b; 2008).

There is evidence that children's academic intrinsic motivation is positively related to environments in which parents encourage children's autonomy and intrinsic motivation, encourage learning, and actively stimulate intellectual interests (A. E. Gottfried, 2008; A. E. Gottfried, Fleming, et al., 1994, 1998; A. E. Gottfried & Gottfried, 2008). Regarding school environments, those that are personally meaningful to students include activities that are moderately and appropriately challenging; encourage mastery; include fantasy, novelty and humor in curriculum; and provide competence feedback and praise that is informational, not just evaluative, should facilitate the development of academic intrinsic motivation in schools (Henderlong & Lepper, 2002; Urdan & Turner, 2005).

These dimensions of academic environment can be considered to be aspects of intrinsic motivational school culture. To the extent that classroom environments are devoid of these dimensions and motivational experiences and opportunities, then school culture would be lacking in the stimulation of academic intrinsic motivation. Some contemporary educational trends that would impede the development of academic intrinsic motivation in school culture might include the ubiquitous use of test score accountability and the adoption of one-size-fits-all scripted curriculum programs. Whereas test scores may be one form of school evaluation, they ought not to be considered the only or best methods. When test scores are predominantly relied on to compare and evaluate students and schools, anxiety of students and teachers may be raised by such high-stakes testing and this accountability utilizes scores as outcomes rather than a way to examine learning processes. Importance is not placed on assessing whether students are enjoying learning, striving, excited, curious, investigative, exploratory, or mastery-oriented. Rather, test score accountability employs externally determined outcomes that often lead teachers to teach to the tests instead of spending time developing academic intrinsic motivation that would ultimately enhance learning and achievement.

Regarding the use of scripted programs, the first author has taught graduate courses in educational psychology and motivation for many years. Many classroom teachers who are pursuing their master's degrees in educational psychology have provided anecdotal evidence indicating that the use of scripted programs in their schools has limited their ability to teach to the individual students' academic and motivational needs. These teachers, whether novice or experienced, are frustrated and unhappy using scripted programs and themselves show impaired intrinsic motivation. Hence, to the extent that the culture of the schools is antithetical to the development of academic intrinsic motivation in students by emphasizing externally derived standards, test accountability, and rigid scripted curriculum programs—but not oriented toward enhancing dimensions of school environment that would facilitate academic intrinsic motivation—then we can expect an increase in at-risk levels of academic intrinsic motivation in the students in the United States.

To the extent that school culture fails to support students' development of academic intrinsic motivation, students will need to look elsewhere for the development of these strivings, perhaps to their parents, home environments, peers, or extracurricular activities (A. Gottfried & Gottfried, 2007). However, this places the responsibility for developing such motivation outside of schools and there are likely to be few children who have these resources available to them. Most children and adolescents are likely to be exposed to a school culture that emphasizes externally determined and rigid expectations but not the development of academic intrinsic motivation. It may take the most intrinsically motivated, perhaps those with gifted motivation (A. E. Gottfried & Gottfried, in press), to overcome the absence of an academic intrinsic motivational culture in the school.

Therefore, to the extent that students evidence extremely low—that is, at-risk—academic intrinsic motivation in addition to the double jeopardy described above, there is a third jeopardy with regard to being in a school cultural context that not only fails to encourage students' enjoyment of the learning process but instead is high in conditions that would be expected to be detrimental to the development of their academic intrinsic motivation. This may have an effect that backfires: Instead of a school culture that encourages the development of strong academic intrinsic motivation, which is a positive factor for students' academic competence and performance, the absence of such a school culture would provide conditions that diminish academic intrinsic motivation. As evidenced by the study results, low academic intrinsic motivation is an adverse and significant factor for lowered school competence and performance. Those at risk because of low academic intrinsic motivation would not be expected to be able to overcome these conditions. We suggest that the presence of school culture that is adverse to the development of academic intrinsic motivation applies to all students—across socio-economic status, ethnicity, and gender.

In conclusion, motivationally at-risk students comprise a unique subgroup from early childhood through adulthood. Notably, motivational risk placed these children at a disadvantage throughout their childhood and adolescent years into early adulthood as they evidenced a history of diminished development and school engagement across a breadth of cognitive, affective, and behavioral outcomes. Being motivationally at risk has significant implications for the development of school culture by emphasizing the need to encourage academic intrinsic motivation. It is essential that motivational risk and its related outcomes be prevented through early identification and intervention focusing on learning experiences emphasizing an optimal degree of challenge, stimulation of students' enjoyment of learning, and development of their mastery strivings. As we have previously said, "Teaching the desire to learn may be as important as teaching academic skills" (A. E. Gottfried & Gottfried, 2004, p. 129). Motivation may well provide its own foundation for future development, and academic and career success.

⚏ Note

[1] For academic anxiety and the GATSB measures, nonsuccess is defined as falling above the mean because these are adverse outcomes.

⚏ Acknowledgment

This research was funded by grants from the Spencer Foundation, Thrasher Research Fund, California State Universities, Fullerton and Northridge, and the Society for the Psychological Study of Social Issues. We gratefully thank the participants and families in the Fullerton

Longitudinal Study for their willingness to be a part of and their continuous support of this extensive investigation. We also acknowledge the previous and ongoing contributions of our colleagues and graduate student assistants to this research.

⠿ References

Achenbach, T. M., & Rescorla, L. A. (2001). *Manual for the ASEBA School-Age Forms and Profiles.* Burlington, VT: ASEBA.

Alexander, K. L., Entwisle, D. R., & Dauber, S. L. (2003). *On the success of failure: A reassessment of the effects of retention in the primary school grades* (2nd ed.). New York: Cambridge University Press.

Anderson, E. S., & Keith, T. Z. (1997) A longitudinal test of a model of academic success for at-risk high school students. *Journal of Educational Research, 90,* 259–268.

Baron, R. M., & Kenny, D. A. (1986). The moderator-mediator variable distinction in social psychological research: Conceptual, strategic, and statistical consideration. *Journal of Personality and Social Psychology, 51,* 1173–1182.

Carr, M., Borkowski, J. G., & Maxwell, S. E. (1991). Motivational components of underachievement. *Developmental Psychology, 27,* 108–118.

Bornstein, M. H., & Bradley, R. H. (Eds.). (2003). *Socioeconomic status, parenting, and child development.* Mahwah, NJ: Lawrence Erlbaum.

Christenson, S. L., & Thurlow, M. L. (2004). School dropouts: Prevention, considerations, interventions, and challenges. *Current Directions in Psychological Science, 13,* 36–39.

Cohen, J. (1988). *Statistical power analysis for the behavioral sciences* (2nd ed.). New York: Academic Press.

Cohen, J., Cohen, P., West, S. G., & Aiken, L. S. (2003). *Applied multiple regression/correlation analysis for the behavioral sciences* (3rd ed.). Mahwah, NJ: Lawrence Erlbaum.

Cool, V. A., & Keith,T. Z. (1991). Testing a model of school learning: Direct and indirect effects on academic achievement. *Contemporary Educational Psychology, 16,* 28–44.

Dai, D. Y. (2002). Are gifted girls motivationally disadvantaged? Review, reflection, and redirection. *Journal for the Education of the Gifted, 25,* 315–358.

Dicintio, M. J., & Gee, S. (1999). Control is the key: Unlocking the motivation of at-risk students. *Psychology in the Schools, 36,* 231–237.

Epstein, S. (1979). The stability of behavior: On predicting most of the people much of the time. *Journal of Personality and Social Psychology, 37,* 1097–1126.

Fredricks, J. A., Blumenfeld, P. C., & Paris, A. H. (2004). School engagement: Potential of the concept, state of the evidence. *Review of Educational Research, 74,* 59–109.

Gottfried, A., & Gottfried, A. (2007, February). *Paths from gifted motivation to leadership.* Paper presented at the 17th Annual Kravis-de Roulet Leadership Conference, Claremont McKenna College, Claremont, CA.

Gottfried, A. E. (1982). Relationships between academic intrinsic motivation and anxiety in children and young adolescents. *Journal of School Psychology, 20,* 205–315.

Gottfried, A. E. (1985). Academic intrinsic motivation in elementary and junior high school students. *Journal of Educational Psychology, 77,* 631–645.

Gottfried, A. E. (1986a). *Children's Academic Intrinsic Motivation Inventory.* Odessa, FL: Psychological Assessment Resources.

Gottfried, A. E. (1986b). Intrinsic motivational aspects of play experiences and play materials. In A. W. Gottfried & C. Brown (Eds.), *Play interactions* (pp. 81–99). Lexington, MA: Lexington Books.

Gottfried, A. E. (1990). Academic intrinsic motivation in young elementary school children. *Journal of Educational Psychology, 82,* 525–538.

Gottfried, A. E. (2008). Home environment and academic intrinsic motivation. In N. Salkind (Ed.), *Encyclopedia of educational psychology* (pp. 485–490). Thousand Oaks, CA: Sage.

Gottfried, A. E., Fleming, J. S., & Gottfried, A. W. (1994). Role of parental motivational practices in children's academic intrinsic motivation and achievement. *Journal of Educational Psychology, 86,* 104–113.

Gottfried, A. E., Fleming, J. S., & Gottfried, A. W. (1998). Role of cognitively stimulating home environment in children's academic intrinsic motivation: A longitudinal study. *Child Development, 69,* 1448–1460.

Gottfried, A. E., Fleming, J. S., & Gottfried, A. W. (2001). Continuity of academic intrinsic motivation from childhood through late adolescence: A longitudinal study. *Journal of Educational Psychology, 93,* 3–13.

Gottfried, A. E., & Gottfried, A. W. (2004). Toward the development of a conceptualization of gifted motivation. *Gifted Child Quarterly. 48,* 121–132.

Gottfried, A. E., & Gottfried, A. W. (2008, March). *Parental motivational strategies differ for motivationally gifted and at-risk children: A longitudinal study.* Paper presented at the meeting of the American Educational Research Association, NY.

Gottfried, A. E., & Gottfried, A. W. (in press). Development of gifted motivation from childhood through young adulthood: Longitudinal research and implications for gifted assessment and education. In L. Shavinina (Ed.), *International handbook on giftedness.* Dordrecht, The Netherlands: Springer Science.

Gottfried, A. E., Marcoulides, G. A., Gottfried, A. W., Oliver, P., & Guerin, D. (2007). Modeling the developmental decline in academic intrinsic math motivation: Childhood through adolescence. *International Journal of Behavioral Development, 31,* 317–327.

Gottfried, A. W. (1985). Measures of socioeconomic status in child development research: Data and recommendations. *Merrill-Palmer Quarterly, 31,* 85–92.

Gottfried, A. W., Gottfried, A. E., Bathurst, K., & Guerin, D. W. (1994). *Gifted IQ: Early developmental aspects.* New York: Plenum.

Gottfried, A. W., Gottfried, A. E., Bathurst, K., Guerin, D. W., & Parramore, M. M. (2003). Socioeconomic status in children's development and family environment: Infancy through adolescence. In M. H. Bornstein & R. H. Bradley (Eds.), *Socioeconomic status, parenting, and child development* (pp. 189–207). Mahwah, NJ: Lawrence Erlbaum.

Gottfried, A.W., Gottfried, A. E., Cook, C., & Morris, P. (2005). Educational characteristics of adolescents with gifted academic intrinsic motivation: A longitudinal study from school entry through early adulthood. *Gifted Child Quarterly, 49,* 172–186.

Gottfried, A. W., Gottfried, A. E., & Guerin, D. (2006). The Fullerton Longitudinal Study: A long-term investigation of intellectual and motivational giftedness. *Journal for the Education of the Gifted, 29,* 430–450.

Guerin, D. W., & Gottfried, A. W. (1994). Developmental stability and change in parent reports of temperament: A ten-year longitudinal investigation from infancy through preadolescence. *Merrill-Palmer Quarterly, 40,* 334–355.

Guerin, D. W., Gottfried, A. W., Oliver, P. H., & Thomas, C. W. (2003). *Temperament: Infancy through adolescence.* New York: Kluwer Academic/Plenum Publishers.

Guerin, D. W., Gottfried, A. W., & Thomas, C. W. (1997). Difficult temperament and behavior problems: A longitudinal study from 1.5 to 12 years. *International Journal of Behavioral Development, 21,* 71–90.

Guide to the assessment of test session behavior (GATSB). (1993). San Antonio, TX: Psychological Corporation.

Hardre, P. L., & Reeve, J. (2003). A motivational model of rural students' intentions to persist in, versus drop out of, high school. *Journal of Educational Psychology, 95,* 347–356.

Henderlong, J., & Lepper, M. R. (2002). The effects of praise on children's intrinsic motivation: A review and synthesis. *Psychological Bulletin, 128,* 774–795.

Hollingshead, A. B. (1975). *Four factor index of social status.* Unpublished manuscript, Yale University, Department of Sociology.

Kagan, J., Snidman, N., & Arcus, D. (1998). The value of extreme groups. In R. B. Cairns, L. R. Bergman, & J. Kagan (Eds.), *Methods and models for studying the individual* (pp. 65–80). Thousand Oaks, CA: Sage.

Lehrer, B. E., & Hieronymus, A. N. (1977). Predicting achievement using intellectual, academic-motivational and selected non-intellectual factors. *Journal of Experimental Education, 45,* 44–51.

Lerner, R. M., Lerner, J. V., von Eye, A., Ostrum, C. W., Nitz, K., Talwar-Soni, R., & Tubman, J. G. (1996). Continuity and discontinuity across the transition of early adolescence: A developmental contextual perspective. In J. A. Graber, J. Brooks-Gunn, & A. C. Petersen (Eds.), *Transitions through early adolescence: Interpersonal domains and contexts* (pp. 3–22). Mahwah, NJ: Lawrence Erlbaum.

Lloyd, J., & Barenblatt, L. (1984). Intrinsic intellectuality: Its relations to social class, intelligence, and achievement. *Journal of Personality and Social Psychology, 46,* 646–654.

Marcoulides, G. A., Gottfried, A. E., Gottfried, A. W., & Oliver, P. (2008, March). *Latent transition analysis of academic intrinsic motivation from childhood through adolescence.* Paper presented at the meeting of the American Educational Research Association, NY.

Marsh, H. W. (1990). *Self-Description Questionnaire II: Manual and research monograph.* San Antonio, TX: Psychological Corporation.

Miserandino, M. (1996). Children who do well in school: Individual differences in perceived competence and autonomy in above-average children. *Journal of Educational Psychology, 88, 203–214.*

Murdock, T. B. (1999). The social context of risk: Status and motivational predictors of alienation in middle school. *Journal of Educational Psychology, 91,* 62–75.

Pintrich, R. R., & Schunk, D. H. (2002). *Motivation in education: Theory, research, and applications.* (2nd ed.). Upper Saddle River, NJ: Merrill Prentice Hall.

Radke-Yarrow, M. (1998). Comments on chapter 4. In R. B. Cairns, L. R. Bergman, & J. Kagan (Eds.), *Methods and models for studying the individual* (pp. 80–82). Thousand Oaks, CA: Sage.

Roberts, B. W., & DelVecchio, W. F. (2000). The rank-order consistency of personality traits from childhood to old age: A quantitative review of longitudinal studies. *Psychological Bulletin, 126,* 3–25.

Rosenthal, R., Rosnow, R. L., & Rubin, D. B. (2000). *Contrasts and effect sizes in behavioral research: A correlational approach.* New York: Cambridge University Press.

Rumberger, R. W. (1987). High school dropouts: A review of issues and evidence. *Review of Educational Research, 57,* 101–121.

Rumberger, R. W. (1995). Dropping out of middle school: A multilevel analysis of students and schools. *American Educational Research Journal, 32,* 583–625.

Rushton, J. P., Brainerd, C. J., & Pressley, M. (1983). Behavioral development and construct validity: The principle of aggregation. *Psychological Bulletin, 94,* 18–38.

Stipek, D. (2002). *Motivation to learn: Integrating theory and practice* (4th ed.). Boston: Allyn and Bacon.

Urdan, T., & Turner, J. C. (2005). Competence motivation in the classroom. In A. J. Elliot and C. S. Dweck (Eds.), *Handbook of competence and motivation* (pp. 297–317). New York: Guilford Press.

Vallerand, R. J., Fortier, M. S., & Guay, F. (1997). Self-determination and persistence in a real-life setting: Toward a motivational model of high school dropout. *Journal of Personality and Social Psychology, 72,* 1161–1176.

Wachs, T. D. (1991a). Environmental considerations in studies with non-extreme groups. In T. D. Wachs & R. Plomin (Eds.), *Conceptualization and measurement of organism-environment interaction* (pp. 44–67). Washington, DC: American Psychological Association.

Wachs, T. D. (1991b). Synthesis: Promising research designs, measures, and strategies. In T. D. Wachs & R. Plomin (Eds.), *Conceptualization and measurement of organism-environment interaction* (162–182). Washington DC: American Psychological Association.

Wechsler, D. (1974). *Manual for the Wechsler Intelligence Scale for Children.* San Antonio, TX: Psychological Corporation.

Wechsler, D. (1981). *WAIS-R manual.* New York: Psychological Corporation.

Wechsler, D. (1991). *WISC-III. Wechsler Intelligence Scale for Children— Third Edition.* San Antonio, TX: Psychological Corporation.

Wigfield, A., Eccles, J. S., Schiefele, U., Roeser, R. W., & Davis-Kean, P. (2006). Development of achievement motivation. In N. Eisenberg (Ed.), *Handbook of child psychology: Vol. 3. Social, emotional, and personality development* (6th ed., pp. 933–1002). New York: Wiley.

Wolters, C. A. (2004). Advancing achievement goal theory: Using goal structures and goal orientations to predict students' motivation, cognition, and achievement. *Journal of Educational Psychology, 96,* 236–250.

Woodcock, R. W., & Johnson, M. B. (1977). *Woodcock-Johnson Psycho-Educational Battery.* Hingham, MA: Teaching Resources.

Woodcock, R. W., & Johnson, M. B. (1989). *Woodcock-Johnson Psycho-Educational Battery—Revised.* Allen, TX: DLM.

PART 2 ⠿

Students' Social Cognitions and Motivational Processes

4 ⠿

Essential Solidarities for Understanding Latino Adolescents' Moral and Academic Engagement

Theresa A. Thorkildsen, Courtney J. Golant,
and Elizabeth Cambray-Engstrom

Feeling part of a group is central to individuals' well-being, especially for adolescents who rely heavily on feedback from group members as they explore possible identities. In adolescence, individuals learn the ramifications of voluntarily associating with groups that reflect civil, nationalistic, and personal interests, and of being assigned to social groups such as those formed around academic or ethnic characteristics. Regardless of whether group membership is chosen or assigned, collective norms influence the solidarities that emerge and become part of adolescents' identities. It is easy to imagine that solidarity with others, real or imagined, plays a role in adolescents' motivation, but it is more difficult to predict which reference groups are critical for understanding moral and academic engagement in school. This chapter discusses a study in which we evaluated Mexican American adolescents' civil, ethnic, and local school identities, and determined which of these three value systems best accounted for the diversity in their educational commitments.

Each of the three identity dimensions compared in our study has been used in other research to reflect individuals' cultural commitments. Despite discrepancies in how culture is defined by researchers, there is congruence in that most definitions refer to some form of self-chosen group solidarity. We are working toward a better understanding of how to communicate with students about their present and future roles in society by determining if Mexican American adolescents' sense of solidarity with those who share similar values is also associated with other indicators of their moral and academic engagement. Studying intra-ethnic variation in these adolescents' views allows us to systematically discern which dimensions of their cultural identity best explain the variance in their personal educational standards and readiness to act on those standards.

⠴ Culture as Solidarity

To see why cultural concerns are important aspects of motivation, we need to accept a few premises that were initially put forth in fields outside of psychology. In earlier work, education was defined as an independent social sphere charged with helping individuals find and understand their place in society (Walzer, 1983). At a psychological level, it was enough to know that individuals construct different conceptions of school and their place within it (Thorkildsen, 1989, 2007). The simplicity of this representation has been more recently challenged by a stronger articulation of the nature and purposes of the civil sphere. Alexander's (2006) thick description of a pluralistic civil sphere led us to wonder whether schools are more accurately construed as civil institutions than as free-standing entities charged with fostering individual growth. To explore the psychological viability of this change, we reconceptualized school's role in society and considered a more multifaceted notion of cultural solidarity than we could imagine in the 1980s. We asked whether adolescents' commitment to broad civil norms coalesced into clear civil identities and if those identities were independent of their ethnic and local identities. These three forms of solidarity were then compared with adolescents' beliefs about an ideal school and their action readiness to identify the role of each in students' moral and academic engagement.

Civil Solidarities

According to Alexander's (2006) new description, the civil sphere is one in which the greater good is preserved by balancing community obligations with respect for personal autonomy and a commitment to justice. Civil activities address the tension between upholding universal moral values and preserving personal autonomy in the struggle to achieve a fully inclusive society. Civil solidarities and their corresponding effect on individuals' identities should be independent of those found in other social spheres because they require thoughtful consideration of norms accepted by people unlike ourselves. Adding further complexity, individuals are represented as autonomous agents who decide which social pressures to embrace and which to reject. Because schools offer a forum for discussions about civil responsibilities, it seems reasonable to think of them as civil institutions charged with helping each agent to define his or her civil identity.

Two Dated Notions of Civility, Citizenship, and Schooling

Although Alexander (2006) did not discuss the role of school in the civil sphere, it is easy to see how educational policy has mirrored his broader discussion. He contrasts a new pluralistic definition of the civil sphere with cultural determinism and capitalistic definitions. These latter two conceptions, albeit dated, are highly salient in educational policy decisions.

The deterministic notion of the civil sphere emerges from the idea that societal institutions are static in nature and that society is a system of hierarchies passed from one generation to the next. Culture and the extant solidarities are represented as a series of traditions, rituals, and rites of passage. Some solidarities, such as those formed around nationality, are still sustained by these ideas. Nevertheless, cultural determinists once assumed that the civil sphere, culture, and nationality were synonymous and intra-cultural variation was a sign of human fallibility. Individuals, in this view, are not autonomous agents; they are products of the society in which they live. Studies of identity serve only to indicate how well individuals embrace appropriate social norms.

When civil society was defined in culturally deterministic terms, schools helped to perpetuate caste systems and other societal hierarchies by rewarding well-situated individuals while ignoring an imperative of justice for all (Kluger, 1975). Individuals succeeded in this sort of civil society by behaving properly and finding ways to subvert their need for autonomy. The movie *Dead Poets Society* illustrates well the motivational struggles adolescents face when such hierarchical notions of civility are applied to education because it illustrates how individuals fail to experience freedom to explore their talents and tastes.

What we are calling the capitalistic notion of the civil sphere represents civility as an epiphenomenon of capitalism in which market forces determine the greater good. As many social critics point out, this second conception can foster a system in which the rich become richer and the poor and disenfranchised are left behind. Societal institutions are constructed and destroyed as individuals and groups endeavor to meet self-interested goals. Individuals are autonomous agents who behave like consumers. Their civil identities reflect the selection of particular values and commitments. Schools have embraced this notion of civility largely by using economic policy to make decisions about what to teach and treating learning as a meritocratic process in which those who achieve well are rewarded with more opportunities (Walberg & Bast, 2003). In this respect, schools and classrooms have often been defined as cultures in which success is tied to workforce demands.

Taking Pluralism Seriously

The newest conception of the civil sphere involves valuing cultural pluralism and the resulting diversity in individuals' civil identities, but this possibility is only becoming acknowledged in education. Nevertheless, our comparison of Alexander's deterministic, capitalistic, and pluralistic conceptions of the civil sphere with educational policies supports the possibility that schools are civil institutions. Civil institutions are places in which individuals and groups with divergent interests collectively negotiate their place within global, national, and local communities. In schools, individuals can meet others with different ideas, examine various definitions of civility, and develop a capacity for social criticism and democratic integration.

Extending Alexander's (2006) ideas to determine which visions of civil participation are salient in school, we began by asking whether adolescents' personal life goals provide insight into their civil identities. We assumed that adolescents who participate in educational activities may experience social as well as intellectual growth when working toward the civil ideal of universal justice and respect for persons. Individuals who understand and work toward this pluralistic ideal could be expected to build socially valuable solidarities as they define their civil responsibilities.

Other Solidarities

In addition to learning about civil solidarities, most adolescents discover the importance of voluntary and assigned solidarities such as those formed around ethnic and local understandings. Again, it may be helpful to understand that these solidarities can be real or imagined by each agent, a possibility that distinguishes them from a sense of belongingness to a tangible group. Voluntary solidarities can be constrained by life experiences and social positions, but the permeability of such group boundaries allows adolescents to choose from among an array of options. For example, the Mexican American adolescents (n = 234) we surveyed could choose allegiance to one or more nationalities. Some adolescents identified primarily with the cultural norms found in Mexico whereas others reported allegiance to two nations, Mexico and the United States. A third group reported allegiance to no particular countries, and interestingly, none of the adolescents reported allegiance only to the United States. These national allegiances offer one rough indication of how these adolescents define their ethnic identity as distinct from their biologically constrained racial classification.

Independent of national identities, racial solidarities also affect individuals' habits of living (Kessing, 1981). Involuntary classifications such as race may have a different effect on adolescents' identities because group boundaries are impermeable (Jackson, Sullivan, Harnish, & Hodge, 1996). As adolescents increasingly attend school in racially homogeneous neighborhoods, solidarity can be strengthened by incorporating corresponding racial and ethnic perspectives into the curriculum. Adolescents may need and benefit from coaching on how to respond to common racial stereotypes and to their emerging understanding of racial status hierarchies, yet the solidarities they invent for themselves seem to influence their moral and academic engagement.

Like others, adolescents also form solidarities around local institutions and the structures within them (Geertz, 1983). Students attend different schools, or as is the case in large schools, they are sometimes assigned to smaller clusters in which individuals are expected to find meaningful relationships with teachers and peers. When smaller academic units are formed within a large school, students can identify with their assigned cohort as well as with the school itself. Similarly, although adolescents select courses from a range of options, they may be tracked according to their academic performance and offered limited opportunities to change tracks or otherwise choose their academic placement. When adolescents find cultural boundaries such as those tied to race or academic standing to be impermeable, they can incorporate these group assignments into their identities or resist them. Nevertheless, most people inevitably accept these group memberships and invariably come to terms with the relative permanence of their assigned classifications.

Comparing Solidarities

These premises about the effects of different solidarities on engagement are speculative, yet the solidarities adolescents imagine seem to play a role in their identities and the personal standards they use to guide decisions in school (Chang, Chen, Greenberger, Dooley, & Heckhausen, 2006; French, Seidman, Allen, & Aber, 2006). Extending earlier findings, adolescents in our research held divergent views about civility and their responsibilities for promoting a civil society. They voluntarily identified with different national allegiances and were assigned to racial and academic groups. When details of these solidarities are consolidated within and across students, clear group norms seem to emerge. We expected to see adolescents' civil identities explaining more motivational variance than racial, ethnic, or local school identities. Even so, each of the solidarities that adolescents build and accept involves a negotiation of where they are and where they would like to position themselves in the world. Full acknowledgment of adolescents' autonomy in the civil sphere involves the acceptance of their freedom to choose which solidarities and corresponding norms are central to their identities and thus contribute to their moral and academic engagement.

∷ The Function of an Ideal School

Our decision to ask adolescents to imagine an ideal school is grounded in a second set of ideas, extrapolated from Alexander's (2006) pluralistic representation of the civil sphere. Schools are sustained by public opinion, cultural codes, and specific institutional practices. They place controls on how individuals offer judgments of particular social norms and so can foster change. Hence schools are places in which most individuals develop, evaluate, and sometimes revise current terms of civil solidarity because most community members are involved with these institutions for at least some portion of their lives.

Solidarities between and within schools facilitate the preparation of a diverse range of individuals for involvement in society. Between schools, educators endorse a number of different means of negotiating social participation. Within schools, students are expected to imagine a universal common good as they regularly participate in interactions calling for civility, criticism, and mutual respect. Educators often teach students to situate themselves in a multifaceted array of solidarities and understand the ramifications of their decisions. Regardless of their structure, schools have become places in which various commitments are examined and evaluated.

By acknowledging everyone in their community, educators and students ideally discover how to understand people they may or may not know and learn to respect on principle the idea that all humans share a common set of values. Principals, counselors, and teachers may also miss or fail to respect essential features of students' cultural identities and introduce distorted social norms. For example, when students see no representatives of their ethnic heritage in the material they are asked to learn, they might mistakenly assume that the boundaries of civil society fail to include them. Similarly, if schools focus only on local or ethnic concerns, participants may not adequately conceptualize and contribute to a broader democratic society. Overrepresentation of certain groups in educational materials could foster attitudes of superiority, eliciting ideologies of domination and oppression in the broader community.

Regular conversations about the boundaries of the civil sphere and the relative inclusiveness of such boundaries already occur in the design of educational activities but could better reflect a commitment to cultural pluralism. Of course, schools cannot completely change boundaries in the civil sphere, but by remaining responsive to different types of solidarity, they can regularly challenge other social spheres and endeavor to restrict domination and oppression. Including students in such conversations can help them clarify their identities and understanding of the norms operating in the larger society.

⠃⠃ Adolescents' Sense of the Ideal

To explore these possibilities, we evaluated adolescents' understanding of how schools contribute to the project of creating a civil society by asking them to evaluate how often particular activities and concerns should be emphasized in an ideal school. These adolescents thought about how schools might promote the common good and participated in rudimentary forms of social criticism. Specifically, they evaluated how often educators should address issues of fairness, epistemology, student motivation, and meta-cognitive strategy use.

Adolescents' fairness judgments represented a mixture of regulative and communicative concerns. Items for this survey emerged from interviews in which students evaluated corrective, distributive, procedural, and commutative justice issues as they related to learning, test, and contest situations (Thorkildsen, 2000; Thorkildsen, Sodonis, & White-McNulty, 2004; Thorkildsen & White-McNulty, 2002). Adolescents evaluated items that were somewhat contradictory. Individuals who indicated that educators should consider most of the included practices offered a complex vision of an ideal school and revealed an awareness of contingencies. For example, adolescents with complex reasoning might see that there are times when teachers should ensure that everyone tries to learn the same material and times when equity distributions would be fairer. Adolescents indicating that educators should consider only some of these contingencies revealed more narrowly focused priorities that reflected a limited sense of the common good.

Adolescents also completed an epistemology survey containing items that emerged from another set of developmental interviewers focusing on students' commitment to different forms of knowledge. (See review in Thorkildsen, 2007.) At relatively young ages (6 or 7), most students understand the differences between matters of logic, intellectual conventions, and personal preferences. It is not until sometime during middle school that most students consistently distinguish controversial and noncontroversial topics. We assumed that the adolescents in our study would be able to distinguish these different forms of knowledge and asked them to evaluate how often teachers should emphasize each form.

Adolescents also completed a motivation strategies instrument on which they evaluated how teachers should help all students sustain a strong motivation to learn. Respondents considered how often teachers should use concrete gestures, thought patterns, and other routine classroom habits that have been recommended in previous research (Thorkildsen & Nicholls, 2002; Thorkildsen, Nolen, & Fournier, 1994; Thorkildsen et al., 2004). Once again, individuals with higher scores on this measure were more concerned with contingencies than were individuals with lower scores.

Adolescents' awareness and use of meta-cognitive strategies, the final dimension in this collection of measures, has not been consistently incorporated into previous research but is sometimes treated as a major explanation for individual differences in academic achievement (Zimmerman, 1989). We asked adolescents to imagine a common tension between obligations in school and in other social spheres. Students who manage their time effectively, keep their materials organized, and understand how to maximize productivity when they have time to study are presumably more likely to do well in school than students without these skills. Some schools help students with these regulative skills using direct instruction whereas other schools leave such teaching up to parents and voluntary organizations. The adolescents in our study evaluated how often schools should accept responsibility for such instruction, and high scores indicated that schools should accept all responsibility whereas low scores indicated that such instruction should occur outside of school.

Taken together, these measures reflect four common ethical features of education. Knowing that engagement is high when there is a strong match between someone's personal standards and opportunities to act on those standards did not allow us to fully imagine adolescents' educational expectations. Measuring adolescents' standards for an ideal school strengthened our knowledge of which standards guided their moral and academic engagement.

⠇⠇ The Engagement Force

A third set of assumptions in need of clarification concerns the concept of engagement. In culture-focused research, a theoretical rift has emerged in how researchers who study the psychology of motivation and those who study educational policy represent this notion, implying conflicts where none may exist. Definitions of engagement seem to reflect different assumptions about what develops. Psychologists focus on human development whereas educational policy research focuses on institutional development.

More specifically, psychologists consider engagement to be an intrapersonal feature of a more complex motivational system that is profoundly affected by individuals' relationships within institutions (Bandura, 1999; Thorkildsen, 2007). As should be apparent by our representation of solidarities, psychologists tend to define engagement by imagining culture as a meaning-making enterprise that serves to regulate human behavior (Oyserman, Bybee, & Terry, 2006; Triandis, 1995). Individuals are assumed to choose which solidarities are central or peripheral to their identities, even though they volunteer for some cultural groups and are assigned to others. Individuals' engagement changes as they learn more about themselves, their relationships with others, and their respective social positions. Nevertheless, their awareness is constrained by their environment.

In educational policy research, engagement is defined in relation to various structural supports for enhancing student participation. The focus is on institutional supports designed to clarify cultural boundaries and improve retention rates (Terenzini, Pascarella, & Blimling, 1996). The resulting institutional definition of development equates engagement with enrollment in courses and other activities (Mahoney, Cairns, & Farmer, 2003; Nakamura, 2001). According to this institutional definition, merely being a member of a group can constitute engagement. It should not be surprising, therefore, that these psychological and educational definitions of engagement emerge from different theoretical leanings and that the resulting studies, in turn, facilitate discrepant findings and conclusions.

Because our assumption is that solidarity choices constrain everyone's understanding of and participation in educational institutions, we adopted an interdisciplinary approach to the study of moral and academic engagement. Starting with psychological assumptions, we defined engagement as a knowledge-driven force that compels participation (Bandura, 1999), comparing adolescents' cultural identities with their beliefs about an ideal school and readiness to act on such beliefs. In this way, we evaluated engagement as a personal system of meaning. We also explored whether variations in broader cultural classifications revealed differences in psychological patterns that are often assumed by researchers working in disciplines like sociology and education policy. Identifying engagement patterns attributable to adolescents' national preferences and immigrant status offered an intra-ethnic exploration of engagement. Knowing that adolescents were also assigned in an unsystematic manner to academic houses and within each house to performance-based tracks, it was possible to determine whether salient patterns of engagement could be attributed to educators' sociocultural notions of solidarity and adolescents understanding of their local school identities. Our initial attempt to consolidate discrepant notions of engagement is reflected in these comparisons of civil, ethnic, and local systems of meaning.

∷ Adolescents' Solidarities and Engagement

Our evaluation of the relations between adolescents' cultural solidarities and engagement offers multifaceted representations of these adolescents' motivation. Table 4.1 outlines the tools we used to assess adolescents'

Table 4–1. Scale Names and Sample Items

SCALE NAME	SAMPLE ITEMS
Individualistic goals *(19 items, α = .86)*	I will feel most successful if I earn enough money to live comfortably; do what my family expects of me. I am most concerned about learning something interesting; discovering more about my abilities.
Communitarian goals *(18 items, α = .92)*	I will feel most successful if I help solve global problems; make sure everyone's rights are protected. I am most concerned about learning how democracy works; studying different cultures.
Personal belief in a just world *(7 items, α = .71)*	When thinking about the world, I assume that I am treated fairly; believe that I typically get what I deserve; believe that most things happening in my life are fair.
Fair school *(41 items, α = .87)*	In an ideal school there should be opportunities to learn challenging ideas; students should follow the rules; students should receive grades; there should be contests.
Epistemology *(19 items, α = .88)*	Teachers should make sure students learn useful facts; spelling rules; about controversial topics; scientific methods.
Sustain motivation *(43 items, α = .91)*	Most students will stay involved if they solve problems by working hard; can monitor their progress; find someone to compete with; have teachers who care about them.
Teach strategies *(20 items, α = .91)*	Students do their best work when they make a list of things to do; take time to write down assignments; outline their notes to make a study guide.
Readiness to work hard *(36 items, α = .93)*	I work hard when I see how I might use the ideas; my teachers care about me; I can figure out problems on my own; rules for behavior are fair; the material fascinates me.

(continued)

TABLE 4–1. Scale Names and Sample Items (*continued*)

SCALE NAME	SAMPLE ITEMS
Readiness to cheat or take shortcuts *(39 items, α = .97)*	I take shortcuts or cheat when I am not sure how to do the work; I don't like my teacher; I can't see why the work is worth doing; the teacher never gave us directions; I want to add fun into my day.
Readiness to address justice *(13 items, α = .89)*	I think I am more affected by justice than most people. Nothing angers me more than seeing injustice. I am especially tormented when I cause injustice.

Note. There were 234 Mexican American adolescents in this sample. Of these 78 (50 males, 28 females) said that Mexican and U.S. norms were part of their ethnic identity, 78 (50 males, 28 females) said that only Mexican norms were part of their ethnic identity, and 78 (50 males, 28 females) said that their ethnic identity was not tied to any countries.

civil identities, beliefs about an ideal school, and readiness to act on their beliefs. The remainder of this chapter illustrates the steps we went through to verify that only the civil identities of these Mexican American students explained variance in their moral and academic engagement.

Distributions of Solidarities

Consistent with Alexander's pluralistic notion of the civil sphere, we represented adolescents' civil identities as profiles of how strongly they endorse individualistic and communitarian norms and believe in a just world (Dalbert, 1999; Oyserman, Coon, & Kemmelmeier, 2002; Triandis, 1995). Assuming that culture is the confluence of multiple solidarities, some of which are voluntary and others assigned, we also compared adolescents' ethnic and local identities to their personal education standards. Adolescents were assigned local identities by being unsystematically placed in academic houses and systematically placed in ability tracks. We concluded that ethnic solidarity was not central to moral and academic engagement because a great deal of variance was evident in adolescents' ideal school standards and action readiness, even though only Mexican American youth from immigrant families were included.

Civil Identities

When cluster analysis was used to classify adolescents according to their civil identities, relatively few adolescents endorsed Alexander's (2006) pluralistic vision, but those with alternative beliefs showed perspectives consistent with historical notions of civil responsibility. One group reported few life goals and the belief that their world is basically unjust, indicative of no obvious civil identity (Table 4.2). A second, and by far the largest group, reported moral tones sometimes attributed to market society by treating the civil sphere as an epiphenomenon of capitalism. They favored the belief that their world is just, shared a desire to attain personal wealth and autonomy, but revealed a disregard for societal obligations. A third group reported a restricted vision of societal boundaries that offered no means of change. They said their world is fundamentally unjust but held strong individualistic and communitarian life goals. The group that endorsed the most pluralistic notion of civil solidarity balanced community obligations and the quest for personal autonomy with the belief that their world is just.

Although less common, this last vision seems optimal because adolescents with balanced life goals and a sense that their world is just seem ready to participate in the civil discourse necessary for improving society and bringing local values more closely in line with an inclusive ideal. Adolescents with balanced life goals who believed their world is unjust could challenge injustices, but they could just as easily avoid democratic participation. Those with unformed or individualistic civil identities were not especially committed to civil discourse.

Other Identities

Along with their civil identities, adolescents incorporated other cultural dimensions into their sense of self. They attended a large school that primarily served Latino families, embraced their Mexican American identity, and were fluent in English and Spanish. Despite this commonality, there was much diversity in how they defined other aspects of their ethnic and local identities (Tables 4.3 and 4.4). Slightly more than half the sample (n = 150) had parents who recently immigrated to the United States while the remaining adolescents (n = 84) reported that their grandparents first immigrated. Independent of their family's immigrant status, these adolescents also identified with different countries, and this choice was not related to their civil identities or immigrant status.

TABLE 4–2. Cluster Descriptions and Mean Scale Scores Validating the Civil Identity Classifications

	SCALES IN THE CLUSTER ANALYSIS		
CLUSTER DESCRIPTION	INDIVIDUALISTIC GOALS	COMMUNITARIAN GOALS	PERSONAL BELIEF IN A JUST WORLD
Unformed identity (n = 37)	3.33 (.28)	2.71 (.51)	3.12 (.74)
These adolescents reported few goals and the belief that their world is more unjust than just.			
Individualistic identity (n = 87)	3.88 (.22)	3.31 (.30)	4.22 (.35)
Consistent with a capitalistic vision of civil society, these adolescents endorsed goals that focused on autonomy and agreed that their world was just.			
Community outsider identity (n = 56)	4.21 (.23)	3.82 (.32)	3.42 (.42)
Consistent with members of disenfranchised groups, these adolescents showed a strong commitment to personal autonomy and a moderate commitment to communal obligations, but saw their world as unjust.			
Pluralistic identity (n = 54)	4.45 (.22)	4.15 (.32)	4.68 (.42)
In addition to reporting mostly positive justice beliefs, these adolescents showed a commitment to both community obligations and personal autonomy.			

Note. The Life Goals measures are outlined in Thorkildsen, Golant, & Richesin (2007) and the Personal Belief in a Just World tool was adapted from Dalbert (1999). For these unstandardized means, the Life Goals scores could range from 1 to 5 and the Personal Belief in a Just World scores could range from 1 to 6. Scores were standardized for the cluster analysis by dividing each participant's mean score by the scale range. Differences between the clusters were significant at $p < .001$.

TABLE 4–3. Distribution of Civil Identity by Local Identity

| | ACADEMIC HOUSE | | | |
CIVIL IDENTITY	GREEN (N = 56)	BLUE (N = 46)	MAROON (N = 62)	GOLD (N = 70)
Unformed identity	9	11	7	10
Individualistic identity	29	15	17	26
Community outsider identity	10	11	17	18
Pluralistic identity	8	9	21	16

Note. There are no differences in civil identities across the four academic houses.

TABLE 4–4. Distribution of Civil Identity by Ethnic Identity

| | COUNTRY PREFERENCE | | |
| | | MEXICO & | |
CIVIL IDENTITY	MEXICO (N = 78)	UNITED STATES (N = 78)	NO PREFERENCE (N = 78)
Unformed identity	14	9	14
Individualistic identity	30	34	23
Community outsider identity	19	18	19
Pluralistic identity	15	17	22

Note. There are no differences in civil identities across the three ethnic groups.

Consistent with findings from research on group membership (Smith & Henry, 1996), adolescents' assignment to different academic houses also produced solidarities, and these were independent of other aspects of their identities. These patterns clearly reflected multiple solidarities and suggest that there is a great deal of intra-ethnic variation in the cultural identities of Mexican American adolescents.

Cultural Identities and Ideal School Beliefs

Interesting patterns of engagement emerged when adolescents' various cultural identities were compared with their beliefs about the practices and obligations of an ideal school. Adolescents reported different personal commitments to both school and the civil sphere, but there were no differences attributable to ethnicity, immigrant status, academic placement, or gender. Our findings are consistent with those of at least one other study (Chang, Chen, Greenberger, Dooley, & Heckhausen, 2006) but contradict those found using sociological methods with other Latino samples (Guzman, Santiago-Rivera, & Haase, 2005). Similarly, the diversity in our sample raises questions about the assumption that adolescents from first- and second-generation immigrant families are all highly committed to education (Fuligni, 1997; Perreira, Harris, & Lee, 2006; Tseng, 2006). Instead, our findings suggest that stronger person-centered research could reveal problems with ethnic and academic stereotypes generated using sociological research designs.

We found marked differences in adolescents' sense of an ideal school that are attributable to their civil identities (Figure 4.1). Adolescents reporting an unformed civil identity showed the simplest understanding of an ideal school whereas adolescents whose identities were most closely aligned with pluralistic goals showed the most complex beliefs. Because surveys included a mixture of positive and negative evaluations, it would be unfair to attribute these findings to optimistic or pessimistic dispositions. A closer look at the beliefs of adolescents who see themselves as unable to influence the boundaries of civil society, for example, suggests that individuals with a critical stance may have a very complex awareness of situational contingencies. Adolescents differed in how seriously they embraced their civil responsibilities, and this was associated with different conceptions of an ideal school. Perhaps adolescents' respect for others and for the importance of civil commitments could be broadened if they had a better understanding of how an ideal school ought to be organized.

Action Readiness in the Engagement Force

Psychological notions of engagement include intentional behavior that reflects an awareness of personal responsibility. We evaluated such awareness by measuring adolescents' action readiness, an intermediary mechanism by which individuals activate their personal standards and become willing to exhibit behavior. We could not assess adolescents' actual behavior, but they reported their readiness to work hard and to cheat or take shortcuts in school as well as their willingness to address justice.[1] Only after individuals' personal standards were integrated with

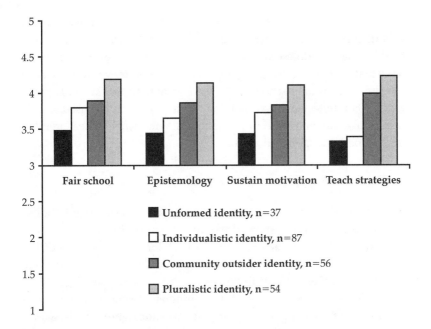

Figure 4-1. Adolescents' civil identities by standards for an ideal school.
Note. The civil identity by standards for an ideal school interaction was significant, $F_{(9,690)} = 1.98$. $p < .05$, $\eta^2 = .03$, observed power = .85. Differences between the clusters were all significant.

their action readiness could we draw conclusions about their moral or academic engagement.

Psychological notions of disengagement contrast with engagement in that disengagement reflects the absence of some part of the engagement system. Individuals may act in ways that do not coincide with their standards, but these impulsive behaviors would be insufficiently predictable to reflect engagement. Similarly, individuals may also hold standards that remain dormant, in which case their actions would remain unintentional. In our study, adolescents who reported few or highly unbalanced civil identities and simple representations of an ideal school showed a moderate form of disengagement. We focused on engagement by evaluating the internal consistency of adolescents' action readiness and educational standards, but those adolescents who reported unfocused personal standards serve as an interesting comparison group because they did not fully integrate personal standards and action readiness.

In our engagement model, action readiness was evaluated using two rather traditional concerns about effort in the classroom. Accentuating the positive, adolescents reported on when they would work hard. Accentuating the negative, they reported on when they might cheat or take shortcuts in their schoolwork. The ethical nature of such readiness was further reflected by combining adolescents' effort-based beliefs with an assessment of their readiness to act on justice issues, adapted from Dalbert and Umlauft (2003).

Cultural Identities and Action Readiness

Comparisons between the different readiness dimensions and adolescents' cultural identities showed the same interesting patterns as those apparent for their beliefs about an ideal school. There were no differences attributable to adolescents' ethnic or academic identities, but there were marked differences attributable to their civil identities (Figure 4.2). Although differences in adolescents' willingness to cheat or take shortcuts were not attributable to their civil identities, individuals with a pluralistic civil identity showed the strongest inclination to work hard and address justice. It is also noteworthy that adolescents with an individualistic civil identity were not especially ready to act on their justice beliefs. Adolescents with an unformed civil identity showed disinterest in justice although they reported some conditions in which they might work hard in school.

These analyses hide some of the variance in adolescents' readiness to work hard and, more important, in their readiness to cheat or take shortcuts. When adolescents' readiness profiles were constructed using nonhierarchical cluster analysis, four meaningful clusters were apparent, reflecting different degrees of engagement and disengagement. Whereas Figure 4.2 might suggest otherwise, 32% (n = 75) of the students said they would definitely cheat or take shortcuts. Furthermore, this group of adolescents differed in whether they were also inclined to work hard and consider justice. Showing signs of disengagement, 13% of this likely-to-cheat group said they would not be ready to work hard or address justice concerns. However, the remaining 87% of those adolescents willing to cheat also said they would work hard and act on justice concerns.

A more ideal form of engagement was apparent among adolescents who said they were committed to justice and working hard but not to cheating (28% of the total sample, n = 66). An apathetic form of disengagement in which adolescents reported no discernible action

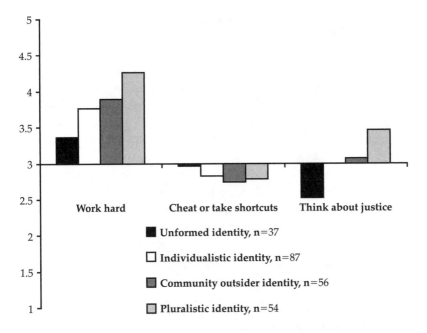

Figure 4-2. Adolescents' civil identities by action readiness.

Note. The civil identity by readiness to act interaction was significant, $F_{(6,460)} = 9.79$, $p < .001$, $\eta^2 = .11$, observed power $= 1.00$. Differences between the clusters were all significant.

readiness was apparent for the remaining unwilling-to-cheat cluster (40% of the total sample, n = 93). Despite this hidden variance, the relations between adolescents' civil identities and their action readiness support our assumption that civil identities account for more of the diversity in adolescents' moral and academic engagement than their ethnic or local school identities.

Validating Relations Between Civil Identities and Engagement

To fully evaluate our engagement model, we tested how well adolescents' ideal school standards and action readiness predicted their civil identities. After verifying that the assessments were sufficiently independent (Table 4.5), we used hierarchical regression and entered ideal school standards and action readiness in two blocks (Table 4.6) to predict adolescents' civil identity cluster assignment. Adolescents' personal standards for an ideal school included strong predictors of their civil identity, and when measures of action readiness were added in a second step, the equation was strengthened further, accounting for 38% of the variance. Each measure contributes to the whole of adolescents' engagement, but their fairness standards and sense that school should teach meta-cognitive strategies explained the most variance when ideal school beliefs were entered alone. When both blocks were entered, adolescents' fairness standards, readiness to work hard, and readiness to address justice accounted for the most variance. This suggests that much of the diversity in these adolescents' engagement could be attributed to their moral rather than their academic expectations.

The strength of this model suggests that school may prepare adolescents to participate in the civil sphere. Those adolescents with complex civil identities recognized greater levels of contingency in how school ought to be organized and were ready to participate fully in educational

TABLE 4–5. Correlations Between Indicants of Civil Identity, Ideal School Standards, and Action Readiness

SCALES BY BLOCKS	1	2	3	4	5	6	7	8	9
Civil identity									
1. Individualistic goals									
2. Communitarian goals	.79								
3. Belief in a just world	.42	.34							
Ideal school									
4. Fair school	.54	.52	.35						
5. Epistemology	.40	.40	.20	.60					
6. Sustain students' motivation	.47	.36	.34	.73	.61				
7. Teach metacognitive strategies	.59	.53	.32	.68	.55	.61			
Action readiness									
8. Work hard	.62	.54	.39	.63	.50	.67	.69		
9. Cheat or take shortcuts	−.10	−.09	.01	−.17	.00	.00	−.17	−.05	
10. Address justice	.47	.49	.34	.38	.39	.40	.48	.49	−.01

Note. Corrections for any violation of distribution assumptions were incorporated into the regression and the within-subjects analysis of variance.

TABLE 4–6. Summary of Hierarchical Regression Analyses Testing the Relation Between Adolescents' Civil Identity, Ideal School Standards, and Action Readiness

STEP AND VARIABLES	B	$SE\ B$	$ß$	t	ADJUSTED $R^2/\Delta R^2$
Step 1					.30/.32
(Constant)	–2.71	.53		–5.09***	
Fair school	.59	.22	.24	2.69**	
Epistemology	.08	.13	.05	.61	
Sustain students' motivation	.23	.19	.10	1.22	
Teach metacognitive strategies	.47	.15	.25	3.21**	
Step 2					.38/.08
(Constant)	–3.19	.58		–5.51***	
Fair school	.53	.21	.22	2.52**	
Epistemology	.04	.12	.02	.29	
Sustain students' motivation	–.06	.19	–.03	–.32	
Teach metacognitive strategies	.09	.16	.05	.60	
Readiness to work hard	.65	.17	.31	3.75***	
Readiness to cheat/ take shortcuts	–.02	.07	–.01	–.24	
Readiness to address justice	.32	.10	.19	3.13**	

Note. *p < .05, ** p < .01, ***p < .001. Adolescents' civil identity was assessed using the results of nonhierarchical cluster analysis that included measures of their individualistic and communitarian life goals and personal belief in a just world. The resulting four identity types reported in Table 4.2 were ranked to reflect students' differing commitment to communal obligations, personal autonomy, and personal beliefs in a just world.

activities. Adolescents with an unformed civil identity reported simpler standards for school and a weaker action readiness, indicating a somewhat alienated disposition.

These psychological patterns confirm the simple idea that some students are highly engaged and others are not, a belief already accepted by researchers interested in institutional change. Nevertheless, they offer more information on the nature of adolescents' engagement. It is adolescents' civil identities rather than their ethnic or local school identities that account for the diversity in their educational commitment. Schools would fail to contribute adequately to the civil sphere if involuntary solidarities like ethnicity and academic status were overlooked, but adolescents might stay committed to schoolwork if they understood the school's role in addressing society's civil obligations.

∷ Nurturing Civil Solidarities

Given that adolescence is an optimal period in which to elicit students' participation in civil discourse, education is one means by which individuals can adjust their choice of solidarities and balance their societal commitments. By intentionally strengthening students' commitment to civil projects, schools can accept responsibility for nurturing universal moral values while sustaining particularistic conversations about how to include everyone in our collective understanding of who matters in the world. Our data add to this agenda by illustrating that engagement is most likely when adolescents align their civil identities with their personal educational standards and readiness to act on those standards. Civil commitments seem not to detract from students' sense of agency and other achievement concerns but to align with an awareness of just how challenging it can be to organize an ideal school.

With these conclusions in mind, two remaining questions are implied by our findings, each concerning where information about students' engagement can be situated in community discussions about the nature and purposes of school. First, it seems reasonable to ask how schools can formulate institutional agendas that allow for shared solidarities such as those reflecting students' racial, ethnic, or academic identities. Second, it also seems worthwhile to explore how educators fulfill communicative and regulative civil functions while remaining respectful of the diverse solidarities in students' civil commitments. Our findings cannot speak to the whole of these concerns, but some specific possibilities emerge.

Educators can better understand adolescents' thoughts about shared solidarities when they identify groups operating within their school and reflect on the usefulness of such groups. In the school where we collected our data, asking adolescents to report their racial classification, country preferences, and family's immigrant status confirmed available demographic information but also extended that information to determine whether individuals of the same race held different ethnic commitments. There was diversity in these adolescents' allegiances, and describing such patterns could help students discover meaningful solidarities within the school. This would be beneficial in that students who feel a sense of belonging are more likely to openly acknowledge their inclusion in this civil institution (Smith & Henry, 1996).

Although educators cannot control someone's identity, the process of education can help students acquire information that may in turn play a role in how they see themselves and plan their lives. Adolescents benefit from tasks that require them to imagine what type of person they would like to be because they can become more intentional about developing the skills needed to become such a person. Those who already articulate life goals may strengthen or revise their goals by reflecting on how well they balance commitments to personal autonomy and societal obligations. In other words, classrooms can operate like local forums for inventing and examining possible life goals and roles in solving social justice problems. Educators who encourage such discourse promote personal and institutional movement toward a fully inclusive and civil society.

Students' understanding of education evolves in age-related cycles. Even though adolescents have been in school for a number of years, educators still have much control over their awareness and understanding of how an ideal school might be organized. If educators take time to discuss the complexity of their daily decisions with students, adolescents can learn more about schools' structures and roles in society. For example, educators could facilitate conversations about fairness by encouraging students to think about different forms of justice as these issues unfold during the year. They might also highlight the different types of knowledge embedded in their curriculum to help students see the importance of each type and how controversial and noncontroversial ideas can be prioritized. In addition, educators can help students monitor how well they organize their school responsibilities, even if more direct instruction on issues like time management, organizational habits, and study skills occurs outside of school. Educators' strategies for offering feedback on students' work and for encouraging personal reflection and teamwork seem to teach students about their own and others' motivation. In unison, such teacher-led efforts could expand adolescents' understanding of their civil responsibilities in school as well as society. When solidarities within a school are widely recognized, educators responsible for connecting school and societal agendas could more readily ensure that both the institution and its members remain full participants in a broader civil discourse.[2]

:: Endnotes

[1] In Thorkildsen, Golant, & Richesin (2007) we called our action readiness scales Agency to Work Hard and Agency to Cheat or Take Short-cuts. Because our definition of engagement is nested within a more general concept of agency, this labeling proved to be confusing to our readers. The action readiness concept that we now use is similar to one explored by Frijda, Kuipers, & ter Schure (1989) in their studies of how individuals experience emotion. This terminology change also allows us an opportunity to compare the two forms of engagement.

[2] We would like to thank Rich Moore, Janice Ozga, and Frank Zarate for their help in initiating a larger school-culture project from which the sample reported in this book was selected. We would also like to thank the students and staff of those high schools in the Chicago area that offered insightful feedback as our project unfolded. This work was funded by the College of Education at the University of Illinois at Chicago.

:: References

Alexander, J. C. (2006). *The civil sphere*. New York: Oxford University Press.

Bandura, A. (1999). Moral disengagement in the perpetration of inhumanities. *Personality and Social Psychology Review, 3,* 193–209.

Chang, E. S., Chen, C., Greenberger, E., Dooley, D., & Heckhausen, J. (2006). What do they want in life? The life goals of a multi-ethnic, multi-generational sample of high school seniors. *Journal of Youth and Adolescence, 35,* 321–332.

Dalbert, C. (1999). The world is more just for me than generally: About the Personal Belief in a Just World Scale's validity. *Social Justice Research, 12,* 79–98.

Dalbert, C. & Umlauft, S. (2003). *Justice Centrality Scale.* Unpublished scale, Martin Luther University of Halle, Wittenberg, Germany.

French, S. E., Seidman, E., Allen, L., & Aber, J. L. (2006). The development of ethnic identity during adolescence. *Developmental Psychology, 42,* 1–10.

Frijda, N. H., Kuipers, P., & ter Schure, E. (1989). Relations among emotion, appraisal, and emotional action readiness. *Journal of Personality and Social Psychology, 57,* 212–228.

Fuligni, A. J. (1997). The academic achievement of adolescents from immigrant families: The roles of family background, attitudes, and behavior. *Child Development, 68,* 351–363.

Geertz, C. (1983). *Local knowledge: Further essays in interpretive anthropology.* New York: Basic Books.

Guzman, M. R., Santiago-Rivera, A. L., & Haase, R. F. (2005). Understanding academic attitudes and achievement in Mexican-origin youths: Ethnic identity, other-group orientation, and fatalism. *Cultural Diversity and Ethnic Minority Psychology, 11,* 3–15.

Jackson, L. A., Sullivan, L. A., Harnish, R., & Hodge, C. N. (1996). Achieving positive social identity: Social mobility, social creativity, and permeability of group boundaries. *Journal of Personality and Social Psychology, 70,* 241–254.

Keesing, R. M. (1981). Theories of culture. In R. Casson (Ed.), *Language, Culture, and Cognition.* New York: Macmillan. (Originally published in 1974.)

Kluger, R. (1975). *Simple justice: The history of Brown v. Board of Education and Black America's struggle for equality.* New York: Vintage Books.

Mahoney, J. L., Cairns, R. B., & Farmer, T. W. (2003). Promoting interpersonal competence and educational success through extracurricular activity participation. *Journal of Educational Psychology, 95,* 409–418.

Nakamura, J. (2001). The nature of vital engagement in adulthood. In M. Michaelson, & J. Nakamura (Eds.), *Supportive frameworks for youth engagement* (pp. 5–18). San Francisco: Jossey-Bass.

Oyserman, D., Bybee, D., & Terry, K. (2006). Possible selves and academic outcomes: How and when possible selves impel action. *Journal of Personality and Social Psychology, 91,* 188–204.

Oyserman, D., Coon, H. M., & Kemmelmeier, M. (2002). Rethinking individualism and collectivism: Evaluation of theoretical assumptions and meta-analyses. *Psychological Bulletin, 128*(1), 3–72.

Perreira, K. M., Harris, K. M., Lee, D. (2006). Making it in America: High school completion by immigrant and native youth. *Demography, 43,* 511–536.

Smith E. R., & Henry, S. (1996). An in-group becomes part of the self: Response-time evidence. *Personality and Social Psychology Bulletin, 22* (6), 635–642.

Terenzini, P. T., Pascarella, E. T., & Blimling, G. S. (1996). Students' out-of-class experiences and their influence on learning and cognitive development: A literature review. *Journal of College Student Development, 37*, 149–162.

Thorkildsen, T. A. (1989). Pluralism in children's reasoning about social justice. *Child Development, 60*, 965–972.

Thorkildsen, T. A. (2000). The way tests teach: Children's theories of how much testing is fair in school. In M. Leicester, C. Modgil, & S. Modgil (Eds.), *Education, culture, and values, Vol. III: Classroom issues: practice, pedagogy, and curriculum* (pp. 61–79). London: Falmer Press.

Thorkildsen, T. A. (2007). The role of personal standards in second graders' moral and academic engagement. In D. Thiessen & A. Cook-Sather (Eds.). *International handbook of student experience in elementary and secondary school* (pp. 193–231). New York: Springer.

Thorkildsen, T. A., Golant, C. J., & Richesin, L. D. (2007). Reaping what we sow: Cheating as a mechanism of moral engagement. In E. M. Anderman & T. B. Murdock (Eds.), *The psychology of academic cheating* (pp. 171–202). San Diego, CA: Elsevier.

Thorkildsen, T. A., & Nicholls, J. G. (with Bates, A., Brankis, N., & DeBolt, T.). (2002). *Motivation and the struggle to learn: Responding to fractured experience.* Boston, MA: Allyn & Bacon.

Thorkildsen, T. A., Nolen, S. B., & Fournier, J. (1994). What's fair? Children's critiques of practices that influence motivation. *Journal of Educational Psychology, 86*, 475–486.

Thorkildsen, T. A., Sodonis, A., & White-McNulty, L. (2004). Epistemology and adolescents' conceptions of procedural justice in school. *Journal of Educational Psychology, 96*, 347–359.

Thorkildsen, T. A., & White-McNulty, L. (2002). Developing conceptions of fair contest procedures and the differentiation of skill and luck. *Journal of Educational Psychology, 94*, 316–326.

Triandis, H. C. (1995). The self and social behavior in differing cultural contexts. In N. R. Goldberger, & J. B. Veroff (Eds.), *The culture and psychology reader* (pp. 326–365). New York, NY: New York University Press.

Tseng, V. (2006). Unpacking immigration in youths' academic and occupational pathways. *Child Development, 77*, 1434–1445.

Walberg, H. J., & Bast, J. L. (2003). *Education and capitalism: How overcoming our fear of markets and economics can improve America's schools.* Stanford, CA: Hoover Institution Press.

Walzer, M. (1983). *Spheres of justice: A defense of pluralism and equality.* New York: Basic Books.

Zimmerman, B. J. (1989). A social cognitive view of self-regulated academic learning. *Journal of Educational Psychology, 81*, 329–339.

5 ⸬

Sources of Influence on the College Goals, Sexual Behavior, and Childbearing Attitudes of Latina Girls in Alternative High Schools

Laura F. Romo, Claudia Kouyoumdjian, and Marguerita Lightfoot

Teenage pregnancy and parenthood reduce the likelihood that adolescents will succeed in school, increasing their chances of living in poverty (Hoffman, 2006). Although these trends are relevant for all youth, Latina girls from low-income backgrounds are at particularly high risk for these adverse consequences. Teenage birthrates among Latinas remain consistently higher than those for same age non-Latino peers (Hamilton, Martin, Ventura, Sutton, & Menacker, 2005). Between 1991 and 2005, the birth rate decreased by only 22% among Latina teens, compared to 48% among African American teens, and 40% among non-Hispanic white teens (Hamilton, Martin, & Ventura, 2006). These findings underscore the need to design school programs that can effectively lower risky sexual behavior among Latina girls living in poor neighborhoods.

Research on academic motivation can contribute to this endeavor. Several studies have shown that educational goals and academic motivation are linked to adolescents' sexual behavior and attitudes (e.g., Billy, Landale, Grady, & Zimmerle, 1988; Miller & Sneesby, 1988; Ohannessian & Crockett, 1993). The mechanism underlying this link can be explained by the expectancy-value model of achievement choices (Eccles et al., 1983; Wigfield & Eccles, 1992). Choices that adolescents make regarding what activities to pursue are influenced by several factors including utility and cost value. Utility value in this model refers to the perceived usefulness of a task in fostering the attainment of short- or long-term goals (Eccles-Parsons et al., 1983). From this perspective, delaying sexual activity or engaging in regular contraceptive use takes on utility value to the extent that it facilitates the adolescents' goals to complete school and pursue desirable careers. Additionally, motivation to engage in self-protective sexual behaviors may be prompted by adolescent concerns over the cost of losing out on educational and career opportunities as a result of teenage childbearing.

Studies focusing predominantly on Latino adolescents are few, but there is some research to suggest that the expectancy-value model plays a role in decisions affecting their sexual behavior and academic outcomes. In two studies, Mexican American adolescents who valued education and felt positive toward school were less likely to engage in early sexual activity (Liebowitz, Castellano, & Cuellar, 1999) and become pregnant (Baumeister, Flores, & Marin, 1995) compared to adolescents who did not report these attitudes. In a Puerto Rican majority sample, adolescents who believed that avoiding sexual activity would enhance their chances of achieving their career goals were more likely to report an intent to remain abstinent (Villarruel, Jemmott, Jemmott, & Ronis, 2004). Considered from the opposite perspective, Unger, Molina, and Teran (2000) found that Latino adolescents who perceived childbearing to have less positive consequences had higher educational expectations in addition to lower levels of experience in risky sexual behavior than adolescents who did not have these perceptions. In sum, Latino adolescents with high educational expectations and positive attitudes toward school tend to avoid early and unprotected sex more consistently than youth who do not hold these attitudes, perhaps because they perceive that early childbearing jeopardizes their chances of achieving their future goals (Ohannessian & Crockett, 1993; Schvaneveldt, Miller, Berry, & Lee, 2001).

In this chapter we examine sources of influence on the educational expectations, childbearing attitudes, and sexual behavior of Latina girls attending alternative high schools. Alternative high schools represent a unique culture in American schooling in that they typically accommodate students who are not allowed to attend traditional schools because of chronic behavior problems, failing grades, and truancy (Aron, 2006). School districts with large minority student populations and high poverty rates are more likely than other districts to have such alternative education programs for deviant youth who have been placed there for disciplinary reasons (Aron, 2003). Additionally, these programs serve students who have difficulty meeting the academic and schedule demands of traditional schools because they are pregnant or parenting, or because they are involved with the juvenile justice system (Aron, 2006). Most students who attend this type of program do so not by choice but because they are mandated by school district policies recommending that deviant youth, along with pregnant or parenting youth, be segregated from mainstream peers (Martin & Brand, 2006). Maintaining high self-efficacy and motivation to succeed are perhaps the greatest challenges affecting students' attendance and retention rates (Aron, 2006; May & Copeland, 1998). This highlights the need to identify sources of influence on the educational goals of this vulnerable student population. Increasing girls' expectancies to succeed in school and supporting their efforts to do so may have an impact not only on academic outcomes, but also on their sexual health decisions.

∷ The Influence of Peer Norms

In alternative schools, youth are segregated from mainstream peers and grouped with other youth experiencing similar academic and behavioral difficulties. This practice is intended to benefit students by providing them with small classroom environments, tailored instruction, and flexible schedules for completing assignments. Some studies suggest that this approach is successful (e.g., May & Copeland, 1998), but to date, few studies have paid attention to its potential drawbacks. For example, aggregating youth with academic and behavioral difficulties can increase the occurrence of problem behaviors through a phenomenon known as peer contagion (Dodge, Dishion, & Landers, 2006). That is, increased exposure to a peer culture where risky behavior is the norm, and peer selection is limited, fosters the opportunity for negative peer influences to shape attitudes and behavior of the group (Dodge et al., 2006). Adolescents in alternative school settings may feel compelled to conform to these attitudes if they believe it will increase their social status within the group and decrease the possibility of social rejection (Cohen & Prinstein, 2006). Peer influence in this context is not necessarily overt but can occur through subtle conversation cues that occur in casual exchanges. Through observational studies, Dishion, Spracklen, Andrews, and Patterson (1996) found that adolescents communicate their approval of deviant behavior in conversations by smiling and laughing, which fosters the acceptance of deviant peer norms for the group. Deviant peer norm setting has occurred in many types of well-intentioned programs. For example, in a longitudinal study examining the experiences of youth in community recreation centers, researchers found that many girls who had not been deviant eventually became so because they were socialized by deviant peers whom they met at the youth center (Persson, Kerr, & Stattin, 2004; Stattin, Kerr, Mahoney, Persson, & Magnusson, 2005).

Deviant-peer involvement also increases the risk of early sexual initiation (French & Dishion, 2003). Several studies have shown that the initiation of first sexual intercourse among high-risk adolescents across ethnic groups is linked to perceptions that their peers are sexually experienced (e.g., Christopher, Johnson, & Roosa, 1993; Miller et al., 1997) and social gains are tied to early sexual intercourse (Kinsman, Romer, Furstenberg, & Schwartz, 1998). These findings raise questions about whether peer affiliations in alternative schools strongly influence the sexual behavior and attitudes of students who are not yet sexually active. About 90% of students in alternative schools report engaging in sexual activity (Grunbaum et al., 1999; Shrier & Crosby, 2003). These students tend to initiate sexual activity at younger ages and have more sexual partners than youth in traditional school environments (DiClemente, Lanier, Horan, & Lodico, 1991; Morris, Harrison, Knox, Tromanhauser, Marquis, & Watts, 1995). Increased exposure to in an environment where risky sexual behavior is normative may reduce adolescent girls' concerns about unprotected sex, increasing their vulnerability to teenage pregnancy.

Likewise, peer group norms in alternative schools may have an impact on teen mothers experiencing a second pregnancy, although this question has not been studied. Approximately 40% to 50% of adolescent mothers experience another pregnancy within 2 years of the first (Coard, Nitz, & Felice, 2000). Antecedents to repeated pregnancies in adolescence include high frequency of sexual intercourse, failure to use effective contraception, and best friends experiencing a pregnancy (Gillmore, Lewis, Lohr, Spencer, & White, 1997). The extent to which the alternative school environment contributes to the likelihood of a second pregnancy is not known. However, school practices that exclude parenting adolescents from regular academic courses and extracurricular activities with mainstream peers can deprive students of peer social capital that can help them succeed (Crosnoe, Cavanagh, & Elder, 2003; Pillow, 2006).

The Influence of Parents

Although sexually active peers can have a negative influence on adolescent sexual behavior and attitudes, this influence can be offset through connectedness with parents. There is growing evidence that Latino adolescents' sexual behavior is influenced by their perceptions of what their parents think. For example, beliefs that their parents had conservative attitudes toward teen sexual behavior was associated with Latino youth reporting less sexual experience (Hovell et al., 1994; Rucibwa, Modeste, Montgomery, & Fox, 2003) and less risky sexual behavior (Kotchick, Miller, & Forehand, 1999; Liebowitz et al., 1999) than adolescents who did not hold these perceptions about their parents. Intentions to have sex have been negatively correlated with Latino adolescents' beliefs that their parents would be proud of them for not having sex (Villarruel, Jemmott, Jemmott, & Ronis, 2004). Longer discussions between Latino adolescents and their mothers about sexuality beliefs and values as a conversation topic predicted adolescents engaging in less intimate sex-related behaviors 1 year later (Romo, Lefkowitz, Sigman, & Au, 2002). A delay in sexual intercourse among Latino adolescents has also been linked to their perceptions of general parental support (e.g., Velez-Pastrana, Gonzalez-Rodriguez, & Borges-Hernandez, 2005).

These findings mirror recent trends related to Latino parents' influence on adolescent academic outcomes. Among a sample of high school students, Plunkett and Bámaca-Gómez (2003) found that adolescents who perceived support and approval from their Mexican immigrant parents tended to be academically oriented and aspired to higher levels of education than youth perceiving less support. Among youth in grades 6–12, social support has been shown to predict high levels of academic well-being in Latino adolescents, including a lower likelihood of school dropout (DeGarmo & Martinez, 2006). Other studies conducted with Latina girls have linked higher academic motivation (Alfaro, Umaña-Taylor, & Bámaca, 2006) and low levels of school behavior problems among early adolescents (Prelow & Loukas, 2003) to academic support, particularly from their mothers. Together, these studies converge to suggest that Latino parents play a prominent role in fostering adolescents' academic success in addition to influencing their decisions about sexual activity.

Latino adolescents' motivation to do well in school and to avoid risky sexual activity are interrelated perhaps because parental messages link them together. Findings from focus groups (e.g., Guilamo-Ramos, Dittus, Jaccard, Goldberg, et al., 2006), in-depth qualitative interviews (e.g., McKee & Karasz, 2006), and conversation analysis of Latino mothers and adolescents (Romo, Kouyoumdjian, Nadeem, & Sigman, 2006) have revealed that daughters are advised or warned that they should delay sex and avoid pregnancy in order to pursue their academic goals and obtain a successful career. Immigrant mothers encourage their daughters to take advantage of educational opportunities available in the United States so they can live a better life than the mothers themselves currently experience or experienced growing up. Some mothers report that they convey these messages to help their daughters avoid making the same mistakes of early childbearing that they did (McKee & Karasz, 2006). Such communication is important given findings by Whitaker and Miller (2000) that although perceptions of peer sexual behavior have an influence on adolescents' sexual health outcomes, the impact can be minimized through open communication between parents and adolescents. These studies offer support against the stereotype that Latino parents do not value education for their children, and they contradict the speculation that Latina mothers socialize their daughters for marriage and childbearing at the expense of their educational goals.

⁞ Parental Influence on Alternative School Student Outcomes

Despite the growing number of adolescents attending alternative schools, almost no attention has been paid to the role of parental influence on these students' sexual behavior and academic outcomes. In one qualitative study, May and Copeland (1998) found that alternative school students listed their parents and friends among the personal factors that fostered their persistence to succeed. In a recent study that included a large proportion of Latino youth, alternative high school students who perceived greater family connectedness were significantly less likely to report that they had ever had sex compared to students who perceived less closeness (Markham et al., 2003). Additionally, among students who were sexually active, family connectedness predicted a lower likelihood of recently having sex without a condom or being involved in a pregnancy. These findings suggest that despite the prevalence of negative peer influences in high-risk environments, parents continue to shape the behaviors and attitudes of their adolescents.

In this chapter, we explore academic achievement motivation through secondary analyses of data derived from two different studies conducted in alternative high schools. Specifically, we were interested in whether the educational goals, childbearing attitudes, and sexual behavior of Latina adolescents are interrelated as the literature suggests is the case for adolescents attending traditional schools. A second question focused on identifying the role of parents and peers as possible sources of influence on these outcomes.

⠃⠃ Study

In Study 1, we analyzed data comprised of a small sample of Latina girls attending two alternative high schools in a semi-rural community in southern California. We examined whether pregnancy status or history was associated with how far the adolescents planned to go to school. We hypothesized that girls who had never been pregnant would aspire to higher levels of education than girls who were, or had been, pregnant. A second question focused on perceived parents' and friends' feelings about the adolescent having a baby in the next year and whether these feelings were associated with the adolescents' college plans and personal feelings about having a baby. We hypothesized that perceived parental attitudes would have an impact on the adolescents' negative perceptions of childbearing, but the influence of friends' attitudes was not clear. Our final question examined how perceived consequences of childbearing might be associated with the adolescents' current use of birth control and the age at which they wanted to have their first child. We expected that sexually active adolescents who were concerned that having a baby would be too much work for them and that a baby would affect their educational opportunities, career options, and financial situation would engage in regular use of birth control and favor having their first child at a later age compared to girls who were not concerned about these potential consequences.

Method

We administered surveys in two alternative high schools to 30 Mexican American adolescent girls in grades 10–12, who ranged in age from 16 to 19 years (M = 17.0 years, SD = 1. 0). Students attended small classes at satellite sites separate from their local traditional high school campuses, as is typical for alternative schools. Whether these students were enrolled at the alternative high school by choice or compulsion was unknown; however three of the adolescent girls (10%) had a child and nine of them (27%) were pregnant or had been pregnant. There were 18 students (63%) who were not sexually active or who were sexually active but had never experienced a pregnancy. The majority of the adolescent girls were U.S. born (87%) with the rest born in Mexico. About half (53%) of their mothers were foreign-born, as were two-thirds (66%) of the fathers. All of the foreign-born mothers and all but one of the fathers were born in Mexico. About half of the adolescents (53%) reported that their home language was Spanish.

The students responded to questions on a paper-and-pencil survey in a quiet space away from the classroom during regular school hours. A researcher was present to answer questions as needed. Upon completing the surveys, the students were given a $5 gift certificate as a way of thanking them for their participation.

The survey contained demographic items asking about the adolescents' age, grade, country of origin, their parents' country of origin, home language, and the ethnic group they identified with. College plans were measured by having the adolescents indicate their ultimate school plans: 1 = *finish high school*, 2 = *attend a junior college*, 3 = *enroll in a 4-year university*, or 4 = *pursue a graduate degree*. The adolescents were asked to rate how they would feel if they became pregnant in the next year on a scale worded and coded as follows: 1 = *I would be devastated*; 2 = *I would be unhappy, but not devastated*; 3 = *I would be happy but not overjoyed*; 4 = *I would be overjoyed*. The same scale was used to rate their perceptions about how their parents and friends would feel if the adolescents had a baby in the next year. Childbearing attitudes were also obtained by asking the adolescents to report the ages at which they would like to have their first child. Concern about the consequences of teenage pregnancy were assessed by four questions asking them to rate on a scale from 1 to 3 the extent to which they were concerned that *"having a baby in the next year would affect (1) educational opportunities; (2) career options; (3) financial situation;* and their concern that *(4) having a baby would be too much work."* Finally, birth control use was assessed by asking the adolescents to report their frequency of birth control use (1 = *never* to 4 = *always*).

Results

As a first step, we compared demographic differences between never-pregnant girls and those who were, or had been, pregnant. Never-pregnant adolescents were significantly younger, $t(28) = -2.99$, $p < .01$, with a mean age of 16.7 (SD = .9) compared to adolescents who had been pregnant (M = 17.7, SD = .9). The two groups also differed significantly ($\chi^2 [1] = 3.77$, $p = .05$) in the proportion of their mothers who were U.S. born. About 75% of the mothers of the pregnant adolescents had been born in the United States compared to 39% of mothers of never-pregnant adolescents. The adolescents did not differ with respect to their country of origin, their use of Spanish as a home language, and their fathers' country of origin.

Regarding their school plans, more than half of the adolescents (56%) reported that they intended to finish high school or attend a community college. The remaining adolescents reported that they intended to enroll in a four-year university and beyond. This demonstrates that girls were generally ambitious about their future school plans, regardless of pregnancy status or history. This is not surprising in the context of research suggesting that for many pregnant adolescents, having a child creates an incentive for them to succeed in school because they want to be good examples for their children (Shanok & Miller, 2005).

The next set of analyses included only the 18 girls who had never been pregnant. We were interested in how their plans for college and feelings about having a baby in the next year were associated with their perceptions of how their parents and friends would feel if they had a child. In reporting their personal feelings, more than half of the adolescents (56%) reported that they would feel happy or overjoyed. In addition, 78% of the adolescents reported that their friends would feel happy or overjoyed, suggesting a high acceptance of teenage pregnancy among their peers. The troubling aspect of this trend is that there was a significantly positive association between the adolescents' personal feelings and their perceptions of their friends' attitudes, $r(19) = .52, p < .05$. Adolescents who reported that they would feel happy if they had a baby believed that their friends would be happy for them.

Adolescents' perceptions of how their parents would feel if their daughters had a baby were quite different. Two-thirds (67%) of adolescents reported that their parents would be unhappy or devastated. Importantly, parental attitudes were congruent with their daughters' attitudes. Perceptions that their parents would feel unhappy if they had a baby were significantly associated with the girls' beliefs that they also would feel unhappy, $r(18) = .51, p < .05$. As hypothesized, girls who perceived that their parents would feel unhappy about a baby were those who aspired to higher educational goals, $r(18) = -.50, p < .05$.

The final set of analyses is displayed in Table 5.1. We conducted a series of correlational analyses between the ages at which never-pregnant adolescents desired to have their first child and their levels of concern that a baby would negatively impact their educational, career, and financial opportunities. For never-pregnant girls who were sexually active

TABLE 5–1. Correlations Between Perceived Consequences Associated With Having a Baby, Use of Birth Control, and Desired Age for First Child Among Never-pregnant Adolescents

PERCEIVED CONSEQUENCES ASSOCIATED WITH HAVING A BABY	USE OF REGULAR BIRTH CONTROL (N = 12)†	DESIRED AGE FOR FIRST CHILD (n = 18)
Would negatively affect my educational opportunities	.68*	.45*
Can affect my career options	.62*	.32
Would negatively affect my financial situation	.41	.56*
Would be too much work for me	.67*	.32

*$p < .05$

† This analysis was conducted only on girls who were sexually active

(n = 12), we performed correlations between their perceptions of these consequences and their frequency of birth control use. We found that never-pregnant girls who reported older desired ages for having a first child expressed higher levels of concern that a baby could negatively impact their educational opportunities and financial situation. Among those who were sexually active, consistent use of birth control was associated with their perceptions that a baby could affect educational and career opportunities and that a baby would be too much work for them. These findings support our hypothesis that greater concern about the consequences of pregnancy would be associated with the adolescents reporting more frequent use of birth control and older desirable ages for having a first child.

Discussion

Despite what is known in the literature about the role of peer affiliations on adolescent sexual behavior, girls' susceptibility to teenage childbearing in alternative high school environments has not been studied. Our findings show that the majority of never-pregnant girls believed that having a baby in the next year would be a positive event and that their friends would be happy for them. These positive perceptions of childbearing may be linked to their exposure to a school culture where teenage pregnancy and parenthood are normative and perhaps in some cases even desirable. Nevertheless, our findings do suggest that parental influence may work against peers' favorable childbearing attitudes leading to an actual pregnancy. Girls who believed that their parents would be unhappy or devastated if their daughters had a baby shared their parents' feelings. Importantly, these perceptions were associated with girls aspiring to complete higher levels of education.

Another source of influence on girls' attitudes toward childbearing was their perception that there would be serious consequences associated with having a baby. Girls who reported older desired ages for having a first child were more concerned that a baby could negatively impact their educational opportunities and financial situation than girls reporting younger desired ages for having a first child. Among girls who were sexually active, consistent use of birth control was associated with their perceptions that a baby could affect their educational and career opportunities and that a baby would be too much work for them. These findings are consistent with the expectancy-value model of achievement choices that adolescents who have expectations for continuing their education are likely to avoid decisions that jeopardize their chances for succeeding in school (Eccles et al., 1983). For these girls, birth control use has high utility value in that it enhances the possibility of achieving their long-term goals by preventing pregnancy.

∷ Study 2

In Study 2, we analyzed data from a sample of Latina girls who attended seven different alternative schools in urban southern California. The sample was part of a larger study (Lightfoot, Comulada, & Stover, 2006). The variables measured in this study were similar to those of Study 1 in that they focused on the adolescents' college plans, sources of influence on educational outcomes, birth control, and sexual behavior. In these schools, only a handful of girls who participated in the study were pregnant, which prevented us from analyzing differences between pregnant and never-pregnant adolescent girls. Instead, we focused on differences between never-pregnant girls who were currently sexually active and those who were not, given research suggesting that family closeness and high-risk adolescent girls' sexual behavior are linked (Markham et al., 2003).

The first research question addressed whether college aspirations and motivation to set and achieve goals were different for sexually active and not currently sexually active adolescent girls. We speculated that girls who were not currently sexually active would be more goal oriented and more optimistic about their chances of attending and graduating from college. The second question focused on whether high-risk youth turn to parents and friends as sources of support for their goals. We expected that parents would have an influence on their daughters' goals and college aspirations, but this association might be different depending on whether their daughters were currently sexually active. It was not clear whether girls in alternative schools seek friends as sources of support for their goals and college plans. Finally, we examined whether girls' college plans and motivation to set and achieve their goals were associated with self-protective practices related to sexual activity.

Method

Sixty-two Latina girls enrolled in 10th through 12th grade at alternative high schools were included in this study. The girls ranged in age from 14 to 18 years, with a mean age of 16.3 years. Four girls were pregnant leaving a sample of 58 adolescents who had never been pregnant. Among the 58 girls, 7 (19%) had been in juvenile hall at some point in their lives, and 12 (21%) of the sample were currently on probation. The majority (83%) of the adolescent girls were U.S. born. About 60% reported that they spoke English extremely well and the remaining girls stated that they spoke English moderately well. For the mothers' education level, 44% of the sample reported that their mothers had attended middle school or less, 46% reported high school, trade, or vocational school attendance for mothers, and 10% reported that their mothers had gone to college. The trend for the father's level of education was similar.

The students used audio computer-assisted self-interviews (ACASI) on laptop computers to complete their surveys. The questionnaire took about 1 hour to complete, and students were given $25 for their participation in the entire study. The measures included demographic items, pregnancy history, number of sexual partners in the last 90 days, and whether the girls were currently sexually active. Current sexual activity was measured by a yes-no question: *"Did you have vaginal or anal sex in the past 90 days?"* College plans were measured by asking the adolescents to rate, on a Likert-type scale from 1 to 5, how much they wanted to go to college, the likelihood that they would go to college, and the likelihood that they would graduate. The latter two questions were collapsed into a single variable assessing their expectations of *"attending* and *graduating from college.*" Motivation to set and achieve goals was measured by summing their responses to two questions and three statements from the Goal Setting Skills scale (Hansen, 1992) (abbreviated): "*How much do you work on goals, How often do you set goals, I don't give up until I achieve my goals, I always give it my best, I think about what I need to do to achieve my goals.*" The adolescents responded using a Likert-type scale from *Never* (1) to *All the time* (3). Parents and friends as sources of influence were measured by four items from the Relative Influence of Parents and Friends scale (1995). On this measure, the girls were asked to report whom they depend on for advice about four important issues: school, personal decisions, health issues, and their outlook on life. The available choices were *Parents most* (1), *Parents and friends the same* (2), and *Friends most* (3). Condom use self-efficacy was measured by the Situation Self-Efficacy for Condom Use Scale (Redding & Rossi, 1999). The scale consisted of 10 questions asking their confidence levels from *(1) Not at all sure* to *(5) Extremely Sure* that they would use condoms in various risky situations, e.g., "*When you are affected by drugs and alcohol, When you are depressed.*"

Results

Of the 58 adolescents, about half ($n = 31$) were currently sexually active and 27 were not. Among youth not currently sexually active, two-thirds reported never having had sex in their lifetime. The two groups of adolescents did not differ in their ages, country of origin, ability to speak English, and parents' educational levels.

In examining their educational goals, we found no significant differences between girls who were currently sexually active and those who were not in how much they desired to go to college or their expectations that they would attend college and graduate. Most of the girls wanted to go to college and most appeared to be optimistic that college was a possibility. On a scale of 1 (low) to 5 (high), the overall mean rating associated with their desire to go to college was 4.2 ($SD = 1.0$). The mean score associated with the likelihood that they would attend and graduate from college was 7.5 ($SD = 1.6$) on a scale from 1 to 10. However, there was a marginal difference in goal setting between girls who were currently sexually active and those who were not; girls not sexually active reported higher motivation to set and achieve their goals ($M = 9.1, SD = 3.3$) in comparison to sexually active girls ($M = 7.5, SD = 3.6$), $t(56) = 1.81, p = .07$. This difference is meaningful given research suggesting that goal orientation influences how much effort and value students place on doing well (Caraway, Tucker, Reinke, & Hall, 2003).

To examine the role of parents and friends as sources of influence on girls' college aspirations and motivation to achieve their goals, we conducted a series of correlation analyses separately for girls who were sexually active and those who were not. Table 5.2 presents the correlations associated with sources of influence on the adolescents' desire to go to college, attend, and graduate from college as well as motivation to achieve their goals. Among girls not sexually active, high levels of desire to go to college and high optimism about attending and graduating from college were associated with their reports that they relied mostly on their parents (as opposed to their friends) for advice about health issues. In addition, those who reported high levels of motivation to set and achieve their goals reported that they depended mostly on their parents for advice related to personal life decisions. None of the remaining correlations reached significance but it is important to note that for girls not sexually active, only two of the 12 coefficients approached zero ($r < .10$) and the remainder were all positive, suggesting that overall parents tend to be more influential than friends for these girls. The pattern for sexually active girls was such that none of the correlations reached significance, and 10 of the 12 coefficients approached zero, indicating less influence from parents on these issues.

The last set of analyses focused only on currently sexually active girls. Two t-tests were conducted to examine differences their college aspirations and desire to achieve their goals by whether a condom was used the last time they had sex and whether they had ever used hormonal birth control methods. The large majority of these girls (78%) reported having just one regular partner in the last 3 months, yet more than half of the sample (54%) reported that they had not used a condom the last time they had sex, and 88% claimed that they had never used hormonal birth control methods. These girls appear to be at high risk for teenage pregnancy due to their low levels of contraceptive use. None of these variables was associated with their college aspirations or goals in the t-test comparisons.

Discussion

Although Latina girls' current sexual behavior did not differentiate girls who desired to go to college or those who perceived that their chances of attending and graduating from college were high, there was a marginal difference in their goal orientation. Currently sexually active girls

TABLE 5-2. Correlations Between Parent/Friend Influences and Education Goals by Whether Girls Were Currently Sexually Active

Depend on most for advice? friends (0), both (1), parents (2)?	NOT SEXUALLY ACTIVE (n = 27)			SEXUALLY ACTIVE (n = 31)		
	DESIRE COLLEGE (n = 22)†	GRADUATE COLLEGE	ACHIEVE GOALS	DESIRE COLLEGE (n = 28)‡	GRADUATE COLLEGE	ACHIEVE GOALS
1. School decisions	.23	.34	.26	.02	.07	-.20
2. Personal life choices	.37	.13	.38*	-.05	.06	.06
3. Health care	.64**	.39*	.27	.03	-.02	-.17
4. Outlook on life	.09	.05	.23	.02	.03	.18

* $p < .05$; ** $p < .01$

† 5 students taking college courses

‡ 3 students taking college courses

reported less motivation to set and achieve their goals compared to girls who were not sexually active, despite similar levels of optimism. Low levels of goal orientation may explain why a large proportion of currently sexually active girls in this study were not engaging in regular use of birth control in contrast to sexually active girls in Study 1 who were motivated by the notion that childbearing would be a hindrance to their future goals. This pattern of findings highlights the important role of future goal orientation on the contraceptive use practices of Latina girls in alternative school settings, in addition to its implications for high school completion and future college attendance. These findings also support the recommendation that pregnancy prevention can be more effective if programs address nonsexual antecedents of risky sexual behavior, such as academic motivation, in addition to teaching about knowledge and skills that are pertinent to contraceptive use (Kirby, 2002).

Similar to Study 1, parents were a key source of influence on girls' attitudes. Advice-seeking from parents about personal life decisions and health issues was associated with a stronger desire to go to college, higher levels of optimism about attendance and graduation from college, and stronger motivation to achieve goals. This finding highlights the role of parental support in helping alternative school students complete their goals, mimicking trends from studies conducted with adolescent populations who attend traditional schools. Note, however, that parental support had a significant influence only on girls who were not currently sexually active, suggesting that sexually active girls in this study had a different relationship with their parents that may include less communication. These findings also support the need for alternative schools to involve parents in their efforts to reduce the risk of teenage pregnancy among nonpregnant adolescents.

∷ Conclusion

Isolating youth from mainstream peers in traditional high schools and placing them in alternative schools with other students experiencing academic and behavioral difficulties is a disciplinary strategy used by many school districts serving ethnic minority students. The potential drawbacks of this practice have not been widely questioned. Aggregating youth who are disruptive, failing in school, and are pregnant and parenting makes it difficult to provide a high-quality program that will address the multiple risks faced by these students. In addition, aggregating youth who engage in deviant or nonconventional behavior creates an opportunity for peer contagion effects to occur (Dodge et al., 2006). Our intent in this chapter was to consider potential peer effects in relation to early childbearing attitudes and risky sexual behavior among adolescent girls. It is clear that being a student in an alternative high school offers them considerably more opportunities to affiliate with pregnant and parenting peers than being a student in a traditional school. Little is known about peer socialization effects that might occur as a result of exposure to this social context. It is possible that alternative school participation increases the vulnerability of nonpregnant girls to teenage parenting if they are not motivated to invest the effort needed to complete their studies. For example, although sexually active girls in Study 2 positively appraised their ability to get a college education, they reported less motivation to set and reach their goals in comparison to girls not sexually active. Not surprisingly then, these girls engaged in low levels of contraceptive use, suggesting a lack of concern about becoming pregnant. Although it is quite reasonable to assume that no one is directly suggesting to girls that they should become pregnant, subtle positive social interaction while discussing pregnancy and parenting situations of their peers may foster acceptance and approval among nonpregnant adolescent girls. The finding that some girls in Study 1 perceived that their friends would be happy for them if they had a baby in the next year indicates that peer influence may be operating in this school environment. Additional research is needed to clarify the mechanisms of peer influence.

The importance of parents' influence in this school culture was strongly supported. Although our data cannot speak to what types of support were the most influential, it is clear that a close relationship with parents characterized by open communication with adolescents is quite effective. As expected, parental support, adolescent sexual behavior, and educational goals were interrelated. In Study 1, parents' negative attitudes toward adolescent childbearing were associated with their daughters' attitudes and their aspirations to attend college. In Study 2, it appeared that girls who were not sexually active were closer to their parents than those who were sexually active, and this was positively associated with their college plans and motivation to reach their goals. These findings highlight the role of parents as key social agents in fostering positive educational and sexual behavior outcomes among their adolescents, two outcomes that are typically studied apart. We agree with one educational policy researcher (Pillow, 2006) who recently called for teenage pregnancy to be studied as an educational issue, not just as a health and social welfare topic studied apart from the arena of education. In doing so, we can identify best practices that prevent adolescent girls from disengaging and dropping out of school.

In summary, our findings support the need to understand factors in alternative schools that can hinder adolescent girls' efforts to achieve their goals. Negative peer influences in this social context could be offset by programs that enhance girls' beliefs about the future, provide a realistic understanding of how childbearing could jeopardize future opportunities, and strengthen connections with significant others in their lives who can support their educational aspirations.

⠶ References

Alfaro, E. C., Umaña-Taylor, A. J., & Bámaca, M. Y. (2006). The influence of academic support on Latino adolescents' academic motivation. *Family Relations: Interdisciplinary Journal of Applied Family Studies, 55*(3), 279–291.

Aron, L. Y. (2006). *An overview of alternative education programs: A compilation of elements from the literature.* Washington, DC: Urban Institute.

Aron, L. Y. (2003). *Toward a typology of alternative education programs: A compilation of elements from the literature.* Washington, DC: Urban Institute.

Baumeister, L. M., Flores, E., & Marín, B. V. (1995). Sex information given to Latina adolescents by parents. *Health Education Research, 10*(2), 233–239.

Billy, J. O. G., Landale, N. S., Grady, W. R., & Zimmerle, D. D. (1988). Effects of sexual activity on adolescent social and psychological development. *Social Psychology Quarterly, 51,* 190–212.

Caraway, K., Tucker, C. M., Reinke, W. M., & Hall, C. (2003). Self-efficacy, goal orientation, and fear of failure as predictors of school engagement in high school students. *Psychology in the Schools, 40*(4), 417–427.

Christopher, F. S., Johnson, D. C., & Roosa, M. W. (1993). Family, individual, and social correlates of early Hispanic adolescent sexual expression. *Journal of Sex Research, 30*(1), 54–61.

Coard, S. I., Nitz, K., & Felice, M. E. (2000). Repeat pregnancy among urban adolescents: Sociodemographic, family, and health factors. *Adolescence, 35*(137), 193–200.

Cohen, G. L., & Prinstein, M. J. (2006). Peer contagion of aggression and health risk behavior among adolescent males: An experimental investigation of effects on public conduct and private attitudes. *Child Development, 77*(4), 967–983.

Crosnoe, R., Cavanagh, S., & Elder, G. H. Jr. (2003). Adolescent friendships as academic resources: The intersection of friendship, race, and school disadvantage. *Sociological Perspectives, 46*(3), 331–352.

DeGarmo, D. S., & Martinez, C. R. (2006). A culturally informed model of academic well-being for Latino youth: The importance of discriminatory experiences and social support. *Family Relations, 55,* 267–278.

DiClemente, R. J., Lanier, M. M., Horan, P. F., & Lodico, M. (1991). Comparison of AIDS knowledge, attitudes, and behaviors among incarcerated adolescents and a public school sample in San Francisco. *American Journal of Public Health, 81*(5), 628–630.

Dishion, T. J., Spracklen, K. M., Andrews, D. W., & Patterson, G. R. (1996). Deviancy training in male adolescent friendships. *Behavior Therapy, 27*(3), 373–390.

Dodge, K. A., Dishion, T. J., & Landers, J. E. (2006). Deviant peer influences in intervention and public policy for youth. *Social Policy Report, 20,* I. The Society for Research on Child Development. New York, NY: Guilford Press.

Eccles-Parsons, J., Adler, T. F., Futterman, R., Goff, S. B., Kaczala, C. M., Meece, J. L., et al. (1983). Expectancies, values, and academic behaviors. In J. T. Spence (Ed.), *Achievement and achievement motivation* (pp. 75–146). San Francisco: Freeman.

French, D. C., & Dishion, T. J. (2003). Predictors of early initiation of sexual intercourse among high-risk adolescents. *Journal of Early Adolescence, 23*(3), 295–315.

Gillmore, M. R., Lewis, S. M., Lohr, M. J., Spencer, M. S., & White, R. (1997). Repeat pregnancies among adolescent mothers. *Journal of Marriage and the Family, 59*(3), 536–550.

Grunbaum, J., Kann, L., Kinchen, S., Ross, J., Gowda, V., Collins, J., et al. (1999). Youth Risk Behavioral Surveillance—national alternative school youth risk behavior survey, United States, 1998. *Morbidity and Mortality Weekly Report, 48* (SS-7), 1–44.

Guilamo-Ramos, V., Dittus, P., Jaccard, J., Goldberg, V., et al. (2006). The content and process of mother-adolescent communication about sex in Latino families. *Social Work Research, 30*(3), 169–181.

Hamilton, B. E., Martin, J. A., & Ventura, S. J. (2006). Births: Preliminary data for 2005. *National Vital Statistics Reports; 55*(11), 1–20.

Hamilton, B. E., Martin, J. A., Ventura, S. J., Sutton, P. D., & Menacker, F. (2005). Births: Preliminary data for 2004. *National Vital Statistics Reports, 54*(8), 1–17.

Hansen, W. B. (1992). School-based substance abuse prevention: a review of the state of the art in curriculum, 1980–1990. *Health Education Research, 7,* 403–420.

Hoffman, S. (2006). *By the numbers: The public costs of teen childbearing.* Washington, DC: National Campaign to Prevent Teen Pregnancy.

Hovell, M., Sipan, C., Blumberg, E., Atkins, C., Hofstetter, C. R., & Kreitner, S. (1994). Family influences on Latino and Anglo adolescents' sexual behavior. *Journal of Marriage and the Family, 56*(4), 973–986.

Jessor, R., Van Den Bos, J., Vanderryn, J., Costa, F. M., & Turbin, M. S. (1995). Protective factors in adolescent problem behavior: Moderator effects and developmental change. *Developmental Psychology, 31*(6), 923–933.

Kinsman, S. B., Romer, D., Furstenberg, F. F., & Schwartz, D. (1998). Early sexual initiation: The role of peer norms. *Pediatrics, 102*(5), 1185–1192.

Kirby, D. (2002). *Effective approaches to reducing adolescent unprotected sex, pregnancy, and childbearing.* Scotts Valley, CA: ETR Associates.

Kotchick, B., Miller, K., & Forehand, R. (1999). Adolescent sexual risk taking in single parent ethnic minority families. *Journal of Family Psychology, 13,* 93–102.

Liebowitz, S. W., Castellano, D. C., & Cuellar, I. (1999). Factors that predict sexual behaviors among young Mexican American adolescents: An exploratory study. *Hispanic Journal of Behavioral Sciences, 21*(4), 470–479.

Lightfoot, M., Comulada, W. S., & Stover, G. (2007). Computerized HIV preventive intervention for adolescents: Indications of efficacy. *American Journal of Public Health, 97*(6), 1027–1030.

Markham, C. M., Tortolero, S. R., Escobar-Chaves, S. L., Parcel, G. S., Harrist, R., & Addy, R. C. (2003). Family connectedness and sexual risk-taking among urban youth attending alternative high schools. *Perspectives on Sexual and Reproductive Health, 35*(4), 174–179.

Martin, N., & Brand, B. (2006). *Federal, state, and local roles supporting alternative education.* American Youth Policy Forum. U. S. Department of Labor, Employment, and Training Administration. http://www.aypf.org/publications/AlternativeEducation2006.pdf

May, H. E., & Copeland, E. P. (1998). Academic persistence and alternative high schools: Student and site characteristics. *High School Journal, 81*(4), 199–208.

McKee, M. D., & Karasz, A. (2006). "You have to give her that confidence": Conversations about sex in Hispanic mother-daughter dyads. *Journal of Adolescent Research, 21*(2), 158–184.

Miller, B. C., & Sneesby, K. R. (1988). Educational correlates of adolescents' sexual attitudes and behavior. *Journal of Youth and Adolescence, 17,* 521–530.

Miller, B. C., Norton, M. C., Curtis, T., Hill, E. J., Schvaneveldt, P., & Young, M. H. (1997). The timing of sexual intercourse among adolescents: Family, peer, and other antecedents. *Youth & Society, 29*(1), 54–83.

Morris, R. E., Harrison, E. A., Knox, G. W., Tromanhauser, E., Marquis, D. K., & Watts, L. L. (1995). Health risk behavioral survey from 39 juvenile correctional facilities in the United States. *Journal of Adolescent Health, 17*(6), 334–344.

National Campaign to Prevent Teen Pregnancy. (2007). A look at Latinos: An overview of Latina teen pregnancy. Washington, DC. Retrieved from http://www. teenpregnancy. org/espanol/PDF/latino_overview. pdf.

Ohannessian, C. M., & Crockett, L. J. (1993). A longitudinal investigation of the relationship between educational investment and adolescent sexual activity. *Journal of Adolescent Research, 8,* 167–182.

Persson, A., Kerr, M., & Stattin, H. (2004). Why a leisure context is linked to normbreaking for some girls and not others: Personality characteristics and parent-child relations as explanations. *Journal of Adolescence, 27,* 583–598.

Pillow, W. (2006). Teen pregnancy and education: Politics of knowledge, research, and practice. *Educational Policy, 20,* 56–84.

Plunkett, S. W., & Bámaca-Gómez, M. Y. (2003). The relationship between parenting, acculturation, and adolescent academics in Mexican-origin immigrant families in Los Angeles. *Hispanic Journal of Behavioral Sciences, 25*(2), 222–239.

Prelow, H. M., & Loukas, A. (2003). The role of resource, protective, and risk factors on academic achievement-related outcomes of economically disadvantaged Latino youth. *Journal of Community Psychology, 31*(5), 513–529.

Redding, C. A., & Rossi, J. S. (1999). Testing a model of situational self-efficacy for safer sex among college students: Stage of change and gender-based differences. *Psychology & Health, 14*(3), 467–486.

Romo, L. F., Lefkowitz, E. S., Sigman, M., & Au, T. K. (2002). A longitudinal study of maternal messages about dating and sexuality and their influence on Latino adolescents. *Journal of Adolescent Health, 31*(1). 59–69.

Romo, L. F., Kouyoumdjian, C., Nadeem, E., & Sigman, M. (2006). Promoting values of education in Latino mother-adolescent discussions about conflict and sexuality. In J. Denner & B. L. Guzmán (Eds.), *Latina girls: Voices of adolescent strength in the United States* (pp. 59–76). New York: New York University Press.

Rucibwa, N. K., Modeste, N., Montgomery, S., & Fox, C. A. (2003). Exploring family factors and sexual behaviors in a group of Black and

Hispanic adolescent males. *American Journal of Health Behavior, 27*(1), 63–74.

Schvaneveldt, P. L., Miller, B. C., Berry, E. H., & Lee, T. R. (2001). Academic goals, achievement, and age at first sexual intercourse: Longitudinal, bidirectional influences. *Adolescence, 36*(144), 767–787.

Shanok, A. F., & Miller, L. (2005). Fighting and depression among poor pregnant adolescents. *Journal of Reproductive and Infant Psychology, 23*(3), 207–218.

Shrier, L. A., & Crosby, R. (2003). Correlates of sexual experience among a nationally representative sample of alternative high school students. *Journal of School Health, 73*(5): 197–200.

Stattin, H., Kerr, M., Mahoney, J., Persson, A., & Magnusson, D. (2005). Explaining why a leisure context is bad for some girls and not for others. In J. L. Mahoney, R. W. Larson, & J. S. Eccles (Eds.), *Organized activities as contexts of development: Extracurricular activities, after-school and community programs* (pp. 211–234). Mahwah, NJ: Erlbaum.

Unger, J. B., Molina, G. B., & Teran, L. (2000). Perceived consequences of teenage childbearing among adolescent girls in an urban sample. *Journal of Adolescent Health, 26*(3), 205–212.

Vélez-Pastrana, M. C., González-Rodríguez, R. A., & Borges-Hernández, A. (2005). Family functioning and early onset of sexual intercourse in Latino adolescents. *Adolescence, 40*(160), 777–791.

Villarruel, A. M., Jemmott, J. B. I., Jemmott, L. S., & Ronis, D. L. (2004). Predictors of sexual intercourse and condom use intentions among Spanish-dominant Latino youth: A test of the planned behavior theory. *Nursing Research, 53*(3), 172–181.

Whitaker, D. J., & Miller, K. S. (2000). Parent-adolescent discussions about sex and condoms: Impact on peer influences of sexual risk behavior. *Journal of Adolescent Research, 15*(2), 251–273.

Wigfield, A., & Eccles, J. S. (1992). The development of achievement task values: A theoretical analysis. *Developmental Review, 12,* 265–310.

6 ⠿

Cultural Continuity Between Home and School as a Predictor of Student Motivation

What We Know, What We Need to Learn, and Implications for Practice

Kristen Bogner Warzon and Marika Ginsburg-Block

As noted elsewhere in this volume, the motivation literature abounds with studies of middle-class, average-achieving, primarily Anglo-American students. Until very recently, however, little has been done to determine whether the findings from earlier research with relatively homogeneous groups extend to less well-studied groups (e.g., students from diverse socioeconomic backgrounds, language minorities, and ethnic minorities). America's schools are increasingly ethnically and linguistically diverse. In 2004, 43% of students enrolled in public schools were from an ethnic minority group, a percentage which has almost doubled since 1972 (National Center for Education Statistics, 2006). Also in 2004, 19% of U.S. students spoke a language other than English at home (National Center for Education Statistics, 2006). Changing demographics alone indicate a clear need to expand the literature to include analyses of motivational processes for diverse learners.

However, there are also other questions about motivation and achievement among learners from diverse backgrounds. Ethnic and language minority students fare, on average, worse than their majority counterparts in many key academic areas including reading achievement and graduation rates (National Center for Education Statistics, 2006; National Research Council, 2002). This achievement and graduation gap has not diminished appreciably over the past several years. The clear, empirically demonstrated relationship between students' academic intrinsic motivation and important school outcomes is yet another indicator of the urgent need to better understand motivational and achievement-related processes for minority students

(Eccles, 1993; Gilman & Anderman, 2006; National Center for Education Statistics, 2006).

Researchers have proposed many reasons for the achievement gap between Anglo-American students and their ethnic and linguistic minority peers (e.g., National Research Council, 2002; Ogbu, 1992). One area that has been given significant consideration in the literature is the role of cultural continuity of educational practices, expectations, and values across home and school in predicting students' motivational and achievement outcomes (e.g., Phelan, Davidson, & Yu, 1998). The term "cultural continuity" indicates a degree of similarity, across home and school settings, in one of the above-mentioned culturally-based beliefs or practices. As in many emerging fields, early work in the area of cultural continuity has been largely theoretical and/or qualitative in nature (e.g., Betancourt & Lopez, 1993; Cummins, 1986; Cureton, 1989). To have a research-based literature relative to motivation and diverse learners, the field needs broad-based analyses of continuity across home and school settings.

Some research has examined isolated aspects of culturally based learning styles and preferences (e.g., verve, communalism) as they relate to achievement and motivation in school (Allen & Boykin, 1992; Bempechat, 1998; Boykin & Bailey, 2000). Ethnographic studies on ethnic and cultural differences (e.g., the tendency to have communalistic versus individualistic family structures) have been used to create measures of these culturally based preferences and subsequently test students in learning situations under various conditions (Allen & Boykin, 1992; Allen & Butler, 1996). For example, Boykin and colleagues (1982; Boykin, Allen, Davis, & Senior, 1997) have studied home-stimulation environments and students' performance under conditions of high and low task variability. Over the course of several studies, Boykin and colleagues have found mixed results; in some cases, only African American students benefited from high task variability while in others, African American and Caucasian students have both benefited from greater task variability, despite African American students' ratings of higher home activity levels (Allen & Boykin, 1991; Allen & Boykin, 1992; Boykin, 1982; Boykin et al., 1997). One outcome of this line of research has been culture/ethnicity-specific teaching practices (e.g., cooperative learning strategies, movement and music as a part of instruction) (Allen & Boykin, 1992; Cureton, 1989; Gibson & Gay, 1989; Haynes & Gebreyesus, 1992; Richardson, 1993).

Other research has directly examined students' perceptions of cultural discontinuity across home and school settings and its impact on students' academic and affective outcomes (e.g., Arunkumar, 1999; Arunkumar, Midgley, & Urdan, 1999). This line of inquiry is grounded in an understanding that the culture of home and school are, for some students, quite similar. For other students, however, the two are very different and sometimes even mutually exclusive, making home and school cultures quite foreign to one another. Phelan and colleagues (Phelan et al., 1998) have pinpointed this discontinuity between home and school as one possible source of difficulty for students who must negotiate discrepant cultural norms and values.

In the research completed to date, students' perceptions of cultural discontinuity have been correlated with their academic and affective outcomes. For example, one study on discontinuity (Arunkumar et al., 1999) did not explicitly ask students about match or mismatch in culturally based learning preferences but about the general feeling that the home and school contexts were, to use the authors' language, "two different worlds" (Arunkumar et al., 1999, p. 448). Students with higher self-reported ratings of discontinuity performed more poorly on all measures of school success. This body of literature appears to nest the concept of cultural continuity within the broad social context of the school (see Goodenow, 1992; Wentzel, 1998, 1999; Wentzel & Berndt, 1999; Wentzel & Watkins, 2002). Conceptualized in this way, cultural continuity has been less well studied than the previously discussed construct of cultural learning styles.

Although the study of cultural continuity is, in many respects, still in its infancy, much debate has already ensued as to the role of culture in students' educational lives. Questions that remain unanswered include these: (1) Do students from diverse backgrounds benefit from culturally relevant and responsive teaching styles (and if so, which aspects of cultural continuity are particularly important for instruction)? (2) Do all students need similar research-based teaching and classroom management practices to thrive in school? (Bempechat, 1998; Kane & Boan, 2005; Keith & Fine, 2005; VanDerHeyden & Burns, 2005). While evidence exists for differential achievement between ethnic groups based on specific teaching styles (e.g., Boykin, 1982), some researchers assert that the same mechanisms predictive of achievement for majority group students also predict outcomes for their minority peers (see Frisby, 1993; Keith & Fine, 2005). Finally, Arunkumar and colleagues

(1999) have demonstrated that students' own perceptions of discontinuity across home and school settings are important predictors of students' outcomes, further complicating the debate.

As for most real-world phenomena, the truth in the cultural continuity debate may lie at some middle ground. Perhaps some research-based teaching practices are beneficial for all students' school outcomes, regardless of cultural background (see Keith & Fine, 2005; VanDerHeyden & Burns, 2005). On the other hand, perhaps cultural continuity across social contexts makes an additional contribution to student outcomes, whether directly through culturally responsive teaching practices or indirectly through some motivational or other social contextual process (Slaughter-Defoe & Carlson, 1997; Vogt, Jordan, & Tharp, 1987).

∷ What We Need to Learn: Cultural Continuity Project—A First Step

Researchers in the field of cultural continuity have thus far examined home cultural values/beliefs, student learning preferences/styles, and students' reports of perceived discontinuity between home and school as these factors relate to student achievement and affective outcomes (e.g., Arunkumar et al., 1999; Boykin et al., 1997). There has also been debate about the importance of culturally specific teaching practices relative to good teaching for all students. However, our review of the literature yielded no empirical studies examining generic good teaching simultaneously with a measure of cultural continuity. Neither did we find work examining cultural continuity as reported by all major stakeholders in children's educational lives: families, teachers, and, of course, the children themselves.

Although researchers have examined the relationship between cultural continuity and students' academic and affective outcomes, the possible connection between cultural continuity and important social contextual variables for students (e.g., relationships between families and schools) is an understudied area. Findings in the area of family-school relationships are unequivocal; relationships between families and teachers matter for students' outcomes (Christenson, Abery, & Weinberg, 1986; Christenson & Sheridan, 2001; Eccles & Harold, 1996; Weissberg & Greenberg, 1998; Zellman & Waterman; 1998). Given the importance of family-school relationships and the possible roadblocks that militate against connectedness for families of diverse backgrounds (e.g., language barriers), working toward successful home-school relationships is especially important with these families. Cultural continuity and family-teacher relationships may be particularly important, if thus far understudied with respect to student academic achievement motivation and outcomes (Castro, Bryant, Peisner-Feinberg, & Skinner, 2004; Christenson & Sheridan, 2001; Raffaele & Knoff, 1999).

In the Cultural Continuity Project, we evaluated both teaching practices and the social contextual dimensions of cultural continuity as they relate to students' motivation and achievement. We also examined the connection between family- and teacher-rated cultural continuity and family and teacher relationship satisfaction. To investigate culture as it may differ within and across ethnic groups, we examined culture as reported by participants; we did not equate culture and ethnicity.

In this study, we investigated not only students' perceptions of continuity/discontinuity, but also the reports of students' families and teachers regarding both cultural continuity and relationship satisfaction. Examining students' perspectives allowed us to evaluate student perceived adjustment—that is, the degree to which students feel that their home and school cultures are similar or different and the degree to which they internalize the values of home and school (e.g., Phelan et al., 1998). By also measuring teacher and family perspectives, we expanded the focus of previous research in this area to include two important socializing contexts for students: home and school (Phelan, Davidson, & Cao, 1991; Phelan et al., 1998; Wentzel & Berndt, 1999).

We also examined the home-school relationship context, a well-established predictor of student success, as it may relate to student outcomes (Christenson, Abery, & Weinberg, 1986; Christenson & Sheridan, 2001; Weissberg & Greenberg, 1998). We examined satisfaction with the home-school relationship based on our hypothesis that continuity and relationship satisfaction are related but not identical concepts. That is, we view perceived cultural discontinuity between families and teachers to be a possible point of relationship stress rather than an automatic indicator of relationship dissatisfaction. Conversely, relationship satisfaction in light of discontinuity may represent a form of resilience on the part of teachers and families, described by some researchers as trust (Adams & Christenson, 2000).

We chose to study students in middle childhood (grades 3 through 5) because this developmental stage represents a point of possible prevention rather than intervention with regard to students' achievement and motivational outcomes. There is clear evidence that for many students, adolescence is a period of declining motivation, grades, and feelings of belonging at school (e.g., Gottfried, Fleming, & Gottfried, 2001). Determining the relationship between cultural variables and outcomes for students at the cusp of the transition to adolescence is an important step in understanding developmental change in motivation and may contribute to the development of prevention efforts.

This study addressed three specific research questions: (1) How do family and teacher ratings of cultural continuity relate to self reports of satisfaction with the home-school relationship? (2) Do the concepts of home-school discontinuity (family, teacher, and student) and family and/or teacher relationship satisfaction predict student motivation and achievement? (3) What role do good teaching practices play in predicting student outcomes?

∷ The Cultural Continuity Project

The Cultural Continuity Project (CCP) was a mixed methods survey development project and descriptive study conducted in an ethnically and linguistically diverse urban school district (see Hitchcock et al., 2006, for information on mixed-methods design). The purpose of this project was to create a measure of educationally relevant cultural beliefs and practices. An important feature of the CCP was the development of separate surveys for families, students, and teachers that would allow for comparable measurement of each rater's perspective. This technique also allowed for measurement of continuity in beliefs across raters. The study took place during the spring of the 2002–2003 academic year.

Participants

The survey development portion of the study included four student focus groups from three elementary schools, two teacher focus groups from two schools, two parent/guardian groups, and one group of community members. Members of the school district's educational equity and diversity committee also participated.

Participants in the descriptive portion of the CCP included 142 third- through fifth-grade students from 35 classrooms in eight different schools. All 35 classroom teachers participated in the study, as did 141 parents/guardians. The mean participation rate by classroom for this study was 20% (participation rates ranged from 4% to 66%).

Student and family ethnic group composition for the CCP was 32% African American, 24% Caucasian, 19% Asian American/Pacific Islander, 14% multiracial, 2% Hispanic, 2% Native American, and 7% "other." Eighty percent of students spoke English as their first and primary language. Approximately 66% of the students in the study were eligible for free or reduced-price lunch. Our sample from the eight participating schools was fairly representative of the school district on percentages of students receiving free and reduced-price lunch and English language learners. Although participants were generally representative of the ethnic diversity in the district, this sample may have underrepresented individuals of Hispanic, African American, and Native American heritage.

Procedures

We developed the Culture and School surveys through participatory action research in collaboration with the participating school district. After a literature review, we met with focus groups. We created open-ended discussion questions and topics and discussed these separately with each focus group. Surveys were then created and discussed by two student groups, one parent group, and the participating school district's educational equity and diversity committee. Their suggestions were incorporated into the surveys. For more information about this process, see Ginsburg-Block and Warzon (2007).

After developing the surveys and securing permission from the appropriate agencies, we requested participation in the descriptive study from principals at 31 elementary schools; the schools were chosen to ensure accuracy of geographic, ethnic, and socioeconomic representation within the school district. Principals at eight schools agreed to participate. After classrooms were identified and participation secured, survey packets and consent forms were sent home with students from the participating eight schools. Translated versions of the survey were made available for families whose first language was Hmong, Somali, or Spanish. For their participation, parents/guardians were given a $5 educational gift certificate and entered into a lottery for a chance to win a $100 educational gift certificate. After parents/guardians completed and returned surveys, we administered surveys to small student groups at school. Students were given a $5 educational gift certificate and a new pencil for their participation. Teachers filled out the teacher survey independently and were given a $5 educational gift certificate. We secured achievement data from archival records.

Measures

Each of the Culture and School surveys (family, teacher, and student versions) has several scales; however, for this study we report only a portion of each family, teacher, and student survey (see Ginsburg-Block & Warzon, 2007, for further information). The student outcomes relevant to this study were oral reading fluency and motivation. Relevant scales from the Culture and School survey included family and teacher satisfaction with the home-school relationship, good teaching practices (teachers' self-reports), and all raters' perceptions of cultural discontinuity.

Our study used CBM probes from the Houghton Mifflin Invitations to Literacy series (1999). CBM oral reading fluency scores reflect the number of words students read aloud correctly in one minute. Criterion-validity studies have demonstrated high correlations between oral reading fluency scores and student performance on standardized, norm-referenced tests of basic reading skills and reading comprehension (e.g., Deno, 1985; Stage & Jacobson, 2001). CBM scores are also reliable and valid measures of reading growth (Deno, 1985).

Our academic motivation inventory (AMI) was developed in earlier research (see Ginsburg-Block & Fantuzzo, 1998) on the basis of the Young Children's Academic Intrinsic Motivation Inventory (YCAMI) with permission of the author (Gottfried, 1990). The YCAMI contains three scales (Reading, Math, and General) and was developed to measure enjoyment of learning, mastery orientation, curiosity, and persistence. The YCAMI was validated with a primarily White, middle-class student population in grades 1–4. The 13-item General scale from the YCAMI was adapted into the AMI. To accommodate the wide range of reading levels found in urban classrooms, some wording was altered and the scale was changed from a 3-point scale to a dichotomous scale with response options of *yes* and *no*. In this study, the AMI's internal consistency reliability coefficient was .83.

Scales for family and teacher satisfaction with the home-school relationship are based on the Parent Satisfaction with Educational Experiences (PSEE) and Teacher Satisfaction with Educational Experiences (TSEE) scales; these were included with permission of the authors

(Fantuzzo, Perry, & Childs, 2006; M. A. Perry, personal communication, April 3, 2007). These scales, consisting of 12 items each, measure family and teacher satisfaction with three aspects of the home-school relationship: teacher contact experiences, classroom contact experiences, and school contact experiences. We chose to include all items from the scale in a single score to examine overall satisfaction. Response options, on a 4-point Likert-type scale, were *strongly disagree, disagree, agree,* and *strongly agree.* The reliability coefficients for the family and teacher scales were .87 and .85, respectively.

To examine continuity between family and teacher satisfaction (i.e., degree of agreement across raters), the parallel teacher item was subtracted from a family item for each of the 12 items. The absolute value was taken for each difference score, and absolute values for each of the 12 difference scores were summed. Finally, the total was divided by 12 to create an average difference score. Absolute value was used to prevent false camouflaging of overall across-rater differences.

A good teaching practices (GTP) scale measured teachers' endorsement of the use of research-based teaching and classroom management practices (e.g., using assessments to tailor instruction to individual student's needs, using questions to check for student understanding). This 12-item scale was created and modified based on a review of the relevant literature (i.e., Ames & Archer, 1988; Cummins, 1986; Elliott & Dweck, 1988; Gibson & Gay, 1989; Holland, 1989; Jagers & Mock, 1995; Pepper & Henry, 1989; Saracho, 1989; Vogt et al., 1987; Willis, 1992). Response options were *rarely, sometimes, often,* and *always.* The internal consistency reliability coefficient was .71.

The cultural discontinuity (CD) construct was measured through two questions about cultural differences between the home and school. Items were adapted from the Home-School Dissonance scale (Arunkumar, 1999; Arunkumar et al., 1999) to fit our population as well as to modify the respondent's perspective from that of student to the family and teacher. For teacher cultural discontinuity, these questions were used: "My students' home cultures are different from our school culture" and "My students' families and I have different ideas on how children should be taught." The family questions were identical except that the wording was changed to reflect the home perspective. A higher score indicates greater perceived discontinuity between home and school. The family CD construct had an internal consistency reliability coefficient of .51; the teacher construct's internal consistency reliability coefficient was .75. For the student Culture and School survey, students responded yes or no to the following statement: "Sometimes my family and teacher disagree on what is important at school" (also adapted from Arunkumar et al., 1999). Responses of "yes" indicated students' endorsement of discontinuity across home and school values; "no" represented a sense of continuity. Students were divided into two groups based on their responses.

:: Data Analysis and Findings

Cultural Discontinuity and Family and Teacher Satisfaction

To provide an answer to the first research question, students were divided into four groups based on family and teacher reports of cultural continuity. The groups were (1) low family and teacher discontinuity (agreement that there is continuity in culture across home and school), (2) low family report and high teacher report of discontinuity (disagreement, with teachers reporting more discontinuity than families), (3) high family and teacher discontinuity (agreement that there is a high level of cultural discontinuity), and (4) high family report and low teacher report of discontinuity (disagreement, with families reporting more discontinuity).

Analysis of variance (ANOVA) showed a statistically significant difference in family satisfaction across family-teacher continuity groups, $F_{(3, 118)} = 3.01$, $p = .03$. Post hoc analysis indicated that families were most satisfied when they rated cultural discontinuity as low but teachers rated it as high; families were least satisfied when families and teachers agreed in high discontinuity across settings, $t_{(45)} = 2.94$, $p = .01$. Teacher satisfaction with the home-school relationship was not related to cultural discontinuity agreement, $F_{(3, 87)} = 1.11$, ns.

Cultural Discontinuity, Motivation, and Reading Fluency

To obtain an answer to question two, cultural discontinuity ratings were correlated with student motivation and reading achievement. Neither family nor teacher ratings of cultural discontinuity correlated significantly with student motivation ($r = -.01$, ns and $r = .06$, ns, respectively). However, student motivation was related to students' responses to the cultural discontinuity item, $t_{(139)} = -2.46$, $p = .02$. Motivation was higher for those students who reported no discontinuity.

Teacher-rated discontinuity correlated positively with students' reading achievement ($r = .26$, $p = .02$); these results are discussed below in relation to good teaching practices and reading fluency. Students' perceptions of discontinuity were related to CBM reading fluency, $t_{(122)} = -2.35$, $p = .02$. Students who reported discontinuity between home and school had lower reading fluency scores (mean CBM score = 107.6 words per minute) than did their peers who reported continuous home-school cultures (mean CBM score = 126.6 words per minute). Families' perceptions of cultural discontinuity were not significantly correlated with students' reading fluency ($r = .13$, ns).

Cultural Discontinuity, Good Teaching Practices, Motivation, and Reading Fluency

To further probe research questions two and three, we examined student- and teacher-rated cultural discontinuity, teacher-perceived good teaching practices, and student motivation and reading achievement. Teachers' ratings of cultural discontinuity (CD) and good teaching practices (GTP) were both positively correlated with students' reading fluency ($r = .26$, $p = .02$ and $r = .28$, $p = .00$, respectively). A regression analysis revealed that teacher-perceived discontinuity ($B = .12$) and good teaching practices ($B = .26$) both independently predicted oral reading fluency, $F_{(2, 96)} = 4.13$, $p = .02$; these variables did not interact to predict reading scores.

Figure 6.1 illustrates the relationship among discontinuity, good teaching practices, and oral reading fluency. Predictor scores (i.e., discontinuity ratings and good teaching practices) are depicted at the mean as well as one standard deviation below and above the mean, as per Cohen and Cohen's guideline (Cohen & Cohen, 1983). The relationship between both predictors and reading was positive; that is, as teachers' endorsement of good teaching practices increased, so did reading fluency scores. Also, the higher teachers rated discontinuity across settings, the higher were students' reading scores. The highest predicted reading scores occurred for teachers who reported using a high level of good teaching practices (+1 standard deviation) and who perceived the highest discontinuity between home and school (+1 standard deviation) (CBM score = 141.75 words per minute). Conversely, the lowest predicted oral reading scores occurred for students whose teachers endorsed the lowest level of discontinuity and the fewest good teaching practices (CBM score = 87.87 words per minute). Good teaching

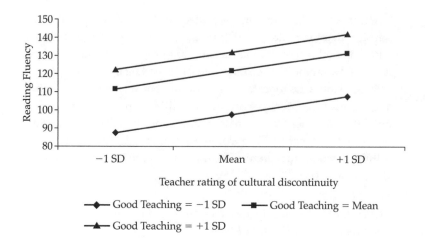

Figure 6–1. Reading fluency as a function of both teacher-reported good teaching practices and cultural discontinuity.

practices did not correlate independently with student motivation, $r = .10$, *ns*.

Family and Teacher Satisfaction, Motivation, and Reading Fluency

Correlations among family and teacher satisfaction and student outcome variables were another aspect of the second research question. Family satisfaction was not related to student motivation ($r = -.02$); however, teacher satisfaction and discrepancy between family and teacher satisfaction were related to motivation ($r = .23$, $p = .02$, $r = -.26$, $p = .02$, respectively) (See Figure 6.2). As in Figure 6.1, predictor scores for Figure 6.2 are depicted at the mean as well as one standard deviation above and below the mean (Cohen & Cohen, 1983).

As is shown in Figure 6.2, the more satisfied a teacher was with the relationship with students' families, the more motivated students were, $F_{(1, 95)} = 5.33$, $p = .02$, $R^2 = .05$. Satisfaction discontinuity was negatively related to motivation; the more similar satisfaction ratings were between teachers and families, the higher was student motivation, $F_{(1,83)} = 5.81$, $p = .02$, $R^2 = .07$. Neither family nor teacher report of relationship satisfaction correlated significantly with students' reading fluency scores ($r = -.10$, *ns*, $r = -.12$, *ns*, respectively).

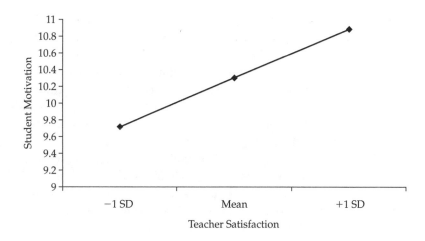

Figure 6–2. Student motivation as a function of overall teacher satisfaction with the home-school relationship.

∷ Discussion of Research Findings

Families reported greatest satisfaction with the family-school relationship when they viewed the home-school setting as relatively continuous and teachers rated it as discontinuous. Families were most dissatisfied when there was agreement that home and school cultures were discontinuous. Although the process behind this satisfaction difference was not investigated, we speculate that in the first instance (high teacher discontinuity, low family discontinuity), families may have been more satisfied because teachers perceived points of cultural discontinuity in the relationship and may have acted more assertively to ensure that potential problems did not strain the relationship, which also explains low family ratings of discontinuity. Conversely, perhaps in the high discontinuity agreement condition, although both teachers and families were aware of cultural differences, no action was taken to ensure that differences were acknowledged and dealt with. In this case, differences in cultural values between home and school did strain relationships, resulting in low family ratings of satisfaction.

It was initially surprising that neither family nor teacher cultural discontinuity ratings were correlated with student motivation. However, as noted above, it has been argued that the mere existence of cultural discontinuity does not necessitate motivational or academic problems for students (Phelan et al., 1998). In the current study, teacher satisfaction and discrepant family-teacher satisfaction were both related to student motivation; families' ratings of satisfaction were not. Based on this finding, perhaps what matters for creating motivating and nurturing classroom environments for diverse students is not whether cultural discontinuity exists (as was shown in the current study) but how teachers feel and react to discontinuity across home and school cultures and how teacher beliefs and actions are perceived by families.

What appears to matter for student motivation and reading achievement are students' perceptions of home-school discontinuity. We found that students who endorsed their home-school environments as continuous in values (one aspect of their respective cultures) scored higher on both motivation and reading achievement measures than did those who rated these contexts as discontinuous. As Arunkumar and colleagues (Arunkumar et al., 1999) demonstrated with fifth-grade students, students' own perceptions of cultural incompatibility across socializing contexts relate to both attitudinal and achievement outcomes.

Although the positive relationship between good teaching practices and student achievement is intuitively clear, our data cannot speak to the precise process by which teachers' perceptions of cultural discontinuity predict higher student reading fluency. In a recent article, Maehr and Yamaguchi proposed that educators' core beliefs likely influence their specific educational practices (Maehr & Yamaguchi, 2001). As all classrooms in the current study were composed of students from diverse backgrounds, perhaps a teacher's higher rating of discontinuity did not represent an objectively larger difference between home and school cultures compared to classrooms in which teachers rated discontinuity as low. Instead, perhaps a high rating indicated a teacher's greater awareness of cultural differences as well as the belief that such differences are important, which, according to Maehr and Yamaguchi's line of thought (2001), may lead to more culturally sensitive and respectful practices in the classroom.

Further, given the relationship between students' reading scores and good teaching practice and teachers' ratings of cultural discontinuity, perhaps cultural awareness is best conceptualized as one aspect of good teaching rather than as a separate skill set for teachers. Given the relationship between student ratings of discontinuity and their academic and motivational outcomes, it may be that teachers' beliefs and classroom practices can either mitigate or exacerbate students' perceptions of home-school discontinuity, which, in turn, influences their motivational and achievement outcomes.

In the current study, we extended the cultural continuity literature by examining the perspective not only of students but also of two important socializing forces in their lives—families and teachers. This research provides additional data to support Arunkumar, Midgley, and Urdan's (1999) findings that subjective measures of continuity are related to students' academic and motivational outcomes, while simultaneously considering the role of good teaching practices. In the this study, we also expanded the earlier finding to include students as young as third grade.

:: Next Steps

While the Cultural Continuity Project has brought us closer to understanding the relationships among indicators of cultural continuity, several limitations and related research questions remain. In planning for prevention and intervention, it will be important to identify which cultural continuity constructs are more or less valid for predicting student learning outcomes. This study examined cultural continuity as an affective measure of interpersonal relations, yet we did not examine behavioral aspects of cultural continuity such as continuity between classroom management strategies and behavior management strategies used at home. Although controversial, research suggests that these specific culturally based differences may also be important points of contrast between home and school and may predict student affective and academic outcomes (e.g., Bempechat, 1998; Boykin & Bailey, 2000). At the very least, these specific cultural continuities/discontinuities are likely related to students' global perceptions of cultural continuity. Given the predictive relationship between student-perceived cultural continuity and important student motivational processes and school outcomes, additional theory building and validity studies in the area of cultural continuity are sorely needed.

In conjunction with the need to further develop and validate the construct of cultural continuity, additional student outcomes related to academic motivation should be examined. For example, the growing theoretical literature on student engagement (e.g., Appleton, Christenson, Kim, & Reschly, 2006; Fredricks, Blumenfeld, & Paris, 2004) seems to suggest that indicators of student engagement may help to explain the relationship between motivation and achievement outcomes. Motivation, according to engagement theorists, may be a form of cognitive engagement explaining *why* students engage or disengage from schooling whereas the study of academic and behavioral engagement provides measurable indicators—that is, the behaviors associated with *how* students withdraw or participate in schooling (e.g., homework completion, attendance). These indicators may be more sensitive to perceived cultural continuity and student motivation than are other measures, such as achievement measures. Thus, it would be important to include indicators of student engagement as either mediating or dependent variables in any model examining the relationship between cultural continuity and student motivation.

The findings of the Cultural Continuity Project are also limited to the participating sample of students, families, and teachers. The extent to which the results of this study can be generalized to other populations is unknown. Future studies with larger and more diverse samples (e.g., greater representation of Latino students) are warranted. While the findings of the Cultural Continuity Project highlighted in this chapter primarily addressed home-school continuity, continuity in cultural values between students and their peers is undoubtedly another important variable in studying student academic motivation. Seminal research with adolescents has identified peer influences as mediating the relationship between family values and educational outcomes (e.g., Steinberg, Dornbusch, & Brown, 1992). For the elementary school sample studied in the Cultural Continuity Project, student-peer continuity as well as home-school continuity may also contribute to student outcomes (Warzon & Ginsburg-Block, 2007). These relationships should be examined in future research and used to inform prevention efforts, given the increasing salience of peers as students develop and work on the role of peers in social motivational processes related to schooling (Phelan et al., 1998; Wentzel, 1998).

The literature on cultural continuity is predominantly descriptive. While experimental studies have been conducted to evaluate programs with family components (e.g., Comer's School Development Program; Haynes & Comer, 1996), very few experimental studies have explicitly targeted specific aspects of cultural continuity or perceptions of discontinuity as causal variables. Component studies may be warranted to identify the causal mechanisms behind the success of interventions aimed at bringing home and school cultures closer together. Descriptive studies should be used to identify the most salient models of cultural continuity as they correspond to student outcomes, yet experimental studies are needed to determine mechanisms through which interventions designated to either enhance cultural continuity (or perhaps the recognition of discontinuity) are effective. While the experimental work of Boykin and colleagues (e.g., Boykin, 1982) was based on instructional modifications, component studies evaluating a range of approaches to addressing cultural continuity are needed.

∷ Implications for Practice

The preliminary findings of the Cultural Continuity Project should be considered a starting point for planning future research. While some interesting and potentially important findings were generated, they must be confirmed before being translated into universal school-based practices. Given this word of caution, the Cultural Continuity Project and the larger body of research examining cultural continuity can generate several worthwhile recommendations.

As documented by current research, perceptions of home and school cultures vary dramatically (e.g., Eccles, Wong, & Peck, 2006). For this reason, schools and communities interested in addressing the issue of cultural continuity should consider conducting site-specific needs assessments to determine whether students, their families, and teachers feel satisfied and accepted. A needs assessment of this nature may be useful in identifying groups that are more or less satisfied and connected. Such information could be used to target specific subgroups or areas of need for intervention. For example, children from families who are culturally and linguistically different from the schools may be at greater risk for decreased motivation and achievement. In another context, busing may reduce the ease with which families access their children's schools, widening the divide between home and school cultures. Numerous precedents have been established for the use of needs assessments in the literature. For example, Fantuzzo, McWayne, and Bulotsky (2003) and others (e.g., Power, 2003) have proposed models for conducting meaningful partnership-based research in vulnerable communities, all of which incorporate community needs assessment.

The composition of public schools, particularly those located in urban areas, will continue to become increasingly culturally diverse. Work to involve family and community members in the schools in meaningful roles—as, for example, mentors and tutors—seems warranted based on both research and theory. There is a developing literature documenting the benefits of involving community members in our schools (e.g., Manz, Power, Ginsburg-Block, & Dowrick, 2007; Power, Dowrick, Ginsburg-Block, & Manz, 2004). While cultural differences across home, peer, and school settings will undoubtedly exist, the incorporation of community members in schools has shown positive effects on student outcomes (e.g., Power et al., 2004). Some of the plausible mechanisms behind these positive findings are an increase in educators' and peers' awareness of the diverse cultures within the schools, resulting in a more welcoming climate (Ingraham, 2000); emphasizing the value of education and positive expectations that both teachers and community members hold for students, thereby enhancing social motivation for academic goals (Wentzel, 1999); and providing culturally similar, positive role models for students to emulate (Schunk, Hanson, & Cox, 1987). Involving community members in the schools appears to be a cost-effective strategy for addressing cultural differences across students' social settings and promoting positive affective and academic outcomes for students.

Teacher responsiveness to working with culturally diverse students and families is a likely influence on student perceptions of discontinuity and may be another focal point for prevention and intervention efforts through preservice and inservice training (Maehr & Yamaguchi, 2001). The Cultural Continuity Project, along with both theoretical and descriptive work on culturally sensitive practices (e.g., Ingraham, 2000), identifies teacher awareness of cultural differences as an important factor related to student motivational processes and outcomes. Pianta and Walsh's (1996) work on the development of strong student-teacher relationships and Christenson and Sheridan's (2001) research on developing the home-school relationship both emphasize the important protective roles of teachers and families for culturally diverse students. Schools and teacher education programs must continue to identify ways to enhance teacher awareness and responsiveness to the diverse nature of students and families they serve.

Efforts such as cultural awareness training for teachers and enlisting community members to fulfill advocacy roles in schools represent the growing recognition that prevention efforts are more viable and less costly than remedial efforts to enhance student outcomes. Simply stated, prevention works better than intervention (e.g., Durlak, 1995). Prevention efforts targeted at elementary students seem wise, given the strong evidence that academic motivation declines significantly after elementary school (e.g., Gottfried, Fleming, & Gottfried, 2001) and that children in grades 3, 4, and 5 (as demonstrated by the Cultural Continuity Project) demonstrate associated drops in motivation when they perceive cultural discontinuity. Research on transitional periods in schooling also substantiates this recommendation (Pianta, Rimm-Kaufman, & Cox, 1999). Schoolwide prevention initiatives focused on school climate, such as Comer's School Development Program (Haynes & Comer, 1996), Slavin's Success for All (Slavin, Karweit, & Wasik, 1994), and Ziegler's Head Start (Ziegler & Styfco, 1993), which have evidence of efficacy and include family components (Lewis, Battistich, & Schaps, 1990), should be strongly considered for adoption by public school systems.

:: Note

We thank the students, teachers, and families who participated in the Cultural Continuity Project, as well as the participating school district.

:: References

Adams, K. S., & Christenson, S. L. (2000). Trust and the family-school relationship: Examination of parent-teacher differences in elementary and secondary grades. *Journal of School Psychology, 38*, 477–497.

Allen, B. A., & Boykin, A. W. (1991). The influence of contextual factors on Afro-American and Euro-American children's performance: Effects of movement opportunity and music. *International Journal of Psychology, 26*, 373–387.

Allen, B. A., & Boykin, A. W. (1992). African-American children and the educational process: Alleviating cultural discontinuity through prescriptive pedagogy. *School Psychology Review, 21*, 586–596.

Allen, B. A., & Butler, L. (1996). The effects of music and movement opportunity on the analogical reasoning performance of African American and White school children: A preliminary study. *Journal of Black Studies, 22*, 316–328.

Ames, C., & Archer, J. (1988). Achievement goals in the classroom: Students' learning strategies and motivation processes. *Journal of Educational Psychology, 80*, 260–267.

Appleton, J. J., Christenson, S. L., Kim, D., & Reschly, A. L. (2006). Measuring cognitive and psychological engagement: Validation of the Student Engagement Instrument. *Journal of School Psychology, 44,* 427–445.

Arunkumar, R. (1999). *Living in the interface of different cultures: Adolescents' experiences of cultural dissonance between home and school.* Unpublished doctoral dissertation, University of Michigan, Ann Arbor.

Arunkumar, R., Midgley, C., & Urdan, T. (1999). Perceiving high or low home-school dissonance: Longitudinal effects on adolescent emotional and academic well-being. *Journal of Research on Adolescence, 9,* 441–466.

Bempechat, J. (1998). *Against the odds: How "at-risk" students exceed expectations.* New York: Wiley.

Betancourt, H., & Lopez, S. R. (1993). The study of culture, ethnicity, and race in American psychology. *American Psychologist, 48,* 629–637.

Boykin, A. W. (1982). Task variability and the performance of black and white schoolchildren. *Journal of Black Studies, 12,* 469–485.

Boykin, A. W., Allen, B., Davis, L. H., & Senior, A. M. (1997). Task performance of Black and White children across levels of presentation variability. *Journal of Psychology, 131,* 427–437.

Boykin, A. W., & Bailey, C. T. (2000). *The role of cultural factors in school relevant cognitive functioning: Description of home environmental factors, cultural orientations, and learning preferences.* Baltimore, MD: Center for Research on the Education of Students Placed at Risk, Johns Hopkins University & Howard University: U. S. Dept. of Education, Office of Educational Research and Improvement, Educational Resources Information Center.

Castro, D. C., Bryant, D. M., Peisner-Feinberg, E. S., & Skinner, M. L. (2004). Parent involvement in Head Start programs: The role of parent, teacher, and classroom characteristics. *Early Childhood Research Quarterly, 19,* 413–430.

Christenson, S. L., Abery, B., & Weinberg, R. A. (1986). An alternative model for the delivery of psychology in the school community. In S. N. Elliott & J. C. Witt (Eds.), *The delivery of psychological services in the schools: Concepts, processes, and issues* (pp. 349–391). Hillsdale, NJ: Erlbaum.

Christenson, S. L., & Sheridan, S. M. (2001). *Schools and families: Creating essential connections for learning.* New York: Guilford.

Cohen, J., & Cohen, P. (1983). *Applied multiple regression/correlation analyses for the behavioral sciences* (2nd ed.). Hillsdale, NJ: Erlbaum.

Cummins, J. (1986). Empowering minority students: A framework for intervention. *Harvard Educational Review, 56,* 18–36.

Cureton, G. O. (1989). Using a Black learning style. In B. J. Shade (Ed.), *Culture, style, and the educative process*. Springfield, IL: Charles C. Thomas.

Deno, S. L. (1985). Curriculum-based measurement: The emerging alternative. *Exceptional Children, 52*, 219–232.

Durlak, J. A. (1995). *School-based prevention programs for children and adolescents*. Thousand Oaks, CA: Sage.

Eccles, J. S. (1993). School and family effects on the ontogeny of children's interests, self-perceptions, and activity choice. In J. Jacobs (Ed.), *Nebraska symposium on motivation: Developmental perspectives on motivation* (pp. 145–208). Lincoln: University of Nebraska Press.

Eccles, J. S., & Harold, R. D. (1996). Family involvement in children's and adolescents' schooling. In A. Booth & J. F. Dunn (Eds.), *Family-school links: How do they affect educational outcomes?* (pp. 3–34). Mahwah, NJ: Erlbaum.

Eccles, J. S., Wong, C. A., & Peck, S. C. (2006). Ethnicity as a social context for the development of African-American adolescents. *Journal of School Psychology, 44*, 407–426.

Elliott, E. S., & Dweck, C. S. (1988). Goals: An approach to motivation and achievement. *Journal of Personality and Social Psychology, 54*, 5–12.

Fantuzzo, J., McWayne, C., & Bulotsky, R. (2003). Forging strategic partnerships to advance mental health science and practice for vulnerable children. *School Psychology Review, 32*, 17–37.

Fantuzzo, J., Perry, M. A., & Childs, S. (2006). Parent satisfaction with Educational Experiences Scale: A multivariate examination of parent satisfaction with early childhood education programs. *Early Childhood Research Quarterly, 21*, 142–152.

Fredricks, J. A., Blumenfeld, P. C., & Paris, A. H. (2004). School engagement: Potential of the concept, state of the evidence. *Review of Educational Research, 74*, 59–109.

Frisby, C. L. (1993). One giant step backward: Myths of Black cultural learning styles. *School Psychology Review, 22*, 535–557.

Gibson, S. E., & Gay, G. (1989). Improving the success in school of poor Black children. In B. J. Shade (Ed.), *Culture, style, and the educative process* (pp. 275–283). Springfield, IL: Charles C. Thomas.

Gliman, R., & Anderman, E. M. (2006). Editorial: Motivation and its relevance to school psychology: An introduction to the special issue. *Journal of School Psychology, 44*, 325–329.

Ginsburg-Block, M., & Fantuzzo, J. (1998). An evaluation of the relative effectiveness of NCTM standards-based interventions for low-achieving urban elementary students. *Journal of Educational Psychology, 90*, 1–10.

Ginsburg-Block, M., & Warzon, K. B. (2007). *The Cultural Continuity Project: An examination of home-school continuity and student outcomes.* Manuscript submitted for publication.

Goodenow, C. (1992). Strengthening the links between educational psychology and the study of social contexts. *Educational Psychologist, 27,* 177–196.

Gottfried, A. E. (1990). Academic intrinsic motivation in young elementary school children. *Journal of Educational Psychology, 82,* 525–538.

Gottfried, A., Fleming, J. S., & Gottfried, A. W. (2001). Continuity of academic intrinsic motivation from childhood through late adolescence: A longitudinal study. *Journal of Educational Psychology, 93,* 3–13.

Haynes, N. M., & Comer, J. P. (1996). Integrating schools, families, and communities through successful school reform: The School Developmental Program. *School Psychology Review, 25,* 501–506.

Haynes, N. M., & Gebreyesus, S. (1992). Cooperative learning: A case for African-American students. *School Psychology Review, 21,* 577–585.

Hitchcock, J. H., Sarkar, S., Nastasi, B. K., Burkholder, G., Varjas, K., & Jayasena, A. (2006). Validating culture- and gender-specific constructs: A mixed method approach to advance assessment procedures in cross-cultural settings. In B. K. Nastasi (Ed.), *Multicultural issues in school psychology* (pp. 13–33). Hawthorne, NJ: Hawthorne Press.

Holland, R. P. (1989). Learner characteristics and learner performance: Implications for instructional placement decisions. In B. J. Shade (Ed.), *Culture, style, and the educative process* (pp. 167–183). Springfield, IL: Charles C. Thomas.

Ingraham, C. L. (2000). Consultation through a multicultural lens: Multicultural and cross-cultural consultation in the schools. *School Psychology Review, 29,* 320–343.

Jagers, R. J., & Mock, L. O. (1995). The communalism scale and collectivist-individualistic tendencies: Some preliminary findings. *Journal of Black Psychology, 21,* 153–167.

Kane, H., & Boan, C. H. (2005). A review and critique of multicultural learning styles. In C. L. Frisby & C. R. Reynolds (Eds.), *Comprehensive handbook of multicultural school psychology* (pp. 425–456). Hoboken, NJ: Wiley.

Keith, T. Z., & Fine, J. G. (2005). Multicultural influences on school learning: Similarities and differences across groups. In C. L. Frisby & C. R. Reynolds (Eds.), *Comprehensive handbook of multicultural school psychology* (pp. 457–482). Hoboken, NJ: Wiley.

Lewis, C., Battistich, V., & Schaps, E. (1990). School-based primary prevention: What is an effective program? *New Directions for Child Development, 50,* 35–59.

Maehr, M. L., & Yamaguchi, R. (2001). Cultural diversity, student motivation, and achievement. In F. Salili, C. Y. Chu, & Y. Y. Hong (Eds.), *Student motivation: The culture and context of learning* (pp. 123–148). New York: Kluwer Academic/Plenum.

Manz, P. H., Power, T. J., Ginsburg-Block, M., & Dowrick, P. (2007). *Community paraeducators: A partnership-directed approach for preparing and sustaining the involvement of community members in central city schools.* Manuscript submitted for publication.

National Center for Education Statistics. (2006). *The condition of education 2006.* Washington, DC: U.S. Department of Education.

National Research Council. (2002). *Minority students in special and gifted education.* Committee on Minority Representation in Special Education, M. Suzanne Donovan and Christopher T. Cross (Eds.). Division of Behavioral and Social Sciences and Education. Washington, DC: National Academy Press.

Ogbu, J. (1992). Understanding cultural diversity and learning. *Educational Researcher, 21,* 5–24.

Pepper, F. C., & Henry, S. (1989). Social and cultural effects on Indian learning style: Classroom implications. In B. J. Shade (Ed.), *Culture, style, and the educative process* (pp. 33–42). Springfield, IL: Charles C Thomas.

Phelan, P., Davidson, A. L., & Cao, H. T. (1991). Students' multiple worlds: Negotiating the boundaries of family, peer, and school cultures. *Anthropology and Education Quarterly, 22,* 224–250.

Phelan, P., Davidson, A. L., & Yu, H. C. (1998). *Adolescents' worlds: Negotiating family, peers, and school.* New York: Teachers College Press.

Pianta, R. C., Rimm-Kaufman, S. E., & Cox, M. J. (1999). Introduction: An ecological approach to kindergarten transition. In R. C. Pianta & M. J. Cox (Eds.), *The transition to kindergarten* (pp. 3–12). Baltimore, MD: Paul H. Brookes.

Pianta, R. C., & Walsh, D. J. (1996). *High-risk children in schools: Constructing sustaining relationships.* New York: Routledge.

Power, T. J. (2003). Promoting children's mental health: Reform through interdisciplinary and community partnerships. *School Psychology Review, 32,* 3–16.

Power, T., Dowrick, P., Ginsburg-Block, M., & Manz, P. (2004). Partnership-based, community-assisted early intervention for literacy: An application of the participatory intervention model. *Journal of Behavioral Education, 13,* 93–115.

Raffaele, L. M., & Knoff, H. M. (1999). Improving home-school collaboration with disadvantaged families: Organizational principles, perspectives, and approaches. *School Psychology Review, 28,* 448–466.

Richardson, T. Q. (1993). Black cultural learning styles: Is it really a myth? *School Psychology Review, 22,* 562–567.

Saracho, O. N. (1989). Cultural differences in the cognitive style of Mexican-American students. In B. J. Shade (Ed.), *Culture, style, and the educative process* (pp. 129–136). Springfield, IL: Charles C Thomas.

Schunk, D. H., Hanson, A. R., & Cox, P. D. (1987). Peer-model attributes and children's achievement behaviors. *Journal of Educational Psychology, 79,* 54–61.

Slaughter-Defoe, D. T., & Carlson, K. G. (1997). Young African American and Latino children in high-poverty urban schools: How they perceive school climate. *Journal of Negro Education, 65,* 60–70.

Slavin, R. E., Karweit, N. L., & Wasik, B. A. (Eds.). (1994). *Preventing early school failure: Research, policy, and practice.* Needham Heights, MA: Allyn and Bacon.

Stage, S. A., & Jacobsen, M. D. (2001). Predicting student success on a state-mandated performance-based assessment using oral reading fluency. *School Psychology Review, 30,* 407–419.

Steinberg, L., Dornbusch, S. M., & Brown, B. B. (1992). Ethnic differences in adolescent achievement: An ecological perspective. *American Psychologist, 47,* 723–729.

VanDerHeyden, A. M., & Burns, M. K. (2005). Effective instruction for at-risk minority populations. In C. L. Frisby & C. R. Reynolds (Eds.), *Comprehensive handbook of multicultural school psychology* (pp. 483–513). Hoboken, NJ: Wiley.

Vogt, L. A., Jordan, C., & Tharp, R. G. (1987). Explaining school failure, producing school success: Two cases. *Anthropology and Education Quarterly, 18,* 276–286.

Warzon, K. B., & Ginsburg-Block, M. (2007). *The role of peers in predicting students' engagement in school.* Manuscript submitted for publication.

Weissberg, R. P., & Greenberg, M. T. (1998). School and community competence-enhancement and prevention programs. In W. Damon & K. A. Renninger (Eds.), *Handbook of child psychology: Volume 4: Child psychology in practice* (5th ed., pp. 877–954). New York: Wiley.

Wentzel, K. R. (1998). Social relationships and motivation in middle school: The role of parents, teachers, and peers. *Journal of Educational Psychology, 90,* 202–209.

Wentzel, K. R. (1999). Social-motivational processes and interpersonal relationships: Implications for understanding motivation at school, *Journal of Educational Psychology, 91,* 76–96.

Wentzel, K. R., & Berndt, T. J. (1999). Social influences and school adjustment: Overview. *Educational Psychologist, 34,* 1–2.

Wentzel, K. R., & Watkins, D. E. (2002). Peer relationships and collaborative learning as contexts for academic enablers. *School Psychology Review, 31*, 366–377.

Willis, M. G. (1992). Learning styles of African American children: A review of the literature and interventions. *Journal of Black Psychology, 18*, 260–278.

Zellman, G. L., & Waterman, J. M. (1998). Understanding the impact of parent school involvement on children's educational outcomes. *Journal of Educational Research, 91*, 370–380.

Ziegler, E., & Styfco, S. (Eds.). (1993). *Head Start and beyond.* New Haven, CT: University Press.

7 ⠿

Cultural Mistrust, Academic Outcome Expectations, and Outcome Values Among African American Adolescent Males

Miles Anthony Irving

Over the last several decades Africans Americans as a group have continued to struggle with academic success, as evidenced by standardized test scores, high school completion rates, and postsecondary completion rates. This evidence suggests that past and current educational reforms have been largely ineffective in rectifying African American students' academic difficulties (Cokley, 2002a; Kaplan, 1999; Tucker, 1999). Recent data from the National Center of Educational Statistics (NCES, 2001) reveals that 65% of African American students have achievement levels that fall below basic skill levels, compared to only 19% of White students. Racism, social inequity, and unequal access to effective schooling have all been clearly implicated in this significant disparity (Fine, 1991; Oakes, 1985).

The breadth of this problem is illustrated by the finding that academic underachievement among African American students is equally problematic among urban and suburban students as well as across the full spectrum of socioeconomic status (SES) (Ogbu, 2003; University of California, Outreach Task Force, 1997). Still, despite these findings, many African American students at all levels of SES are quite successful in school (Ford, 1998; Hilliard, 2003). Thus, we must look beyond the obvious inequities in educational and economic opportunities that confront ethnic minorities in this country to develop a richer, more flexible description of the broad range of influences on students' educational outcomes.

⠴ Seeking Solutions to Underachievement

Research on student motivation has been a particularly robust area of research in examining student underachievement. However, the influence of race and culture on African American student motivation did not began to receive significant attention in literature until the 1990s. A seminal literature review by Graham (1994) highlighted the differences between African American and Caucasian students in self-esteem, self-concept, and other motivational constructs. Motivational studies with African American students have largely been grounded in social learning, social cognitive, or cultural ecological frameworks (Bandura, 2002; Hilliard, 1992; Kromhout & Vedder, 1996). However, relatively little specific attention has been paid to the consequences of membership in a marginalized cultural group on students' own beliefs about school achievement and academic motivation. This chapter describes research at that nexus by exploring the relationship between beliefs about cultural barriers to success and beliefs about educational achievement in a sample of African American high school students.

⠴ Motivation and Student Beliefs

Since the 1970s, the expectancy value model of motivation has generated a substantial empirical literature. Research guided by this general model has illustrated that human behavior is strongly influenced by two factors: an individual's expectancy of a successful outcome when engaging in a particular behavior and the subjective value of that successful outcome (Weiner, 1992). Further, expectancy of success and perceptions of value will influence one's willingness to overcome challenges and persevere toward a particular goal (Eccles & Wigfield, 2002; Lord, Hanges, & Godfrey, 2003). In the academic domain, students are motivated to persist in their achievement striving if they expect to succeed and if those strivings to result in outcomes that they desire and deem favorable.

One set of motivational beliefs, outcome expectancies, has been found to influence a range of motivated behaviors. For example, early laboratory research with young children demonstrated that high expectancies for success were related to higher persistence on an assigned task (Mahrer, 1956). More recent school-based research has revealed that expectancies predict grades, course-taking decisions, and occupational aspirations (Nauta & Epperson, 2003). For example, among high school students in advanced mathematics classes, expectancies for success predicted subsequent classroom grades as well as effective use of learning strategies (Pokay & Blumenfeld, 1990). Research has also found that perceptions of competence and outcome expectancy predict successful high school completion when measured as early as sixth grade (Eccles, Vida, & Barber, 2004; Jacobs, Lanza, Osgood, Eccles, & Wigfield, 2002).

Academic outcome value represents the importance and desirability that students perceive for outcomes that are possible as a result of a formal education (Wigfield & Eccles, 2000). If expectancy beliefs answer the question "Can I accomplish this?" achievement values answer the question "Do I want this?" If outcomes that are commonly associated with success in formal education are not perceived as useful or attractive, a student's motivation to achieve those outcomes may be undermined (Anderman & Midgley, 1997; Wigfield & Eccles, 2002). Even students who believe they can accomplish particular outcomes are less likely to work diligently if they perceive the attractiveness or utility of the outcome as negligible (Shell, Murphy, & Bruning, 1989). Adolescents who devalue academic achievement striving are more likely to direct their attention and efforts to nonacademic pursuits (personal dress and grooming, athletic prowess, dating success) that may not be conducive to academic success (Graham, Taylor, & Hudley, 1998).

◼ The Sociocultural Environment

The sociocultural environment is another key influence on motivational beliefs and values. In the United States, race, economic status, and social stratification are sociocultural factors that may impact an individual's outcome expectancies and outcome values (Darley & Gross, 1983; Williams, Davis, Cribbs, Saunders, & Williams, 2002). In a society plagued by racism and classism as is U.S. society (Hacker, 1992), those who perceive barriers to social mobility to be motivated by race, ethnicity, or social class may have little expectation that success can be achieved through academic strivings (Weis & Fine, 1993). For example, a body of motivational research had consistently attempted to connect chronic school failure among African Americans to low expectancy and negative academic beliefs (see review in Graham, 1994). However, the causal relationship between self-beliefs and achievement beliefs is complex and not well understood.

Research has not successfully specified a causal direction among academic achievement, expectancy beliefs, and self-beliefs in African American students. For example, van Laar (2000) found that among African American college students, declines in academic outcome expectancies are driven primarily by the growing belief that opportunities are proscribed by racial inequality rather than individual motivation or measured achievement. Similarly, in a national survey, African American adults expressed the belief that racial discrimination rather than individual failure accounts for low career and educational success among members of ethnic minority groups (Hughes & Demo, 1989). Collectively, these data represent compelling evidence of the impact of the sociocultural environment as a primary influence on expectancy beliefs.

Turning to achievement value, work on social stereotypes suggests that African American adolescents may be particularly vulnerable to pervasive cultural stereotypes that portray them as intellectually incompetent and socially belligerent (Hudley & Graham, 2001; Steele, 1997). These cultural stereotypes are widely known to their adolescent targets (Brown, 1995) and may lead adolescents to a process of psychological disidentification (Steele, 1997). The theory of stereotype threat proposes that members of negatively stereotyped groups may fear being judged or treated according to that stereotype. Given this social-psychological threat, African American youth may devalue achievement striving and reject identification with school, irrespective of their academic competence, in response to racist stereotypes (Major et al., 2002; Steele & Aronson, 1998). In sum, although research has identified a number of self-beliefs that govern outcome expectancies and outcome values, I argue here that these two critical determinants of achievement motivation are moderated by the broader sociocultural environment in which students must enact their achievement strivings. Membership in a marginalized ethnic group that is victimized simultaneously by racial discrimination and hostile cultural stereotypes may negatively impact both outcome expectancies and achievement values.

∷ Cultural Mistrust

The psychological construct of cultural mistrust may be useful in operationalizing the influence of social inequity on motivational beliefs

(F. Terrell & Terrell, 1981). Cultural mistrust has been described as the tendency for African Americans to distrust Whites in institutional, personal, or social contexts. Such distrust, fueled by the pervasive influence of racism, saps African Americans' confidence and trust in White Americans and White-controlled institutions (Feagin & McKinney, 2003; Larson & Ovando, 2001). From slavery until the advances gained through the civil rights movement of the early 1960s, the majority of African Americans were economically relegated to a lower or underclass status in the United States. Since the civil rights movement, although many more African Americans have secured meaningful and respected work within the dominant culture, opportunities for promotion are still limited by what is commonly known as a "glass ceiling" (Grodsky & Pager, 2001). Currently, qualified African Americans continue to earn less in dollars than White males with the same qualifications and credentials (Staveteig & Wigton, 2000).

Cultural mistrust has developed in response to years of racial and economic inequality and oppression. African Americans with high levels of cultural mistrust will therefore expect that members or institutions of the dominant culture will not treat them in a fair manner (Ogbu, 1991). For example, many African Americans, confronted with manifestly inferior schools (Kozol, 1991), do not trust public schools to provide an adequate education for their children (Ogbu, 1991). Many African American families and communities may perceive structural and political barriers such as neglected community infrastructure and deficient schooling as racially constructed neglect (Gadsen, Smith, & Jordan, 1996). Adolescents may similarly interpret structurally imposed racial disadvantages as indicators that there is little relationship between academic achievement striving and economic and social opportunities in life (Mickelson, 1990). This lack of trust that African Americans will receive equal access to the opportunity structure in the United States may create both lowered educational outcome expectations and a devaluing of achievement striving (Ogbu, 1991).

Cultural mistrust has been researched in the clinical and counseling area for several decades, dating back to the introduction of the construct of "healthy cultural paranoia" (Grier & Cobbs, 1968). Clinical research has typically addressed the relationship between cultural mistrust and attitudes toward mental health services. These studies suggest that African Americans who are high in cultural mistrust tend to have more negative attitudes toward therapy with White clinicians and greater expectations of bias from the mental health system (Phelps, Taylor, & Gerard, 2001;

Terrell, Daniloff, Garden, Flint-Shaw, & Flowers, 2001; Thompson, Nevelle, Weathers, Postin, & Atkinson, 1990; Whaley, 2001a, 2001b).

Fewer studies have investigated the relationship between cultural mistrust and academic functioning. However, our current knowledge, albeit limited, suggests that mistrust is detrimental to academic functioning. Prior research has demonstrated a negative relationship between occupational expectations and cultural mistrust among African American junior high school students (F. Terrell, Terrell, & Miller, 1993). As well, adolescents both in this country and abroad with higher levels of cultural mistrust self-report higher levels of deviant behavior, which may have a negative influence on school performance (Biafora et al., 1994). In sum, upward social and economic mobility has been a powerful incentive supporting academic achievement motivation for many Americans (Larson & Ovando, 2001). However, for African Americans as a group, several hundred years of racial, social, and economic discrimination may undermine academic achievement motivation by negatively impacting academic outcome expectancy and academic achievement values.

∷ Examining Cultural Mistrust

To expand our understanding of sociocultural influences on academic achievement and motivation, the data presented here measured the relationship between cultural mistrust, academic achievement values, academic outcome expectations, and academic achievement among a sample of African American high school students. The goal of this study was to determine whether effects of cultural mistrust are similar across geographic regions. In a prior study, our research team found substantial effects for high school students on the west coast (Irving & Hudley, 2005); however, there is reason to wonder whether we would find similar effects for high school students in the southeastern United States. The southeastern United States has a particularly painful history demarcated along racial lines. The Deep South was essentially the front lines of the civil rights movement in the 1960s. Today, many African American communities in the South remain racially isolated, impoverished, and economically disenfranchised. As well, many schools in African American communities continue to be segregated and substandard.

Historical and continuing racial issues in the southeastern United States make it an ideal place to study cultural mistrust, motivation, and school achievement. High school students are an especially important population to study, given that important academic and career decisions take on an increased urgency as students progress from middle school to high school. Based on prior research with high school and middle school students, I expected to find inverse relationships between cultural mistrust and outcome expectations, cultural mistrust and outcome value, and cultural mistrust and academic achievement. Based on classic motivation theory, I also expected outcome expectancy and outcome value to be strongly intercorrelated and both to be correlated to academic achievement. Finally, I expected cultural mistrust and academic outcome expectations to each uniquely predict school achievement.

:: Participants and Setting

Participants in the study were African American male high school students (N = 105) in grades 9–12, with mean ages ranging from 14.5 for ninth graders to 17.0 for 12th graders. Prior research indicates that variables included in this study may operate differently as a function of gender (Fordham, 1996; Osborne, 1997). Therefore, consistent with our previous study (Irving & Hudley, 2005), only male respondents were included in this study. The students were enrolled in a public high school in a large metropolitan city in the southeastern United States. The school's student population is 99% African American and the total adult staff (including faculty, administrators, and staff) of the school is 85% African American. All African American male students in the school were eligible for participation, and all participants were fluent in English. Students were recruited from high-, medium-, and low-track classes to avoid any potential achievement level selection bias. Written informed consent was obtained from the participants as well as the parent or legal guardian of all students under 18 years of age.

:: Measures

Cultural Mistrust

The Revised Cultural Mistrust Inventory (CMI) (Irving & Hudley, 2000; Irving, 2002) is a measure of African Americans' mistrust of the dominant culture (Terrell & Terrell, 1981). Originally, the Cultural Mistrust

Inventory was a 48-item measure with four subscales: Politics and Law, Business and Workplace, Education and Training, and Interpersonal Relationships. However, previous research demonstrated high intercorrelations for subscales, ranging from r = .75 to r = .88 (Irving & Hudley, 2005). A factor analysis revealed that the one-factor model explained 43% of the variance, and I made the decision to analyze the Cultural Mistrust Inventory as a single, composite score. I also reduced the number of items by eliminating items with low factor loadings and selecting the 10 questions that best reflected a general description of mistrust toward the dominant culture. After eliminating items from the original scale, I verified that the scale reliability remained at an appropriate level ($\alpha = .91$). In the revised scale, low scores represent a low level of mistrust whereas high scores reflect a high level of mistrust.

Outcome Expectation and Outcome Values

Outcome expectations were assessed using the African American Academic Outcome Expectations Scale (Irving, 2002). This 20-item measure has two subscales, one measuring the benefits respondents expect to gain from academic achievement and the other how much they value these outcomes. High scores indicate a high outcome expectation or a high valuation of a given item. Reliabilities for expectations and value were $\alpha = .89$ and $\alpha = .91$, respectively (Irving & Hudley, 2005).

Academic Achievement

Students' academic achievement was measured using their cumulative academic grade point average (GPA). The academic GPA does not take in consideration nonacademic electives like physical education or the extra grade point available in advanced placement (AP) courses.

✠ Results

The relationship between cultural mistrust and academic outcome expectations was assessed using Pearson's correlations; results were only partially consistent with the first hypothesis. As predicted, cultural mistrust demonstrated a significant inverse relationship with academic achievement, $r = -.16$, $p < .05$. However, the relationships between cultural mistrust and outcome expectations, $r = .36$, $p < .01$, and cultural mistrust and outcome value, $r = .23$, $p < .05$, although significant, were in the opposite direction of my hypotheses. As predicted, measures of outcome expectations and outcome value were related to academic achievement, $r = .29$, $p < .01$, and $r = .27$, $p < .05$, respectively. Finally, as expected outcome expectancy demonstrated a strong relationship to outcome value, $r = .79$, $p < .01$. I used a multiple regression analysis to examine the fourth hypothesis, using cultural mistrust and outcome expectation as the predictor variables and academic achievement as the dependent variable. Due to the high intercorrelation of outcome value and outcome expectation only outcome expectation was added to the model. The overall model was significant, and the predictor variables accounted for 11% of the variance in academic achievement (see Table 7.1). As hypothesized, both cultural mistrust and outcome expectations remained significant in the equation predicting educational achievement.

TABLE 7–1. Multiple Regression for Academic Achievement. (N = 105)

VARIABLE	R^2	F	B	SE B	β	T
	.11	5.56**				
(Constant)						3.6**
Cultural Mistrust			−.57	.21	−.30	−2.6*
Outcome Expectations			.54	.19	.33	2.9*

*$p < .05$.
**$p < .01$.

∷ Discussion

Few quantitative studies have established a relationship between perceptions of cultural barriers, educational outcome expectations, and outcome value. Prior research has looked separately at beliefs concerning educational outcomes among African Americans (Arroyo & Zigler, 1995; Honora, 2003) and African Americans' value of education (Graham et al., 1998). One of the few earlier studies (Terrell et al., 1993) found a relationship between expectations for low-paying careers and high levels of cultural mistrust among African American junior high school students. The data I discuss here are able to extend those findings by documenting a relationship between three constructs (i.e., expectancy, achievement, and mistrust). Several factors might explain this relationship.

In this study cultural mistrust was positively related to both outcome expectations and outcome value and negatively related to academic achievement. In addition, cultural mistrust and outcome expectations both uniquely predicted academic achievement. Contrary to predictions, cultural mistrust was not related to academic outcome expectations or outcome value in the direction predicated. As stated previously the direction of these hypothesis was based on the author's previous research with a sample attending an ethnically diverse school (Irving & Hudley, 2005). However, the students in the present study attend a school that maintains a virtually all African American student body and a predominantly African American staff, administration, and faculty. In addition, these students live in predominantly African American environments. My previous research found that students in a diverse school did not anticipate being able to use education to avoid significant discrimination (Irving & Hudley, 2005). It may be that for African American students living in segregated environments and attending racially segregated schools, cultural mistrust operates as a realistic and normative response to years of oppression in a White-dominated society. Thus, this study and our current knowledge, albeit limited, suggest that the relationship between cultural mistrust, motivational variables, and achievement outcomes may depend on the sociocultural environment and historical circumstances of the students (F. Terrell et al., 1993).

As stated in the introduction, the concept of cultural mistrust has been researched in the clinical and counseling dating back to the introduction of the construct of "healthy cultural paranoia" (Grier & Cobbs, 1968). Healthy cultural paranoia was essentially conceptualized to be a normative or healthy protective mechanism African Americans would employ to buffer themselves and the community against racial mistreatment and malpractice in a deeply racist society. Few studies have investigated the relationship between cultural mistrust and academic functioning. However, this study and our current knowledge, albeit limited, suggest that the extent to which cultural mistrust is a negative influence on attitudes toward achievement outcomes may depend on the sociocultural environment of the students (F. Terrell et al., 1993). If as theorized, cultural mistrust among African Americans is a normative or healthy response to racial inequality and mistreatment, then students who live in more oppressive and segregated environments are more likely to employ protective strategies against institutions and social structures controlled or sanctioned by the dominant culture. Perhaps for students living in racially segregated and marginalized environments, the relationship between cultural mistrust and outcome expectations may represent a realistic perception of the sociocultural challenges that they must overcome and their understanding of the importance of academic success in that challenging environment.

As expected, cultural mistrust did maintain a negative relationship to academic achievement. Consistent with findings from other regions of the country, cultural mistrust may undermine achievement striving for these students because they do not expect academic effort to yield personal benefits. Further, high levels of effort that do not lead to success also convey a message of personal incompetence, leading to diminished self-worth (Harter, Waters, & Whitesell, 1998). Rather than risk feeling personally incompetent, students who perceive structural barriers to be unyielding to personal effort and achievement may discount the academic domain as a place to achieve success in favor of other areas that can denote competence such as social or athletic activities (Hudley, 1995). Another social cognitive construct, stereotype threat (Steele, 1997), posits that a process of disidentification with academic achievement striving is the product of racist stereotypes rather than perceived racism per se. Recall that pervasive stereotypes of African American males include strong messages of academic incompetence. Rather than running the risk of confirming those stereotypes, African American male students may psychologically disidentify with academic activities and efforts. Stereotype threat theory is consistent with findings from this study of an inverse relationship between cultural mistrust and academic achievement. However, the positive relation between cultural mistrust and academic outcome expectancy seems to contradict this theory. An admittedly speculative interpretation is that students who are growing up in an environment of racial oppression may be simultaneously more aware of racial stereotypes and more aware of the need to overcome those stereotypes.

John Ogbu's cultural ecological theory provides yet another lens for examining the findings from this study. Ogbu's theory identifies how historical and current cultural and ecological experiences with racism and discrimination have contributed to the development of survival strategies among African Americans. These strategies include resistance to the social norms of the dominant cultural. Ogbu held that the historical and continued experiences of acts of racial violence and racial aggression against African Americans that are perpetuated by members of and institutions of the dominant culture have led to the development of mistrust of Whites. This mistrust has prompted African Americans to develop alternative frames of reference for appropriate values and beliefs (Ogbu, 1991). Rather than adopt the values and practices of the dominant culture of the oppressor, groups that he refers to as involuntary minorities, including African Americans, frame cultural values in opposition to or resistant to the dominant culture to preserve their own identity (Ogbu & Simons, 1998). Thus, viewed through the lens of cultural ecological theory, cultural mistrust is inversely related to academic achievement because students do not endorse the values of the dominant culture that support academic achievement and achievement striving (Fordham, 1996).

Finally, even in this potentially challenging environment, African American male students' outcome expectations did maintain a positive relationship with academic achievement, consistent with prior research. Students who maintained higher academic outcome expectations perhaps were less susceptible to the resistant cultural attitudes described in Ogbu's research. However, for the students in this study who maintained lower outcome expectations and lower academic achievement, the same forces of racism and oppression that shape a resistant identity may also constrain outcome expectations and lead to the devaluing of activities that are approved and encouraged by the dominant culture (i.e., academic achievement striving).

Limitations and Future Research

Overall, this study provided additional evidence for the development of a model of African American achievement motivation that is powerful enough to account for both personal beliefs and sociocultural influences. However, this study examined a restricted set of variables. Although the findings shed light on the school achievement of African American male students, cultural mistrust alone is not sufficient to fully explain the relationship between African American students' perceptions of the opportunity structure and academic achievement motivation. Additional constructs are necessary to develop a valid and comprehensive understanding of sociocultural influences on academic achievement motivation among African American students. Self-concept, attributions, and stereotype threat are all theoretically important constructs that must guide future research. As well, this sample was limited to male students, and I am acutely aware that African American females have equal although unique challenges to success in American society. Thus, research must eventually develop a theoretical framework comprising motivational and sociocultural variables that is appropriate for both genders.

A measure of ethnic or racial identity will be critical for future research that examines achievement motivation in sociocultural context. The process of ethnic/racial identity development may have a significant influence on motivational orientations toward education. For example, recent research on racial self-schemas suggest that African American students who are more in-group oriented are less academically oriented and display lower levels of academic achievement (Oyserman, Kemmelmeier, Fryberg, Hezi, & Hart-Johnson, 2003). However, there is current disagreement among scholars as to whether having a strong racial or ethnic identify promotes high levels of academic achievement, engagement, and attainment among African Americans (Chavous et al., 2003; Sanders, 1997; Smith, Atkins, & Connell, 2003; Spencer, Noll, Stoltzfus, & Harpalani, 2001). Additional research is needed to explore the intersections of African American racial and cultural identification, academic achievement motivation, and the sociocultural contexts in which success must be achieved.

∷ Implications

The findings of this study have implications for policy makers, educators, and parents of African American males living in potentially challenging environments. A clearer understanding of students' experiences that contribute to low academic outcome expectations and a mistrust of the dominant culture will enable educators to identify methods to reduce the development of cultural mistrust and poor school performance in African American males. The variables of cultural mistrust, educational outcome expectations, and outcome value may assist school personnel by identifying students who are ideal for an educational intervention. Early detection of students' low education expectations would help educators recognize students who are at risk of school failure. Programs designed to help students proactively become change agents in the current system while simultaneously creating successful educational experiences may help students with high levels of cultural mistrust develop a more progressive cultural identification.

African American students who live in segregated and marginalized environments may benefit from culturally relevant and empowering experiences in the school system. Teachers are in a position to implement curriculum and lesson plans that support and empower students of color. However, many teachers lack the training to work effectively with students of color. The inclusion of instructional theory focused on the social and cultural values of African Americans in the core curriculum of teacher education programs may provide important preparation for future teachers of African American children. The creation of learning environments that are affirming, nurturing, and accepting for students would encourage more students to feel that they are a part of the formal educational system and could reduce their level of mistrust of those very systems.

The findings of this research also highlight the importance of implementing multicultural educational theory in the curriculum. For too many schools, implementation of multicultural curricula is limited to Black history month or other specific holidays and concentrates on displays of ethnic food and artifacts. For multicultural education to become more effective, reform must begin at the epistemological level to reflect the validity and authenticity of diverse worldviews, beliefs, and experiences that students from diverse backgrounds bring to school. One of the major limitations of many current multicultural approaches today is that the theoretical orientation of many multicultural teachings is derived from a framework that is rigidly grounded in a Western European worldview (Sue, 2001). Research has suggested that implementing alternative cultural competencies, psychological frameworks, and sociological perspectives are needed to effectively improve the achievement of diverse learners (Jones, 1991; Sue, 2001). This could include expanding the forms of literacy and use of language that are validated in the classroom, incorporating the diversity in the construction of knowledge that exists within different ethnic groups, and utilizing examples and perspectives toward learning that are grounded in the social reality of children of color in challenging environments (Abell, 1999). Without a grounding in and commitment to divergent epistemological paradigms, multicultural educational reform will continue to fall short in meeting the needs of many African American students.

∷ References

Abell, P. K. (1999). Recognizing and valuing difference: Process considerations. In E. R. Hollins & E. I. Oliver (Eds.), *Pathways to success in school: Culturally responsive teaching* (pp. 175–196). Mahwah, NJ: Lawrence Erlbaum.

Anderman, E. M., & Midgley, C. (1997). Changes in achievement goal orientations, perceived academic competence, and grades across the transition to middle-level schools. *Contemporary Educational Psychology, 22*(3), 269–298.

Arroyo, C. G., & Zigler, E. (1995). Racial identity, academic achievement, and the psychological well being of economically disadvantaged adolescents. *Journal of Personality & Social Psychology, 69,* 903–914.

Bandura, A. (2002). Social cognitive theory in cultural context. *Applied Psychology: An International Review, 51*(2), 269–290.

Brown, R. (1995). *Prejudice: Its social psychology.* Oxford, England: Blackwell.

Chavous, T. M., Bernat, D. H., Schmeelk-Cone, K., Cladwell, C. H., Kohn-Wood, L., & Zimmerman, M. A. (2003). Racial identity and academic achievement among african american adolescents. *Child Development, 74*(4), 1076–1090.

Cokley, K. O. (2002). Ethnicity, gender and academic self-concept: A preliminary examination of academic disidentification and implications for psychologists. *Cultural Diversity & Ethnic Minority Psychology, 8*(4), 378–388.

Darley, J. M., & Gross, P. H. (1983). A hypothesis-confirming bias in labeling effects. *Journal of Personality & Social Psychology, 44*(1), 20–33.

Eccles, J. S., Vida, M., & Barber, B. (2004). The relation of early adolescents' college plans and both academic ability and task-value beliefs to subsequent college enrollment. *Journal of Early Adolescence, 24*(1), 63–77.

Eccles, J. S., & Wigfield, A. (2002). Motivational beliefs, values, and goals. *Annual Review of Psychology, 53*(1), 109–132.

Feagin, J. R., & McKinney, K. D. (2003). *The many costs of racism.* Lanham, MD: Rowman and Littlefield.

Fine, M. (1991). *Framing dropouts: Notes on the politics of an urban high school.* Albany, NY: SUNY Press.

Ford, D. (1998). The underrepresentation of minority students in gifted education: Problems and promises in recruitment and retention. *Journal of Special Education, 32,* 4–14.

Fordham, S. (1996). *Blacked out: Dilemmas of race, identity, and success at Capital High.* Chicago, IL: University of Chicago Press.

Gadsden, V., Smith, R., & Jordan, W. (1996). The promise of desegregation: Tendering expectation and reality in achieving quality schooling. *Urban Education, 31,* 381–402.

Graham, S. (1994). Motivation in African Americans. *Review of Educational Research, 64*(1), 55–117.

Graham, S., Taylor, A., & Hudley, C. (1998). Exploring achievement among ethnic minority early adolescents. *Journal of Educational Psychology, 90,* 606–620.

Grier, W. H., & Cobbs, P. M. (1968). *Black rage.* New York: Basic Books.

Grodsky, E., & Pager, D. (2001). The structure of disadvantage: Individual and occupational determinants of the black-white wage gap. *American Sociological Review, 66*(4), 542–567.

Hacker, A. (1992). *Two nations: Black and white, separate, hostile, unequal.* New York: Maxwell Macmillan International.

Harter, S., Waters, P., & Whitesell, N. R. (1998). Relational self-worth: Differences in perceived worth as a person across interpersonal contexts among adolescents. *Child Development, 69* (3), 756–766.

Hilliard, A. G. (1992). Behavioral style, culture, and teaching and learning. *Journal of Negro Education, 61,* 370–377.

Hilliard, A. G. (2003). No mystery: Closing the achievement gap. In T. Perry, C. M. Steele, & A. G. Hilliard (Eds.), *Young, gifted, and black: Promoting high achievement among African American students.* Boston: Beacon Press.

Honora, D. (2003). Urban African American adolescents and school identification. *Urban Education, 38*(1), 58–76.

Hudley, C. (1995). Assessing the impact of separate schooling for African American male adolescents. *Journal of Early Adolescence, 15,* 38–35.

Hudley, C., & Graham, S. (2001). Stereotypes of achievement striving among early adolescents. *Social Psychology of Education: An International Journal, 5,* 201–224.

Hughes, M., & Demo, D. (1989). Self-perceptions of Black Americans: Self-esteem and personal efficacy. *American Journal of Sociology, 95,* 132–159.

Irving, M. A. (2002). Oppositional identity and academic achievement among African American males. *Dissertation Abstracts International, 63*(06), 2129 (UMI No. AAT 3055998).

Irving, M. A., & Hudley, C. (2005). Cultural mistrust, academic outcome expectations and outcome value among African American males. *Urban Education, 40*(5).

Jacobs, J. E., Lanza, S., Osgood, D. W., Eccles, J. S., & Wigfield, A. (2002). Changes in children's self-competence and values: Gender and domain differences across grades one though twelve. *Child Development, 73*(2), 509–527.

Jones, J. M. (1991). Racism: A cultural analysis of the problem. In R. L. Jones (Ed.), *Black psychology* (pp. 609–636). Berkeley, CA: Cobb & Henry.

Kozol, J. (1991). *Savage inequalities: Children in American's schools.* New York: Crown.

Kromhout, M., & Vedder, P. (1996). Cultural inversion in Afro-Caribbean children in the Netherlands. *Anthropology & Education Quarterly, 27*(4), 568–586.

Larson, C. L., & Ovando, C. J. (2001). *The color of bureaucracy: The politics of equity in multicultural school communities.* Belmont, CA: Wadsworth.

Lord, R. G., Hanges, P. J., & Godfrey, E. G. (2003). Integrating neural networks into decision-making and motivational theory: Rethinking VIE theory. *Canadian Psychology, 44*(1), 21–38.

Mahrer, A. (1956). The role of expectancy in delayed reinforcement. *Journal of Experimental Psychology, 52,* 101–106.

Major, B., Gramzow, R. H., McCoy, S. K., Levin, S., Schmader, T., & Sidanius, J. (2002). Perceiving personal discrimination: The role of group status and legitimizing ideology. *Journal of Personality & Social Psychology, 82*(3), 269–282.

Mickelson, R. A. (1990). The attitude-achievement paradox among black adolescents. *Sociology of Education, 63,* 44–61.

National Center for Education Statistics. (2001). *Digest of education statistics, 2001.* Washington DC: NCES.

Nauta, M., & Epperson, D. L. (2003). A longitudinal examination of the social-cognitive model applied to high school girls' choices of nontraditional college majors and aspirations. *Journal of Counseling Psychology, 50*(4), 448–457.

Oakes, J. (1985). *Keeping track: How schools structure inequality.* New Haven, CT: Yale University Press.

Ogbu, J. (1991). Minority coping responses and school experience. *Journal of Psychohistory, 18,* 433–456.

Ogbu, J., & Simons, H. D. (1998). Voluntary and involuntary minorities: A cultural-ecological theory of school performance with some implications for education. *Anthropology & Education Quarterly, 29,* 155–188.

Ogbu, J. (2003). *Black American students in an affluent suburb: A study of academic disengagement.* Mahwah, NJ: Erlbaum.

Osborne, J. (1997). Race and academic disidentification. *Journal of Educational Psychology, 89,* 728–735.

Oyserman, D., Kemmelmeier, M., Fryberg, S., Hezi, B., & Hart-Johnson, T. (2003). Racial-ethnic self-schemas. *Social Psychology Quarterly. 66*(4), 333–347.

Phelps, R. E., Taylor, J. D., & Gerard, P. A. (2001). Cultural mistrust, ethnic identity, racial identity, and self-esteem among ethnically diverse black students. *Journal of Counseling & Development, 79*(2), 209–216.

Pokay, P., & Blumenfeld, P. C. (1990). Predicting achievement early and late in the semester: The role of motivation and use of learning strategies. *Journal of Educational Psychology, 82*(1), 41–50.

Sanders, M. G. (1997). Overcoming obstacles: Academic achievement as a response to racism and discrimination. *Journal of Negro Education, 66*(1), 83–93.

Shell, D. F., Murphy, C. C., & Bruning, R. H. (1989). Self-efficacy and outcome expectancy mechanisms in reading and writing achievement. *Journal of Educational Psychology, 81*(1), 91–100.

Smith, E., Atkins, J., & Connell, C. M. (2003). Family, school, and community factors and relationships to racial-ethnic attitudes and academic achievement. *American Journal of Community Psychology, 32*(1/2), 159–173.

Staveteig, S., & Wigton, A. (2000). *Racial and ethnic disparities: Key findings from the national survey of America's families. Series b, no. B–5.*

Steele, C. M. (1997). A threat in the air: How stereotypes shape intellectual identity and performance. *American Psychologist, 52*(6), 613–629.

Steele, C. M., & Aronson, J. (1998). Stereotype threat and the test performance of academically successful African Americans. In C. Jencks & M. Phillips (Eds.), *The black-white test score gap* (pp. 401–427). Washington DC: Brookings Institution Press.

Sue, D. W. (2001). Multidimensional facets of cultural competence. *Counseling Psychologist, 6,* 790–821.

Terrell, F., Terrell, S., & Miller, F. (1993). Level of cultural mistrust as function of educational and occupational expectations among black students. *Adolescence, 28,* 572–578.

Terrell, F., & Terrell, S. L. (1981). An inventory to measure cultural mistrust among blacks. *Western Journal of Black Studies, 3,* 180–185.

Terrell, S. L., Daniloff, R., Garden, M., Flint-Shaw, L., & Flowers, T. (2001). The effect of speech clinician race and Afro-American students' cultural mistrust of clinician-child conversation. *Clinical Linguistics & Phonetics, 15*(1–2), 169–175.

Thompson, C. E., Nevelle, H., Weathers, P. L., Postin, W. C., & Atkinson, D. R. (1990). Cultural mistrust and racism reaction among African American students. *Journal of College Student Development, 31,* 162–168.

van Laar, C. (2000). The paradox of low academic achievement but high self-esteem in African American students: An attributional account. *Educational Psychology Review, 12,* 33–61.

Weiner, B. (1992). *Human motivation: Metaphors, theories, and research.* Newbury Park, CA: Sage.

Weis, L., & Fine, M. (Eds.). (1993). *Beyond silenced voices: Class, race, and gender in United States schools.* Albany: State University of New York Press.

Whaley, A. L. (2001a). Cultural mistrust and mental health services for African Americans: A review and meta-analysis. *Counseling Psychologist, 29*(4), 513–531.

Whaley, A. L. (2001b). Cultural mistrust: An important psychological construct for diagnosis and treatment of African Americans. *Professional Psychology: Research & Practice, 32*(6), 555–562.

Wigfield, A., & Eccles, J. S. (2000). Expectancy-value theory of achievement motivation. *Contemporary Educational Psychology, 25*(1), 68–81.

Wigfield, A., & Eccles, J. S. (2002). Students' motivation during the middle school years. In J. Aronson (Ed.), *Improving academic achievement: Impact of psychological factors on education* (pp. 159–184). San Diego, CA: Academic Press.

Williams, T. R., Davis, L. E., Cribbs, J. M., Saunders, J., & Williams, J. H. (2002). Friends, family, and neighborhood: Understanding academic outcomes of African American youth. *Urban Education, 37*(3), 408–431.

8

Responding to Self-Threats

Understanding Stigma in the Academic Domain

Collette P. Eccleston and Brenda Major

In 2002, President Bush signed into law the No Child Left Behind Act of 2001. This new law was intended to improve the performance of the nation's primary and secondary school children and to close the gap in achievement between European American and ethnic minority students. Closing the achievement gap was declared a national priority that would be achieved by holding schools specifically accountable for the annual progress of ethnic minority students. The new law proclaimed: "Schools must have high expectations for every child—the soft bigotry of low expectations is no longer tolerated" (U.S Department of Education, 2005). Despite these bold declarations and undoubtedly good intentions of many, the academic achievement gap remains a persistent problem in American schools. On the 2005 National Assessment of Educational Progress, the average reading score of African American eighth-grade students was 28 points lower and the average math score was 34 points lower than that of European American students. More practically, only 52% of African American eighth graders meet the basic level of achievement expected for eighth graders in reading and only 42% reach the basic level of math. Among European American students, 82% and 80% of students achieve these levels in reading and math, respectively (Perie, Grigg, & Dion, 2005).

Beyond secondary school, differences in academic achievement persist; the college graduation rate among African American students is 42% compared to 62% among European American students (U.S. Department of Education, 2007). Though more limited in scope, a similar problem has been observed with respect to the academic achievement of women relative to men in the domains of math and science. In 2006, the average score of male students on the quantitative section of the Scholastic Aptitude Test was approximately 34 points (one-third of a standard deviation) higher than the average score of female students. Whereas male students represent approximately 46% of test takers, they represent 57% of those scoring above the 75th percentile in math (College Board, 2006). In 2004, women earned 57.6% of all bachelor's degrees; yet, of the bachelor's degrees awarded in mathematics and statistics, only 45.9% were awarded to women. The underrepresentation of women is even more pronounced for advanced degrees; only 28.4% of the doctoral degrees in mathematics and statistics were earned by women (National Science Foundation, 2007).

How are we to understand these persistent differences between ethnic and gender groups in academic achievement? We propose that the differences in academic achievement between ethnic minority and European American students and between men and women in math and science domains may be partially explained by the fact that ethnic minorities and women are stigmatized. That is, within academic contexts, they "possess (or are believed to posses) some attribute or characteristic that conveys a social identity that is devalued" (Crocker, Major, & Steele, 1998, p. 505). Membership in a group that is stigmatized in academics, a domain that is of importance in social life, poses a potential threat to an individual's personal and social identity. Furthermore, because maintaining the integrity of the self is a primary motivation, individuals develop various methods of coping with these threats, some of which have negative repercussions for motivation. In this chapter we discuss factors that exacerbate the extent to which local academic environments can be threatening to the self. We also discuss coping strategies in response to stigmatization that have implications for motivation and performance. Finally, we consider how local cultures can be shaped so that they are less threatening to the self-integrity of students who belong to academically stigmatized groups. We draw from an extensive literature in social psychology, most of which focuses on the effects of stigmatization among African Americans and women. Although our discussion focuses primarily on these two groups, the processes we discuss apply more generally to members of a variety of groups that experience stigmatization.

:: Stigma and Self-threats

Those who possess a stigmatized identity are more likely to experience situations that threaten their social identity and ultimately their sense of self. Major and O'Brien (2005) present a model of stigma-induced identity threat as a way of understanding the psychological effects of stigma. According to this model, the extent to which individuals appraise particular situations as threatening is a function of the collective representations of the individual's group, cues present in the immediate social situation, and the individual's personal characteristics. "Stigma–induced identity threat results when an individual appraises the demands imposed by a stigma-relevant stressor as potentially harmful to his or her social identity and exceeding his or her resources to cope with those demands" (p. 402).

Cultural Beliefs About African Americans and Women as a Source of Threat

Culture includes feelings, beliefs, and attitudes that are shared by a group of people (Triandis, 1989). Therefore, stereotypes—beliefs about the traits and characteristics of individuals who belong to a social group—can be considered part of culture. For groups that are the most profoundly stigmatized, there is widespread knowledge of the negative characteristics that are presumed to be descriptive of the group. Individuals who are members of these stigmatized groups are not immune to this cultural knowledge; they are quite aware of the negative beliefs about their group (Crocker et al., 1998). Within American society, stereotypes that African Americans are unintelligent, uneducated, and lazy are widely known. Individuals are equally knowledgeable about these cultural stereotypes regardless of their personal attitude or feelings about African Americans (Devine, 1989; Devine & Elliot, 1995). Negative stereotypes about women are also pervasive. Of particular relevance to academic performance, women are stereotyped as having less ability than men in math and math-related domains (Eccles, Jacobs, & Harold, 1990; Swim, 1994). The former president of Harvard University, Lawrence Summers, suggested that women's lack of ability may explain why fewer women succeed in science and math careers—an indication of the pervasiveness of this stereotype.

These negative cultural beliefs about the abilities of African Americans and women in the academic domain are often paired with devaluation of these groups. They are perceived as less valuable and worthwhile, and stigmatized group membership lowers an individual's status in the eyes of others (Crocker et al., 1998; Link & Phelan, 2001). This devaluation is likely to be experienced as threatening, as demonstrated by the presence of physiological markers of stress (see Dickerson & Kemeny, 2004). Furthermore, low social status places individuals at risk for poor or unfair treatment, discrimination, and ultimately exclusion (Major & Eccleston, 2005). Because performance in academics is highly valued in our society, the potential threat to the self posed by being negatively stereotyped and devalued in the academic domain is high.

Within social psychology, a growing body of research demonstrates that the existence of negative stereotypes relevant to one's performance is indeed a potential source of threat with important implications for performance. Stereotype threat is the psychological state experienced when individuals are concerned about confirming negative stereotypes of their group or are concerned that others may evaluate their performance in terms of these negative group stereotypes (Steele & Aronson, 1995; Steele, Spencer, & Aronson, 2002). When a negative group stereotype can be applied to an individual's performance, members of negatively stereotyped groups perform poorly compared to members of groups that are not negatively stereotyped. This effect has been demonstrated among African Americans (e.g., Steele & Aronson, 1995), women (e.g., Spencer, Steele, & Quinn, 1999), people of low socioeconomic status (Croizet & Claire, 1998) and the elderly (Chasteen, Bhattacharyya, Horhota, Tam, & Hasher, 2005; O'Brien & Hummert, 2006). Research demonstrates that individuals who are highly identified with the group are more likely than those who are low in group identification to suffer performance decrements when negative group stereotypes are activated. These findings offer support for the idea that decreased performance is due to a threat to social identity (Schmader, 2002).

A number of involuntary responses to stereotype threat are likely to play a role in performance decrements. When individuals believe that a negative stereotype may be seen as relevant to their performance, this belief can consume cognitive resources that are necessary for performing the given task. In turn, limited cognitive resources to devote to the primary task at hand decreases performance (Schmader & Johns, 2003). Concern with one's performance may also lead to a pattern of physiological arousal that impairs cognitive functioning and disrupts performance (Blascovich, Spencer, Quinn, & Steele, 2001; Croizet et al., 2002). Psychological processes stemming from anxiety, self-doubt, and lowered performance expectations may also mediate stereotype-induced performance decrements. Voluntary responses to stereotype threat can also contribute to decrements in performance. For example, the presence of negative stereotypes might lead individuals to engage in self-handicapping behaviors such as a decrease in the amount of effort they expend in affected domains, which in turn harms performance (Keller, 2002). (See Steele et al., 2002, for a review of possible mediators of the relationship between negative stereotypes and performance.) In sum, because of the negative stereotypes and devaluation of women and African Americans that are part of American culture, members of these groups are at risk for experiencing a threatened social identity in academic contexts.

Aspects of Academic Culture as Sources of Threat

Culture operates on multiple levels. We can think about culture broadly as it applies to the shared practices, values, and beliefs of individuals in a country or set of countries (e.g., the Western world). In addition, there is also local culture within a given country, for example, that describes the shared practices, values, and beliefs of individuals in a particular region or a particular institution. Thus, a school may have its own local culture. Because broad culture affects local culture, we would expect the societal stereotypes about African Americans and women to be present also in schools. In fact, because many of the stereotypes about these two groups have particular relevance in academic settings, events that occur in these settings may be especially likely to be viewed in terms of negative cultural stereotypes. For example, it is likely that the negative stereotype about women's math ability will come to mind and influence perceptions and judgments of a female student more often in her math class than outside of the classroom setting.

For African Americans and women, several aspects of academic contexts may further exacerbate the extent to which they experience identity threat. One is being in the numerical minority. Individuals in the numerical minority are more likely to feel distinctive, to feel that they stand out from the surrounding environment. In addition, the less well represented a group is in a particular setting, the more likely the individual group member will be reminded of the group membership that makes him or her distinct (McGuire, McGuire, & Winton, 1979). As well, when a group membership is made salient, the negative stereotypes associated with the group are also likely to come to the group member's mind. That is, a female student is more likely to be thinking of her gender identity in her advanced math class, where women are likely to be in the numerical minority, compared to classes where women are less likely to be in the numerical minority. These cognitive consequences of being in the numerical minority can be considered markers of stereotype threat and may help to explain why being in the numerical minority is often related to poor performance (Inzlicht & Ben-Zeev, 2000; Saenz & Lord, 1989; Thompson & Sekaquaptewa, 2002). Further, to the extent that distinctiveness leads to performance decrements in the domains in which individuals are negatively stereotyped, it may contribute to increased underrepresentation of academically stigmatized individuals. Ironically, high-achieving academically stigmatized students are particularly likely to find themselves in academic settings where they are distinctive; ethnic minority students are underrepresented in advanced or gifted programs (Ford, 1998) and women are especially likely to be underrepresented in advanced math and science courses (National Center for Education Statistics, 2000). Thus, even academically stigmatized students who have achieved some measure of success are susceptible to identity threats.

Feeling distinctive within academic settings because of one's gender or ethnicity is a predicament experienced by faculty as well as students. For example, only between 3% and 15% of full professors at top engineering and science departments are women (Beutel & Nelson, 2005). Among senior faculty members at colleges and universities in 1993, only 4.4% were African American (Magner, 1996). For stigmatized students, models of success in the academic domain at the postsecondary level are unlikely to be members of their own group. This lack of role models with whom one shares a group membership also contributes to identity threat in the academic domain (Marx & Roman, 2002).

Underrepresentation of women and/or minorities among faculty or top academic scholars can lead others to justify the system by using negative stereotypes. People are strongly motivated to perceive prevailing social systems as just and fair, to perceive what "is" as what "ought" to be (Lerner; 1980; Jost & Banaji, 1994). For example, rather than considering the social factors that contribute to the underrepresentation of African Americans in higher education, individuals may justify this situation by invoking the stereotype that African Americans are unintelligent. Women's absence in top management positions may be attributed to their lack of leadership skills, emotional unpredictability, or indecisiveness.

∷ Stigmatized Group Membership and Determinants of Motivation

Theorists have long emphasized the importance of expectations and values in determining motivation (e.g., Atkinson, 1964; Eccles et al.,

1983; Rotter, 1966). Individuals are postulated to be more motivated to obtain an outcome the more they *expect* they can successfully obtain the outcome and the more they *value* attaining the outcome. Evidence shows that individuals who expect to be successful are in fact more persistent and exert greater effort than those who do not expect success (Feather, 1962; Pyszczynski & Greenberg, 1983). The extent to which performing well in the domain is important also predicts motivation. For example, Meece, Wigfield, and Eccles (1990) found that the strongest predictor of middle school children's motivation and intention to enroll in mathematics was how much they valued math. The extent to which individuals expect to do well in and value a domain also affects performance in the domain. Meece and colleagues (1990) also found that children got higher math grades the more they expected to do well at math, even when the researchers controlled for past performance.

Stigma and Expectations for Success

Awareness of the negative perception of their group in the academic domain may lead women and African Americans to expect less success in these domains. There are several routes by which this may occur. One possibility is that members of stigmatized groups integrate the negative images of their group that are dominant in society into how they view their group and ultimately how they view themselves (Allport, 1954; Cooley, 1956; Mead, 1934). Thus, an African American who endorses the negative stereotypes that the group is lazy and unintelligent may come to expect that he or she will not be successful in academics. Members of negatively stereotyped groups are, at times, just as likely as out-group members to engage in stereotyping when evaluating members of their own groups (e.g., Hudley & Graham, 2001; Judd, Park, Ryan, Brauer, & Kraus, 1995). For instance, ethnic minority boys who evaluated low- and high-achievement behaviors reported that low-achievement behaviors (e.g., fooling around in class, doing just enough to get by) were more likely to be performed by ethnic minority boys than White boys or any girls overall (Hudley & Graham, 2001).

Even when individuals accept negative traits ascribed to their group as true of the group in general, they often reject the negative traits as being true of themselves as individuals (Biernat, Viesco, & Green, 1996; Pickett, Bonner, & Coleman, 2002). Nonetheless, negative group stereotypes can still have a negative effect on individuals' expectations. Whereas positive feedback or previous successful experiences generally lead individuals to believe that they will perform well in the future, activating negative stereotypes can undermine the effect of prior success on expectations of future success (Stangor, Carr, & Kiang, 1998). Stangor and colleagues investigated this possibility among a group of college women. Among women for whom stereotypes had *not* been activated, those who received positive feedback on a first task estimated that they would perform better on a second task than those who received ambiguous feedback. However, when negative stereotypes about women's ability were activated, women who received positive feedback did not expect to perform any better than those who received ambiguous feedback. Thus, the presence of these negative stereotypes diminished the effect of previous success. Even if one has managed to achieve some measure of success, the possibility of confirming negative stereotypes is always looming (Steele, 1997; Steele & Aronson, 1995).

Stigma and Valuing

People are more likely to value domains in which they experience positive rather than negative outcomes (James, 1890; Taylor & Brown, 1988; Tesser & Campbell, 1980). Crocker and Major (1989) proposed that this tendency to differentially value domains as a function of performance in the domain may also operate at the group level. As a result of one's group being relatively unsuccessful at obtaining outcomes in stigma-relevant domains, members of stigmatized groups might come to place less value on these domains in an effort to maintain self-esteem. There is evidence to suggest that individuals personally devalue a domain in response to a group threat (e.g., Schmader & Major, 1999; Wagner, Lampen, & Syllwasschy, 1986). For example, Schmader and Major (1999) found that participants who were given no feedback about their own personal performance on a test of a personality trait valued the trait less when they learned other members of their in-group had performed worse than members of an out-group in comparison to feedback that the in-group performed better than the out-group. Although these studies demonstrate that individuals devalue a domain in response to poor group performance, both studies were laboratory studies in which the domain that was being devalued probably was not of great overall importance to participants. Domains such as academics that are highly culturally valued and perceived as being useful in attaining success are less readily devalued (Schmader, Major, Eccleston, & McCoy, 2001). Although devaluing academics overall might not be a common response to negative stereotyping, to the extent that it occurs, it leads to decreased motivation to pursue success in the domain. Lower valuing of male-dominated fields, for example, is related to women not maintaining career aspirations in those fields (Frome, Alfeld, Eccles, & Barber, 2006).

Disengagement and Disidentification

Individuals have at their disposal a variety of strategies that enable them to maintain their sense that they are valued and worthwhile individuals in the face of devaluation. Crocker and Major (1989) proposed that members of stigmatized groups might regard as less important for self-definition dimensions in which the stigmatized in-group experiences negative outcomes. In a similar vein, Claude Steele and his colleagues (Steele, 1992; Steele & Aronson, 1995) argued that devaluation of one's group in a particular domain may lead individuals to be reluctant to allow that domain to be the basis of self-evaluation. Individuals may disengage their self-esteem from or cease identifying with domains where they expect to be viewed or treated negatively. Disengagement of self-esteem can reduce the individual's vulnerability to threat by decreasing the demands of the situation—in particular, the necessity to perform well in the domain. Individuals who do not identify with the domain in which their group is negatively stereotyped (women who report that it is not important to them to do well in math, for example) do not experience performance decrements in response to the salience of a negative group stereotype (Spencer et al., 1999).

Psychological disengagement of self-esteem from domains in which negative outcomes are experienced has been frequently offered as an explanation for the seeming paradox between high self-esteem and low academic achievement among African American students. There is some evidence to suggest that this coping strategy is often used by African American students. Hare (1985) found that the self-esteem of African American boys was just as high as that of their European American classmates, although the African American boys had lower achievement test scores. The African American boys tended to place greater emphasis on relationships with peers than academic performance. Further support for the idea that African American students detach their self-esteem from academic outcomes appears in a correlational study by Osborne (1995). He found that the relationship between self-esteem and academic outcomes weakens over time among African American students but remains stable among European Americans. Major et al.

(1998) demonstrated a similar effect experimentally. In this experiment, African American and European American students took a test on which they subsequently received either failure or success feedback. Among European American students, self-esteem was lower following failure feedback than following success feedback. Among African American students, however, self-esteem did not differ as function of performance feedback. A second study that examined the effects of chronic disengagement revealed that among African American students, those who had self-esteem that was chronically disengaged from academics were especially likely to maintain high self-esteem in the face of failure. Thus, the self-esteem of African American students appears less contingent than that of European American students on performance on tests; nonetheless, there is variability in the extent to which disengagement is employed with stigmatized groups.

Disengagement of one's self-esteem from a domain in which one's social identity is viewed negatively protects self-esteem, but one negative consequence of this coping strategy may be reduced motivation to succeed in the domain. As Steele (1999) states: "Pain is lessened by ceasing to identify with the part of life in which the pain occurs. . . . But not caring can mean not being motivated" (p. 46). However, this outcome is not necessarily a foregone conclusion. It is important to specify whether disengagement is chronic versus situation specific (Crocker et al., 1998). Individuals whose self-concept does not include being a good student and whose self-esteem is not at all dependent on academic performance would be considered chronically disengaged. It is unlikely that these individuals would be motivated to perform well in academics if the domain has no implications for their self-views. On the other hand, situational disengagement reflects the extent to which the individual's self-views are affected by a particular academic outcome. Nussbaum and Steele (2007) argue that detaching self-esteem from performance in a particular situation might enable individuals to continue to be motivated in the domain overall. They demonstrated that when African American students were given negative feedback on a task that was ostensibly diagnostic of ability, the *more* they disengaged their self-esteem from the feedback, the more likely they were to persist on the task. That is, if students who are stigmatized in the academic domain can maintain their belief that they are intelligent or gifted at math, despite the results of a particular test, they may be more likely to remain motivated.

Decreased motivation may be an indirect result of disengagement; but it may also be a direct response to stigmatization. The presence of negative stereotypes can lead individuals to take on an avoidance or prevention focus in domains where they are negatively stereotyped (Seibt & Forster, 2004). Rather than being motivated to pursue positive outcomes in the domain, individuals with a prevention focus are motivated to avoid risks and losses, and they can achieve this by avoiding situations where negative stereotypes apply and failure is a possibility. Davies, Spencer, Quinn, and Gerhardstein (2002) examined whether reminding women of their societal devaluation leads them to withdraw from domains in which their group is negatively stereotyped, such as math. Women in this study were college students who had previously indicated that they were good at math and it was important to them to do well in math. They were either exposed to gender stereotypic television commercials or television commercials with neutral content. Participants then completed a time-limited task that contained both math and verbal problems. Among women for whom math was important, those who watched the television commercials with neutral content completed more math problems than verbal problems. However, when these women watched gender-stereotypic commercials, they avoided math problems in favor of verbal problems. This avoidance of math problems occurred even though none of the commercials specifically made reference to the stereotype about women and math ability. In a second study, women exposed to gender-stereotypic commercials also demonstrated less interest in pursuing careers that require mathematical skills to succeed (e.g., engineering). Reminding the women of the devalued identity of women caused them to remember a variety of negative stereotypes, even those that were not specifically mentioned in the setting. In turn, to the extent that negative stereotypes about women's math ability came to mind, women were less motivated to pursue outcomes in the domain.

Individuals have greater expectations of encountering prejudice and discrimination in domains where they are negatively stereotyped (O'Brien, Kinias, & Major, in press), and this might also explain why calling to mind negative stereotypes decreases their motivation. Prejudice and discrimination are cues that individuals will not be given a fair chance at attaining desired outcomes. In domains in which their group is devalued, stigmatized individuals have little control over whether their efforts will be rewarded. However, they can exert control by choosing to withdraw effort from these domains and dedicating their efforts to domains in which they are likely to be treated fairly. Thus, decreasing motivation may give individuals an opportunity to reexert control and thereby reduce the threat associated with these situations.

In a recent study, we directly investigated the possibility that expecting to be the victim of prejudice decreases motivation (Eccleston & Major, 2007). Female college students were led to believe that they (along with a male applicant) were being evaluated by either a prejudiced or an unprejudiced male evaluator for a management position. As part of the evaluation process, they completed an anagram task. Performance on this task was ostensibly related to problem-solving tasks that participants would perform in the management position. Participants were led to believe that the evaluator would use his discretion in the extent to which he considered performance on the anagram task in making his choice for the management position. When participants thought the evaluator was prejudiced, they expected to be treated unfairly and believed that the evaluator's personal preferences rather than their performance on the anagram task would determine his evaluation. Even though women who thought the evaluator was prejudiced believed they had the ability to perform as well on the anagram task as those with the unprejudiced evaluator, these women reported being less motivated to attain the position for which they were applying. Expecting prejudice also led to worse performance on the anagram task.

Similarly, expecting unfairness and discrimination affects students who are stigmatized in the academic domain. For example, Schmader, Major, and Gramzow (2001) found that the more African American students perceived discrimination against their group, the less they valued academic success and the more they discounted the validity of academic feedback. If students expect their academic outcomes to be unfair and invalid indicators of their abilities, they are likely to be unmotivated to attain these outcomes.

In summary, negative stereotypes about African Americans in academics and women in math and science are widely known in society at large, including by individuals who belong to these groups. Students who belong to these groups must contend with academic cultures that often reinforce the negative images of their group. Consequently, the predominant academic culture can be threatening to the identities of stigmatized students. Threats to identity posed by negative stereotypes, devaluation, and discrimination can decrease stigmatized students' expectations of success, diminish the value they place on succeeding at school, and lead them to disengage their self-esteem from academic domains. Decreased motivation may be an unintended consequence of these strategies.

⠃⠃ Resilience

Although the preceding discussion is bleak, many African Americans succeed scholastically and many women succeed in math and science. What are the factors that enable these students to remain motivated to pursue their academic goals? We discuss characteristics of the situation and the person below.

Just as situations can be threatening to the identities of students stigmatized in the academic domain, they can also be made safer for social identity (Steele et al., 2002). The threat posed by an academic environment may be lessened by challenging the extent to which negative stereotypes about academic ability are perceived as valid, relevant, or acceptable. The most direct and explicit way that this can be done is by simply stating that the stereotype is untrue or does not apply in a particular situation (e.g., Davies, Spencer, & Steele, 2005; Spencer et al., 1999). For example, women are negatively stereotyped as having less leadership ability, and when negative stereotypes about their identity are made salient, women are less likely to aspire to leadership positions (Davies et al., 2005, Study 1). However, Davis, Spencer, and Steele (2005, Study 2) created an identity-safe environment by simply telling women that their research had revealed no gender differences on the leadership task participants were to complete. As a result, female participants for whom negative stereotypes about women were salient but for whom the environment had been made safe did not show lower leadership aspirations than men. While it may not be possible to eliminate negative stereotypes entirely, individuals may be buffered from their negative effects if they feel that the stereotypes do not apply in a given situation or setting.

Negative stereotypes about academic ability are powerful in part because they imply that poor academic performance is a reflection of inalterable characteristics, such as ability. When groups are thought of as having a core essence, as is often true for ethnicity and gender, the characteristics associated with those groups tend to take on special meaning and be seen as immutable (Prentice & Miller, 2006). Further, to the extent that personal attributes are seen as fixed, stereotyped traits are more likely to be seen as being due to inborn group qualities rather than environmental factors (Levy, Stroessner, & Dweck, 1998). Thus, even characteristics that may generally be thought of changeable (e.g., laziness) are seen as less changeable if they are associated with negatively stereotyped, essentialized groups. In the face of academic difficulties, believing that intelligence is fixed leads students to experience more anxiety, to exert less effort, and to exhibit decreased academic engagement (Dweck, 1986). Similarly, if poor performance is seen as confirmation of the negative stereotype, it may set off a chain of low expectations, disengagement, and decreased motivation.

For academically stigmatized students, threat can be reduced to the extent that intelligence is perceived by them and represented by others in the environment as malleable and the result of factors that are under the individual's control (Aronson, Fried, & Good, 2002; Dar-Nimrod & Heine, 2006; Dweck, 1986). Women performed better on a math task when they were exposed to information suggesting that gender differences in math performance were due to experience (and therefore changeable) rather than genetic factors (Dar-Nimrod & Heine, 2006). In a similar vein, African American students who were encouraged to view intelligence as a capacity that can increase with hard work reported greater enjoyment of the educational process and greater identification with academics, and they earned better grades compared to those not encouraged to see intelligence as malleable (Aronson et al., 2002; Good, Aronson, & Inzlicht, 2003). Being encouraged to think that intelligence is malleable also led European American students to earn better grades, supporting the notion that reducing threats to self-integrity that may be posed by the possibility of poor academic performance is beneficial for all students.

The potency of negative stereotypes can also be reduced by educating students about how they may be affected by the presence of negative stereotypes about their group. Students who are stigmatized in the academic domain are likely to feel anxious in performance situations and attribute this anxiety to their own ability. However, the reality is that the presence of negative stereotypes is likely to be responsible for some of this anxiety. Informing students about this possibility reduces the threat they feel. Women who believed they were taking a math test that assessed gender differences experienced less threat if they had been told that anxiety could be due to the negative stereotypes that exist about women rather their own ability when compared to women who were not given an alternate attribution for their anxiety (Johns, Schmader, & Martens, 2005).

Changing the composition of academic settings so that they are more representative of a variety of groups is certain to be a long-term process. Nonetheless, small changes can have an effect on students who are stigmatized in the academic domain. Specifically, the presence of role models who are stigmatized group members who have achieved success in the academic domain can reduce the threat. Such role models challenge the accuracy of the negative stereotype and thus may increase individuals' expectations of success in the domain (Marx & Goff, 2005; Marx & Roman, 2002). Individuals in situations that are typically threatening to their social identity (e.g., women taking a difficult math test, African Americans taking a test diagnostic of ability) perform better in the presence of an in-group member whom they believe to excel in the domain than in the absence of such an individual. Role models are more likely to be a source of inspiration if their achievements seem relevant and attainable, and if the individuals who are to be inspired believe that their own ability can improve over time (Lockwood & Kunda, 1997). This emphasizes once again the importance of a belief system that academic outcomes are not simply a result of fixed levels of intelligence but rather involve factors such as hard work, which can change over time.

In addition to challenging the validity of negative stereotypes, resilience in the face of a threatening academic culture can be promoted by strategies that restore students' self-integrity but not at the expense of academic engagement. One strategy for doing so is affirming that the individual is good and worthwhile. Self-affirmations include reflections on personally important and overarching values that are unrelated to the domain in which threat may be experienced (Sherman & Cohen, 2006; Steele, 1988). Recent research by Cohen, Garcia, Apfel, and Master (2006) suggests that affirmation helps to reduce the threat stigmatized students face in the classroom. Participants in this study were African American and White seventh-grade students who were randomly assigned to either a self-affirmation or a control condition. At the beginning of the academic term, participants in the self-affirmation condition wrote about their most important value(s); children in the control group wrote about their least important value(s). At the end of the term, African American students who received the self-affirmation manipulation received higher grades than those in the control condition. In the control condition, African American students' grades tended to decrease over time, but the self-affirmation manipulation buffered students against that negative effect. Interestingly, self-affirmation did not have beneficial effects on grades for European American students. This may have occurred because European American students were experiencing less threat and thus were less vulnerable to that particular cause of performance decrements over time.

The strategy used in this self-affirmation intervention can be considered part of what psychologist Claude Steele calls wise schooling, schooling that is "made to see value and promise in [stigmatized] students and act accordingly" (Steele, 1992, p. 75). Thus, it is important that aspects of the school environment help students who are stigmatized to feel valued. The study by Cohen et al. (2006) demonstrates that this can be done in very simple and straightforward ways and yet produce impressive results.

Conclusions

Culture, both broad and local, influences the psychological experience of students who are stigmatized in the academic domain. Cultural beliefs that emphasize negative stereotypes and devalue these students' ability in academic contexts place stigmatized students at risk for experiencing threats to the integrity of their social selves. Attempts to reduce the negative outcomes associated with membership in such groups must address the psychological predicament in which these students often find themselves. The key dilemma is how to maintain self-integrity while aligning one's self with a domain that constantly poses a threat to one's value and worth. Thus it is important that interventions acknowledge the impact that these negative cultural beliefs can have but challenge and invalidate the negative stereotypes by, for example, providing students with role models. Most important, when students feel valued and worthwhile, they may be able to cope with challenging academic contexts.

References

Allport, G. (1954/1979). *The nature of prejudice.* New York: Doubleday Anchor.
Aronson, J., Fried, C. B., & Good, C. (2002). Reducing the effects of stereotype threat on African American college students by shaping theories of intelligence. *Journal of Experimental Social Psychology, 38,* 113–125.

Atkinson, J. W. (1964). *An introduction to motivation.* Princeton, NJ: Van Nostrand.

Ben-Zeev, T., Fein, S., & Inzlicht, M. (2005). Arousal and stereotype threat. *Journal of Experimental Social Psychology, 41,* 174–181.

Beutel, A. M., & Nelson, D. J. (2005). Gender and race-ethnicity of faculty in top science and engineering research departments. *Journal of Women and Minorities in Science and Engineering, 11,* 389–403.

Biernat, M., Vescio, T. K., & Green, H. L. (1996). Selective self-stereotyping. *Journal of Personality and Social Psychology, 71,* 1194–1209.

Blascovich, J., Spencer, S. J., Quinn, D., & Steele, C. (2001). African Americans and high blood pressure: The role of stereotype threat. *Psychological Science, 12*(3), 225–229.

Chasteen, A. L., Bhattacharyya, S., Horhota, M., Tam, R., & Hasher, L. (2005). How feelings of stereotype threat influence older adults' memory performance. *Experimental Aging Research, 31,* 235–260.

Cohen, G. L., Garcia, J., Apfel, N., & Master, A. (2006). Reducing the racial achievement Gap: A social-psychological intervention. *Science, 313*(5791), 1307–1310.

College Board. (2006). *2006 college-bound seniors: Total group profile report.* Retrieved May 25, 2007, from http://www.collegeboard.com/prod_downloads/about/news_info/cbsenior/yr2006/national-report.pdf.

Cooley, C. H. (1956). *Two major works: Social organization. Human nature and the social order.* Glencoe, IL: Free Press.

Crocker, J., & Major, B. (1989). Social stigma and self-esteem: The self-protective properties of stigma. *Psychological Review, 96,* 608–630.

Crocker, J., Major, B., & Steele, C. M. (1998). Social stigma. In D. Gilbert, S. T. Fiske, & G. Lindzey (Eds.), *The handbook of social psychology* (4th ed., Vol. 2, pp. 504–553). Boston: McGraw-Hill.

Croizet, J.-C., & Claire, T. (1998). Extending the concept of stereotype and threat to social class: The intellectual underperformance of students from low socioeconimic backgrounds. *Personality and Social Psychology Bulletin, 24*(6), 588–594

Dar-Nimrod, I., & Heine, S. J. (2006). Exposure to scientific theories affects women's math performance. *Science, 314,* 435.

Davies, P. G., Spencer, S. J., Quinn, D. M., & Gerhardstein, R. (2002). Consuming images: How television commercials that elicit stereotype threat can restrain women academically and professionally. *Personality and Social Psychology Bulletin, 28,* 1615–1628.

Davies, P. G., Spencer, S. J., & Steele, C. M. (2005). Clearing the air: Identity safety moderates the effects of stereotype threat on women's leadership aspirations. *Journal of Personality and Social Psychology, 88,* 276–287.

Devine, P. G. (1989). Stereotypes and prejudice: Their automatic and controlled components. *Journal of Personality and Social Psychology, 56,* 5–18.

Devine, P. G., & Elliot, A. J. (1995). Are racial stereotypes really fading? The Princeton trilogy revisited. *Personality and Social Psychology Bulletin, 21,* 1139–1150.

Dickerson, S. S., & Kemeny, M. E. (2004). Acute stressors and cortisol responses: A theoretical integration and synthesis of laboratory research. *Psychological Bulletin, 130,* 355–391.

Dweck, C. S. (1986). Motivational processes affecting learning. *American Psychologist 41,* 1040–1048.

Eccles-Parsons, J., Adler, T. F., Futterman, R., Goff, S. B., Kaczala, C. M., Meece, J. L., & Midgley, C. (1983). Expectancies, values, and academic behaviors. In J. T. Spence (Ed.), *Achievement and achievement motivation* (pp. 75–146). San Francisco: W. H. Freeman.

Eccles, J. S., Jacobs, J. E., & Harold, R. D. (1990). Gender role stereotypes, expectancy effects, and parents' socialization of gender differences. *Journal of Social Issues, 46,* 183–201.

Eccleston, C. P. & Major, B (2007). *An expectancy/value perspective on the demotivating effects of prejudice.* Unpublished manuscript, Syracuse University.

Feather, N. T. (1962). The study of persistence. *Psychological Bulletin, 59,* 94–115.

Ford, D. Y. (1998). The underrepresentation of minority students in gifted education: Problems and promises in recruitment and retention. *Journal of Special Education, 32,* 4–14.

Frome, P. M., Alfeld, C. J., Eccles, J. S., & Barber, B. L. (2006). Why don't they want a male-dominated job? An investigation of young women who changed their occupational aspirations. *Educational Research and Evaluation, 12,* 359–372.

Good, C., Aronson, J., & Inzlicht, M. (2003). Improving adolescents' standardized test performance: An intervention to reduce the effects of stereotype threat. *Journal of Applied Developmental Psychology, 24,* 645–662.

Hare, B. R. (1985). Stability and change in self-perception and achievement among Black adolescents: A longitudinal study. *Journal of Black Psychology, 11,* 29–42.

Hudley, C., & Graham, S. (2001). Stereotypes of achievement striving among early adolescents. *Social Psychology of Education, 5*(2), 201–224.

Inzlicht, M. B., & Ben-Zeev, T. (2000). A threatening intellectual environment: Why females are susceptible to experiencing problem-solving deficits in the presence of males. *Psychological Science, 11,* 365–371.

James, W. (1890/1950). *The principles of psychology* (Vol. 1). New York: Dover.

Johns, M., Schmader, T., & Martens, A. (2005). Knowing is half the battle: Teaching stereotype threat as a means of improving women's math performance. *Psychological Science, 16*, 175–179.

Jost, J. T., & Banaji, M. R. (1994). The role of stereotyping in system-justification and the production of false consciousness. *British Journal of Social Psychology Stereotypes: Structure, Function and Process, 33*, 1–27.

Judd, C. M., Park, B., Ryan, C. S., Brauer, M., & Kraus, S. (1995). Stereotypes and ethnocentrism: Interethnic perceptions of African American and White American college samples. *Journal of Personality and Social Psychology, 69*, 460–481.

Keller, J. (2002). Blatant stereotype threat and women's math performance: Self-handicapping as a strategic means to cope with obtrusive negative performance expectations. *Sex Roles, 47*, 193–198.

Lerner, M. J. (1980). *Belief in a just world: A fundamental delusion.* New York: Plenum.

Levy, S. R., Stroessner, S. J., & Dweck, C. S. (1998). Stereotype formation and endorsement: The role of implicit theories. *Journal of Personality and Social Psychology, 74*, 1421–1436.

Link, B. G., & Phelan, J. C. (2001). Conceptualizing stigma. *Annual Review of Sociology, 27*, 363–385.

Lockwood, P. U., & Kunda, Z. (1997). Superstars and me: Predicting the impact of role models on the self. *Journal of Personality and Social Psychology, 73*, 91–103.

Magner, D. K. (1996, February 2). The new generation: Study shows proportions of female and minority professors are growing. *Chronicle of Higher Education*, pp. A17–A18.

Major, B., & Eccleston, C. P. (2005). Stigma and social exclusion. In D. Abrams & M. A. Hogg (Eds.), *The social psychology of inclusion and exclusion* (pp. 63–87). New York: Psychology Press.

Major, B., & O'Brien, L. T. (2005). The social psychology of stigma. *Annual Review of Psychology, 56*, 393–421.

Major, B., Spencer, S., Schmader, T., Wolfe, C., & Crocker, J. (1998). Coping with negative stereotypes about intellectual performance: The role of psychological disengagement. *Personality and Social Psychology Bulletin, 24*, 34–50.

Marx, D. M., & Goff, P. A. (2005). Clearing the air: The effect of experimenter race on target's test performance and subjective experience. *British Journal of Social Psychology, 44*, 645–657.

Marx, D. M. H., & Roman, J. S. (2002). Female role models: Protecting women's math test performance. *Personality and Social Psychology Bulletin, 28*, 1183–1193.

McGuire, W. J., McGuire, C. V., & Winton, W. (1979). Effects of household sex composition on the salience of one's gender in the spontaneous self-concept. *Journal of Experimental Social Psychology, 15,* 77–90.

Mead, G. H. (1934). *Mind, self and society: From the standpoint of a social behaviorist.* Chicago, IL: University of Chicago Press

Meece, J. L., Wigfield, A., & Eccles, J. S. (1990). Predictors of math anxiety and its influence on young adolescents' course enrollment intentions and performance in mathematics. *Journal of Educational Psychology, 82,* 60–70.

National Science Foundation (NSF). 2007. *Women, minorities, and persons with disabilities in science and engineering: 2007* (NSF 07–315). Arlington, VA: Author.

National Center for Education Statistics (NCES). 2000. *The digest of education statistics 1999.* NCES 2000–031. Washington, DC: U. S. Department of Education, Office of Educational Research and Improvement.

Nussbaum, A. D., & Steele, C. M. (2007). Situational disengagement and persistence in the face of adversity. *Journal of Experimental Social Psychology, 43,* 127–134.

O'Brien, L. T., Kinias Z., & Major, B. N. (in press). How status and stereotypes impact attributions to discrimination: The stereotype-asymmetry hypothesis. *Journal of Experimental Social Psychology.*

O'Brien, L. T., & Hummert, M. L. (2006). Memory performance of late middle-aged adults: Contrasting self-stereotyping and stereotype threat accounts of assimilation to age stereotypes. *Social Cognition, 24,* 338–358.

Osborne, J. W. (1995). Academics, self-esteem and race: A look at the underlying assumptions of the disidentifcation hypothesis. *Personality and Social Psychology Bulletin, 21,* 449–455.

Perrie, M., Grigg, W., & Dion, G. (2005). *The nation's report card: Mathematics 2005* (NCES 2006–453). U.S. Department of Education, National Center for Education Statistics. Washington, DC: U.S. Government Printing Office.

Pickett, C. L., Bonner, B. L., & Coleman, J. M. (2002). Motivated self-stereotyping: Heightened assimilation and differentiation needs result in increased levels of positive and negative self-stereotyping. *Journal of Personality and Social Psychology, 82,* 543–562.

Prentice, D. A., & Miller, D. T. (2006). Essentializing differences between women and men. *Psychological Science, 17,* 129–135.

Pyszczynski, T., & Greenberg, J. (1983). Determinants of reduction in intended effort as a strategy for coping with anticipated failure. *Journal of Research in Personality, 17,* 412–422.

Rotter, J. B (1966). Generalized expectancies for internal versus external control of reinforcement. *Psychological Monographs: General & Applied. 80*(1), 1–28.

Saenz, D. S., & Lord, C. G. (1989). Reversing roles: A cognitive strategy for undoing memory deficits associated with token status. *Journal of Personality and Social Psychology, 56,* 698–708.

Schmader, T. (2002). Gender identification moderates stereotype threat effects on women's math performance. *Journal of Experimental Social Psychology, 38*(2), 194–201.

Schmader, T., & Johns, M. (2003). Converging evidence that stereotype threat reduces working memory capacity. *Journal of Personality and Social Psychology, 85*(3), 440–452.

Schmader, T., & Major, B. (1999). The impact of ingroup vs. outgroup performance on personal values. *Journal of Experimental Social Psychology, 35*(1), 47–67.

Schmader, T., Major, B., Eccleston, C. P., & McCoy, S. K. (2001). Devaluing domains in response to threatening intergroup comparisons: Perceived legitimacy and the status value asymmetry. *Journal of Personality and Social Psychology, 80,* 782–796.

Schmader, T., Major, B., & Gramzow, R. H. (2001). Coping with ethnic stereotypes in the academic domain: Perceived injustice and psychological disengagement. *Journal of Social Issues, 57,* 93–111.

Seibt, B., & Förster, J. (2004). Stereotype threat and performance: How self-stereotypes influence processing by inducing regulatory foci. *Journal of Personality and Social Psychology, 87,* 38–56.

Sherman, D. K., & Cohen, G. L. (2006). The psychology of self-defense: Self-affirmation theory. In M. P. Zanna (Ed.) *Advances in experimental social psychology* (Vol. 38, pp. 183–242). San Diego, CA: Academic Press.

Spencer, S. J., Steele, C. M., & Quinn, D. M. (1999). Stereotype threat and women's math performance. *Journal of Experimental Social Psychology, 35,* 4–28.

Stangor, C., Carr, C., & Kiang, L. (1998). Activating stereotypes undermines task performance expectations. *Journal of Personality and Social Psychology, 75,* 1191–1197.

Steele, C. M. (1988). The psychology of self-affirmation: Sustaining the integrity of the self. In L. Berkowitz (Ed.), *Advances in experimental social psychology: Vol. 21. Social psychological studies of the self: Perspectives and programs* (pp. 261–302). San Diego, CA: Academic Press.

Steele, C. M. (1992). Race and the schooling of Black Americans. *Atlantic Monthly, 269*(4), 68–78.

Steele, C. M. (1997). A threat in the air: How stereotypes shape intellectual identity and performance. *American Psychologist, 52*(6), 613–629.

Steele, C. M. (1999, August). Thin ice: "Stereotype threat" and black college students. *Atlantic Monthly, 284,* 44–47, 50–54.

Steele, C. M., & Aronson, J. (1995). Stereotype threat and the intellectual test performance of African Americans. *Journal of Personality and Social Psychology, 69,* 797–811.

Steele, C. M., Spencer, S. J., & Aronson, J. (2002). Contending with group image: The psychology of stereotype and social identity threat. In M. P. Zanna (Ed.), *Advances in experimental social psychology* (Vol. 34, pp. 379–440). San Diego, CA: Academic Press.

Taylor, S. E., & Brown, J. D. (1988). Illusion and well-being: A social psychological perspective on mental health. *Psychological Bulletin, 103,* 193–210.

Tesser, A., & Campbell, J. (1980). Self-definition: The impact of the relative performance and similarity of others. *Social Psychology Quarterly, 43,* 341–347.

Triandis, H. C. (1989). The self and social behavior in differing cultural contexts. *Psychological Review, 96,* 506–520.

Thompson, M., & Sekaquaptewa, D. (2002). When being different is detrimental: Solo status and the performance of women and racial minorities. *Analyses of Social Issues and Public Policy, 2,* 183–203.

U. S. Department of Education. (2005). *How No Child Left Behind benefits African-Americans.* Retrieved from http://www.ed.gov/nclb/accountability/achieve/nclb-aa.pdf.

U. S. Department of Education, National Center for Education Statistics. (2007). *Placing college graduation rates in context: How 4 year college graduation rates vary with selectivity and the size of low-income enrollment: Postsecondary education descriptive analysis report.* Retrieved from http://nces.ed.gov/pubsearch/pubsinfo.asp?pubid=2007161.

Wagner, U., Lampen, L., & Syllwasschy, J. (1986). In-group inferiority, social identity, and out-group devaluation in a modified minimal group study. *British Journal of Social Psychology, 25,* 15–23.

9 ⠶

Cultures in Contrast

Understanding the Influence of School Culture on Student Engagement

Cynthia Hudley and Annette M. Daoud

Today's students will need to become active participants in their own lifelong learning to meet the demands of an ever more rapidly changing landscape of knowledge and skills. Postsecondary education as well as lifelong learning and retraining will be minimum requirements for those who will participate fully in the new economy. Schools must prepare our children and youth now for that world of the future, and the future is upon us already. However, the most rigorous, enriched school curriculum delivered by academically expert professionals will result in high levels of student achievement only to the extent that students are motivated to engage and persist in learning activities. The ways students engage in school learning have a great deal to do with how they experience the school context and how they fare in school, and the institutional culture of school is one important determinant of student engagement and student outcomes. Thus, student engagement and school culture are in a continuing transactional relationship, and this relationship has significant consequences for academic motivation and school success.

In this chapter we discuss the relationship between school culture and student outcomes. We begin by describing our understanding and use of the terms *school culture* and *student engagement* and their relevance to school practices and students' academic achievement motivation. We then present data, quantitative and qualitative, drawn from our research on student academic motivation to illustrate the connections between school culture as perceived by students, teachers' perceptions of students, and student engagement in learning. We conclude with a consideration of the implications of our findings for education, including classroom and school practices as well as programs of teacher preparation.

∷ School Culture

Our research has been guided by a definition of school culture that is consistent with a more global view of culture. Following the systems view of culture (Kitayama, 2002), we define school culture as a set of variable, loosely organized systems of meanings (e.g., beliefs, values, goals) that organize group members' perceptions, behaviors, and interpersonal processes (e.g., expectations, social norms, communication styles) within the particular ecocultural niche of the school (i.e., the cultural and ecological context in which people in the school community live out their daily lives). This view of culture is particularly valuable for examining the relationship between school culture and student engagement as it links the institutional context of school in meaningful ways to student and teacher behavior as well as to the larger cultural context in which the school is embedded.

It is important to note at the outset that our operationalization of the construct is quite distinct from other, prevalent uses of the term *school culture* that refer to the academic content of schooling (e.g., vocational schools, college preparatory academies; Conchas, 2001) or to the peer culture of high school (Steinberg, 1996). However, our perspective on school culture is similar if somewhat broader than that of other researchers who have operationalized culture as specific to classrooms (e.g., Weinstein, 2002) or to school organization (Hobby, 2004). Our use of the term is also similar to another construct, *school climate,* that has featured prominently in research on achievement motivation. Early research on school climate focused on multiple dimensions of relationships, classroom management, and pedagogy in the classroom setting (Moos, 1979), using the traditional business management definition that located climate within the local work unit (Burke & Litwin, 1992). More recent research on school climate has expanded to examine the whole school context (Hoy & Hoy, 2003; Smerdon, 2002) as well as a broad range of motivational variables that are relevant to a student's personal development (e.g., autonomy, efficacy, self-regulation) (for a review see Wigfield, Eccles, Schiefele, Roeser, & Davis-Kean, 2006). In this chapter, we are interested in the ways a school's systems of meanings (i.e., culture) reflect the broader culture of the society in which it is embedded as well as how students' perceptions of the school culture influence their attitudes and behaviors.

School culture is driven by the beliefs, values, and goals that members of the school community bring with them into the setting, and these cultural values have substantive consequences for school practice and organization. Instantiated in the school context, the cultural values of the broader society shape norms of appropriate behavior and interaction, rewards and sanctions for those behaviors and interactions, and relationships in which those norms and rewards are enacted. For example, the values of the dominant culture in the United States strongly favor freedom of choice and the ability to make one's own decisions. However, one consequence of that value is that teachers with the greatest experience and expertise are typically teaching higher level and Advanced Placement classes; such classes typically enroll more White, middle-class students than students of color and low-income students (Brown et al., 2003). This disparity in teacher expertise has a demonstrated negative impact on the quality of education, students' conduct problems, and academic achievement motivation (Miller & Garran, 2007).

Related to the value of personal freedom, U.S. culture strongly values individualism, individual achievement, and personal independence ("rugged individualism") (Stewart & Bennett, 1991). As a consequence, particularly in secondary school cultures there is often a deemphasis on a communal orientation, interpersonal warmth, and nurturance and an increased emphasis on competition, content knowledge, and hierarchical structures. However, when the school culture is perceived by students as orderly, with teachers who hold high expectations of all students, more nurturing interpersonal relationships with teachers reduce conduct problems (Kasen, 1990) and promote student achievement motivation (Wentzel, 1997) among early adolescents. Although the broader U.S. cultural milieu has a potent influence on school culture, the unique character of local school culture influences student attitudes and behaviors.

A school culture that duplicates certain values and beliefs of the dominant U.S. culture can be especially challenging for low-income and language minority students. For example, a highly salient belief represented in the dominant culture is the importance of wealth and consumerism. Those who are less economically successful are believed somehow to be personally responsible for their circumstances (Wilson, 1995), a belief that reflects our cultural emphasis on personal achievement ("rags to riches") and a persistent blindness to the cultural barriers of institutional classism and racism (Miller & Garran, 2007). Low-income students who do not have access to culturally valued symbols of wealth (expensive clothing, electronic gadgets) may perceive rejection from peers as well as school staff (Brantlinger, 1993) and experience a sense of alienation from the school culture that can undermine their academic engagement (Patrick, Ryan, & Kaplan, 2007) at school. Further, children and youth in impoverished, isolated urban and rural communities may simply be unable to see the advantage of long-term educational solutions to the immediate problems of economic disadvantage that surround them on a daily basis. Paradoxically, sustaining achievement motivation and the attendant belief that school success is important to their future life chances is especially important for children who lack the social opportunities and privileges that are implicit in the lives of their more affluent peers.

Children who are English learners also experience alienation and rejection while trying to "fit in" to a school culture that reflects broader social stereotypes that portray low-income people, ethnic minorities, and especially immigrants as academically incompetent (Hudley & Graham, 2001) and an economic burden on society (Suárez-Orozco & Suárez-Orozco, 2001). Latino students sometimes also function in a cultural milieu both at school and in the larger society that perceives Spanish-English bilingualism as a problem to be eradicated (Hunt, 2007). Although many countries and cultures view multilingualism as a strength and their schools require exposure to at least two languages by the completion of compulsory schooling, U.S. school culture and U.S. culture more broadly sometimes devalue bilingual education and sees Spanish in particular as a barrier to school success (Bali, 2001; Rossell & Baker, 1996). This cultural value, when embodied in a school's language policies, can lead to the segregation of English learners into separate classes and programs that undermine their academic efficacy beliefs (Ryan & Patrick, 2001), leave them socially and psychologically distanced from their English speaking peers (Dornbusch & Kaufman, 2001; Olsen, 1997), and unable to access an intellectually challenging curriculum that can prepare them for postsecondary education.

English learners' perceived lack of acceptance by their peers, perhaps because of school policies and pervasive cultural stereotypes, may lead them to isolate themselves socially at school (Daoud & Quiocho, 2005; Gibson, Gandara, & Koyama, 2004). Further, the low-level, intellectually impoverished curriculum available to English learners may not only distance them from peers but also distance them from a belief that education provides opportunities and access to good jobs and a good life. For recent immigrant students in particular, segregation by language ability also limits opportunities for peer socialization into the school culture as well as broader U.S. cultural values, beliefs, and behaviors that provide the foundation for the school culture that these newly arrived students are expected to embrace. The education system in the United States now serves increasing numbers of students who confront the dual burdens of economic disadvantage and language minority status. When discussing academic achievement and motivation for these young people, the discourse typically highlights the culture of the child (e.g., cultural compatibility, cultural discontinuity). It would be wise to turn our lens from the individual to the institution to understand the ways school culture can support achievement motivation among all students, including those who are not currently well served.

⠋ Student Engagement and Perceived School Culture

Student motivation and achievement does not happen in a vacuum; school is one (but not the only) important context in which students' motivation is either nurtured or suppressed. Engagement, a motivational construct that indexes the persistence and quality of students' involvement in learning activities, is a concept that links the individual student to the classroom or institutional context of school. Because of this ability to link context and individual, engagement is a potentially useful construct for an examination of individual outcomes that are strongly influenced by the school culture. The definition of engagement in our work comprises two components: behavior and affect (Skinner & Belmont, 1993). Behavioral engagement represents what students do to remain involved in learning. For example, such engagement at school would be reflected by low rates of disciplinary problems (Ekstrom, Goertz, Pollack, & Rock, 1986) and absenteeism (Hudley, 1995) and high rates of task completion (Conchas, 2001; Hudley, 1995). Affective engagement represents attitudes or feelings about the pursuit of learning (Skinner & Belmont, 1993). Students who are affectively engaged at school hold positive attitudes toward academic activities and achievement striving. Affective engagement is somewhat similar to intrinsic motivation, as an intrinsically motivated student will perceive the learning task to be a source of enjoyment (Deci & Ryan, 1987). As well, the effects of school culture on any particular student are typically determined by that student's perceptions and understandings. Thus in our work on student engagement, we have been especially interested in students' perceptions of the school culture, including their peers and their teachers. We have been examining student engagement in a sample of Latino and White secondary school students to understand the relationships between perceived school culture and student outcomes such as school adjustment, attitudes toward school, academic achievement, and expectations about the future.

Recent research tells us that engagement is related to perceived school culture as well as student outcomes. Research in urban school districts, for example, has revealed that students' perceptions of teacher support and a positive school culture are positively related to behavioral engagement (e.g., attendance, reduced dropout) and academic success in high school (Finn & Rock, 1997; Gambone, Klem, Summers, Aken, & Sipe, 2004). High school students' perceptions of interpersonal relations on campus have also been positively related to affective engagement, measured as positive attitude toward learning, as well as to students' GPA (Gilman & Anderman, 2006). Similarly, a positive perception of school culture in middle school has been concurrently related to affective engagement, measured as school connectedness (Loukas, Suzuki, & Horton, 2006). Early school leaving, which forecloses traditional opportunities to develop important competencies for a successful career trajectory, may be the final act for high school students who have become progressively alienated by and disengaged from the school culture (Alexander, Entwistle, & Kabbani, 2001; Conchas, 2001). Because ethnic minority students are most likely to leave high school early (NCES, 2000), understanding how the school culture influences high school engagement for these students seems especially important.

In examining student perceptions of high school culture, our focus has been on two specific elements: teacher support and cultural sensitivity. Those who study classroom climate and culture have defined teacher support as a nurturing, respectful attitude toward students that conveys a personal interest and expectations for success (Blumenfeld, 1992; Wentzel, 1997). Thus teacher support comprises both emotional and academic support for students. Prior research indicates that perceived teacher support is related to both behavioral and affective engagement in middle school (Wentzel, 1997) and elementary school (Furrer & Skinner, 2003), and this is particularly true for ethnic minority adolescents (Hudley, 1995, 1997, 1998; Murdock, 1999). These effects are evident even when researchers control for general motivational orientation (e.g., control beliefs) and overall adjustment (Furrer & Skinner, 2003; Wentzel, 1997).

We were especially interested in possible ethnic differences in the relationship between perceived support and engagement, given pervasive disparities in the treatment of ethnic minorities in the dominant U.S. culture and the troubling empirical evidence that this cultural bias is duplicated in teachers' views of students. For example, classic studies in the sociology of education have written about disparities in opportunity and "dysconscious racism" (King, 1991); such disparity is embedded in the normative cultural framework that tacitly awards advantages to those with white skin and middle-class status (i.e., White privilege) in the United States (King, 1991; Rains, 1998). These normative advantages (e.g., ability to obtain credit, freely select a neighborhood of residence, experience a school curriculum that teaches that your race is the architect of civilized democracy) are typically invisible to those who enjoy them exactly because they are represented as normative for American culture, or "just the way things are" (McIntosh, 1992). These cultural values are manifested in schools through treatment that varies by student background (Gollnick, 1992). Low-income and ethnic minority children who struggle in school are more often treated as unmotivated or conduct disordered, while struggling affluent, White children are provided services (e.g., counseling, tutoring) to improve their learning (Bowles & Gintis, 1976). Research in multicultural education has found that teachers across all grade levels may perceive African American and Latino students as more behaviorally (i.e., discipline problems) and affectively (i.e., don't care about education) disengaged than other groups, regardless of objective similarities in behavior across groups (Kalin, 1999; Katz, 1999). Evidence for a similar bias has been found in preservice teachers as well (King, 1991).

Biased attitudes may reciprocally influence engagement to the extent that they represent a school culture that is perceived as alienating. Bandura's concept of reciprocal determinism (1978) captures the process through which people and environments mutually shape one another; an individual student's reactions can be elicited by biases directed at personal characteristics (e.g., language status, race). A negative reaction elicited by bias affects both target and perceiver, as the target's elicited response may maintain and confirm the initial biases of the perceiver. Consider the example of a student who perceives her ethnic group to be unfairly treated or marginalized in school. This student may resist instruction from those she perceives as unfair, leading to a cycle of reduced achievement, low school staff expectations, progressive disengagement from school, and increased behavioral problems (Cummins, 1996). Prior research on the positive side of reciprocal determinism has found that a school culture that supports students' ethnic identities and home cultures promotes academic achievement among Latino high school students (Tan, 2001; Trueba, 1988) and more positive relations generally across ethnic groups for both students and teachers (Tatum, 1997). Examining how ethnicity moderates perceived culture and student engagement may be useful for understanding the mechanisms linking school culture variables to student outcomes.

⋈ One American High School

We have undertaken our study of student engagement in a small, suburban community on the central coast of California. Nowhere are the issues of educating language minority students more complex and consequential than in California. At both the national level and in California, ideologies, policies, and practices toward English learners are largely negative. In recent years, California voters have approved propositions that call for the elimination of services to undocumented workers (predominantly from Mexico) and their children (Proposition 187) and drastic limits for bilingual education in the public schools (Proposition 227). However, Spanish-speaking students are a substantial and growing population that approaches a majority of enrolled students in California's public schools (48%, approximately 3 million students), and the subgroup learning English comprises 25% (approximately 1.6 million) of the total enrollment. Further, English learners are overrepresented in the cohort that is just entering the educational system (39% of kindergarteners) (California Department of Education, 2007). Punitive beliefs and policies will not reduce the need to consistently and effectively serve these students in public schools.

We gathered the data in a community with a single comprehensive high school. Our high school site had an enrollment of 840 students in the spring of 2001 when we collected these data, with an average class size of 25, and a student-teacher ratio of 20 to 1. Of that total student population, 47% were females, and the ethnic composition was 54% Latino, 43% White, and 3% other (African American, Asian, and Native American). As well, 26% or 216 students were classified as English learners, all of whom spoke Spanish as their first language, and virtually all were Mexican immigrant students (California Department of Education, 2007).

The community was a small town of approximately 14,500 residents with a population of approximately 59% White, 38% Latino, and 3% other (U. S. Census Bureau, 2000). The structure of the community reflects many of the realities and tensions that are represented statewide and nationally. Employment ranged from lucrative positions in the computer industry to low-paying agricultural jobs such as farm worker. The per capita annual income for employed White residents in the community was right at the state average of $22,000, but the comparable figure for Latino community residents was $12,000, or just over half that for White residents (U.S. Census Bureau, 2000). Due to its seaside location and proximity to a resort town, the cost of living was high, and the average home price was in the $400,000 to $650,000 range and rapidly rising. Rents were equally high, ranging from $600 for a small studio apartment to at least $2,000 for a three-bedroom house. Thus low-income families faced disproportionate obstacles to providing their children with the material and social resources necessary to support academic achievement.

⠃ Examining Student Engagement

Our investigation incorporated both quantitative and qualitative methods to examine students' behaviors and affect in school as a function of their perceptions of the school culture. In this chapter we discuss results that were guided by two specific research questions. The overarching question we asked was how does the culture of the school influence student engagement? Two specific hypotheses explored that question: (1) We expected that perceptions of teacher and peer support would be positively related to both behavioral and affective engagement, but the pattern of relationships would differ for Latino and White students. (2) We also expected perceptions of ethnic relations at school to be positively related to both behavioral and affective engagement for all students, but again this result would be moderated by ethnicity. Although the classroom and the broader school environment are both important contexts for manifestations of school culture, we were interested in these two hypotheses to determine whether effects of the classroom culture might differ from those of the broader school culture. We also wondered how students' perceptions of the school would differ as a function of ethnicity, consistent with our earlier discussion of the invisibility of

White privilege. Thus we specifically examined the qualitative meaning of perceived school culture for both Latino and White students.

Our sample (N = 190) was approximately equally balanced by ethnicity (46% Latino and 54% White) and gender (53% girls and 47% boys); the gender balance was similar across ethnicity. Using free lunch status as a proxy for socioeconomic status (SES), we found that 44% of Latino students (n = 39) and 4% of White students (n = 4) received free or reduced-price lunch. Our English learners (N = 24), all of whom qualified for free lunch, comprised 27% of the Latino sample and 62% of the low SES, Latino sample. Thus ethnicity, language status, and class were relatively confounded in the sample, due to the disproportionate concentration of the English learners at the lower end of the SES spectrum in the Latino sample.

⁜ Sources of Quantitative Data

We collected quantitative survey data from students with a 53-item instrument that assessed both students' and teachers' perceptions of student engagement, and students' perceptions of teacher support, campus ethnic attitudes, and intergroup interactions. Students also provided demographic information (age, grade, gender, and ethnicity). Our measure of behavioral engagement combined teacher report and archival data. Each participant's English or English as a Second Language (ESL) teacher rated two behaviors: how often the student got "in trouble because of inappropriate behavior" and how often the student failed to complete class assignments. These questions were combined into a single teacher index (α = .73) in which higher numbers represent lower engagement (i.e., more problem behavior). A review of school records yielded days of detention and suspension, which were combined into a single discipline index (α = .85), which was scaled similarly so that higher numbers represent lower engagement (i.e., more detentions and suspensions). We also collected attendance for the academic year. Affective engagement was measured by a combination of teacher and student report. Teachers rated students on a single item asking how often the student "enjoys learning new things." Students responded to 11 items (α = .68) assessing attitudes toward achievement (e.g., "I like to do easy assignments; I think it is interesting to do work in science"), adapted from the School Attitude Measure (SAM) (Wick, 1990) and the Children's Academic Intrinsic Motivation Inventory (CAIMI) (Gottfried, 1986).

Perceived teacher support was assessed with seven items ($\alpha = .69$) tapping both emotional ("this teacher really cares about us") and academic ("my teacher thinks I am a good student") support. Five items measured students' perceptions of ethnic attitudes at school ($\alpha = .67$) covering both teacher ("some teachers don't like it when students speak Spanish") and peer ("how well do White students and students learning English get along") attitudes. Three items ($\alpha = .67$) tapped the amount of students' own intergroup interactions ("I have friends at school who are of different ethnic groups than my own"). Finally, we collected students' GPA for the prior academic year as our measure of achievement.

⠃ Sources of Qualitative Data

We conducted a series of open-ended focus group interviews with Latinos who were English learners, Latinos who were English fluent, and White students to explore in greater depth their opinions and attitudes about their schooling experiences. Focus groups were selected as the most effective means to encourage interaction between students in discussion that would elicit more elaborated responses. The interviews, all conducted by the second author, lasted approximately 45 minutes and comprised questions on five specific topics related to our survey measures of student engagement: their own academic performance, their perceptions of their teachers, their college and career aspirations, their friends, and typical interactions across student groups on campus. Fifty-four students, including 20 White and 34 Latino students participated in 18 focus group interviews. We included all 24 English learners in the full sample (all 24 were low-income, Mexican immigrant youth) in our interview sample. The balance of the focus group participants were randomly selected from the remaining students in the full sample who volunteered to participate in interviews ($n = 71$).

⠃ Results

Because of the substantial confound of ethnicity and class we used a measure of free lunch eligibility to divide the sample for quantitative analysis into three groups: White, Latino mid SES, and Latino low SES. The three groups differed on four of five measures of engagement, one measure of perceived ethnic relations, and GPA. Generally, but not uniformly, mid-SES Latinos and Whites were more similar in self-report measures, and mid-SES and low-SES Latinos were more similar in teacher and archival measures. However, preliminary analyses determined that our groups did not differ significantly by gender, so gender was dropped from subsequent analyses.

Support and Engagement

We began by testing the relationship between perceived support and behavioral engagement. An ANOVA using teacher-rated behavioral engagement as the dependent variable and perceived teacher support (used as a categorical variable with three levels) and our three ethnic/class groups as independent variables yielded a significant interaction ($F[4, 168] = 2.79$, $p < .05$) of ethnic/class and perceived support (see Figure 9.1). The perception of low levels of teacher support negatively impacted students' teacher-rated behavioral engagement, and this effect

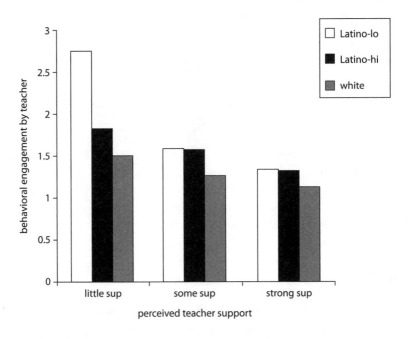

Figure 9-1. Teacher rated behavioral engagement by perceived teacher support.

Note. Higher numbers reflect more problem behaviors.

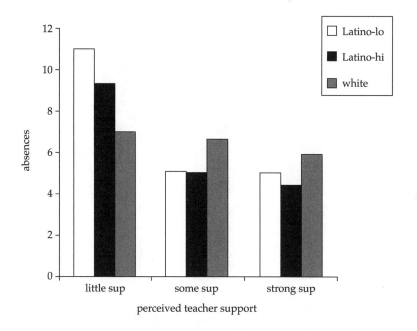

Figure 9-2. Student absences by perceived teacher support.

was most pronounced for low-SES Latino students. As well, teachers rated White students as most behaviorally engaged. Using attendance as the dependent variable, we again found a significant interaction $(F[4, 174] = 3.12, p < .01)$. Low perceived levels of teacher support undermined attendance for Latino students, and those at low income most severely (see Figure 9.2). Finally, we found a main effect of perceived teacher support on number of student detentions $(F[3, 171] = 2.72, p < .05)$ in the expected direction. Perceived peer academic support ("students like to work together") was unrelated to any measures of behavioral engagement.

We examined affective engagement using similar analyses. Low perceived teacher support significantly negatively impacted teacher-rated affective engagement $(F[3, 160] = 4.67, p < .01)$ for all students. However, using self-reported affective engagement, we found a marginally significant interaction $(F[4, 174] = 1.79, p < .11)$. Low levels of perceived teacher support were more detrimental to high-SES Latino students' self-reported affective engagement than to low-SES Latino students, while White students fell somewhere in between (see Figure 9.3). Perceived peer academic support was unrelated to teacher-rated affective

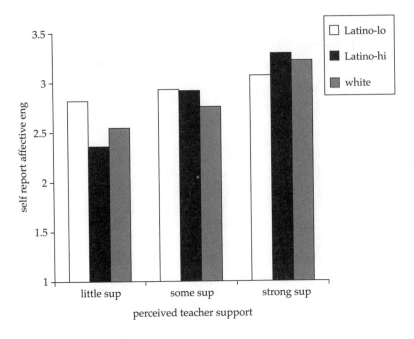

Figure 9–3. Self-reported affective engagement by perceived teacher support.

engagement but significantly ($F[3, 168] = 3.29$, $p < .05$) related to self-reported affective engagement for all students.

Engagement in the local classroom setting, somewhat unsurprisingly, was more strongly related to teacher-student relationships than to relations with peers. We have concluded elsewhere (see Hudley & Daoud, 2007) that the local classroom is instrumental in shaping student engagement in academic tasks. Teachers have the primary responsibility for managing relationships in the classroom and therefore positive relations with teachers should reasonably be expected to influence students' willingness to engage in classroom activities. As well, although we did find hypothesized interactions with ethnicity, relationships in the classroom are clearly important for all students, a point to which we shall return.

Ethnic Relations in School

As discussed earlier, for the analyses of student engagement presented here, we were primarily interested in the contrast between the effects of the immediate classroom and the effects of the broader school culture. We elected to focus our examination of school culture on perceptions of ethnic attitudes, as we expected the school culture might be shaped by patterns of ethnic differences prevalent in the larger U.S. culture. The analyses are similar to those used to test our first hypothesis. An ANOVA using number of absences as the dependent variable and perceived ethnic attitudes at school (transformed into a categorical variable with three levels) and our three ethnic/class groups as independent variables revealed a significant interaction ($F[6, 169] = 2.36, p < .05$) (see Figure 9.4). We found a similar interaction for teacher-rated behavioral engagement ($F[6, 167] = 2.79, p = .01$). Students who held more negative perceptions of ethnic attitudes on campus had more days absent and were rated less behaviorally engaged by teachers, and this effect was very strong for low-SES Latino students No other effects on behavioral engagement were significant.

For teacher-rated affective engagement, we found main effects of both perceived ethnic attitudes ($F[2, 167] = 2.83, p = .06$) and ethnic/class group ($F[3, 167] = 4.13, p < .01$). More positive perceptions of ethnic

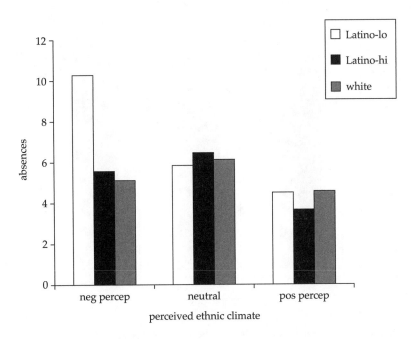

Figure 9-4. Student absences by perceived ethnic climate.

attitudes on campus were related to higher teacher-rated engagement, and generally, White students were rated as more affectively engaged. For self-reported affective engagement, our analysis revealed a significant ethnic/class interaction ($F[6, 169] = 2.13$, $p = .05$) with perceived ethnic attitudes, with effects again strongest for low-SES Latino students (see Figure 9.5).

In addition to examining perceptions of general attitudes, we also analyzed engagement as a function of intergroup relations on campus. Again we found a significant interaction of ethnicity/class and students' interpersonal relations (transformed into a categorical variable with three levels) on teacher-rated behavioral engagement ($F[6, 169] = 2.16$, $p = .05$) and teacher-rated affective engagement ($F[6, 169] = 2.01$, $p = .07$), and effects were again strongest for low-SES Latino students. Most interestingly, self-reported affective engagement also revealed a significant interaction ($F[6, 167] = 3.24$, $p < .01$) of ethnicity/class and students' interpersonal relations. When intergroup relationships were very limited or nonexistent, low-SES Latino students reported the lowest

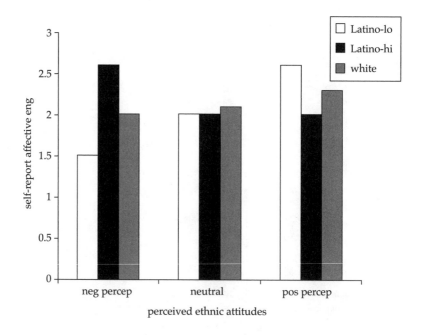

Figure 9–5. Self-reported affective engagement by perceived ethnic climate.

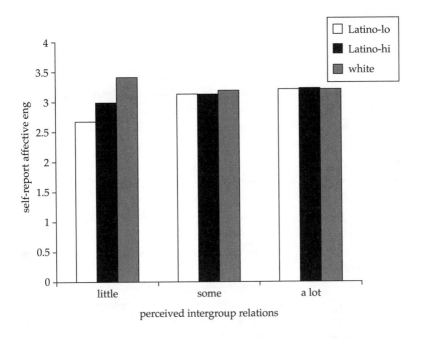

Figure 9–6. Self-reported affective engagement by perceived intergroup relations.

affective engagement of all students but White students reported the highest affective engagement of all students (see Figure 9.6).

Our comparison of classroom and school-level perceptions suggests similar effects on behavioral engagement, whether measured with teacher reports or archival records. Students behave in a more school-appropriate manner when they feel supported and valued in the classroom and the school as a whole. However, findings for affective engagement, or positive attitudes toward school and learning, were more complex. Teacher effects were strongly related to teacher-perceived affective engagement and peer effects were strongly related to self-reported attitudes for all students. Self-reported attitudes were negatively affected by perceived lack of teacher support most strongly for mid-SES Latino students and least affected for low-SES Latino students. Conversely, perceived ethnic relations more powerfully influenced low-SES Latino students' attitudes toward school. Finally, personal interethnic relationships supported positive attitudes for low-SES Latino students but worked against such attitudes for White students. These findings suggest that perceptions of support are critical, but the influences depend on how engagement is defined as well as the nature of the support. As we expected, local classroom support (i.e., teachers) exerted influences that were distinct from the broader campus (i.e., ethnic relations). Teachers are apparently most instrumental in determining behavioral engagement in the classroom, but peers seem to have an equally powerful but more complex influence on more general attitudes toward school.

⚉ The Qualitative Meaning of School Culture

Given the differences we found for perceptions of teacher, peer, and school supportive attitudes as influences on our measures of engagement, we took particular care to examine our qualitative data for possible elaborations on our quantitative findings of differences by status group. For example, perceived teacher support was especially influential on low-SES Latino students' behavioral engagement. In the focus groups, many of the Latino students reported that teachers told them to speak only English in their classrooms, and most of the students who reported being rebuked were immigrant English learners, who also represented the majority of our low-SES Latino sample. Some of these students said simply that teachers "got mad" when they spoke Spanish, and others explained more fully that teachers told them that it was rude to speak Spanish in class. Students typically interpreted this to mean that some teachers did not like students speaking Spanish in the classroom because they could not understand what was being said and felt threatened. In the following example, three Latino immigrant students enrolled in an advanced ESL class are discussing their interactions with teachers in "mainstream" classes. Two students interpreted the reaction from their math teacher, who told them not to speak Spanish in her class because she thought they were "saying bad words."

> RESEARCHER: Do teachers ever say anything to you when you speak Spanish in class?
> DANIEL: Yeah. In math.
> OMAR: Yeah, math.
> RESEARCHER: What does your math teacher say to you?
> OMAR: She is like, "Don't speak Spanish." She thinks that we are saying bad words. (all laugh) So she doesn't want me to speak Spanish.

RESEARCHER: Are you saying bad words?
OMAR: No. (all laugh)
RESEARCHER: So she just doesn't understand you.
DANIEL: Yeah.
OMAR: She thinks that we are talking bad about her. So she doesn't want to hear it.

Similarly, native-born Latino students, who represented the majority of our mid-SES group, also reported negative reactions from teachers. Recall that the influence of perceived teacher support on attitudes toward school was greatest for this group. Two male students interpreted this attitude as a negative value on the Spanish language.

FRANCISCO: Yeah, especially last year. Especially in English class, she would get mad.
LUIS: Yeah.
FRANCISCO: Even if you are talking about the subject. Like she was off doing something else and we would talk in Spanish, she would turn around, "This is an English class!"
LUIS: Most people will say it is rude or something.

In another interview group, an English fluent, native born Latina reported that her math teacher got mad when she spoke Spanish to her friend. However, she stated that they spoke Spanish because they felt like outsiders in the class.

I had one teacher who told me like it is not cool to speak Spanish in front of other people. It is kind of rude because I had a math class, and there are usually two of us who speak Spanish. We just hang out together because we don't feel comfortable in that class because we are the only ones who speak Spanish. We're like outsiders. We are communicating the same in Spanish what we would usually speak in English.

Thus our qualitative data provide insight into our findings that teachers influence behavioral engagement more so for low-SES Latinos and affective engagement for mid-SES Latinos. Latino culture has often been described as interdependent with strong values favoring interpersonal relationships over formalized professional roles (Suárez-Orozco & Suárez-Orozco, 2001). Thus, a warm relationship with teachers may be particularly important in sustaining school-appropriate behavior for Latino students, and we speculate that this effect might be strongest for immigrant students who have had the least exposure to contrary assumptions of the dominant U.S. culture (e.g., individualism). If teachers do not provide a positive interpersonal relationship, immigrant Latino students may become more negative in the relationship and either give the teacher a "bad time" or cancel the relationship (i.e., by not attending school). However, Latino students who have had more consistent exposure to the dominant culture might not have such a strong behavioral reaction. Rather, as our informants reported, they may feel emotionally disconnected and more like outsiders in their own classrooms because their bilingualism is seen as a negative, rather than a strength, and a skill that they and their culture values pushes them into a category of "other" in the school culture.

Our interview data also shed interesting light on peers' contributions, both academic support and interpersonal relations, to affective engagement and did so in a manner that partially explained our quantitative findings. Recall that both perceived academic support and cross-ethnic relations related to affective engagement for all students but in very different ways. Three Latina English learners who discussed problematic peer relationships in some of their honors classes felt that classmates resented their presence in these high-achieving classes because these classmates did not think the girls' immigrant status gave them the right to be there. The girls perceived that White peers did not feel they had worked as hard to get there, and as a result, White students separated themselves in class and would not interact with them socially outside of class. Because classmates did not know anything about their backgrounds or prior schooling, these Latinas believed that students were not judging them fairly.

> RESEARCHER: You said you feel like an outsider. How do other students treat you, like, in an honors class?
> ANNA: Well, they just look at us different because I guess we haven't been around them the whole time. I just got here and I think they think it's just not fair because they have been working harder than we have for their whole lives. And we just got here, and we are able to pick up the subjects and whatever, and we just got in there.
> RESEARCHER: So do you all kind of keep to your own?
> LORENA: Separate. When you are in there, they, like, don't talk to you. But then when they need something from you, they will

talk to you. And it is like, "You never talk to me, and now you want something and you talk to me. I don't know."

RESEARCHER: How does that make you react?

VERONICA: I just feel like I'm judged unfairly. Because one, they haven't talked to me. They don't know me that well. And I guess they just don't have to judge me the way other people react. We're not all the same. They just react unfairly.

Among White student respondents, there was evidence that students who spoke Spanish were sometimes resented. For example, two White respondents discussed their dislike for their Latina soccer teammates as well as the coach. One student, Marissa, stated that the teammates' and the coach's use of Spanish and their preference for Mexican music was troublesome for her. Another soccer player, Lindsay, added that the coach liked Mexican players on the team better than Whites but stressed that she was not racist. She was also troubled that the coach and her teammates did not speak English all the time.

LINDSAY: We had a bad coach in girls' soccer. I didn't like him.

MARISSA: Yeah.

LINDSAY: He is kind of like, discriminatory I suppose. He is Mexican and he tends to like the Mexicans more. I have nothing against racial...like I'm not racist at all and I like everybody. But when he discriminates against the five White people on his team, it is kind of like, "Oh, great."

MARISSA: Like when I played soccer, when I was a freshman, I definitely noticed that they talked Spanish all the time. He gave directions in Spanish sometimes even, and they played Mexican music. It was just really, really uncomfortable.

RESEARCHER: Because it was hard to understand?

MARISSA: Yeah. I didn't like him anyways. But like, we are in America. And this is like an English school, and we are supposed to speak English. And like, just because there are more Mexicans on the team and he is like Mexican....And he kind of like acted mean too. Kind of like, "Oh you are White, so what are you doing here?"

LINDSAY: Spanish people are like better at soccer because it is like grown up more in their culture. But like, I like soccer and I consider myself a decent player. But you can definitely tell, when you look at the bench, who is sitting out. And I don't know if that's abilities, if he is actually judging them. I don't think so. You can see all the people in the stadium and on the team. And it is like, "O. K. " If there are five White people on the team and there are three on the bench, and everyone else out there is just, Mexican. And you know that not everyone out there is better than everyone else. It just gets annoying.

Our data also yielded a number of similar albeit briefer statements from the great majority of White respondents, and especially from White males. Responses to the question "what should White students change about their behavior" included "White students shouldn't take as much...from the Mexicans as they do. Everybody just needs to be equal. The Mexicans think they are better than us" from a White male and "White people at my school need to start acting White" from another White male. In response to the parallel question "what should Latino students change about their behavior," 60% of all responses from White students specifically referenced the need to speak English: "Learn English and not always talk about how great Mexico is. If they like it so much, why don't they move back?" (response from a White male). In contrast, among Latino responses to this same question only one person mentioned "speak more English." Other responses (22%) were equally negative about White peers: "Stop taking insults from White people" (response from a Latino), and some respondents did indicate that Latino students need to reach out to their White peers: "Many have the attitude 'screw all White people that I don't know.' They should change that" (response from a Latino).

Taken together, these data offer a viable interpretation of the relationships between interethnic contact and attitudes toward school that we found in our quantitative data. The negative perceptions of Spanish-English bilingual students in classrooms, extracurricular activities, and general interpersonal interactions is quite consistent with the quantitative finding that greater interethnic contact related to less positive attitudes toward school among White students. Conversely, data from our three Latina respondents in honors classes seem consistent with survey results that greater contact related to more positive attitudes among Latino students. These young women seem open to opportunities to interact with their White peers in honors classes ("They haven't talked to me. They don't know me that well"). It is important to note that our three immigrant Latina honors students were a true rarity in their high school. Few middle-income Latinos were in honors classes and virtually no immigrant or low-income Latino students were placed in the honors track. The three Latinas in our focus group are in contact with White peers but apparently this interaction is problematic for Whites, who, if they have been in honors classes through high school, may have had little previous contact with Latino students. Conversely, White students who do have consistent contact and friendships with Latino students may be troubled by negative perceptions that some of their White peers express toward Latino students.

∷ Conclusions and Implications

Our findings support both research hypotheses. The two elements of perceived school culture that we examined were indeed important for engagement, and we found these perceptions sometimes differed for our ethnic/class groups. Our most interesting finding in these analyses was that intergroup relations had divergent effects on attitudes toward school. Greater interpersonal contacts across ethnic groups moved attitudes in a positive direction for our low-SES Latino students but in a negative direction for White students. Social psychological theory provides a useful lens for interpreting these contrasting effects in the context of the culture in which the school is embedded.

Social identity theory (Tajfel & Turner, 1986), perhaps the best-known theory of social influence, argues that all people construct their sense of a social self from memberships in groups. Group membership implicitly requires an endorsement of the normative standards of the group as well as a sense of obligation for members of the in-group to fulfill those norms. Thus we would expect our student respondents to respond to intergroup contact in a manner that is normative for their particular in-group, and in our data these normative understandings are an important part of the systems of meanings that comprise the culture of the school. As well, it is reasonable to expect local peer group norms to be influenced by normative standards that exist in the systems of meanings that comprise the larger culture in which the school is embedded (Hudley & Graham, 2001).

In California and in the United States, the goal of language policy has been to transition students from their native language to English as quickly as possible (Hornberger, 1990), and California's Proposition 227 (passed in 1998) mandated that all children in California public schools must be taught in English (Crawford, 1999). An English only philosophy argues that English must become the nation's official and only language to preserve the identity of the United States (Wiley & Lukes, 1996), and this ideology is amply reflected in the qualitative responses from our White, English-speaking respondents. The majority of responses from these students explicitly articulated an English only philosophy; similarly, Latino students' reports suggested that at least some teachers also espoused an English only philosophy. According to our data, such a philosophy is as normative on the high school campus as it is in the broader society, where roughly 60% of respondents to public opinion polls over the past decade have approved of English only in government (e.g., voting) and education (e.g., English immersion programs).

Thus, the normative understanding that U.S. identity is defined by the English language is recapitulated on campus in peer groups and supported by influential adults who similarly link social identity to the normative expectation that peers should speak only English. When students categorize themselves as a member of a group (in this case, Americans who speak English), they are influenced by the norms of that group and maintain group cohesion by positive valuing of the in-group at the expense of any out-groups. Increased contact with peers who are bilingual and speak English intermittently or perhaps have a limited ability to speak English might, according to social identity theory, lead to derogation of the out-group in an effort to maintain group cohesion and positive attitudes toward the in-group (Hewstone, Rubin, & Willis, 2002). Thus, more in-group contact leads to more positive attitudes while greater out-group relationships create more negative attitudes toward school. Marissa and Lindsey amply demonstrate this principle of social identity theory in their comments about their experiences with the soccer team.

Conversely, for Latino students, particularly our low-SES respondents who are predominantly English learners and immigrants from Mexico, intergroup contact might have an entirely different meaning that can be understood as a function of their immigrant status. Particularly for adolescents, prior research suggests that immigrant students realize that how well they speak English also plays an important part in their social status on campus (Tse, 2001). These youth are also acutely aware of the normative demands of the larger society that they transition to English. As they learn English they also learn the normative value that speaking English has over speaking other languages (Daoud & Quiocho, 2005). Thus, our English learners might judge, consistent with social identity theory, that more frequent positive contact with students of other ethnicities would bring them into the peer culture of the school and improve the tools they need to function in the new culture, both in the broader society and at school (language fluency, content knowledge, the ways and mores of U.S. schooling). However, we must also consider the influences that John Ogbu has demonstrated with cultural ecological theory (Ogbu & Simons, 1998). Immigrant minorities typically understand that they have to learn the language and cultural practices of the host society because they have voluntarily come to the United States in the hope of personal advancement. Their desire for intergroup contact is not a repudiation of their cultural identity but a pragmatic strategy for getting ahead. The concept of segmented assimilation (Portes & Rumbaut, 2001) similarly postulates that immigrants can adapt certain norms of the host culture while maintaining home cultural values and practices.

More generally, these findings are consistent with a deep and growing literature that attests to the importance of relationships between teachers and students for academic achievement and motivation (e.g., Bryk & Schneider, 2002; Koplow, 2002). Perceived relationships with teachers seem to strongly influence engagement, whether measured as attitudes or behavior, and teacher relationships had some form of influence on engagement for all students. Peer support also related to attitudes toward school (i.e., affective engagement) for all students, and as discussed earlier, the quality of intergroup relations strongly affected how peer support is enacted in the classroom and on campus. Motivational theorists have long understood that people have the desire to be connected to others, and this desire for affiliation is one of the key motivational constructs that propels engagement (Deci & Ryan, 1987). Affiliation can also represent the positive side of the previously described principle of reciprocal determinism. Students who are positively affiliated with teachers and peers elicit a more positive interpersonal culture that allows relationships to strengthen and deepen, and this cycle should contribute positively to growth in academic engagement and success.

Although different groups of students seem to be influenced in different ways by the relationship (behavioral vs. affective engagement), the importance of relationships stands out, and the implications for schools, teachers, and multicultural education are considerable. Teacher preparation as well as inservice training might profitably focus on motivating students through the power of personal relationships. For example, Ooka Pang (2005) has defined an approach to multicultural education that foregrounds the teacher-student relationship. She characterizes a caring-centered approach to multicultural education as an interpersonal relationship between teacher and students that addresses students' needs with explicit attention to the students' cultural contexts. A caring-centered approach allows teachers to support students where they are, with appropriate respect for their cultural values, resulting in academic success for all children (Ooka Pang, 2005).

Through multicultural education curricula, teachers can not only foster relationships with their students but also develop respectful relationships among students. Such relationships will be supported by incorporating and honoring all students' cultures and backgrounds, and using students' cultural and linguistic knowledge as resources to be shared rather than deficits or barriers to inclusion (Nieto, 2004). This implication is again consistent with principles of social psychological theory on group formation and group dynamics. According to the classic contact hypothesis, hallmarks of positive group relations include equal status contact and cooperation to achieve shared goals (Allport, 1954). However, rather than simple contact, more recent formulations of the theory suggest that friendship and its attendant positive emotions across racial and ethnic lines are particularly powerful in shaping peer norms that value intergroup contact (Pettigrew, 1998). Thus, when teachers provide activities that require cooperative, equal status and continuing contact, the classroom culture may provide a smaller, more intimate setting in which friendships might develop. Research has shown that simply knowing that members of one's group have personal friendships with members of other groups can sometimes predict positive intergroup attitudes (Wright, Aron, McLaughlin-Volpe, & Ropp, 1997) and shift group norms that can have significant influences on school culture and student engagement. Consistent with the contact theory, we also argue that on the high school campus, other adults (counselors, administrators, office staff) also influence school culture as it relates to intergroup relations to the extent that these respected authority figures publicly value and support such systems of belief.

In these analyses we have examined a very specific, some might say narrow, definition of school culture. Our interest in the school engagement and adjustment of immigrant students and English learners has driven the manner in which our analyses have proceeded. As a result of these initial analyses, we will continue to pursue more complex analyses of these data to examine additional dimensions of the school culture (e.g., counselor assistance, course-taking behavior) to determine how they interact with the dimensions of interest in the analyses reported here. However, these analyses add a new dimension to the motivational literature that has studied culture as a phenomenon of individual children, classrooms, and schools by broadening our focus to the culture of the society in which the school is embedded.

∷ Note

We would like to thank the students and staff of our participating high school for their enthusiastic cooperation. We would also like to thank our graduate students, Rosina Wright-Castro, Ted Polanco, and Rachel Hershberg, for their hard work to help bring this project to fruition. This research was funded by a generous grant from the Wells Fargo Foundation.

∷ References

Alexander, K., Entwisle, D., & Kabbani, N. (2001). The dropout process in life course perspective: Early risk factors at home and school. *Teachers College Record, 103,* 760–822.

Allport, G. (1954). *The nature of prejudice.* Reading, MA: Addison-Wesley.

Bali, V. (2001). Sink or swim: What happened to California's bilingual students after Proposition 227? *State Politics & Policy Quarterly, 1,* 295–317.

Bandura, A. (1978). The self system in reciprocal determinism. *American Psychologist, 33,* 344–358.

Blumenfeld, P. (1992). Classroom learning and motivation: Clarifying and expanding goal theory. *Journal of Educational Psychology, 84,* 272–281.

Bowles, S., & Gintis, H. (1976). *Schooling in capitalist America.* New York: Basic Books.

Brantlinger, E. (1993). *The politics of social class in secondary school: Views of affluent and impoverished youth.* New York: Teachers College Press.

Brown, M., Carnoy, M., Currie, E., Duster, T., Oppenheimer, D., Shultz, M., & Wellman, D. (2003). *Whitewashing race: The myth of a colorblind society.* Berkeley: University of California Press.

Bryk, A., & Schneider, B. (2002). *Trust in schools: A core resource for improvement.* New York: Russell Sage Foundation.

Burke, W., & Litwin, G. (1992) A causal model of organizational performance and change. *Journal of Management, 18,* 523–545.

California Department of Education. (2007). *Educational data partnership.* Retrieved from http://www.ed-data.k12.ca.us.

Conchas, G. (2001). Structuring failure and success: Understanding the variability in Latino school engagement. *Harvard Educational Review, 71*, 475–504.

Crawford, J. (1999). *Bilingual education: History, politics, theory, and practice.* Trenton, NJ: Crane.

Cummins, J. (1996). *Negotiating identities:Education for empowerment in a diverse society.* Los Angeles, CA: CABE.

Daoud, A., & Quiocho, A. (2005). I can't see you if I don't know you: How students create inequality. *Multicultural Perspectives, 7(4)* 3–12.

Deci, E., & Ryan, R. (1987). The support of autonomy and the control of behavior. *Journal of Personality and Social Psychology, 53*, 1024–1037.

Dornbusch, S., & Kaufman, J. (2001). The social structure of the American high school. In T. Urdan & F. Pajares (Eds.), *Adolescence and education* (pp. 61–91). Greenwich, CT: Information Age Press.

Ekstrom, R. B., Goertz, M. E., Pollack, J. M., & Rock, D. A. (1986). Who drops out of high school and why? Findings from a national study. *Teachers College Record, 87*, 356–373.

Finn, J., & Rock, D. (1997). Academic success among students at risk for school failure. *Journal of Applied Psychology, 82*, 221–234.

Furrer, C., & Skinner, E. (2003). Sense of relatedness as a factor in children's academic engagement and performance. *Journal of Educational Psychology, 95*, 148–162.

Gambone, M., Klem, A., Summers, J., Aken, T., & Sipe, C. L. (2004). *Turning the tide: The achievement of the first things first education reform in Kansas City, Kansas public school district.* Philadelphia: Youth Developmental Strategies.

Gibson, M., Gandara, P., & Koyama, J. (2004). The role of peers in the schooling of U.S. Mexican youth. In M. Gibson, P. Gandara, & J. Koyama (Eds.), *School connections: U.S. Mexican youth, peers, and school achievement.* New York: Teachers College Press.

Gilman, R. & Anderman, E. (2006). The relationship between relative levels of motivation and intrapersonal, interpersonal, and academic functioning among older adolescents. *Journal of School Psychology, 44*, 375–391.

Gollnick, D. (1992). Understanding the dynamics of race, class, and gender. In M. E. Dilworth (Ed.), *Diversity in teacher education* (pp. 63–78). San Francisco: Jossey-Bass.

Gottfried, A. (1986). *Manual for children's academic intrinsic motivation inventory.* Odessa, FL: Psychological Assessment Resources.

Hewstone, M., Rubin, M., & Willis, H. (2002). Intergroup bias. *Annual Review of Psychology, 53*, 575–604.

Hobby, R. (2004). *A culture for learning: An investigation into the values and beliefs associated with effective schools.* London, UK: Hay Group.

Hornberger, N. (1990). Bilingual education and English-only: A language planning framework. In C. Cazden & C. Snow (Eds.), *Annals of the American Academy of Political and Social Science* (pp. 12–26). Newbury Park, CA: Sage.

Hoy, A., & Hoy, W. (2003). *Instructional leadership: A learning-centered guide.* Needham Heights, MA: Allyn and Bacon.

Hudley, C. (1995). Assessing the impact of separate schooling for African-American male adolescents. *Journal of Early Adolescence, 15,* 38–57.

Hudley, C. (1997). Supporting achievement beliefs among ethnic minority adolescents: Two case examples. *Journal of Research on Adolescence, 7,* 133–152.

Hudley, C. (1998, February). *Urban minority adolescents' perceptions of classroom climate.* Paper presented at the annual meeting of the Society for Research on Adolescence, San Diego, CA. (ERIC Document Reproduction Service No. ED 419 880)

Hudley, C., & Daoud, A. (2007). High school students' engagement in school: Understanding the relationship to school context and student expectations. In F. Salili & R. Hoosain (Eds.), *Culture, motivation and learning: A multicultural perspective* (pp. 365–389). New York: Information Age Press.

Hudley, C., & Graham, S. (2001). Stereotypes of achievement striving among early adolescents. *Social Psychology of Education: An International Journal, 5,* 201–224.

Hunt, K. (2007, April 1). Gingrich: Bilingual classes teach "ghetto" language. *Washington Post,* p. A05.

Kalin, W. (1999). How White teachers perceive the problem of racism in their schools: A case study in "liberal" Lakeview. *Teachers College Record, 100,* 724–750.

Kasen, S. (1990). The impact of school emotional climate on student psychopathology. *Journal of Abnormal Child Psychology, 18,* 165–177.

Katz, S. (1999). Teaching in tensions: Latino immigrant youth, their teachers, and the structures of schooling. *Teachers College Record, 100,* 809–840.

King, J. (1991). Dysconscious racism: Ideology, identity, and the miseducation of teachers. *Journal of Negro Education, 60,* 133–146.

Kitayama, S. (2002). Culture and basic psychological processes—Toward a system view of culture. *Psychological Bulletin, 128,* 89–96.

Koplow, L. (2002). *Creating schools that heal.* New York: Teachers College Press.

Loukas, A., Suzuki, R., & Horton, K. (2006). Examining school connectedness as a mediator of school climate effects. *Journal of Research on Adolescence, 16,* 491–502.

McIntosh, P. (1992). White privilege and male privilege: A personal account of coming to see correspondences through work in women's studies. In M. Anderson & P. Collins (Eds.), *Race, class, and gender: An Anthology* (pp. 70–81). Belmont, CA: Wadsworth.

Miller, J., & Garran, A. (2007). *Racism in the United States: Implications for the helping professions.* Belmont, CA: Thompson Brooks/Cole.

Moos, R. (1979). *Evaluating educational environments.* San Francisco: Jossey-Bass.

Murdock, T. (1999). The social context of risk: Status and motivational predictors of alienation in middle school. *Journal of Educational Psychology, 91,* 62–75.

National Center for Education Statistics (NCES). (2000). *The condition of education 2000.* Washington, DC: U.S. Government Printing Office.

Nieto, S. (2004). *Affirming diversity: The sociocultural contexts of multicultural education* (4th ed.). Boston, MA: Allyn and Bacon.

Ogbu, J., & Simons, H. (1998). Voluntary and involuntary minorities: A cultural-ecological theory of school performance with some implications for education. *Anthropology & Education Quarterly, 2,* 155–188.

Olsen, L. (1997). *Made in America: Immigrant students in our public schools.* New York: New Press.

Ooka Pang, V. (2005). *Multicultural education: A caring-centered, reflective approach* (2nd ed.). Boston, MA: McGraw-Hill.

Portes, A., & Rumbaut, R. (2001). *Legacies: The story of the immigrant second generation.* New York: Russell Sage Foundation.

Patrick, H., Ryan, A., & Kaplan, A. (2007). Early adolescents' perceptions of the classroom social environment, motivational beliefs, and engagement. *Journal of Educational Psychology, 99,* 83–98.

Pettigrew, T. (1998). Intergroup contact theory. *Annual Review of Psychology, 49,* 65–85.

Rains, F. (1998). Is the benign really harmless: Deconstructing some "benign" manifestations of operationalized White privilege. In J. Kincheloe, S. Steinberg, N. Rodriguez, & R. Chennault (Eds.), *White reign: Deploying Whiteness in America* (pp. 77–101). New York: St. Martin's Press.

Rossell, C., & Baker, K. (1996). The effectiveness of bilingual education. *Research in the Teaching of English, 30,* 7–74.

Ryan, A., & Patrick, H. (2001). The classroom social environment and changes in adolescents' motivation and engagement during middle school. *American Educational Research Journal 38,* 437–60.

Skinner, E., & Belmont, M. (1993). Motivation in the classroom: Reciprocal effects of teacher behavior and student engagement across the school year. *Journal of Educational Psychology, 85,* 571–581.

Smerdon, B. (2002). Students' perceptions of membership in their high schools. *Sociology of Education, 75*, 287–305.

Steinberg, L. (1996). *Beyond the classroom.* New York: Simon and Schuster.

Stewart, E., & Bennett, M. (1991). *American cultural patterns: A cross-cultural perspective.* Yarmouth, ME: Intercultural Press.

Suárez-Orozco, C., & Suárez-Orozco, M. (2001). *Children of immigration.* Cambridge, MA: Harvard University Press.

Tajfel, H., & Turner, J. C. (1986). The social identity theory of intergroup behavior. In W. G. Austin & S. Worchel (Eds.), *The social psychology of intergroup relations* (2nd ed., pp. 7–24). Chicago: Nelson-Hall.

Tan, G. (2001). "I want my teachers to like me": Multiculturalism and school dropout rates among Mexican Americans. *Equity & Excellence in Education, 34*, 35–42.

Tatum, B. (1997). *"Why are all the Black kids sitting together in the cafeteria?" and other conversations about race.* New York: Basic Books.

Trueba, H. (1988). Peer socialization among minority students: A high school dropout prevention program. In H. Trueba & C. Delgado-Gaitan (Eds.), *School and society: Learning content through culture* (pp. 201–217). New York: Praeger.

Tse, L. (2001). *"Why don't they learn English?": Separating fact from fallacy in the U. S. language debate.* New York: Teachers College Press.

U.S. Census Bureau. (2000). *American factfinder.* Retrieved from http://factfinder.census.gov/servlet/DTTable?_ts=66248380187.

Wentzel, K. (1997). Student motivation in middle school: The role of perceived pedagogical caring. *Journal of Educational Psychology, 89*, 411–419.

Weinstein, R. (2002). *Reaching higher: The power of expectations in schooling.* Cambridge MA: Harvard University Press.

Wick, P. (1990). *School Attitude Measure.* Chicago: American Testronics.

Wigfield, A., Eccles, J., Schiefele, U., Roeser, R., & Davis-Kean, P. (2006). Development of achievement motivation. In N. Eisenberg, W. Damon, & R. Lerner (Eds.), *Handbook of child psychology: Vol. 3, Social, emotional, and personality development* (6th ed., pp. 933–1002). Hoboken, NJ: Wiley.

Wiley, T., & Lukes, M. (1996). English-only and standard English ideologies in the US. *TESOL Quarterly, 30*, 511–535.

Wilson, W. (1995). *When work disappears: The world of the new urban poor.* New York: Knopf.

Wright, S. C., Aron, A., McLaughlin-Volpe, T., & Ropp, S. (1997). The extended contact effect: Knowledge of cross-group friendships and prejudice. *Journal of Personality and Social Psychology, 73*, 73–90.

Part 3 ⠿
Interventions to Enhance
Academic Motivation

10 ::

Scholar Identity and Academic Achievement in African American Adolescents

Is There a Connection?

Olga M. Welch

When one talks about marginality and otherness one must always ask, marginal to what? other to whom?

— R. FERGUSON

As Ferguson (1993) reminds us, questions about marginality and otherness are difficult to answer, since "the place where power is exercised is often a hidden place" (p. 9). Hanson (1996) also notes that

> expectations are based on knowledge of the real world. For youths in more disadvantaged social positions, these expectations may start out high, but tend to be lowered over time as the youths observe the successes and failures of others like themselves. (p. 160)

In essence, as Bourdieu (1973) has suggested, an unacknowledged selection process occurs in educational systems that ensures a status quo based on categories. These categories ensure that individual talent alone does not guarantee advancement; rather, systems "identify, select, process, classify, and assign individuals according to externally imposed criteria" (Kerckhoff, as cited in Hanson, 1996, p. 160).

In her own study of this phenomenon, Hanson (1996) examined data from the nationally representative High School and Beyond (HSB) survey (NCES, 1986), using a subset of men and women who showed signs of early talent as measured by scores on standardized mathematics and reading tests. She found that when students who demonstrate signs of early talent (1) have educational expectations that fall short of their aspirations, (2) have reduced expectations over time, or (3) are not able to realize their early expectations, a loss of talent occurs. Interestingly, minorities who show early talent and by their senior year of high school expect to earn a college degree are more likely than White youths to attend college. Apparently, ethnic minority students who beat the odds by showing early talent and maintaining expectations for college are less likely to "be cooled out" by an oppressive, hidden selection bias and thus fail to attend college (Hanson, 1996, p. 180).

However, even with the development of several well-intentioned enrichment initiatives to increase minority access to postsecondary education, overall increases in minority enrollment in colleges have not kept pace with that of Whites. The immediate college enrollment rate for White high school completers was roughly 50% between 1972 and 1978 and increased to 68% by 1997, where it has remained. The immediate college enrollment rate for Black high school completers was also roughly 50% between 1972 and 1977, but it reached only 60% by 1998 and has remained steady since then. For Hispanic high school completers, the immediate enrollment rate was not measurably different from 50% in 1972, but it has fluctuated greatly over time. Between 1972 and 2003, the average trend for Hispanics has been flat in contrast to a linear increase for Whites; thus, the gap between Whites and Hispanics has widened (National Center for Educational Statistics, 2005). Moreover, although the high school completion rates for Black and White individuals are essentially the same among adults aged 24 to 34 (85% of African Americans and 88% of Whites), there is currently a 50% dropout rate in many inner-city schools (Conley, 1999). Many discussions of such educational disparities focus on characteristics of students as the source of the problem. Poor and minority children are often characterized as unmotivated, noncompetitive, and culturally disadvantaged products of inadequate families. But such discussions ignore the social and structural barriers that often weigh heavily on these young people and present barriers that are insurmountable for too many.

This brief introduction highlights the importance of understanding the development of an academic identity, particularly for students who experience marginality and otherness. Thus, we began a 9-year longitudinal study, Project EXCEL (Encouraging Excellence in Children Extends Learning). We examined how educationally disadvantaged adolescents (predominantly but not exclusively African American) who had the potential to attend college defined themselves as "scholars" and how that definition related to their achievement. We defined educationally disadvantaged students as those who had the potential and the desire to attend college but faced barriers of low performance and weak educational backgrounds. Like Ferguson (1993), we held that the development of an identity that incorporated academic success for educationally disadvantaged adolescents, particularly those of color, involves issues of marginality and otherness that must be explored if appropriate academic interventions are to be developed. For African American EXCEL students, we viewed the construction of their own scholar identities as a possible counterbalance to the negative messages of Black intellectual inferiority that they might encounter. Other researchers have examined identity construction within students who, whether based on race, gender, class, or ableness, define themselves or are defined as being in the margins of school life (Apple, 1990; Cross, 1991; Hall, 1992; Hudak, 1993; McCarthy, 1990). We situate our work within a construct—scholar identity—which emerged in our own academic development.

As two African American female professors at a large research institution who had been identified early in life as college material, our ability to succeed academically in the face of systemic racial and gender barriers involved the development of a "scholar identity." This scholar identity, which we both trace to adolescence, evolved as a series of negotiations and reconstructions of our identities that we used to counteract stereotypic messages of Black intellectual inferiority and limited career and educational options. The powerful nature of the scholar self in our own academic lives became the catalyst for the 9-year investigation of the relationship between academic achievement and identity construction. The initial study (Welch & Hodges, 1997) placed academic achievement at its center and used McClelland's seminal definition of achievement motivation as the point of departure. McClelland's definition suggests that achievement motivation exists as a "stable personality trait possessed only by those individuals whose culture (including race, environment, child-rearing practices, religious values, and social class) stress competition with standards of excellence" (McClelland, as cited in Castenell, 1984, p. 436). For us, however, this definition fails to account for individuals who succeed academically despite disadvantaged backgrounds. The definition also implies that achievement motivation cannot be cultivated in some populations, even if academic enrichment is provided, thereby calling into question the premise that such enrichment can significantly improve postsecondary admissions for educationally disadvantaged African American adolescents.

:: The Development of a Scholar Identity

Working with three small cohorts (10–13 students) of primarily African American adolescents in two high schools, Project EXCEL examined the development of scholar identity in high school juniors and sophomores who identified themselves and were identified as college bound by teachers and guidance counselors. The first cohort consisted of rising juniors who participated in a university-sponsored enrichment program that emphasized reading, writing, and foreign language study (either German or French). Based on the findings from the pilot study with the first cohort, both the second and third cohorts were composed of rising sophomores.

In designing the full study, we focused on two specific questions. Can a transition program build a scholar identity in educationally disadvantaged African American and European American college-bound students? What combination of subjects and classroom experiences are most critical to the development of a scholar identity? These questions represented our belief that, in addition to pre-college preparation, educationally disadvantaged adolescents had to develop a self-defined scholar identity in order to achieve academically. Even with White adolescents who presumably enjoy unearned privilege (McIntosh, 1992), a scholar identity could not be assumed to develop. This development of self-constructed definitions of scholar became central to all the goals in Project EXCEL.

Moreover, in exploring this concept of scholar identity, we chose to concentrate on students who did not represent those with the highest academic qualifications. Instead, the participants in all three cohorts were those students who expressed a desire to attend college and who exhibited academic promise but did not achieve the grade point averages or standardized test scores generally used as strong predictors of college success. Nor were all of these students economically disadvantaged. Some were the children of college graduates; others had parents and/or relatives who held clerical jobs, worked in construction, or had entry-level managerial positions. Our decision to work with these students was not accidental. Rather, it represented the opportunity to test our tacit theory that the development of an identity grounded in scholarship required not only course work, study skills, and role modeling but also a personal commitment to excellence that emerged through engagement in challenging intellectual tasks and career goal setting. We refer to this commitment as scholar ethos, or an academic identity based on a recognition that exclusion from educational opportunities may be unrelated to either potential or performance.

For EXCEL students to build this identity meant intentionally engaging in individual explorations of the meaning of scholar and scholarship in concert with an academic program of study in reading, writing, and foreign language. We purposefully attended to these literacy components rather than to equally important math, science, or computer studies because of their cross-curriculum application. Success in a post-secondary institution requires the ability to articulate ideas in both oral and written communication in a wide variety of courses. We believed that EXCEL students, armed with these skills and their individually crafted definitions of themselves as scholars and of scholarship, might undertake the "border crossing" activities advocated by Giroux (1992), such as the ability to use formal or informal English depending on the conversational context.

Moreover, this border crossing involved making explicit the culture of power that members of marginalized groups must understand if they are to integrate with mainstream culture without relinquishing their own cultures (Collins, 1993). Certain ways of self-representation, talking, interacting, and writing, for example, can serve to facilitate or hinder individual success within mainstream institutions that are dominated by individuals from the majority culture. Children from middle-class homes tend to do better in school than those from non-middle-class homes because the culture of school is based on the culture of the upper and middle classes of the group in power (Delpit, 1995). Often culture-of-home advocates fail to acknowledge the importance of minority students' access to the culture of power; however, minority parents' resistance to an education that exclusively promotes the culture of home is a stark reminder. We further conjectured that, depending on its use, scholar identity might become a mechanism of student agency for our African American students, since to be a success in America is largely viewed as an aberration for these youth. This social stereotype is grounded in a pathology of racism that skews black ambition; low expectations can both limit and drive black ambition (Edwards & Polite, 1992).

Thus, our African American EXCEL students undertook academic work from which each evolved a personalized construction as a scholar. Their interviews suggested a belief that relinquishing their cultural self was unnecessary for their successful matriculation in schools. Nor did they identify a conflict between the academic self and a cultural self, sometimes called "acting white" (Fordham & Ogbu, 1986). Instead, in concert with increased individual efficacy in reading, writing, and foreign language, for some EXCEL students the scholar identity became part of an identity that confronted messages of academic inferiority and discrimination (Cross, 1991).

∷ Implementation of EXCEL in a Community High School

In our first book (Welch & Hodges, 1997), we described the research design, questions, and findings related to scholar identity and achievement motivation with the first two cohorts of Project EXCEL students who participated in a summer enrichment, university-based program. This chapter focuses on the third cohort of EXCEL students from Augustana High School, who participated in a school-based program implemented throughout the academic year. Although Augustana faculty and counselors had participated in the recruitment of students into Project EXCEL from its inception, this move represented an important change. We wanted to investigate the efficacy of EXCEL as a component of the "regular" college preparatory program at the school.

At the time of the study, Augustana High School was a center city high school. Its population of 670 was 95% African American, with only one English class at each grade level designated honors/college preparatory. Augustana is located in a business district. The major road through this section of town boasts several churches, homes, a middle school from which Augustana derives the bulk of its population, business establishments, nightclubs, and a large subsidized housing development. Some of the nightclubs and the housing development periodically appear in the local newspaper as scenes of violence. At the time of the study, much of the main road was being repaved, making it bumpy and difficult to travel. A local community group was attempting to attract new businesses to the area, and a new convenience store had been built at the corner. Despite this small influx, turnover of new businesses remained high. Even so, some businesses were considered community staples, including a dry cleaner and barbershop that had been in the same locations for 25 years.

Augustana, several blocks down this major road, is the product of a merger that occurred in the early 1970s between an all African American school and an all White school. The school merger resulted in White flight, leaving Augustana with a predominantly Black student body. The school, a large brick building on the right side of the street with trees and grass bordering the sidewalk, is next to a dry cleaner, with a funeral home and residences directly across the street. The school addition, containing a state-of-the-art basketball gymnasium, extends Augustana to the corner, and a large parking lot for faculty and staff is behind a wire fence. Three signs appear in the front yard of the school: two refer to past basketball championships won by the school and the third is a marble sign that says a mind is a terrible thing to waste. Over the main door in the school building a blue sheriff's sign appears next to a yellow sign found in all Clarksville schools about the illegality of carrying firearms.

Prior to implementing the EXCEL program, we held planning meetings with Augustana's administrators, both the principal and the assistant principal of curriculum and instruction. In subsequent faculty meetings, we also talked with college preparatory English and foreign language teachers to identify those who wanted to participate in the study. Augustana's administrators made it clear that teacher participation was voluntary, with no penalties should any teacher choose not to be included in the study. Those teachers who indicated their desire to participate completed the appropriate informed consent forms and were provided with college-level materials in English and French that mirrored those given to first- and second-year students at the local university. All the teachers received inservice training on how to integrate EXCEL activities with those already required in their college preparatory classes. We expected that the EXCEL model would draw on good teaching practices that both beginning and more senior-level teachers from accredited teacher education programs could be expected to know and/or to have implemented in their own classrooms.

In the English classes, EXCEL students completed weekly writing assignments from first-year, college-level literature texts. Students also engaged in small and large group discussions about these selections and were tested on retention of factual knowledge, comprehension of themes and characters, and critical analyses. The tests contained essay as well as short-answer questions so that students became familiar with test formats and response requirements. Since Augustana offered French and Spanish, but not German, a 25-year-old White male who had taught introductory-level German as a graduate student was hired with research funds to teach the German classes for Project EXCEL students and any non-EXCEL students who wished to take the language as an elective. In the French and German classes, teachers were asked to speak the target language as often as possible, requiring students to respond in kind. Rather than concentrating on grammar and syntax exclusively, all students in both the French and German classes also became familiar with German/French culture, history, art, and literature, along with engaging in student-to-student dialogues. Thus, the EXCEL model that systematically implements instructional practice to build a "scholar identity" also provides instruction that has been identified as "best practices" with African American youth (Delpit, 1995; Foster, 1997; Hale, 2001; Irvine, 1990; Ladson-Billings, 1994).

In describing what she perceives as a limitation of researchers' explanations of African American underachievement, Irvine (2001) speaks of their failure to acknowledge appropriately the influence of culture on the teaching and learning processes. She refers to this as "seeing with the cultural eye," or the ability of African American teachers to see themselves not as the reason for the existence of the Black-White achievement gap but rather as one strategy for closing it (Irvine, as cited in Pollard & Welch, 2006, p. 104). Irvine extends this metaphor of sight or vision by asserting that African American teachers view their world and situate their work both professionally and personally within a construct intentionally dedicated to addressing the problem of Black students' underachievement. Thus, she contends that African American teachers regard teaching as telling, guiding, and facilitating the mastery of mandated content standards but they also define teaching as caring, "other mothering," "believing," "demanding the best," and a "calling and disciplining" (Irvine, as cited in Pollard & Welch, 2006, p. 107).

In a real sense, Irvine's theoretical construct of "seeing with the cultural eye" represents a potential interpretation of what we observed in one English classroom containing EXCEL students. In the remainder of this chapter, I describe the findings from one facet of the Project EXCEL study, the examination of the process of identity construction in both EXCEL and non-EXCEL student participants in a 10th-grade honors English course at Augustana High School.

∷ Collecting and Analyzing Data in Honors English

In this English class we sought to understand how students as well as the 10th-grade English teacher interpreted the meanings of and the expectations and motivations related to academic achievement in the class. Such an investigation would allow us to test the role, if any, of scholar identity in the academic achievement of these students. Thus, our broad research question concerning the optimal combination of subjects and classroom experiences was more narrowly defined for this portion of the study. We wondered how EXCEL students in this English class might come to understand and respond to academic expectations. How are the terrains of expectations (with respect to achievement and scholarship) negotiated among everyone in the classroom?

In collecting and analyzing our data we recognized how "the other" is constructed by those who conduct qualitative research and speak "of and for others while occluding ourselves and our own investments, burying the contradictions that percolate at the self-other hyphen" (Fine, 1994, p. 70). We were conscious that despite our shared racial identity with most of the students, we needed self-consciously to "work the hyphen," that is, as Fine (1992) suggests, not to seek to "shelter ourselves in the text, as if we were transparent" (p. 74) but rather to recognize the hyphen between us and the EXCEL participants. To "work between" for us meant collaborating with EXCEL students, their parents, and their teachers in the analysis and interpretation of our data and attempting through that process to resist "othering" even as we accepted that our "work would never 'arrive' but must always struggle 'between'" (Fine, 1994, p. 75).

We chose participant observation as the primary methodology and interviews with EXCEL students and the classroom teacher as secondary sources to emphasize what occurred in the English classroom and the meanings derived from it for the students and teacher. In this chapter, I focus exclusively on reporting the student and teacher comments during the class. Analysis of the data focused on the interaction patterns among all students and the teacher as well as the themes that appeared in discussions. Using key words, concepts, and patterns as brackets, we found that categories as well as related themes emerged. This inductive method of analysis ensured that experiences were not labeled but rather discovered.

The class participants for this phase included 13 EXCEL students and nine non-EXCEL students. All students in the class were African Americans, except one female student and the teacher, who were White. The Project EXCEL students were all categorized as honors and college preparatory students. Our observation data were drawn from interactions related to discussion of text selections from *The Little Brown Reader* (Stubbs & Barnett, 1993), an anthology of essays used in first- and second-year university English classes. To answer our research question, we focused on how knowledge was constructed in the class and how participants perceived themselves and their experiences as they worked through the material.

The English classroom was on the second floor of the school at the end of the hallway. The hallway was painted pale blue, the floors were clean, and the lights in the room bright. Brown metal lockers, with and without locks, lined the hallway. The class met in Room 213 from 8:45 to 9:50 A.M. In the class, the emphasis was on college preparatory reading and writing assignments, and instruction was handled by one teacher, Ms. Young. This White female, about 40 years old with over 10 years' experience, had been transferred into Augustana as part of the board of education plan to integrate faculty across the city. The teacher evaluated and graded written work based on each student's academic level, but in discussions all students were encouraged to express their opinions, all of which were given equal weight. While these discussions were central to classroom activity and the interactions among students and teachers, in-class papers, role play, small group activities, and journal writing were other instructional strategies.

⠶ Major Themes

The major themes that emerged centered on the classroom functioning as a community of respect. This community of respect facilitated respect for self and others (Theme One), supported the expression of opinions (Theme Two), and encouraged the establishment of identities (Theme Three). The data suggested that a community of respect existed in the 10th-grade honors English class at Augustana High School. However, what occurred between the teacher and students was also influenced by what occurred outside the classroom. The following discussion, drawn from analysis of the data, focuses on how each of the three themes was enacted in the class.

Respect for Self and Others

Ms. Young considered her placement at Augustana an opportunity to work with students whom she considered misrepresented as academically incapable. Attention to issues of respect for self and others was a priority, as reflected in the patterns of interaction that occurred between the English teacher and the students. Initially, the respect was reflected in the greetings by name exchanged by the teacher and students at the beginning of each class. The significance of this ritual to the development of a community of respect was illustrated in a series of exchanges between Ms. Young and students before the class began.

Cynthia (one of the non-EXCEL honors students) arrives in class and observes, "Ms. Young, you not at the door." Luke (a Project EXCEL student) comes and asks about the last papers the students submitted. Ms. Young tells him they are in one of the trays next to the door. Cynthia repeats her earlier comment, adding, "Good morning. Ms. Young, You're not at the door." Ms. Young responds, "I'm looking something up." Clearly, a ritual of greeting students by name and handling pre-class problems had been established in the classroom. Whenever that ritual was violated, the students in the class noticed and commented.

During class discussions, Ms. Young also demonstrated respect for students by asking questions that invited a wide range of opinions and also by sharing her own opinions with the students. This aspect of community was illustrated clearly in a discussion on faith related to one of the readings. The teacher and students had written in their journals and then began to talk about their experiences and opinions. Ms. Young shared two incidents in her life but reminded students, "[This] is my own perspective; respect that, don't treat it as gospel, just that way for me." After her comments, four EXCEL and two non-EXCEL students expressed their opinions about the role of faith in their lives and questioned other students in the class and each other. As the discussion developed, the teacher reminded the students about the expectation of respect for others: "Let me interject, when we go over this section on religion...feelings [can] get hurt [if you're not sensitive]. When you make comments...everybody has to be respectful." At this point, Rachelle (EXCEL) says, "Oh, did I say it mean or something?"

Rachelle mentions that talking about religion is like talking about race. Ms. Young says, "Ya'll have been real good about not being rude. When we're discussing religion, we need to be extra careful." Another student, Linda (non-EXCEL), a practicing Jehovah's Witness, discussed the tenets of her faith in a polite conversation with the other students. Much later in the discussion, Ms. Young brought up the Crusades and jihad. Rufus (non-EXCEL) asked what the teacher's definition of jihad was, and Ms. Young replied, "Holy war." Rufus responded that it meant to struggle. Ms. Young answered, "I've been misinformed...thank you, Rufus."

This was typical of discussions observed in which the teacher and students shared a wide range of experiences without apparent strain and discomfort. In the choice of language, Ms. Young's expectation of respect for self and others was reflected as she thanked students for contributions to the discussion, apologized to them when she believed she had wronged them, and included "please" with any request, even reminders of inappropriate behavior (e.g., "Ya'll listen, please"). Frequently, both Ms. Young and the students would say, "Excuse me," implying that people were talking and not listening to what was being said.

Ms. Young was equally clear about the expectation that people would demonstrate respect rather than disrespect for others. Often she could be heard saying, "We don't do that in this classroom" when students made comments that could be categorized as put-downs, or personal arguments, or laughing at or making fun of one another. On three occasions, Ms. Young asked students to leave the room when they got into personal arguments with each other. She also interjected the words "Be respectful" which seemed to imply a rule and expectation for both the students and herself. In turn, the students' behaviors suggested that they had internalized this rule, as they raised their hands to speak, listened to the opinions of others whether they agreed or disagreed, and addressed each other by name. In interviews, Ms. Young made several observations about respect in class discussions.

> I want them to learn to respect each other, I mean me, of course, too, but to respect each other. Well, just as I would want to give them the respect for their opinions, I want other people in the class to do the same thing. Now whether you agree with their opinions or not, you need to let them say what's on their minds and we don't put each other down, we don't tell each other to "shut up," and if someone says something that you disagree with, it's okay to disagree but don't put them down because you disagree. And, those are our general guidelines for discussions at the beginning of the year and after a while they get into it and they understand. I think that they like that. Well, you can't have a learning environment, if you don't have respect, I don't think.

These comments, in concert with the class observations, suggested that the expectation of respect for self and others was a core value that Ms. Young had deliberately set about to model and to require of the students. In turn, respect for self and others contributed to the community of respect by facilitating thinking and expressing differing and occasionally controversial opinions (by both students and the teacher).

Expression of Opinions

A second theme that emerged revealed that community respect facili-tated the expression of a wide range of opinions on a variety of topics. Much of the class discussion grew out of the articles in *The Little Brown Reader*. One of these discussions centered on the prison system and grew into a spontaneous role play in which several students spent time in a cell while other students asked questions. After class, Rachelle approached the teacher and said, "Great discussion. We love this class." Ms. Young re-sponded, "I thought you all said you didn't like it." Rachelle looked, ges-tured toward the work on the board, and said, "We don't like all that."

Students did not hesitate to convey their opinions and thoughts to Ms. Young (e.g., Rufus's explanation of the word *jihad*). For example, in a discussion of the Studs Terkel essay, "Three Workers," which described the experiences of a prostitute, Regina (EXCEL) believed the word *inti-macy* meant to have sex. Two other female students and Ms. Young em-phasized that the word could also mean sharing innermost thoughts. As the discussion progressed, Regina went to a dictionary while Suzanne (EXCEL student) looked up the word in her thesaurus, both without prompting from the teacher.

Still another example involved the discussion of the Confederate flag. Rachelle and other students stated that it symbolized slavery. Ms. Young explained that when she was growing up the flag symbolized the South for her but that she had been enlightened. Ms. Young also asked the students if they felt pride in being from Tennessee and they responded, "No." Toward the end of the discussion of the flag and other examples related to issues of free speech, Ms. Young said:

> All I want you [to understand] (pause) [It's a] hard time talking
> about difficult subjects. Basically what I want you to see (pause)
> [there are] so many gray areas. Everybody agrees this is okay, this
> is not...draw a line in what you think about it, not black and white
> related to freedom of speech.

Later she added, "This has been a difficult class period, but you all have been real patient." In a follow-up interview the teacher had this to say about the discussion:

> I found out a lot about them, you know, when I said, "Don't
> you feel pride being from the South and being from Tennessee?"
> and they were like, "Well, no." I was astounded, absolutely

astounded. It was a very difficult discussion. The kids handled it pretty well. I thought, you know, they could have turned on me easily and I knew where I was going with that and that was a possibility, and I felt like they stuck with me that day at times when it was very difficult and I appreciate it but it was hard on all of us.

Another example of differing opinions expressed within the community occurred in a discussion of work, welfare, and child support. At one point in the discussion, Alisha (non-EXCEL student), Shanda (EXCEL student), and a chorus of other female students became involved in a heated argument about mothers who work, go to school, and spend time with their children. Alisha told the other girls across to shut up, and they retorted that she had an attitude. The girls' statement seemed aimed at reminding Alisha of the rule that differing opinions could be expressed without censure. At another point, Tommy (EXCEL student) was trying to add his opinion to discussion and twice said, "Excuse me" when he was interrupted. Ms. Young reinforced Tommy's right to speak with "He has the floor."

Although grammar was not emphasized in the honors curriculum, Ms. Young reviewed grammatical problems that she found in the students' papers. She also talked about the importance of grammar on the writing test required in all 11th-grade Advanced Placement classes in the state. However, as Ms. Young assisted students in developing and refining their writing skills, she emphasized respect for their opinions. As she handed back each paper, she mentioned to the students that most of her comments appeared on the front rather than in the body of the paper and that the papers did not take as long to grade as previous efforts (demonstrating that their mastery of grammar and punctuation was improving). Quietly, she added, "Please don't take it as I'm putting you down" and emphasized that she wanted to help them develop strengths in writing while working on weaknesses. She cited Shanda's feedback on two occasions that students needed more positive feedback on their work than they were receiving from the teacher. In the follow-up interview, Ms. Young reflected on her response to Shanda:

Well, I wanted her to know that I listened to what she said to me and I didn't want to take up class time in the first instance because she was angry, and this could have degenerated into a "You don't like me" kind of thing, and I didn't want it to degenerate to that. I wanted to diffuse that and say, "Well, we need to talk about that later." I knew she probably was not going to come back, but if she did I would have talked about it to her privately and probably apologized that I didn't put a positive comment on her paper. Since she didn't, I felt like the next time I gave out papers that it would be a good thing for her to hear me say "I heard you and I'm sorry," and now she's away from the anger but it also empowers her…it empowers her when she feels that she has been slighted and can say "I've been slighted." And that is important in life.

In the class, respect for differing opinions appeared to support students' freedom and self- confidence to express their ideas and permitted them to practice appropriate ways to respond to those with whom they disagreed.

Establishment of Identity

The community of respect also appeared to facilitate identity construction among the students. This finding emerged most strongly when students were asked to read aloud their papers about identity, followed by a student-led discussion about the issues that they confronted as they prepared the papers. The assignment required students to discuss in a creative essay how their identities had changed during the years. Several said they were more confident and had matured. For the oral presentations, students stood at a podium while the teacher sat at her desk and admonished the rest of the class to "demonstrate your utmost respect for your classmates." Several phrases and quotes reflect the students' perceptions of the changes in their identities.

> REGINA (EXCEL): "I have learned to speak and think about others…and stopped being so hostile."
> RICHARD (EXCEL): "I am interested in going other places," "have a greater urge to compete," "comfortable arguing with caution."
> ROGER (EXCEL): Doesn't "sit in the corner like in the eighth grade," "plays sports and talk on the phone more," not too many people like his friends, but he does "because they are my people," "take nothing from no one."
> DIANE (EXCEL): "I am a Black woman who has achieved a lot, loves and gets along better with her mother."
> JULIUS (EXCEL): "learned to go places he never thought about"
> LUKE (EXCEL): "interested in mind states, not identities. Identities are superficial."

CYNTHIA (non-EXCEL): "I have more confidence...expressing myself more...and doing what is best for me."

LINDA (non-EXCEL): "I'm more interested in what is out there on other planets. My hopes and dreams are my identity."

Students applauded at the conclusion of the feedback, and Ms. Young encouraged the class to continue to take stock of themselves and their goals. "[It's a] good way to give yourself a pat on the back."

Identities Related to Community of Respect

Two of the three discussions that occurred in the classroom suggested that student perceptions of identity were closely related to the community of respect. One discussion focused on the different ways that Augustana and its students are represented in Clarksville. Keely said, "I understand that we're a Black school...put us on TV...[there is] more going on." Ms. Young suggested that being a Black school and having more television exposure were not necessarily connected and encouraged Keely not to think of herself or of the school negatively. Keely responded, "That's not how I was making..." (and was interrupted by other students' verbal affirmations). Ventura added, "People down our school, expect us to do bad stuff." She mentions specifically how the school is presented on television. Ventura also discussed how "bad kids" were sent to Augustana, those who were frequently involved with the juvenile justice system. Shanda expressed similar sentiments.

Ms. Young asked, "How can you change the school's image?" The students offered examples of positive activities occurring at the school, including the science fair, and Ms. Young mentioned that she had seen the names of students in the class and from the school in the local newspaper. Another student countered that the school was mainly recognized for its athletics (football and basketball teams). Luke continued by pointing out that when Ryan (a school that began as all White and later became interracial—60% White and 40% Black—and had been closed 2 years ago) was open, all that was discussed about either school was their rivalry in athletics, not academics. Ms. Young introduced the topic of academic identity, observing that in the first 2 years she taught at Augustana, no male senior qualified academically to become "Mr. Augustana," an award given for academic excellence. Glancing pointedly at a group of male students, she added, "I know we have kids who will qualify."

The discussion continued with issues of power, representation, and action becoming topics. The students expressed frustration with how little had been accomplished by the current class officers. Nicole said that voting for class officers to address Augustana's image problem was "favoritism to me." Luke replied, not loudly but clearly, "I did not vote." Ms. Young said, "I know you feel powerless at times" but questioned whether the students would want teachers rather than themselves to select candidates or officers. The class began to brainstorm ways that they could increase class activities. Luke mentioned wanting to go to on field trips as a possibility, and Victoria voiced her desire to make a senior trip. Again, students blamed sponsors and officers who did not appear to be taking responsibility. To help the students think of the problem differently, Ms. Young asked, "Shanda, you play basketball. What would you do if someone on the team mishandled the ball?" Shanda replied, "Get it." Luke and Shanda noted that other people might take the credit for their initiative and for the work, but Ms. Young emphasized the importance of the end result. Luke talked about "getting started" and field trips. In an authoritative voice, Victoria turned to him and said, "Pay first, then get buses." As the discussion moved to other activities, Nicole asked if the students could have a meeting of "the whole 10th-grade class" in Ms. Young's room, and Ms. Young replied, "Yes...I am happy to help you, I want you to do well and to have things for yourselves." Until the bell rang, the students formed committees.

In the follow-up interview, Ms. Young expressed similar frustration about Augustana's and the students' images:

> I think the population at large sees Augustana as a failure as far as schools are concerned. I think they associate Augustana with violence and ignorance. I just want it to be perceived as another high school in the county. I mean it's that simple. I feel the kids sometimes see themselves the way Clarksville at large sees Augustana, not the [one section of the city] but Clarksville at large. And I have had many experiences where I have gone to people and they say where do you teach? And I say Augustana, and they go, "Oh," you know like, "I feel so sorry for you."

In addition to demonstrating how the students moved from discussion to action, this vignette also reflects a shared dissatisfaction with the representations of the school and its students as well as the actions students might take to secure ownership of a more positive identity and better opportunities for themselves.

⬛ Conclusions About EXCEL: The Meaning of Success

Nieto (1996) has presented conditions that define a successful student. These include (1) remaining in school and planning to complete high school or recently graduated, (2) achieving well although not necessarily at the top of the class, (3) motivated and engaged in school, (4) planning effectively for the future, (5) able to critically analyze their own school experiences and those of their peers, and most important, (6) describing themselves as successful. Applying Nieto's conceptual framework to our own data, the students who participated in EXCEL can be considered successful. All graduated from high school and attained the necessary grades to attend college if they so chose. A major criterion for EXCEL involved the desire to go to college and a minimum GPA of 2.5 when the student entered the program. In addition to demographic and transcript information, students were asked to write about their future college aspirations as well as their reasons for wanting to be considered for EXCEL.

Over the 3-year period for Cohort #3, in classroom observations and interviews, we learned that the students enjoyed their school experiences and had no difficulty identifying and critiquing the systemic school and community barriers they believed contributed to ineffective instruction in their classes. In the 10th-grade English class and particularly in their observations of instruction in their 12th-grade Advanced Placement English class, they described their school experiences and how those experiences affected their perception of teacher expectations relative to their own achievement. In the follow-up interview conducted 1 year after graduation from high school, all of the EXCEL students offered suggestions about how their school experiences could have better prepared them for either college or the world of work. In most cases these discussions centered on the inadequate academic preparation they had received in high school (e.g., insufficient mathematics and science course offerings).

The EXCEL students were also well aware of the barrier of largely negative community perception of their school and its effects on the school's academic resources. As one student commented in an interview, "Shipley, Holt, Sharp, and Thompson [other schools in the community with low black enrollments] get publicity that tends to be positive. When they talk about Augustana, they mention shooting and fighting." Another student remarked during a discussion of a newspaper article comparing Augustana with its peer schools. "They put less money in black schools. We have a new gym but other parts of the building are crumbling. The families at Shipley, Holt, Sharp, and Thompson have more money and get more done for their schools than people in this school."

By focusing on scholar identity we hoped to understand how it might contribute to academic achievement in our participants in spite of the barriers that they faced. Most important, those who developed scholar identity described themselves as successful. "[Being a scholar means] a mature way of looking at things like schoolwork...like you have to be on top of your schoolwork, pay attention in class, be respectful to teachers and classmates...a professional type attitude." Students also mentioned leadership ability and self-respect as a part of that identity. While some of our participants did not develop a scholar identity, those who did tended to complete college, military, or job training. Although our data cannot speak to a causal relationship between scholar identity and achievement, we believe that explorations of these kinds of personal adaptations that might contribute to school success can be useful because families, schools, and communities together can influence such conditions for success (Nieto, 1996).

▪ Beyond EXCEL: The Centrality of Effective Pedagogy

An unanticipated but powerful finding from our study of the EXCEL program on a regular high school campus was the importance of teachers in facilitating student success in a very challenging environment. We presented the 10th-grade classroom because our data suggest that Ms. Young fits Irvine's description of an "experienced and masterful pedagogue" who is "seeing with the cultural eye" (Irvine, 2001). Collins (1991) called adults who felt a sense of personal attachment to the low-income African American students they taught "other mothers" or teachers who adopted hundreds of students each year. In Ms. Young's class, building a community of respect meant reminding the students consistently of classroom expectations as well as the teacher's absolute belief in their ability to achieve at a high level. The teacher-student dialogues we recorded suggest that Mrs. Young felt a sense of "ownership" for the students' progress and the kind of investment in that progress that the term *other mothering* would seem to embody.

Teaching Is Believing and Demanding the Best

Irvine (2001) suggests that teachers who are committed to the achievement of African American students also exhibit persistence and resilience in their practice. "In the face of obstacles and seemingly overwhelming odds against them, these teachers do not give up on their students; they have confidence in their ability to teach and they believe their students can learn" (p. 250). For all of the students in the English honors class, challenging academic assignments and the expectation that the students would and—more important—could complete those assignments appears to confirm the importance of effective and creative instruction for supporting student success (Irvine, 2001). These findings remind us of the strong empirical links among teacher efficacy, student achievement, and students' attitudes toward school.

As our data suggest, in Ms. Young's class the expectation of excellence was communicated, particularly in her insistence on mutual respect (e.g., the exchange with Rufus regarding "Holy war") and her often repeated phrase, "We don't do that in this classroom" whenever students made statements that could be construed as rude or argumentative. Demanding the best from educationally disadvantaged students can be especially difficult since they remain burdened by many factors beyond their control, including inadequately equipped schools lacking the resources to offer the experiences that are routinely provided to better prepared students. Their undeveloped potential continues to be neglected because of grade point averages that do not rank in the top 10% or scores on standardized tests that do not exceed the norms. Moreover they are sometimes, but not always, restricted by lower income levels that prohibit them from taking advantage of supplementary programs and materials to improve their skills. However, both the EXCEL and non-EXCEL students received messages of respect for their potential conveyed by Ms. Young's demand for their best, particularly in an honors class. This message was especially important, given the reality that African American students are sometimes educated in an environment in which they are constantly told to achieve but too often experience assaults on their competence.

Teaching as Disciplining

Vasquez (1988) called teachers who are strong but compassionate disciplinarians "warm demanders"—committed, respectful, dedicated, and competent educators who are not afraid, resentful, or hostile toward their pupils. Ms. Young demonstrated her belief in the students by modeling respect for them and, in turn, requiring them to display the same respect for each other:

> I want them to learn to respect each other, I mean, me, of course too, but to respect each other…just as I would want to give them the respect for their opinions, I want other people in the class to do the same thing.

With both EXCEL and non-EXCEL students, Ms. Young had created a shared environment that was shaped by respect. Although aware of the pressure and prejudices that circumscribe the wider community's perceptions of them and Augustana, the students also saw themselves as worthy of respect. The expression of differing opinions fostered during class discussions assisted them in learning to understand each other and the emergence of each evolving identity. However, what occurred in the classroom was influenced not only by this community of respect but also by what occurred outside the classroom. Our data suggest that future research should more closely investigate the interface between the school community and the larger community within which it is situated and how that interface influences students' continued identity construction.

The Larger Community

This chapter presented a conversation between the EXCEL students and Ms. Young about the different ways Augustana and its students were represented in Clarksville. In the course of the discussion, the students suggested that because Augustana was a "Black" school, its exposure in the media was disproportionately negative, with the inference that "bad kids," that is, those who were frequently involved with the juvenile justice system, were the ones who matriculated at Augustana. Moreover, because of this perceived population, there was a tendency to expect the worst from students. The students also recognized that the school was mainly considered a sports academy because of the success of its football and basketball teams. However, students also noted that this image was partially the result of apathy on the part of the students toward academic excellence. For example, they expressed frustration with how little had been accomplished by the class officers they had elected. They also blamed sponsors who did not facilitate the kind of activist agenda they felt was needed to change Augustana's image with internal and external constituencies.

Recall that Ms. Young also suggested in a follow-up interview that the image of Augustana within the larger community was tied to "violence and ignorance." Comments by Ms. Young and the EXCEL students suggest an awareness of the barriers that low expectations pose for students who seriously engage in academic pursuits at Augustana. Our findings underscore those presented by other studies suggesting a link between student perception and academic achievement among Black adolescents. However, we also found that students, whether EXCEL or non-EXCEL, did not identify with this larger community that attempted to stereotype and marginalize them, even though they lived and were educated there.

This identity illustrates Hudak's concept of marginalized representation, which is adopted from the work of Foucault (1988) in which the constitution of identity is not a matter of choice but rather is a process imposed by the culture, society, and social group within which the individual is situated. Hudak describes his participants' strategies for conducting themselves within socially established limits that marginalized them. For those who are excluded or ostracized, constructing an identity at the margins that permits them to survive in contexts where they are powerless is an act of "radical social action" (hooks, 1990). For both the Excel students and non-Excel students in Ms. Young's class, constructing an identity to counter the existing narrative that ostracized them and their school provides one example of Hudak's survival strategies.

Similarly, as adolescents from marginalized groups complete the normative developmental task of identity development, they do so in a mainstream culture that may view them unfavorably, and for African American youth in particular the task is especially complicated because they have arguably been most heavily stigmatized and marginalized (Blinder, 2007; Spencer & Dornbush, 1990). Therefore, the developmental tasks of academic achievement and social responsibility require these youngsters to develop strategies for negotiating in settings that question their ability to succeed. One strategy, we believe, is the development of a resilient, scholar identity that, consistent with resilience theory (Masten, 1990), allows them to successfully adapt despite risk and adversity. For these African American youngsters, academic resilience is connected with successful formation of an identity as a competent scholar.

Finally, we agree with others that too much research has tended to focus on the academic failure of African American students (Thernstrom & Thernstrom, 1997). Smith, Gilmore, Goodman, and McDermott (1993) suggest that we now see a "failure of failure." "Once we recognize that the task of schooling is not to explain which students do or do not learn, learning becomes easy for most. This will require the dismantling of the elaborate apparatus we have erected for documenting the failures of our children and redirecting the energies taken by that enterprise into organizing more learning" (p. 19).

Thus, although our overall study may provide some insight into the role of scholar identity in academic achievement, we are concerned that in focusing on individual success alone, we may be inadvertently contributing to a body of literature that "blames the victim" (i.e., the students who do not succeed academically). We are concerned that our research might inadvertently support policies that make academically unsuccessful students "casualties of educational systems that cannot 'see' them" (Nieto, 1996, p. 19) because their problems remain personal, unconnected to the larger structural barriers they confront. Thus, the data from this phase of Project EXCEL underscore the need to continue research on the dynamics of social and cultural relations as well as the representations of self that exist in school settings. Further, we argue for investigation of the impact of such dynamics on the construction of a scholar identity as a central component of academic achievement.

∷ Notes

Portions of this chapter were reprinted by permission from *Making Schools Work: Negotiating Educational Meaning and Transforming the Margin* by Carolyn R. Hodges and Olga M. Welch. © 2003 Peter Lang, New York. All rights reserved.

The author acknowledges with appreciation her EXCEL research collaboration with Dr. Carolyn Hodges, Dean of the Graduate School and Vice-Provost for Graduate Studies, University of Tennessee.

∷ References

Apple, M. W. (1990). *Ideology and curriculum* (2nd ed.). New York: Routledge.

Apple, M. W. (1993). Constructing the "other": Rightist reconstructions of common sense. In C. McCarthy & W. Crichlow (Eds.),

Race, identity and representation in education (pp. 24–39). New York: Routledge.

Bourdieu, P. & Passeron, J. C. (1973). Cultural Reproduction and Social Reproduction. In R. K. Brown (Ed.), *Knowledge, Education and Cultural Change.* London: Tavistock.

Castenell, L. (1984). A cross-cultural look at achievement motivation research. *Journal of Negro Education, 53,* 435–443.

Collins, P. H. (1991). Black feminist thought: Knowledge, consciousness, and the politics of empowerment. New York: Routledge & Kegan Paul.

Collins, R. L. (1993). Responding to cultural diversity in our schools. In C. McCarthy & W. Crichlow (Eds.), *Race, identity and representation in education* (pp. 115–208). New York: Routledge.

Conley, D. (1999). Being *Black, Living in the Red: Race, Wealth, and Social Policy in America.* Berkley, CA: University Press.

Cross, W. E., Jr. (1991). *Shades of black: Diversity in African-American identity.* Philadephia: Temple University.

Delpit, L. (1995). Other people's children: Cultural conflict in the classroom. New York: New Press.

Edwards, A., & Polite, C. K. (1992). *Children of the dream: The psychology of black success.* New York: Doubleday.

Ferguson, R. F. (1993). Outcomes of mentoring: Healthy identities for youth. *Journal of Emotional and Behavior Problems 3*(2), 19–22.

Fine, M. (1994). Working the hyphen: Reinventing self and other. In M. K. Denzen & Y. S. Lincoln (Eds.), *Handbook of Qualitative Research* (pp. 70–82). Newbury Park, CA: Sage.

Foucault, M. (1988). *Technologies of the self: A seminar with Michael Foucault.* Amherst: University of Massachusetts Press.

Fordham, S., & Ogbu, J. (1986). Black students' school success: Pragmatic strategy or pyrrhic victory? *Harvard Educational Review, 58*(1), 54–84.

Foster, M. (1997). *Black Teachers on Teaching.* New York: The New Press.

Giroux, H. A. (1994). *Between borders: Pedagogy and the politics of cultural studies.* New York: Routledge.

Giroux, H. A. (1992). *Border Crossings: Cultural Workers and the Polictics of Education.* New York; London: Routledge.

Goetz, J. P., & LeCompte, M. D. (1984). *Ethnography and qualitative design in educational research.* New York: Academic Press.

Hale, J. E. (2001). *Learning while Black: Creating educational excellence for African American children.* Baltimore, MD: John Hopkins University Press.

Hall, S. (1992). Cultural studies and its theoretical legacies. In Gossberg, Nelson, & Treichler (Eds.), *Cultural studies* (pp. 227–294). New York: Routledge.

Hanson, S. L. (1996). *Lost talent: Unrealized educational aspirations and expectations among U.S. youths.* Philadelphia: Temple University Press.

Hatch, J. A. (1985). *Naturalistic methods in educational research.* Paper presented at the meeting of the Centro Interdisciplinario de Investigacion y Docencia en Educacion Tecnica, Queretaro, Qro. Mexico.

hooks, b. (1990). *Yearning: Race, gender, and cultural politics.* Boston, MA: South End Press.

hooks, b. (1994). *Teaching to transgress: Education as the practice of freedom.* New York: Routledge.

Hudak, G. M. (1993). Technologies of marginality: Strategies of stardom and displacement in adolescent life. In C. McCarthy & W. Crichlow (Eds.), *Race, identity and representation in education* (pp. 172–187). New York: Routledge.

Irvine J. J. (2001). *Caring, Competent Teachers in Complex Classrooms.* Washington, D.C.

Irvine J. J. (2001). *Educating Teachers for Diversity: Seeing With the Cultural Eye.* New York: Teachers College Press.

Irvine, J. J. (1999). The education of children whose nightmares come both day and night. *Journal of Negro Education, 68(3),* 244–253.

Kozol, J. (1991). *Saving inequalities.* New York: Crown.

Ladson-Billings, G. (1994). *The Dream Keepers: Successful Teachers of African AmericanChildren.* San Francisco: Jassey-Bass, Inc.

Lipman, P. (1998). *Race, class and power in school restructuring.* New York: State University of New York Press.

Lorde, A. (1984). *Sister outsider: Essays and speeches.* Freedom, CA: Crossing.

Masten, A. S. et.al. (1990). Resilience and development: Contributions from the study of children who overcome adversity. Development and Psychotherapy 2, 425–444.

McCarthy, C. (1990). *Race and curriculum:* London: Falmer.

McCarthy, C., & Crichlow, W. (1993). Introduction: Theories of identitiy, theories of representation, theories of race. In C. McCarthy and W. Chrichlow (Eds.), *Race, identity and representation in education* (pp. xiii–xxix). New York: Routledge. McClelland, D. C. (1953). *The achievement motive.* New York: Appleton-Century-Crofts.

McIntosh, P. (1992). White privilege and male privilege. A personal account of coming to see correspondences through work in women's studies. In M. L. Andersen & P. H. Collins (Eds.), *Race, class, and gender: An anthology* (pp. 359–376). Belmont, CA: Wadsworth.

National Center for Education Statistics (2005). Digest of Education Statistics. Washington, DC: U.S. Department of Education.

Nieto, S. (1992). *Affirming diversity: The sociopolitical context of multicultural education.* New York: Longman.

Nieto, S. (1994). Lessons from students on creating a chance to dream. *Harvard Educational Review, 64*(4), 392–426.

Nieto, S. (1996). *Affirming diversity: The sociopolitical context of multicultural education* (2nd ed.). New York: Longman.

Oakes, J. (1985). *Keeping track: How schools structure inequality.* New Haven, CT: Yale University.

Ogbu, J. (1978). *Minority education and caste: The American system in cross-cultural perspective.* New York: Academic Press.

Ogbu, J. (1998). Class stratification, race stratification, and school. In L. Weis (Ed.), *Class, race and gender in American education.* Albany: State University of New York Press.

Pollard, D. S., & Welch, O. M. (Eds.). (2006). *From center to margins: The importance of self-definition in research.* Albany: State University of New York Press.

Spencer, M.B. (1986). Risk & Resilience: How Black Children Cope With Stress. Social Science, 71(1) 22–26.

Spencer, M. B. & Dornbush, S. M. (1990). Challenges in studying minority youth. In S. Feldman and G. Elliott (Eds.), at the threshold: The developing adolescent (pp. 123–146). Cambridge, MA: Harvard University Press.

Stubbs, M. & Barnett, S. (1992). *The Little Brown Reader.* Addison Wesley Publishing Company.

Thernstrom, S. & Thernstrom, A. (1997). Skills, Tests, and Diversity. America in black and white, one nation, indivisible: Rage in Modern America (p. 352). New York: Simon & Schuster.

U. S. Department of Education, National Center for Education Statistics. (1996). *The condition of education, 1996* (NCES 96–304). Washington, DC: Author.

Vasquez, J. A. (1988). Contexts of Learning for Minority Students. Educational Forum, 52, 243–253.

Waxman, H. C., Padron, Y. N., & Gray, J. P. (Eds.). (2004). *Educational resiliency:Student, teacher, and school perspectives.* Greenwich, CT: Information Age.

Welch, O. M., & Hodges, C. R. (1997). *Standing outside on the inside: Black adolescents and the construction of academic identity.* New York: State University of New York Press.

Welch, O. M., & Hodges, C. R. (2003). *Making schools work: Negotiating educational meaning and transforming the margins.* New York: Peter Lang.

Welch, O. M., Hodges, C. R., & Warden, K. (1989). Developing the scholar ethos in minority college-bound students: The vital link. *Urban Education, 24*(1), 59–76.

Wexler, P. (1992). *Becoming somebody: Toward a social psychology of school.* Washington, DC: Falmer.

11 ⠶

Peer-Assisted Learning

An Academic Strategy for Enhancing Motivation Among Diverse Students

Marika Ginsburg-Block, Cynthia Rohrbeck, Nancy Lavigne, and John W. Fantuzzo

Theorists propose that socialization experiences with peers have a powerful influence on both student academic motivation and achievement (e.g., Piaget & Inhelder, 1972; Wentzel, 1999). The mechanism by which social experiences give rise to learning likely involves cognitive, behavioral, and motivational channels. From a Vygotskyian perspective, learning is a social enterprise, which may be enhanced further through peer models operating within comparable *zones of proximal development* (Vygotsky, 1978). Behaviorally, peer-led instructional strategies promote greater opportunities for active learning by providing active roles for students such as tutor or evaluator (e.g., Ginsburg-Block & Fantuzzo, 1997) as opposed to passive recipient. Also consider the process of social motivation. When peer influences provide students with positive messages about academic accomplishments, changes in school culture are likely to occur whereby students increasingly accept academic values and pursue learning tasks and goals leading to enhances in achievement (Wentzel, 1999).

Peer-assisted learning (PAL) refers to peer-led strategies that focus on academic content, such as dyadic peer tutoring (e.g., Greenwood, Maheady, & Delquadri, 2002) and small group cooperative learning (e.g., Johnson & Johnson, 1989). The effectiveness of PAL in promoting both academic and affective outcomes has been illustrated in the empirical literature (e.g., Ginsburg-Block, Rohrbeck, & Fantuzzo, 2006; Rohrbeck, Ginsburg-Block, Fantuzzo, & Miller, 2003), demonstrating particular promise for students traditionally at risk for poor school outcomes (e.g.,

Haynes & Gebreyesus, 1992). Although mechanisms reflecting social-emotional learning seem likely to underlie PAL's success, its effectiveness has been measured mainly in terms of academic outcomes. PAL appears to bring together both strong academic learning strategies and strong social-emotional strategies, addressing academic learning needs while simultaneously enhancing social-emotional outcomes for students. A recent research synthesis examining social, emotional, and behavioral outcomes of PAL has confirmed that PAL strategies are indeed effective in promoting each of these outcomes (Ginsburg-Block et al., 2006). Several causal mechanisms were suggested that involve motivational processes, including the use of structured roles, opportunities for autonomy, group contingencies, and individualized evaluation procedures, yet academic motivation was not specifically included as an outcome variable.

This chapter provides a review of the theoretical and empirical basis for considering PAL as an intervention to enhance student motivation. The research literature offers multiple definitions of PAL, but for this chapter, discussion of PAL includes peer-led strategies that focus on academic content. We exclude primarily nonacademic peer-mediated strategies, such as peer counseling or peer mentoring, that are often included in discussions of PAL (Ginsburg-Block, Rohrbeck, Fantuzzo, & Lavigne, 2006; Topping & Ehly, 1998). However, student-led cooperative learning strategies are included in our definition. In some instances, cooperative learning approaches have been excluded from definitions of PAL; this is probably because in their generic form they may simply include small group instructional arrangements that lack peer-led interaction (Topping & Ehly, 1998).

Motivation is considered in the context of peer-assisted learning as both an independent and a dependent variable. With motivation as an independent variable, we present research linking motivational strategies commonly found in PAL (e.g., opportunities for autonomy) to student outcomes. With motivation as a dependent variable, we present research examining academic motivation as an outcome of PAL. Results of a meta-analysis of experimental studies examining the effects of PAL interventions on the motivation of elementary students are also offered. In this case, motivational outcomes have included motivation as a global construct as well as subject-specific motivation. PAL is also discussed as an intervention for promoting motivation among diverse youth from both a theoretical and an empirical standpoint. Several evidence-based PAL programs shown to promote motivation are described, including reciprocal peer tutoring and cooperative learning. The chapter concludes with implications for future research.

⠙ Theoretical Basis for PAL's Effectiveness

Multiple theories have been proposed to explain the success of PAL. These theories rely on cognitive, behavioral, and social-emotional explanations. Developmental theorists including Vygotsky, Piaget, Bandura, and others have proposed that social processes play a key role in cognitive development (Bandura, 1977; Piaget & Inhelder, 1972; Vygotsky, 1978). According to Vygotsky, peer-assisted learning activities promote cognitive development because same-age children are most likely operating within the same *zone of proximal development* or learning potential and are better able to learn from one another than independently or from an adult (Crain, 1992; Slavin, 1990). Piaget also saw great educational value in social interactions, particularly those between peers, where an atmosphere of equality results in optimal learning. Piaget hypothesized that the benefit of social learning accrues from cognitive conflict and exposure to differing perspectives, resulting in a reexamination of one's own ideas. This mechanism leads to higher levels of reasoning and learning (Crain, 1992; Webb & Palincsar, 1996). Similarly, the work of Bandura and others on social learning theory suggests that observational learning, particularly from peer models with whom children most identify, results in the adoption of new behaviors, which constitutes evidence of learning (Crain, 1992; Schunk, Hanson, & Cox, 1987).

Modern researchers exploring the mechanism by which social processes give rise to cognitive processes (e.g., Webb & Palincsar, 1996) have also emphasized the academic value of enabling children to explain or teach concepts to one another. Empirical evidence supporting these theories shows that peer tutors actually display more gains than the students they teach (Greenwood, Carta, & Hall, 1988) and that providing explanations as opposed to simple feedback on the accuracy of a response increases students' retention of information (Webb, 1985). It appears that PAL facilitates cognitive restructuring among peers with somewhat comparable cognitive structures as these students discuss and challenge each other's ideas over a period of time (e.g., Foot & Howe, 1998). Regardless of the precise mechanisms, theories and research in the literature on cognitive development support the cognitive role that peers play in learning.

From a behavioral perspective, PAL strategies appear to enhance task engagement, resulting in positive student outcomes. Social learning necessarily requires more active engagement in the learning process, providing more varied tasks for students (e.g., presenting information, providing feedback) than traditional learning arrangements that place the teacher in the active role and students in a more passive one. Ginsburg-Block and Fantuzzo (1997) compared the interactions of elementary students who were experienced and inexperienced in PAL. Students experienced in PAL were indeed significantly more actively engaged in academic activity than their inexperienced peers. Consistent with the literature on academic learning time (Gettinger, 1989), academic engagement in this study was linked to greater achievement in mathematics. Greenwood and colleagues have also found that peer-mediated as opposed to teacher-led instruction produces a greater variety of academic responses in students (Greenwood et al., 1984). Both observational and experimental studies of PAL provide evidence that academic interactions among peers promote student engagement in learning in terms of both quantity and quality.

While cognition and behavior seem amenable to peer influence and may explain how PAL leads to academic outcomes, motivational explanations may actually provide a glimpse at the underlying processes that enable cognitive and behavioral changes to take place. In the context of PAL, both social motivation and intrinsic motivation seem to play key roles. Consistent with theories of social motivation (Wentzel, 1999), it has been suggested that PAL encourages the adoption of pro-academic norms (Slavin, 1990), an aspect of school culture. The use of group contingencies, often found in applications of PAL, may further aid in establishing pro-academic norms by reinforcing academic behavior and learning at the group rather than the individual level. The group's best interests reside in ensuring the learning of each of its members. In contrast, traditional reward structures (e.g., individualistic, competitive) can promote competition among students and may create a classroom environment or school culture in which academic achievement is not promoted by the peer group (Slavin, 1990). In a traditional classroom context, successful students are likely to be interested in lessening their competition whereas the least successful students who are rarely reinforced for their efforts may be interested in preserving their self-esteem or social status. Either scenario may result in anti-academic norms and behaviors, particularly for marginalized students. Empirical evidence supports the notion that social learning opportunities may introduce pro-academic social motivation that results in greater academic engagement, and this process may be reinforced by classroom arrangements such as group contingencies. An experimental study conducted by Fantuzzo, King, and Heller (1992) showed that group (versus individualistic) reward contingencies administered in the context of reciprocal peer tutoring resulted in better student behavior as reported by classroom teachers.

Concerning intrinsic motivation, PAL with its opportunities for active social learning may be inherently more appealing to students than teacher-led instruction. At the root of this appeal are the many strategies employed by PAL that represent student-centered instruction, a concept that has been linked to student motivation (e.g., Ryan & Deci, 2000). These theoretically important, student-centered motivational practices include (1) individualizing the curriculum on the basis of student instructional levels (e.g., Daly, Martens, Kilmer, & Massie, 1996), (2) establishing mastery goals for students based on individual improvement (rather than group norms) (e.g., Ames, 1992; Schunk, 1996), (3) scaffolding learning as opposed to imposing rigid or unstructured learning opportunities (e.g., Fantuzzo et al., 1992; Koestner, Ryan, Bernieri, & Holt, 1984), and (4) providing students with opportunities for autonomy (e.g., Stipek, 1996).

Both self-determination theory and achievement goal theory are helpful for linking these instructional practices to intrinsic motivation. Self-determination theory posits that the degree to which students are intrinsically motivated is related directly to fulfilling three needs: competence, relatedness, and autonomy (Ryan & Deci, 2000). PAL, with its use of student-centered learning practices, likely contributes to intrinsic motivation by meeting all three of these needs. Achievement goal theory draws attention to the purpose of achievement as it is defined in the classroom, offering *mastery* and *performance* goals as two contrasting achievement goal constructs (Ames 1992). A mastery goal is focused on improving learning with the belief that academic effort will result in achievement. Conversely, a performance goal is concerned with doing better than others, reflecting the belief that ability leads to success. Empirical studies have linked mastery goals to increases in adaptive academic behaviors such as on-task behavior (Butler, 1987), positive attitudes toward learning (Ames & Archer, 1988), task persistence (Elliot & Dweck, 1988), self-efficacy, and motivation (Schunk, 1996). Conversely, performance goal orientation has been linked to task avoidance (Elliot & Dweck, 1988) and attributing failure to lack of ability (Ames & Archer, 1988). Student-centered instructional practices employed by

PAL support mastery goals through attention to the structure of classroom tasks, authority, and evaluation.

Research Examining Motivational Components as a Causal Mechanism

Evidence exists to support an argument that cognitive, behavioral, and motivational processes all contribute to the effectiveness of PAL strategies. Consistent with the theme of this volume, in this chapter we focus closely on the evidence supporting motivational processes as a pivotal causal mechanism in PAL's effectiveness. Although the general instructional literature has linked student-centered learning practices to motivational and academic outcomes in the classroom (e.g., McCombs, 1993; Ryan & Deci, 2000), two recent meta-analyses of controlled studies of PAL explored the relationship between socially and intrinsically motivating PAL components and academic and nonacademic outcomes for elementary students. The first meta-analysis (Rohrbeck et al., 2003) included 81 studies evaluating PAL's academic effects; the second (Ginsburg-Block, Rohrbeck, & Fantuzo, 2006) included 36 studies evaluating PAL's social, self-concept, and behavioral effects. Results of these research syntheses showed small to moderate effects for PAL across academic, social, self-concept, and behavioral outcomes. Given the extreme variability in effects across individual studies included in these meta-analyses, the overall effect sizes were considered less meaningful than the study of individual moderators (Shadish & Haddock, 1994). Key findings exploring the role of moderators are presented here as they relate to the role of motivational processes in PAL.

Supporting the role of social motivation in PAL, results of these empirical research syntheses showed that PAL strategies employing interdependent group reward contingencies were associated with significantly greater academic, social, and self-concept effects for students than PAL strategies employing individual or no reward contingencies (Ginsburg-Block, Rohrbeck, & Fantuzo, 2006; Rohrbeck et al., 2003). These findings were congruent with the cooperative learning literature (e.g., Johnson & Johnson, 1989; Slavin, 1990) suggesting that the role of social motivation in peer learning is true for both cooperative learning arrangements (i.e., small group) and peer tutoring (i.e., dyadic) arrangements. In addition, based on this collective literature, group reward contingencies appear to strengthen pro-academic norms among students, thereby reinforcing the social motivational processes underlying PAL.

Intrinsically motivating PAL components examined in this series of meta-analyses were also linked to academic and nonacademic student outcomes. First, structured (rather than unstructured or rigid) PAL interventions that provided roles for students yielded significantly greater social and self-concept gains but not academic effects for their participants (Ginsburg-Block, Rohrbeck, & Fantuzo, 2006; Rohrbeck et al., 2003). These findings were consistent with the research on informational classroom structures, in which students have a clear understanding of teacher expectations. Work on classrooms has repeatedly linked structure to higher levels of intrinsic motivation, perceived competency, exploration, and self-worth (e.g., Koestner et al., 1984; Ryan & Stiller, 1991). It is plausible that informational structures typical of PAL strategies enhance students' feelings of competence, which leads to greater levels of intrinsic motivation. Although there is reason to believe that structure would also be associated with academic outcomes in PAL, the meta-analytic findings are not conclusive; additional research is needed to further examine whether these relationships are indeed indirect, operating through student motivation.

Second, meta-analytic results showed that individualized as opposed to common curricula provided in the context of PAL were linked to greater social outcomes for students, including student self-reports and peer nominations of social competence (Ginsburg-Block, Rohrbeck, & Fantuzo, 2006; Rohrbeck et al., 2003). Similarly, research on classroom instruction has shown that curricula matched to students' individual instructional levels provides opportunities for self-directed learning and increases in students' mastery of academic skills (Daly et al., 1996). It is possible that individualizing curriculum materials in the context of PAL and allowing students to work at their own pace may reduce social comparison among the students. In a classroom setting relatively free of social comparison, students may feel more socially efficacious and judge their peers more positively, thus producing measurable social gains. Additional research is needed to test this hypothesis and to better understand findings relating social outcomes to a more individualized curriculum.

Third, PAL evaluation strategies emphasizing student task mastery were associated with academic, self-concept, and behavioral effects twice as large as those for PAL programs employing evaluation strategies based on normative performance (Ginsburg-Block, Rohrbeck, &

Fantuzzo, 2006; Rohrbeck et al., 2003). These findings support previous achievement motivation studies that have shown the benefit of
using evaluation procedures based on individual improvement and
mastery of material rather than traditional competitive models based
on comparison and norm-based performance (e.g., Ames, 1992; Stipek,
1996).

Finally, the largest intervention effects by far were seen in PAL
studies incorporating greater versus fewer opportunities for student
autonomy. PAL interventions with more student self-management (e.g.,
self-evaluation, self-reward) produced academic, social, and self-concept
effects three times greater than interventions with less self-management.
Both theory and research on the benefits of self-management support
these PAL specific findings. Theoretically, autonomy plays a key role in
the development of students' academic intrinsic motivation. According
to self-determination theory, intrinsic motivation is dependent in great
part on fulfilling one's need for autonomy (Ryan & Deci, 2000). Similarly,
achievement goal theory emphasizes the use of student self-directed
learning as an instructional strategy to promote classroom mastery goal
orientation, which has been linked to motivational gains (Ames, 1992;
Ames & Archer, 1988).

An earlier review of 42 experimental studies of classroom-based
self-management strategies (Fantuzzo & Polite, 1990) found a positive
relationship between the degree of self-management employed in the
intervention and the treatment effect size. Schunk (1996) found that
fourth-graders who were provided with opportunities to engage in self-
evaluation in the context of a learning environment that emphasized effort over ability evidenced increases in their academic skills, self-efficacy,
motivation, and task goal orientation. In the context of PAL, students
who are given opportunities to perform self-management tasks such as
setting their own goals, monitoring and evaluating their own performance, and selecting and administering their own rewards are likely to
have more opportunities to practice their skills with peers, feel more efficacious, and be more intrinsically motivated, which together may lead
to greater task engagement and student achievement outcomes. Overall,
two recent meta-analyses examining the relationship between socially
and intrinsically motivating PAL components and student outcomes
support the idea that motivational processes play an important role in
PAL (Ginsburg-Block, Rohrbeck, & Fantuzo, 2006; Rohrbeck et al., 2003).
Consistent with both motivational theories and research, it appears that
both social and intrinsic motivation may contribute to cognitive and

behavioral engagement in PAL, indirectly resulting in positive academic outcomes.

✳ Motivation as an Outcome of PAL: A Meta-analysis

The two recent meta-analyses (Ginsburg-Block, Rohrbeck, & Fantuzo, 2006; Rohrbeck et al., 2003) showed small to moderate effects for PAL across academic, social, self-concept, and behavioral outcomes for elementary students while pinpointing the likely role of key social and intrinsically motivating components of PAL. However, motivation was not examined as an outcome of PAL. We now turn to a meta-analysis of 15 studies that measured elementary student motivation as an outcome of PAL (Ginsburg-Block & Rohrbeck, 2007).

Fifteen group comparison studies of the effects of PAL on elementary student motivation were identified through a database search of the Psycinfo and ERIC online databases for abstracts included from the inception of the databases (1966) through 2000. Abstracts identified through this search were then screened for meeting these inclusion criteria: (a) used elementary students as participants, (b) focused on a student-led peer-assisted learning (PAL) strategy, (c) were implemented in a school, (d) applied PAL to an academic subject(s), (e) reported a motivation outcome, (f) included an actual evaluation of the PAL intervention, (g) used either an experimental (i.e., random assignment of individuals or groups to treatment conditions) or quasi-experimental (i.e., nonequivalent) group design, and (h) used an intervention that lasted for at least 1 week.

Categories and codes were developed for independent and dependent variables of interest. Independent variables were dichotomized so that comparisons between groups could be made. Demographic characteristics of the sample that were coded included minority status (coded as either less than 50% of the sample was minority or 50% or more of the sample was minority), income status (coded as either less than 50% of the sample was low income or 50% or more of the sample), and school setting (urban or suburban/rural).

Categories for motivational components of the PAL interventions included interdependent group rewards (versus no rewards), structure (versus no structure), individualized curriculum materials (versus common group curriculum materials), individualized evaluation procedures (versus normative group comparisons), and opportunities for autonomy (less or more autonomy). Interventions with 0–2 opportunities for autonomy were considered to have less autonomy, while those with 3 or more (out of 5 coded) were considered to have more autonomy. Autonomy opportunities were only coded in the presence of reward contingencies and included student goal selection, reward selection, monitoring performance, evaluating goal attainment, and administering rewards.

Three general categories of motivational outcomes were identified based on the target of student motivation, including motivation for school (e.g., liking school/classroom), motivation for the content area (e.g., enjoyment of mathematics), and motivation for learning in general (e.g., interest in academic activities). Satisfactory interrater reliability was established for each category and code ranging from 79% to 100% ($M = 92\%$).

Effect sizes (i.e., standardized mean differences between treatment and comparison conditions) were calculated for all outcome variables measuring motivation in each study. We computed Hedges g_u, which is the difference between treatment and comparison group scores divided by the pooled standard deviation of the two groups (Hedges, 1981). ESs were calculated so that a positive effect size indicated a favorable outcome for the intervention group. Table 11.1 includes information about the demographic and motivational features of each study, along with an effect size for each of the motivation outcomes reported. Four studies reported on the effects of PAL on motivation for school, while nine studies reported on motivation for a particular content area and three studies reported on motivation for learning in general. Note that one study reported outcomes for two motivational categories.

Motivation effects varied across studies, ranging from –.28 (moderately negative) to 1.0 (highly positive), with 11 studies reporting positive effects, one study reporting no effect, and three studies reporting negative effects for PAL. Of the studies reporting positive effects, six reported large effects (i.e., above .50), two reported moderate effects (i.e., ranging from .30 to .50), and three reported small effects (i.e., ranging from .10 to .30) (Cohen, 1977).

Analysis of the magnitude and direction of effects revealed that the use of interdependent reward contingencies stood out as a potentially effective moderator. Positive effects were achieved for seven of eight studies employing such reward contingencies whereas positive effects were achieved for only three of six studies without these reward contingencies. Studies with more motivational components (e.g., individualized curriculum materials) also tended to yield higher effects than studies with fewer motivational components. The average effect size for the five studies with three or more components was large (.56); the average effect size for the nine studies with fewer than three motivational components was small (.21).

These findings largely provide support for PAL as a strategy for enhancing student motivation. Greater attention to incorporating motivational strategies within PAL, such as the use of interdependent group reward contingencies, individualized curriculum materials and evaluation strategies, structured roles for students, and opportunities for self management, appears to yield greater motivational outcomes among elementary students. In particular, the link between the use of interdependent group reward contingencies and motivational outcomes was apparent, likely supporting the important role of social motivation in PAL. Replication of these findings with a larger sample of studies will lend greater support to the generalizability of these findings to the PAL literature as a whole.

Studies conducted with vulnerable student groups were associated with greater motivation effects, consistent with the findings reported in recent meta-analyses examining PAL's academic, social, self-concept, and behavioral effects (Ginsburg-Block, Rohrbeck, & Fantuzo, 2006; Rohrbeck et al., 2003). The average motivation effect size for the three studies conducted with predominantly (i.e., greater than 50%) minority students was moderate (.41); the average effect size for the six studies conducted with fewer (i.e., less than 50%) minority students was small (.25). Similar findings were found for studies conducted with students schooled in urban versus suburban or rural settings, with effect sizes of .44, (a moderate effect) and .20, (a small effect), respectively. A similar, but less dramatic trend was seen for studies conducted with children from low-income versus middle- and higher-income families. These findings suggest that PAL may be more effective in promoting motivation among vulnerable student groups. Again, replication of these findings with a larger sample of studies would lend greater support to the generalizability of these findings to the PAL literature as a whole.

‖ PAL as an Intervention for Diverse Youth

Given the seemingly universal importance of peers as social influences on student motivation and achievement, why might the effectiveness of PAL differ across student groups? For example, in evaluations of

Success for All, a schoolwide prevention program employing PAL and aimed at improving academic achievement, the largest effects have been found for children at the greatest risk of academic failure (Durlak, 1995). A likely explanation of the superior effects demonstrated by minority, low-income, and urban students may be PAL's integration of both social-emotional and academic components (Ginsburg-Block, Rohrbeck, & Fantuzo, 2006; Rohrbeck et al., 2003). For students who are particularly vulnerable to disengaging from school, instructional practices like PAL that work at the systems level to enhance the school culture around learning are likely to produce greater effects on indicators of school engagement such as motivation.

When peer interactions such as those encouraged by PAL strategies provide students with positive messages about academic accomplishments, students may be more likely to accept the values of the school and pursue academic tasks and goals. In schools, peer socialization toward achievement is particularly important for high-risk children who may be receiving conflicting messages from home, school, and peers about both their own competence and the value of schooling. In addition to creating social motivation for achievement, the success of PAL methods has also been attributed to the continuity that PAL creates between the culture of the school and the child's home culture. For example, some scholars have hypothesized that the cooperative approach to learning may explain the effectiveness of PAL with African American and Latino students because cooperative strategies are more consistent with the value of communalism (i.e., a commitment to social connectedness) whereas U.S. school culture more typically values individualism and competitiveness (Ellison, Boykin, Tyler, & Dillihunt, 2005; Rothstein-Fisch, Trumbull, Isaac, Daley, & Perez, 2003). The proposed mechanisms by which both social motivation and continuity between home and school culture contribute to enhancing student motivation in the context of PAL are examples of how culture and academic motivation may be interrelated.

Both social and intrinsic motivational processes seem to provide a foundation for PAL's effectiveness in allowing students to engage in learning. Once students accept pro-academic messages and become engaged in the learning process, PAL's behavioral and cognitive mechanisms may further support learning resulting in enhanced achievement effects. Thus, for students with fewer risk factors who are more likely to be engaged in learning at the outset, the effects of PAL may not appear as dramatic as they do for students at risk for academic disengagement.

Collectively, the results of the meta-analysis presented in this chapter and those of the previous meta-analyses are consistent with the recent emphasis in the educational literature on social-emotional learning as a strategy for improving student achievement. Empirically based models of academic achievement have suggested that student characteristics, such as social skills, likely share both direct and indirect relationships with achievement outcomes (DiPerna, Volpe, & Elliott, 2001; Zins, Bloodworth, Weissberg, & Walberg, 2004). In contrast to those who have portrayed PAL as a progressive strategy that may bolster affective gains while sacrificing academic gains (Chall, 2000) or those who suggest that certain implementations of PAL may in fact highlight the disparities between student groups (Rubin, 2003), data generated by the recent meta-analytic studies of PAL support its use with minority, low-income, and urban elementary children.

⠅⠅ Evidence-based PAL Programs

Two specific PAL strategies associated with moderate to large effects on motivation for elementary students are reciprocal peer tutoring (RPT; Ginsburg-Block & Fantuzzo, 1998; Heller & Fantuzzo, 1993) and cooperative learning (CL; Brush, 1997; Johnson, Brooker, Stutzman, Hultman, & Johnson, 1985; Slavin, Leavey, & Madden, 1984). These strategies are presented as examples but are not exhaustive of the PAL literature.

Reciprocal Peer Tutoring (RPT)

RPT, developed by Fantuzzo and colleagues (e.g., 1992), employs same-age student pairs of comparable ability, unlike strategies that rely on mixed-ability pairing strategies, with the primary objective of keeping students actively engaged in academic activity. RPT was specifically developed for dyads of low-achieving urban elementary students. This strategy has been applied primarily to elementary mathematics instruction in the areas of computation and problem solving with children in grades 3 through 6 (Ginsburg-Block, Rohrbeck, Fantuzzo, & Lavigne, 2006).

While RPT provides numerous opportunities for student self-management, the roles of both students and the classroom teacher are critical. Classroom implementation of RPT involves preparation, teamwork training, RPT training, and supervision of the RPT intervention

(Fantuzzo & Ginsburg-Block, 1998). Preparation activities include the development of curricular materials, such as flash cards and drill sheets, and the assessment of student skill levels. Training involves approximately five 45-minute sessions during which students become familiar with teamwork as well as with the specific procedures for RPT. Sessions are held twice weekly for 30–45 minutes and have been implemented for periods of 10 weeks to 5 months with positive results (Ginsburg-Block, Rohrbeck, Fantuzzo, & Lavigne, 2006).

Each session of RPT includes a 20-minute, student-led, problem-solving practice session in which students alternate between the roles of teacher and student. The student teacher presents his or her student with flash cards selected to match the skill areas in which the student needs strengthening (as determined through curriculum-based assessments). Each flash card has a problem on one side and the answer and solution steps on the reverse side. Students solve these problems on a structured worksheet divided into sections: Try 1, Try 2, Help, and Try 3. The student teacher provides the student with performance feedback and provides assistance after two unsuccessful attempts while the student is encouraged to attempt the problem a total of three times (Ginsburg-Block, Rohrbeck, Fantuzzo, & Lavigne, 2006).

This problem-solving session is followed by the completion of individualized problem drill sheets (i.e., matched to student instructional levels), which are traded and scored within the student dyad. Dyads then compute a team score based on the scores of both team members. Team scores are compared with student-selected team goals to determine whether the team has met its goal and won for the day. Students select their own goals from a set of limited choices that reflect improvement from their baseline performance. After a predetermined number of wins, teams earn their rewards. A list of acceptable rewards is compiled by the classroom teacher and usually consists of special privileges rather than tangible items. Student dyads select their desired reward from those available choices (Ginsburg-Block, Rohrbeck, Fantuzzo, & Lavigne, 2006).

The operative components of RPT include structured peer interactions, an interdependent group reward contingency, and peer-led instruction. Each component appears to provide a unique and significant contribution to the effectiveness of RPT. In component studies conducted by RPT's developers, the informational structure used by RPT was linked to higher levels of academic and behavioral competence in students, the group reward contingency was linked to higher conduct reports from classroom teachers, and active reciprocal peer instruction was linked to achievement gains (Fantuzzo & Ginsburg-Block, 1998).

In addition, two controlled studies (See Table 11.1) demonstrated PAL's large effect on intrinsic motivation for learning among urban elementary school students (Ginsburg-Block & Fantuzzo, 1998; Heller & Fantuzzo, 1992). RPT has been successfully implemented with low-achieving urban students as a pullout program, with entire classrooms of students, and with English language learners. Extensive experimental research supports RPT's effectiveness, yielding impressive results in the areas of achievement, self-concept, behavior, and motivation (Fantuzzo & Ginsburg-Block, 1998).

Cooperative Learning (CL)

In cooperative learning, the objective is to engage groups of learners in accomplishing mutual learning goals. The classroom teacher provides students with a learning task followed by small group work. Students in each group work through the task until all group members successfully understand and complete it. CL is most suitable when learning goals or mastery and retention of material are essential, a task is complex, problem solving or higher level reasoning strategies are required, creativity is desirable, or high-quality performance is expected (Johnson & Johnson, 1994).

While the precise instructional format varies from model to model, all CL models are based on five core components. *Positive interdependence* refers to the two main responsibilities of students engaged in cooperative learning: to learn the material and to make certain that all group members learn the material. This is achieved through a combination of goal interdependence, in which the group is working toward a common group goal, and reward interdependence, in which each group member receives a reward when the group achieves its goals. *Face-to-face interaction* allows group members to encourage and assist each other reach group goals by using feedback, challenging each other's ideas, and sharing materials and results. *Individual accountability* requires each member of the group to provide an individual contribution. Keeping groups small, testing students individually, randomly calling upon individual group members to respond, closely monitoring groups, assigning roles to each member, and having each member teach a partner

TABLE 11-1. Summary Information on Demographic Characteristics and Intervention Components for Interventions in Meta-Analysis (N = 15)

STUDY	DEMOGRAPHICS	INTERVENTION COMPONENTS	Tx n[a]	SCHOOL ES[b]	CONTENT ES	LEARNING ES	ALL ES
Brush (1997)	40% minority 75% low SES urban	individualized curriculum, group evaluation, group reward (less autonomy), structure	44	.	.86	.	.86
Gardner (1978)	75% minority urban 75% low SES urban	group curriculum, no reward, structure	52	-.28	.	.	-.28
Ginsburg-Block & Fantuzzo (1998)	89% minority 100% low SES urban	individualized curriculum & evaluation, group reward (more autonomy), structure	13 pairs	.	.	1.0	1.0
Heller & Fantuzzo (1993)	100% minority 85% low SES urban	individual curriculum & evaluation, group reward (more autonomy), structure	26	.	.	.51	.51
Jacobs et al. (1996)	unknown	group curriculum, individual & group eval., group reward (less autonomy), no structure	135	.	.28	.	.28
Johnson et al. (1985)	suburban	group curriculum, no reward, structure	28	.	.74	.	.74
Manning & Manning (1984)	33% low SES	individual curriculum, no reward, no structure	103	.	.57	.	.57

Study	Demographics	Treatment	Tx n[a]				ES[b]
Moskowitz et al. (1983)	6% minority 0% low SES suburban	group curriculum, no reward, no structure	147	0.0	0.0	.	0.0
Peterson & Janicki (1979)	rural	group curriculum, no reward, no structure	49	.	.14	.	.14
Peterson et al. (1981)	rural	group curriculum, no reward, no structure	48	.	-.10	.	-.10
Slavin & Karweit (1981)	rural	group curriculum & evaluation, group reward (less autonomy), no structure	212	.30	.	.	.30
Slavin et al.— Study 1 (1984)	20% minority 0% low SES suburban	individual curriculum, group evaluation, group reward (less autonomy), structure	147	.	.55	.	.55
Slavin et al.— Study 2 (1984)	45% minority 50% low SES suburban	individual curriculum group evaluation, group reward (less autonomy), structure	192	.	-.14	.	-.14
Wright & Cowen (1985)	25% minority 0% low SES suburban	group curriculum, no reward, no structure	40	.30	-.03	.	.14
Zahn et al. (1986)	urban 33% minority	group curriculum, individual evaluation, group reward (less autonomy), no structure	164	.	.	.09	.09

[a] Tx n = sample size of the treatment group. [b] ES = unweighted effect size using Hedges G_u formula.

263

are strategies used to maintain individual accountability in CL. *Interpersonal and small group skills* may be challenging or foreign to many students. Training, practice, and reinforcement is necessary to ensure that students acquire and use the skills necessary for working together in a group. Finally, *group processing* is a technique used in CL to improve group effectiveness. This may involve group members discussing how well the group worked together, identifying what worked well and what did not, and making decisions about how to continue (Johnson & Johnson, 1994). What follows are brief descriptions of four specific CL strategies that have yielded moderate to large effects on motivation among elementary students, based on the meta-analysis presented in this chapter.

Learning Together (LT)

Learning Together (LT), developed by the Johnsons at the University of Minnesota, engages groups of four to five students in a group assignment with an interdependent group reward contingency. In LT, each group completes an assignment together and returns one product to the teacher. Students are then tested individually and their scores are averaged. The group total is compared to a predetermined criterion score to determine the group's grade. Praise and rewards are provided at the group level (Yager, Johnson, Johnson, & Snider, 1986). Brush (1997) found that LT produced large effects on student content area motivation in mathematics in the context of work employing an integrated computer learning system.

Academic Controversy (AC)

Academic Controversy (AC), another cooperative learning strategy developed by the Johnsons, uses intellectual conflict to enhance student learning (Johnson & Johnson, 1995). This method involves five distinct steps: (1) Students develop a set of arguments in favor of a position, (2) each student presents his or her argument, (3) the group discusses the positions, (4) students reverse their positions and present the case for the opposing position, and (5) students relinquish all positions and work to reach a consensus position. The work of Johnson and colleagues (1985) has linked AC to large effects on student motivation for content area learning in science.

Student Team Learning

Student Team Learning consists of several methods (two of which are described here) developed by Slavin and colleagues at Johns Hopkins University. All methods use team rewards, individual accountability, and equal opportunities for success based on individualized performance expectations for student improvement rather than normative achievement levels (Slavin, 1990). Student Teams–Achievement Divisions (STAD) uses heterogeneous groups of four members who work together over three to five class periods. The learning sequence consists of teacher presentation of a lesson, teamwork that encourages mastery of material for all members, and finally individual quizzes on the material. Points are assigned on the basis of individualized performance expectations, which enables all students to be successful, regardless of ability level. Teams earn rewards on the basis of the total points earned by all group members. Several controlled studies have demonstrated moderate effects of STAD on student motivation for both school in general (Slavin & Karweit, 1981) and content area learning in mathematics (Jacobs, Watson, & Sutton, 1996).

Team-Assisted Individualization (TAI)

Team-Assisted Individualization (TAI) was designed specifically for mathematics instruction in grades 3–6 (Slavin, 1990). TAI shares the teaming and reward features of the STAD method; however, it also incorporates an individualized instruction component and comes with instructional materials. Students are placed individually in an instructional sequence according to their skills, and they complete the units at their own pace. Team members check one another's practice problems and provide assistance. Final unit tests are taken individually and used to determine team point totals. In a study by Slavin et al. (1984 — study 1), TAI produced large effects on motivation in mathematics.

Overall, CL has been applied across all academic content areas; across grade levels, including preschool and graduate school; with diverse populations of learners, including students with disabilities, those at risk for school failure, bilingual, and gifted students; and across educational settings, including regular and special education classrooms, after-school programs, and nonschool educational programs (Johnson &

Johnson, 1994). Cooperative learning environments result in better social acceptance and social competence, mental health, and self-esteem compared with competitive and individualistic settings. CL experiences have produced large effect sizes (ranging from 0.62 to 0.65) when students' opinion of the methods is measured (Johnson & Johnson, 1989). Finally, while studied to a lesser degree, CL strategies including LT, AC, STAD, and TAI have been linked to significantly greater motivational outcomes in group comparison studies in which CL is compared to a traditional instructional condition (Brush, 1997; Jacobs et al., 1996; Johnson, Brooker, Stutzman, Hultman, & Johnson, 1985; Slavin & Karweit, 1981; Slavin et al., study 1—1984).

❏ Implications for Future Research

Although recent research has clarified the range of outcomes, salient components, and groups for which PAL is effective, questions concerning PAL's underlying processes remain. Theoretical models explaining the effectiveness of PAL in general and for specific student groups were explored in this chapter. It seems likely that the effectiveness of PAL relies on cognitive, behavioral, and motivational processes. In this chapter we have suggested further that the social and intrinsic motivational processes inherent in PAL may facilitate cognitive and behavioral growth that directly leads to academic gains. With regard to PAL's effectiveness with vulnerable student groups, these processes may be even more effective given the combination of social-emotional and academic learning. The empirical evidence supports the use of PAL as a strategy for enhancing both social-emotional and academic outcomes and a strategy that is particularly effective for vulnerable student groups, but additional research is needed to verify the theoretical models proposed in this chapter. It is important to understand the mechanisms behind effective instructional strategies such as PAL so that the principles discovered may be applied broadly in developing programs for vulnerable youth.

Although there has been a growing recognition of the importance of addressing students' social-emotional as well as academic needs through the process of schooling, widespread adoption of PAL, an integrated strategy proven to accomplish these objectives, has yet to take place. Small group and dyadic grouping strategies are commonly used in classrooms, but research-based PAL strategies are *not* widely used by educators. In a recent survey of classroom teachers, although two-thirds of teachers employed opportunities for weekly student interaction, less than one-fifth used specific empirically supported PAL strategies (Henke, Chen, & Goldman, 1999).

PAL is a versatile set of strategies that relies on peers, a readily available resource in schools. However, preparation, instructional materials, and teacher time are required for its implementation. These commodities are increasingly difficult to obtain in schools given the numerous demands placed on teachers to move through existing curricula and prepare students for high-stakes tests. PAL researchers have addressed these challenges in several ways. The Fuchs and their colleagues have developed a PAL curriculum that includes accessible training materials and a computerized formative evaluation system using curriculum-based measurement for progress monitoring (Fuchs, Fuchs, Phillips, Hamlett, & Karns, 1995). Slavin and colleagues have imbedded Cooperative Integrated Reading and Comprehension, a PAL strategy, into the Success for All (SFA) cooperative learning curriculum. SFA is a widely researched and disseminated school change program designed for low-achieving elementary schools (Slavin, Karweit, & Wasik, 1994). Thus, attempts have been made to overcome barriers to the implementation of PAL, including the development of computer-assisted curricula and the integration of PAL within schoolwide reform programs.

Along with these strategies for streamlining PAL for adoption in the schools, there has been a growing recognition in the intervention literature that for programs to work they must be implemented using a partnership approach (Power, 2003). This approach acknowledges the long-standing gap between evidence-based practices described in the educational research literature and practices employed in schools. Partnership approaches differ from traditional approaches in recognizing that educators' and other stakeholders' acceptance of and investment in an educational program are equally as important as the demonstrated effectiveness of that program. Ginsburg-Block and colleagues (Ginsburg-Block, Rohrbeck, Fantuzzo, & Lavigne, 2006) have proposed a partnership model for the development of PAL interventions. This model recognizes that partnership is essential to building the foundation for lasting and effective PAL programming—in particular, partnerships formed with systems that are salient to child development: peers, teachers, parents, and community members. Key aspects of the model include the evaluation of program effectiveness based on the unique ecology of each classroom, school, or school district, and the use of this information for program improvement, enhancement, and extension.

Integrated interventions that are capable of producing social-emotional and academic outcomes may be more effective and less costly than separate, individual approaches. Thus, efforts to increase PAL's acceptability and accessibility, perhaps through the use of partnership models, are needed. Future research should address the scale-up requirements associated with PAL, identifying the most effective strategies for increasing the use of PAL in the schools.

∷ References

Ames, C. (1992). Classrooms: Goals, structures, and student motivation. *Journal of Educational Psychology, 84,* 261–271.

Ames, C., & Archer, J. (1988). Achievement goals in the classroom: Students' learning strategies and motivation processes. *Journal of Educational Psychology, 80,* 260–267.

Bandura, A. (1977). *Social-learning theory.* Englewood Cliffs, NJ: Prentice Hall.

Brush, T. A. (1997). The effects on student achievement and attitudes when using integrated learning systems with cooperative pairs. *Educational Technology Research and Development, 45,* 51–64.

Butler, R. (1987). Task-involving and ego-involving properties of evaluation: Effects of different feedback conditions on motivational perceptions, interest, and performance. *British Journal of Educational Psychology, 58,* 1–14.

Chall, J. S. (2000). *The academic achievement challenge: What really works in the classroom.* New York: Guilford Press.

Cohen, J. (1977). *Statistical power analysis for the behavioral sciences* (Rev. ed.). New York: Academic Press.

Crain, W. (1992). *Theories of development* (3rd ed.). Englewood Cliffs, NJ: PrenticeHall.

Daly, E., Martens, B., Kilmer, A., & Massie, D. (1996). The effects of instructional match and content overlap on generalized reading performance. *Journal of Applied Behavior Analysis, 29,* 507–518.

DiPerna, J. C., Volpe, R. J., & Elliott, S. N. (2001). A model of academic enablers and elementary reading/language arts achievement. *School Psychology Review, 31,* 298–312.

Durlak, J. A. (1995). *School-based prevention programs for children and adolescents.* Thousand Oaks, CA: Sage. Elliot, E. S., & Dweck, C. S.

(1988). Goals: An approach to motivation and achievement. *Journal of Personality and Social Psychology, 54,* 5–12.

Ellison, C., Boykin, A. W., Tyler, K., & Dillihunt, M. (2005). Examining classroom learning preferences among elementary school students. *Social Behavior and Personality, 33,* 699–708.

Fantuzzo, J. W., & Ginsburg-Block, M. (1998). Reciprocal peer tutoring: Developing and testing effective peer collaborations for elementary school students. In K. J. Topping & S. Ehly (Eds.), *Peer assisted learning* (pp. 121–144). Hillsdale, NJ: Erlbaum.

Fantuzzo, J. W., King, J. A., & Heller, L. R. (1992). Effects of reciprocal peer tutoring on mathematics and school adjustment: A component analysis. *Journal of Educational Psychology, 84,* 331–339.

Fantuzzo, J. W., & Polite, K. (1990). School-based self-management interventions with elementary school children: A component analysis. *School Psychology Quarterly, 5,* 180–198.

Foot, H. & Howe, C. (1998). The psychoeducational basis of peer-assisted learning. In K. J. Topping & S. Ehly (Eds.), *Peer assisted learning* (pp. 27–43). Hillsdale, NJ: Erlbaum.

Fuchs, L. S., Fuchs, D., Phillips, N. B., Hamlett, C. L., & Karns, K. (1995). Acquisition and transfer effects of classwide peer-assisted learning strategies in mathematics for students with varying learning histories. *School Psychology Review, 24,* 604–620.

Gardner, W. E. (1978). Compeer assistance through tutoring and group guidance activities. *The Urban Review, 10,* 45–54.

Gettinger, M. (1989). Effects of maximizing time spent and minimizing time needed for learning on pupil achievement. *American Educational Research Journal, 26,* 73–91.

Ginsburg-Block, M., & Fantuzzo, J. (1997). Reciprocal peer tutoring: An analysis of "teacher" and "student" interactions as a function of training and experience. *School Psychology Quarterly, 12,* 134–149.

Ginsburg-Block, M, & Fantuzzo, J. W. (1998). An evaluation of the relative effectiveness of NCTM standards-based interventions for low-achieving urban elementary students. *Journal of Educational Psychology, 90,* 1–10.

Ginsburg-Block, M., & Rohrbeck, C. (2007). *The effects of peer assisted learning on elementary student motivation.* Manuscript submitted for publication.

Ginsburg-Block, M., Rohrbeck, C., & Fantuzzo, J. W. (2006). A meta-analytic review of the social, emotional and behavioral outcomes of peer assisted learning. *Journal of Educational Psychology, 98*(4), 732–749.

Ginsburg-Block, M., Rohrbeck, C., Fantuzzo, J. W., & Lavigne, N. C. (2006). Peer assisted learning strategies. In G. Bear & K. Minke (Eds.), *Children's needs III: Understanding and addressing the developmental needs of children* (631–645). Bethesda, MD: National Association of School Psychologists.

Greenwood, C. R., Carta, J. J., & Hall, R. V. (1988). The use of peer tutoring strategies in classroom management and educational instruction. *School Psychology Review, 17,* 258–275.

Greenwood, C. R., Dinwiddie, G., Terry, B., Wade, L., Stanley, S. O., Thidabeau, S., & Delquadri, J. C. (1984). Teacher-versus peer mediated instruction: An ecobehavioral analysis of achievement outcomes. *Journal of Applied Behavior Analysis, 17,* 521–538.

Greenwood, C. R., Maheady, L., & Delquadri, J. (2002). Classwide peer tutoring programs. In M. R. Shinn, H. M. Walker, & G. Stoner (Eds.), *Interventions for academic and behavior problems II: Preventive and remedial approaches* (pp. 611–649). Bethesda, MD: National Association of School Psychologists.

Haynes, N. M., & Gebreyesus, S. (1992). Cooperative learning: A case for African-American students. *School Psychology Review, 21,* 577–585.

Hedges, L. V. (1981). Distribution theory for Glass's estimator of effect size and related estimators. *Journal of Educational Statistics, 6,* 107–128.

Heller, L. R., & Fantuzzo, J. W. (1993). Reciprocal peer tutoring and parent partnership: Does parent involvement make a difference? *School Psychology Review, 22,* 517–534.

Henke, R. R., Chen X., & Goldman, G. (1999). *What happens in classrooms? Instructional practices in elementary and secondary schools, 1994–1995.* Washington, DC: U.S. Department of Education, National Center for Education Statistics.

Jacobs, D. L., Watson, T. G., & Sutton, J. P. (1996). Effects of a cooperative learning method on mathematics achievement and affective outcomes of students in a private elementary school. *Journal of Research and Development in Education, 29,* 195–202.

Johnson, R., Brooker, C., Stutzman, J., Hultman, D., & Johnson, D. (1985). The effects of controversy, concurrence seeking, and individualistic learning on achievement and attitude change. *Journal of Research in Science Teaching, 22,* 197–205.

Johnson, D. W., & Johnson, R. T. (1989). *Cooperation and competition: Theory and research.* Edina, MN: Interaction.

Johnson, R. T., & Johnson, D. W. (1994). *An overview of cooperative learning.* Retrieved August 17, 2004, from http://www.co-operation.org/pages/overviewpaper. html.

Koestner, R., Ryan, R. M., Bernieri, F., & Holt, K. (1984). Setting limits on children's behavior: The differential effects of controlling versus informational styles on intrinsic motivation and creativity. *Journal of Personality, 52,* 233–248.

Manning, G. L., & Manning, M. (1984). What models of recreational reading make a difference? *Reading World, 23,* 375–380.

McCombs, B. (1993). Learner-centered psychological principles for enhancing education. In L. A. Penner, G. M. Batsche, H. M. Knoff, & D. L. Nelson (Eds.), *The challenge in mathematics and science education: psychology's response* (pp. 287–313). Washington, DC: American Psychological Association.

Moskowitz, J. M., Malvin, J. H., Schaeffer, G. A., & Schaps, E. (1983). Evaluation of a cooperative learning strategy. *American Educational Research Journal, 20,* 687–696.

Peterson, P., & Janicki, T. C. (1979). Individual characteristics and children's learning in large group and small group approaches. *Journal of Educational Psychology, 77,* 219–312.

Peterson, P. L., Janicki, T. C., & Swing, S. R. (1981). Ability X treatment interaction effects on children's learning in large-group and small-group approaches. *American Educational Research Journal, 18,* 453–473.

Piaget, J., & Inhelder, B. (1972). *The psychology of the child.* New York: Basic Books.

Power, T. J. (2003). Promoting children's mental health: Reform through interdisciplinary and community partnerships. *School Psychology Review, 32,* 3–16.

Rohrbeck, C. A., Ginsburg-Block, M. D., Fantuzzo, J. W., & Miller, T. R. (2003). Peer-assisted learning interventions with elementary school students: A meta-analytic review. *Journal of Educational Psychology, 95*(2), 240–257.

Rothstein-Fisch, C., Trumbull, E., Isaac, A., Daley, C., & Perez, A. (2003). When "helping someone else" is the right answer: Bridging cultures in assessment. *Journal of Latinos and Education, 2,* 123–140.

Rubin, B. (2003). Unpacking detracking: *When progressive pedagogy meets students' social worlds. American Educational Research Journal, 40*(2), 539–573.

Ryan, R. M., & Deci, E. L. (2000). Self-determination theory and the facilitation of intrinsic motivation, social development, and well-being. *American Psychologist, 55,* 68–78.

Ryan, R. M., & Stiller, J. (1991). The social contexts of internalization: Parent and teacher influences on autonomy, motivation, and learning. In M. L. Maehr & P. R. Pintrich (Eds.), *Advances in motivation and achievement* (Vol. 7, pp. 115–149). Greenwich, CT: JAI.

Schunk, D. H. (1996). Goal and self-evaluative influences during children's cognitive skill learning. *American Educational Research Journal, 33,* 359–382.

Schunk, D. H., Hanson, A. R., & Cox, P. D. (1987). Peer-model attributes and children's achievement behaviors. *Journal of Educational Psychology, 79,* 54–61.

Shadish, W. R., & Haddock, C. K. (1994). Combining estimates of effect size. In H. Cooper & L. V. Hedges (Eds.), *Handbook of research synthesis* (pp. 261–281). New York: Russell Sage Foundation.

Slavin, R. E. (1990). *Cooperative learning: Theory, research, and practice.* Englewood Cliffs, NJ: Prentice Hall.

Slavin, R. E., & Karweit, N. L. (1981). Cognitive and affective outcomes of an intensive student team learning experience. *Journal of Experimental Education, 50,* 29–35.

Slavin, R. E., Karweit, N. L., & Wasik, B. A. (Eds.). (1994). *Preventing early school failure: Research, policy, and practice.* Needham Heights, MA: Allyn and Bacon.

Slavin, R. E., Leavey, M. B., & Madden, N. A. (1984). Combining cooperative learning and individualized instruction: Effects on student mathematics achievement, attitudes, and behaviors. *Elementary School Journal, 84,* 409–422.

Stipek, D. (1996). Motivation and instruction. In D. C. Berliner & R. C. Calfee (Eds.), *Handbook of educational psychology* (pp. 85–113). New York: Simon and Schuster Macmillan.

Topping, K., & Ehly, S. (1998). Introduction to peer assisted learning. In K. J. Topping & S. Ehly (Eds.), *Peer assisted learning* (pp. 1–23). Hillsdale, NJ: Lawrence Erlbaum.

Vygotsky, L. S. (1978). Mental development of children and the process of learning (M. Lopez Morillas, Trans.). In M. Cole, V. John-Steiner, S. Scribner, & E. Souberman (Eds.), *L. S. Vygotsky: Mind in society* (pp. 7–8). Cambridge, MA: Harvard University Press. (Original work published 1935)

Webb, N. (1985). Student interaction and learning in small groups: A research summary. In R. E. Slavin, S. Sharan, S. Kagan, R. Hertz-Lazarowitz, C. Webb, & R. Schmuck (Eds.), *Learning to cooperate, cooperating to learn* (pp. 147–172). New York: Plenum.

Webb, N. M., & Palincsar, A. S. (1996). Group processes in the classroom. In D. C. Berliner & R. C. Calfee (Eds.), *Handbook of educational psychology* (pp. 841–873). New York: Simon and Schuster Macmillan.

Wentzel, K. R. (1999). Social-motivational processes and interpersonal relationships: Iimplications for understanding motivation at school. *Journal of Educational Psychology, 91,* 76–96.

Wright, S., & Cowen, E. L. (1985). The effects of peer-teaching on student perceptions of class environment, adjustment, and academic performance. *American Journal of Community Psychology, 13,* 417–431.

Yager, S., Johnson, R. T., Johnson, D. W., & Snider, B. (1986). The impact of group processing on achievement in cooperative learning groups. *Journal of Social Psychology, 126*, 389–397.

Zahn, G. L., Kagan, S., & Widaman, K. F. (1986). Cooperative learning and classroom climate. *Journal of School Psychology, 24*, 351–362.

Zins, J. E., Bloodworth, M. R., Weissberg, R. P., & Walberg, H. J. (2004). *Building academic success on social and emotional learning: What does the research say?* New York: Teacher's College, Columbia University.

PART 4 ⚏

Conclusions and Commentary

12 ⠒

Academic Motivation and the Culture of School

Thematic Integration

Cynthia Hudley

Chapters in this volume elaborate on a worthy tradition of the study of school culture that, until recent years, has not been in the forefront of educational research. No less than 35 years ago (Saranson, 1971; Trickett & Todd, 1972), scholars in both educational and developmental psychology were calling for "an integrative perspective... of the school as a coherent whole rather than a series of discrete classrooms and interpersonal relationships" (Trickett & Todd, 1972, p. 28). This concept of school culture was modeled on a variant of organizational behavior theory that came from the corporate sphere and had been previously used in literatures on counseling and social psychology.

However, education research of this type grew out of a need to understand and refashion school cultures in the context of rapid social and legal changes; thus educational applications melded school culture and societal culture into a reciprocal system. The 1960s and 1970s brought the apex of school desegregation, mandated school busing, school closures, interdistrict mergers for the purpose of school integration—all conducted against a backdrop of fierce opposition to this inevitable cultural shift in American civil society. Education scholars and practitioners at the time were appropriately focused on the twin goals of healthy student development and long-range organizational development of schools in manifestly changing times.

As the turmoil surrounding the implementation of school desegregation and integration began to wind down, American society and schools were thrust into the reality of racial and ethnic pluralism that required serious attention to multicultural education. Both research and practice began working to understand the cultural backgrounds and strengths that students brought with them to previously monocultural schools (e.g., Cross, Long, & Ziajka, 1978), important work that continues to this day. Although this shift has tended to move the concept of school culture into the background in favor of a focus on students' home cultures, school culture is patently a construct that is distinct from student culture, cultural diversity, and a number of other variants on the construct of culture that have become visible in educational research. However, school culture should not be understood as a decontextualized phenomenon. As pointed out in Chapter 1, school culture is the product of norms, expectations, behaviors, and relationships that are specific to the local setting yet a function of the broader cultural milieu in which the school is instantiated.

Earlier research in educational psychology and educational leadership using a narrower construct of school culture that lacks a consideration of the larger society in which it is embedded (e.g., Maehr & Anderman, 1993; Stolp, 1994) concurs that school culture and student motivation are powerfully intertwined. However, this volume has returned to the study of school culture at the nexus of local and societal norms and beliefs, examining both the local school and the broader culture that influences the actors—students, teachers, parents—in the local setting. Using this concept of school culture as a shared lens, each chapter has examined academic achievement motivation. The chapters are grounded in a variety of theoretical perspectives; they address students of diverse ethnicities and social classes and examine processes of school culture at several developmental periods. This integrative chapter first examines consistent themes within each of the three divisions that organize the chapters in this volume: developmental and contextual aspects of student motivation over time; students' social cognitions, motivational processes, and outcomes in school; and interventions to enhance academic motivation. I conclude with a discussion of cross-cutting themes and implications for research and practice that this volume brings to light.

∷ Examining Motivation Over Time

The chapters in this section offer an interesting contrast on academic motivation and school culture across age and grade, classroom contexts, and ethnicity. Notably, the differences between the populations studied provide findings that converge on a number of conclusions regarding the intersection of developmental period, academic motivation, and school culture. Perhaps the most interesting of these conclusions is that the culture of school and the nature of children's motivation are somewhat robust across different levels of education, although school culture and motivation itself become increasingly more complex as children mature.

Chapter 2 and 3 revealed that students' motivation consistently relates to the culture of the school, even though the construct was conceptualized and measured according to the developmental level of the participants. For example, the Rouse and Fantuzzo chapter conceptualized preschool children's competence motivation as initiative, confidence, and an eagerness to understand. Anyone who has spent time with a 4-year-old child answering endless, seemingly random questions will recognize this construct as an accurate description of young children's motivation to understand and learn about the world around them. Children high in competence motivation were more successful in preschool, rated higher in readiness for kindergarten, and were more successful in first grade. This measure of motivation accurately reflects the culture of the American preschool classroom, a context that is deliberately designed to favor independence, exploration, and autonomy. A statement of best practices in early childhood settings prominently features such characteristics as initiative, individualization, and confident problem solving (Bowman, Donovan, & Burns, 2000).

The Gottfried et al. chapter presents a self-reflective construct of motivation, consistent with the age of the participants. Their study defines academic intrinsic motivation as curiosity, persistence, and self-confidence in preferring more challenging tasks—a description similar to that of Rouse and Fantuzzo but a more differentiated one that acknowledges students' self-awareness of their level of motivation. Again, low intrinsic motivation measured in adolescence related to a long-term history of poorer academic achievement and a more negative self-perception of academic abilities.

The cultural values that shape American schools, including autonomy and individual interests, are visible in these results. In both chapters, students' ability to thrive in school seems related to their adjustment to a culture that foregrounds the individual. As many researchers in multicultural education have noted, individualism is an overarching although sometimes unacknowledged culturally constructed value in American society that is clearly reflected in the schools. The chapters diverge, however, as Gottfried et al. note, in that preschool culture differs from our contemporary K–12 school culture with its emphasis on standardized test scores as the ultimate measure of educational success. Although the current allure of standardized testing is consistent with a cultural emphasis on the individual, it fosters a school culture that may undermine, not promote, academic motivation among students who are unable to adjust, for whatever reason, to the prevailing cultural emphases.

∷ Students' Social Cognitions

The chapters on social cognitions remind us that the influence of school culture is most visible at the intersection of the individual and the context. The effects of the school culture are largely a function of how students perceive and interpret that culture. Students who perceive the beliefs, norms, and expectations that make up a school culture to be supportive of and consistent with their own aspirations and achievement are more likely to experience that culture as motivational. Conversely, motivation is compromised when students perceive messages from the school culture that counter or devalue their identities, goals, and beliefs. This section presents data that span the age spectrum, examine a broad variety of motivational constructs and school settings, and still converge on the conclusion that the path from the culture of the school to an individual student's motivation passes through the eye of the beholder.

In the Thorkildsen et al. chapter, Mexican American adolescents who reported higher levels of motivation and engagement in school (defined as the willingness to work hard vs. a preference for shortcuts and cheating) were those with pluralistic civil identities (i.e., beliefs in democratic integration, universal justice, and respect for persons). Further, civil identities accounted for a greater share of the variance in adolescents' motivation than did other identities measured in this study. Most important for this discussion, these motivated students also consistently articulated a particular vision of an ideal school culture, and this perception of school culture was also strongly related to motivation. In essence, those students with the strongest beliefs in justice and respect for others were not only the most motivated but were also aware that a school culture that supported them in these beliefs could motivate and engage them in academic activities.

Romo and colleagues provide a look at a unique school culture and examine a very different set of influences on motivation including sexual behavior, attitudes toward childbearing, and use of birth control. They found that in alternative schools for youth experiencing motivational or behavioral difficulties or for girls already pregnant, parenting, or sexually active, the school culture is strongly informed by negative peer influences and the lack of motivated and academically oriented peers. Although some girls perceived the school culture in a way that supported risky sexual behavior and depressed academic motivation, other girls, largely through the help of parents, perceived the school culture as one that supported motivated behavior and a second chance to achieve their academic goals and aspirations.

Warzon and Ginsburg-Block examine school culture as perceived by families and teachers as well as by students. Their discussion of cultural continuity between home and school extends one of the very familiar themes in multicultural education to a consideration of children's academic motivation. Their novel contribution provides surprising findings. Contrary to the traditional view in multicultural education that discontinuity is "bad," their more nuanced description again affirms the salient theme in this section of our edited volume: What matters for motivation is how students, teachers, and parents perceive the continuity or lack thereof between home and school culture. Perceptions are the foundation for action, and apparently the manner in which adults handle perceived discontinuity is one contributor to student behavior. When students perceive that adults successfully manage that all important connection between home and school, they display significantly higher rates of motivation.

Irving's chapter is one that clearly places school culture within the context of the broader culture. His examination of cultural mistrust, defined as the tendency of African Americans to distrust White American institutions, including schools, demonstrates that perceived bias in the larger culture influences attitudes and perceptions of the local school culture as well as academic motivation among African American male high school students. Interestingly, his comparison of the work he has done in several different geographic regions of the country crystallizes the importance of understanding the school culture as well as the local culture in which it is embedded to fully understand how student perceptions shape academic motivation.

Similar to the Irving chapter, Eccleston and Major also address the role of the broader culture as an influence on school culture and student motivation. Their discussion of stereotype threat makes clear that when students who are also members of negatively stereotyped groups perceive their school culture to implicitly or explicitly endorse these social stereotypes, their academic motivation and performance are often undermined. The two chapters provide complementary understandings of the special challenges for students from marginalized and stigmatized groups. A mainstream school culture that may often reflect prevailing stereotypes, although in subtle and unconscious ways, can destabilize students' self concept of ability, increase cultural mistrust, and decrease achievement striving.

The research by Hudley and Daoud makes a similar point with a sample of Latino and Anglo high school students. Students with a negative perception of school ethnic climate show significantly lower levels of school engagement, and negative perceptions were most detrimental for Latino students of lower socioeconomic status. Complex relationships between student ethnicity, socioeconomic status, and perceptions again bring home the point that the effects of school culture are processed through student perceptions. Even within ethnicity, students may perceive school culture differently depending on their life experiences and beliefs about the nature of school. The interviews reported by Hudley and Daoud flesh out the unfavorable perceptions of school culture that are held by both Latino and Anglo students. However, these negative perceptions, unsurprisingly, are more detrimental to student motivation for Latino than Anglo students.

Across the diverse groups of participants studied in this section, students' perceptions of the school culture significantly influenced motivation, behavior, and achievement. Conversely, the complexity of findings across chapters indicates that such perceptions are also influenced by the larger culture and the various actors in the environments in which the student is a part, including peers, teachers, family, surrounding neighborhood, and even distal influences such as media stereotypes. As research on school culture is extended and amplified, an ecological approach (e.g., Bronfenbrenner, 1979) that attends simultaneously to multiple levels of influence will best explain the complex interactions among student and teacher characteristics, school culture, the broader culture, and academic motivation.

∷ Interventions to Enhance Motivation

The work by Welch emphasizes the importance of teacher-student interactions and a class community of respect as a means of providing a supportive culture that enhances the academic motivation of primarily African American students. Interestingly, the success of their intervention in creating a supportive classroom culture led to a reversal of the direction of effects that we have seen in prior chapters. Rather than the school culture being influenced by the broader culture, students in this classroom culture planned to affirmatively shape the broader community culture by changing the community's perception of the school from athletically successful and academically inferior to academically successful.

Ginsburg-Block et al. focused on the role of peers rather than teachers as change agents for school culture and student motivation. Consistent with cognitive social learning theory (Bandura, 1997), peer interaction is successful in promoting school engagement and academic motivation because student models of persistence, motivation, and school appropriate behavior are more similar to their peers than are the adults in the school environment. The authors suggest that peer-assisted learning develops social motivation for academic norms as well as emphasizing collaborative views of learning rather than competition and individualistic reward structures. Such values are also more consistent with the family values of students of color. Taken together, these interventions suggest multiple routes to changing the culture of school in a manner that enhances student motivation. Whether teachers or peers are the initial agents of change, both interventions identify changes in the classroom as the starting point for changes in the students' perceptions, changes in the school culture, and changes in students' motivation and achievement.

:: Conclusions: Academic Motivation and the Culture of School

No matter which motivation-relevant variables are studied, no matter what the methodology, these chapters all confirm the importance of attending to the too often unexamined areas of school and community culture as well as the more familiar areas of family and classroom culture. Across all ages, academic motivation is related to school culture, which is influenced by the broader social and cultural context. The good news is that school culture can be changed, and the direction of change seems to be from the microsystem of the classroom outward to the culture of the school and community.

The consistent themes present in this volume also speak to educational practice. All of the material leads to a unified conclusion that educators must be aware not only of the home cultures of their students, the admittedly important understanding that is typically foregrounded in discussions of multicultural education. An understanding of the local school culture and its links to the broader cultural milieu, including social stereotypes and inequitable access to the opportunity structure should improve educators' ability to support and enhance the motivation, learning, and quality of education of all students. Only then will teaching and learning be most effective, and with that sensitivity educators will be in a potent position to become change agents for student beliefs and attitudes as well as for classroom and school culture. Among many possible actions for change, teachers can also teach their students to become critically aware and successful change agents as well.

Finally, evidence-based interventions to create a school culture that can successfully support the achievement strivings of all children will require a coordinated effort among researchers who contribute the kind of knowledge represented in this edited volume; academic faculty involved with teacher education and professional development; school personnel (administrators, teachers, school psychologists, and counselors), families, students, policy makers, and the media. With the combined efforts of all stakeholders, a multidisciplinary approach can refine our understanding of the links between student motivation, the culture of school, and the influence of the broader societal culture. In this, way science and practice can converge to improve the developmental outcomes and the life chances for all children and for our society as a whole.

∷ References

Bandura, A. (1997). *Self-efficacy: The exercise of control.* New York: W. H. Freeman.

Bowman, B., Donovan, S., & Burns, S. (2000). *Eager to learn: Educating our preschoolers.* Washington DC: National Research Council.

Bronfenbrenner, U. (1979). *The ecology of human development: Experiments by nature and design.* Cambridge, MA: Harvard University Press.

Cross, D., Long, M., & Ziajka, A. (1978). Minority cultures and education in the United States. *Education and Urban Society, 10,* 263–276.

Maehr, M., & Anderman, E. (1993). Reinventing schools for early adolescents: Emphasizing task goals. *Elementary School Journal, 93,* 593–610.

Sarason, S. (1971). *The culture of the school and the problem of change.* Boston: Allyn and Bacon.

Stolp, S. (1994). *Leadership for school culture: ERIC Digest number 91.* Eugene, OR: ERIC Clearinghouse on Educational Management. (ERIC Document Reproduction Service No. ED370198)

Trickett, E., & Todd, D. (1972). The high school culture: An ecological perspective. *Theory into Practice, 11,* 28–37.

13 ⠿

Academic Motivation and the Culture of Schooling

Integration of Findings

Adele Eskeles Gottfried

This volume presents a discussion of school culture as a construct that plays a potentially causal role in the academic competence of diverse students. Maehr and Fyans (1989) conceptualized motivational culture as pertaining to individual differences between group members regarding their perceptions of the motivational academic environment. The present volume expands beyond this by examining the motivational culture of particular dimensions of schooling from a variety of theoretical perspectives—across varying ethnicities, developmental periods, and school contexts. Hence, motivational culture of schooling is addressed as a multifaceted construct. In this integration, findings are examined across the chapters focusing on developmental and contextual aspects of motivation in diverse groups of students; students' social cognitions, motivational processes, and outcomes in school; and interventions to enhance academic motivation.

The chapters by Rouse and Fantuzzo; Gottfried, Gottfried, Morris, and Cook; and Thorkildsen, Golant, and Cambray-Engstrom address developmental and contextual aspects of academic motivation and school culture across age and grade, classroom context, and ethnicity. What is notable is that despite differences among the investigations regarding populations studied, socioeconomic status, ethnicity, gender, and specific type of academic motivation examined, the findings converge on similar conclusions regarding the developmental role of academic motivation in children's school achievement and competence, and in helping to defining motivational school culture. Among the convergences are these: (1) Motivational culture of schooling is not uniform but can be expected to differ with regard to subgroups in the school population. (2) Students with low academic motivation are likely to be at risk with respect to their school competence from childhood through early adulthood. (3) Motivational school culture comprises classroom and school environments that may facilitate or impede competence motivation, academic intrinsic motivation, and student commitment to both autonomous and collective goals.

With regard to the first point, that motivational culture of schooling is not uniform, across these chapters, subgroups of students evidenced motivational differences that were related to varying levels and types of engagement in the schooling process. For example, in the Rouse and Fantuzzo chapter, children who were stronger in competence motivation were more successful in their transitions from Head Start to kindergarten and first grade. In the Gottfried et al. chapter, the students with at-risk academic intrinsic motivation evidenced a long-term history of poorer academic competence from childhood through early adulthood. In the Thorkildsen et al. chapter, adolescents with pluralistic civil identities (justice beliefs; commitment to community obligations and personal autonomy) endorsed justice aspects of an ideal school more strongly than adolescents in any of the three other identity statuses and were more likely to endorse working hard as an activity in which they engage. At the other extreme, adolescents with an unformed identity (few goals; belief that world is unjust) were the least engaged in school and the least likely to endorse ideal school aspects or working hard. The latter students may be similar to those who are motivationally at risk. From preschool through early adulthood, across diverse ethnicities, socioeconomic statuses, classrooms, geographic locations, and gender, differences in children's academic motivation were found to be significantly related to their academic achievement, beliefs, self-concepts, postsecondary educational accomplishments, and perceptions of student roles. Hence, the motivational culture of school is different for children who vary in these aspects inasmuch as their interactions with their school environments will elicit different outcomes. Even for students within the same classroom or school, their level of academic motivation per se is likely to play a significant role in defining their individual perspectives on motivational school culture.

With regard to the second point about at-risk motivation as related to educational performance, note first that academic motivation was a statistically significant and independent factor with regard to children's academic success. For example, Rouse and Fantuzzo cited evidence that compared to other learning behaviors (attention/persistence and attitude toward learning), competence motivation during preschool was a better predictor of learning readiness and achievement through grade 1; they also cite evidence that competence motivation is distinct from general intelligence. A. E. Gottfried et al. provide data revealing that from childhood through adolescence, children evidencing at-risk academic intrinsic motivation showed a pervasive and long-term history of poorer school competence across a wide range of indices including achievement, intellectual performance, motivation, classroom functioning, test-taking skills, self-esteem, academic anxiety, and later, significantly less post-secondary educational accomplishment. Moreover, at-risk motivational status and lower IQ were found to be statistically independent of each other, a finding consistent with others as discussed in their chapter indicating that academic intrinsic motivation contributes to the prediction of achievement independently of IQ and consistent with findings cited in Rouse and Fantuzzo's chapter. In the Thorkildsen et al. chapter, students with more diffused identity status were least likely to endorse working hard in school, which suggests being academically at-risk. Relating these findings to the issue of motivational school culture in general, one can conclude that children and adolescents with lower competency motivation and academic intrinsic motivation or those who are more disengaged in goal orientation with regard to their identity status are significantly compromised in academic competence and performance, and these findings generalize across demographic groups. Regardless of whether children were from socieconomically depressed families, as for Head Start children (Rouse & Fantuzzo), from a wide middle socio-economic class range (Gottfried et al.), or from a diverse group of Latino adolescents (Thorkildsen et al.), the poorer the motivation, the lower is the student's school competence. Regardless of ethnicity, gender, or SES status, low motivational status places children at risk for compromised school achievement and more limited educational progress.

The effect of low motivation may be progressive—that is, it may increase as students move through schooling. This was suggested by Rouse and Fantuzzo, and also by Gottfried and colleagues who report in their chapter that stability of academic intrinsic motivation increases during adolescence making it more likely that these students will enter adolescence with low motivation. On the positive side of motivation, Rouse and Fantuzzo suggest that early and strong competence motivation serves as a buffer against potential school failure. Thorkildsen and colleagues suggest that students with a pluralistic form of identity evidence the highest school engagement. Pluralistic identity appears to be more adaptive for developing an academic role. Gottfried and colleagues report that from childhood though early adulthood, those with high motivation are consistently more likely to excel across a wide range of academic accomplishments.

With regard to the motivational school context, all three chapters argue for and elaborate on creation of classroom environments that facilitate motivational processes to enhance children's academic competence. The emphasis across these chapters concerns teachers' roles in enhancing curiosity, mastery, and commitment to group and autonomy goals. All three chapters discuss development of curriculum to support students' self-initiated, or autonomous, learning competencies. Therefore, primary emphases regarding motivational school culture from the perspective of these chapters converge on the nature of school environment, teacher behaviors, and curriculum emphasizing interest, curiosity, mastery, justice, and reflection.

Several chapters examined student perceptions of cultural bias and stigmatization as members of underrepresented and often marginalized groups and how such perceptions affect students' academic motivation, achievement, and school engagement. In addition, the roles of teachers, parents, and peers are considered as influences on such perceptions. Another focus across chapters concerns the degree of continuity or discontinuity between students' perceptions and school contexts regarding academic motivation and expectations in relation to cultural group membership and identity along with the impact of such continuities and discontinuities on students' educational attainment.

In the Eccleston and Major chapter, the groups focused on are those shown to predominantly experience stereotype threat, primarily African American and female students. Hudley and Daoud's sample comprised Latino and Anglo-American high school students. Romo, Kouyoumdjian, and Lightfoot studied Latina girls attending alternative high schools, some of whom were pregnant or already mothers. Irving's population comprised African American male high school students. The ethnicities of the Warzon and Ginsburg-Block sample were diverse, including African American, Anglo-American, Asian American/Pacific Islander, Hispanic, multiracial, Native American, and other students. Interestingly, across these divergent groups, there was similarity in the way motivational processes affected academic motivation and performance. This similarity pertains to the impact of the students' perceptions of cultural, normative, stereotyped, or stigmatizing views held by others on their school engagement and academic performance. Across diverse groups, to the extent that students perceived discrimination and bias, these perceptions were adversely related to academic outcomes.

There are, however, important differences among the content of such perceptions as each chapter carefully delineates. Eccleston and Major discussed a large body of evidence regarding the effects of stereotype threat on student performance. According to the authors, when negative stereotypes of abilities are associated with cultural group membership, such as for African Americans or women, these negative perceptions are likely to diminish the academic engagement and performance of affected students through anxiety produced by their perception of the stereotype. Therefore, to the extent that the academic environment implicitly or explicitly conveys such views, they are likely to be perceived as associated with negative academic outcomes.

The research by Hudley and Daoud clearly makes this point with regard to Latino and Anglo high school students. Their research provides evidence that students who had low perceived levels of teacher support and negative views of ethnic school climate showed significantly less school engagement, such as higher absenteeism and number of detentions. These negative perceptions were most detrimental for Latino students of lower socioeconomic status. Complex relationships among perceptions, student ethnicity, and socioeconomic status again bring home the point that motivational school culture is not a uniform entity. Even within ethnicity, students may hold different views of motivational school culture depending on their experiences and perceptions of acceptance by teachers and peers. Interestingly, in the interviews presented by Hudley and Daoud, members of underrepresented and mainstream ethnic groups reported adverse perceptions about the cultural atmosphere of the school. This needs to be addressed if schools are to create a synergistic cultural atmosphere among students in which all are able to express, elaborate, and collectively address often conflicting perspectives.

Irving's chapter concerns perceptions of cultural mistrust in African American male high school students and their impact on academic expectations and values using an expectancy-value perspective of motivation. Cultural mistrust is defined in this research as the tendency of African Americans to distrust White Americans in institutional, personal, or social contexts. It concerns the perception of racism and relegation to underclass status. Results were complex, showing that cultural mistrust was associated with higher outcome expectation but lower academic achievement. This complexity may indicate that cultural mistrust works in both positive and negative fashion to increase efforts to achieve and overcome racial stereotypes; at the same time it is possible that cultural mistrust activates perceptions of stereotype threat that has been shown to adversely affect academic achievement. Again, the cultural context of schools does not have a uniform effect on motivation and achievement but can be expected to play a different role with regard to distinct motivational indices, such as academic outcome expectations and achievement.

Romo, Kouyoumdjian, and Lightfoot's work emphasized the importance of both peer culture and parental attitudes as influences on attitudes toward pregnancy and academic aspirations in Latina girls attending an alternative high school. Their results showed that the peer group has a pervasive influence on such attitudes, particularly with regard to the desirability of pregnancy and teenage parenthood. Girls' attitudes toward pregnancy and parenthood were most favorable and their academic aspirations lowest when they perceived their friends as positive toward pregnancy and parenthood. Girls who perceived their own parents' attitudes as negative regarding teenage pregnancy and parenting had the strongest aspirations to pursue higher education. Overall, these findings bring home the importance of peers and parents as sources of students' value perceptions and as influencing academic aspirations. Romo et al. link these perceptions to the norms of the school culture of the alternative school the girls attended inasmuch as there was a normative presence of teenage pregnancy and parenthood in the school. Despite this, parents may play an important role as well. Relating this to an expectancy-value model of motivation, the authors suggested that such perceptions affect students' values and choices regarding furthering their education.

The research by Warzon and Ginsburg-Block also shows the complexity of cultural continuity and discontinuity perceptions in the context of family-school relationships. They report on a Cultural Continuity Project, a study including an ethnically mixed sample, in which the perceptions of parents, teachers, and students were related to students' academic motivation and reading fluency. The results of their research show divergence depending on the respondent. For example, families reported the greatest satisfaction with the family-school relationship when they perceived the family-school environment as continuous, and when the teachers perceived family-school relationships as discontinuous. Warzon and Ginsburg-Block suggested that perhaps teachers' perceptions of discontinuity helped them work to create a more continuous and sensitive classroom experience for the families. Regarding students, the more home-school continuity they perceived, the more positive was their academic motivation and the higher was their reading fluency. As in the other chapters, student perceptions of cultural school environment are important for student motivation and achievement. The authors propose that cultural awareness may best be considered as a component of good instructional practices in order for teachers to be sensitive to cultural discontinuity and to create culturally sensitive classes.

These chapters advance knowledge regarding the importance of the cultural context of the school environment with regard to student engagement, motivation, and achievement. One conclusion that can be made is that across the diverse ethnicities studied, continuities and discontinuities between students' perceptions of home and school environments can be expected to be significantly related to various aspects of school engagement, achievement, and behaviors. Conversely, the complexity of findings across chapters indicates that such perceptions are likely to be modified by the specific aspects of school environments in which students, peers, teachers, families, and even surrounding neighborhoods play a role in shaping perceptions. Therefore, an ecological approach (e.g., Bronfenbrenner, 1979) is needed to understand the intricacies of interactions between students' academic motivation and motivational school culture. There is likely to be much distinction between schools, and it is important for such specificities to be accounted for in theory, research, and practice.

Intervention programs are addressed by Welch, and Ginsburg-Block, Rohrbeck, Lavigne, and Fantuzzo. Welch described an intervention project that emphasized the important role of the teacher in facilitating a shared community of respect essential to students' development of a scholar identity that can provide a pathway to academic and life success. This project was conducted in the context of a 9-year study, Project EXCEL, aimed at helping educationally disadvantaged adolescents learn to define themselves as scholars and to pursue higher education. For African American students, this included an effort to counteract stereotypes regarding intellectual inferiority. This project also included other students who saw themselves on the outskirts of school life. The focus of the intervention program was on teacher-student interactions that emphasized an atmosphere of inquiry and respect for self and the diversity of others with regard to the development of students' self-concepts of scholarship.

In the chapter, descriptions of classroom processes are presented involving questioning and sharing of opinions and personal perspectives. Students' contributions were valued, and misperceptions were clarified in class. Welch concludes that the class community of respect helps develop a scholar identity. Students were asked to write a paper describing how their identities had changed over the year. Examples provided emphasized an increase in students' curiosity for new experiences. Positive self-concept of racial identity and achievement were also focused on. Students' desire to change the community's perception of the school from an institution of underachievers to a place of academic accomplishment was also discussed.

Welch reported that all EXCEL students graduated from high school and were qualified to attend college. Students who had attained a scholar identity described themselves as successful and were likely to attend college, enter the military, or begin job training. Welch suggested that teacher training may benefit from analyzing a community of respect as part of school culture. Consistent with the ecological analysis offered above, the author discussed the role of the school in the larger community. Students were aware of the adverse views of the school held by the larger community and believed these negative views were reasons the school received fewer resources. Nevertheless, in seeking to define their scholar identity, they needed to understand such views and to go beyond them.

Ginsburg-Block, Rohrbeck, Lavigne, and Fantuzzo advance the theoretical and empirical bases for peer-assisted learning as a means to enhance academic motivation among diverse students. As proposed in their chapter, in the context of theory, peer interaction is facilitative of children's learning because the students involved are in the same zone of proximal development (Vygotsky) and provide each other the cognitive conflict necessary for moving to a higher level of learning (Piaget). Social learning theory is also a foundation for peer-assisted learning as peers are likely to be suitable models for one another in learning new behaviors (Bandura). Practices based on a peer-assisted curriculum include individualizing curriculum, establishing mastery goals based on individual improvement instead of group goals, scaffolding learning, and providing for autonomy. A host of results are cited in this chapter supporting the importance of peer-assisted learning instruction as a facilitator of academic motivation and performance including achievement, intrinsic motivation, social and self-concepts, competence, and behaviors. Based on the results of two meta-analyses examining motivation as an independent variable with regard to the effects of peer-assisted learning, the authors conclude that the social (e.g., pro-academic norms among students) and intrinsic motivational aspects of peer-assisted instruction significantly contribute to cognitive and behavioral engagement that thereby indirectly enhance academic outcomes.

Ginsburg-Block et al. present a third meta-analyses in which motivation is examined as an outcome of rather than a contributor to peer-assisted learning in elementary school students. Results of this meta-analysis indicate positive effects of peer-assisted learning on motivation, with stronger effects for samples they term as vulnerable including students who are of minority status, of lower socioeconomic status, and attending urban schools. Programs including multiple features that would be expected to enhance motivation had stronger effects than those with fewer components. The authors suggest incorporating motivational strategies within peer-assisted learning programs, such as interdependent reward contingencies, individualized curriculum materials and evaluation strategies, structured student roles, and self-management. With regard to school culture, Ginsburg-Block et al. suggest that peer-assisted learning develops social motivation for academic norms as well as emphasizing communal views of learning rather than competition and individualistic reward structures. Communal values were noted to be more consistent with the values of the homes of underrepresented students such as African American and Latino families. Because peer-assisted learning appears to incorporate social and intrinsic motivation processes, the authors further suggest that for children already strong in those areas, peer-assisted learning is less likely to have an effect. A number of different peer-assisted models are described.

∷ Conclusions: Academic Motivation and the Culture of Schooling

Whereas these two latter chapters address, describe, and cite evidence for the effectiveness of specific program models designed to enhance academic motivation in diverse populations of students, there are also intervention implications that emanate from the other studies in this volume. If one were to define an optimal motivational culture of schooling, collectively, all of the studies converge on the importance of the motivational environment of educational settings including the various ecological levels of schools as a whole, classrooms, families, peers, and students. The implications for practice pertain to teacher training. For example, it is important for teachers' motivational strategies to enhance student academic motivation in its various theoretical orientations that may include opportunities to experience excitement about learning and student autonomy; students' perceptions of teachers' supportiveness, respect, and understanding of their cultural background; and enhancement of collective efficacy and identity among students to promote the norm of student academic engagement. All chapters also stress that educators must be sensitive to students' motivations, identities, and social perceptions—their sense of competence, being at risk for academic intrinsic motivation, stereotype threats regarding ethnicity and gender, marginalization and oppression, influence of peer norms, and disengagement. In essence, teachers must learn how to take the role of the students and perceive the school environment as their students do. Learning activities, curriculum, and classroom and school motivational activities need to be planned accordingly.

Based on the contributions of each author, it can be concluded that there is no single motivational culture of schools. Generalizations can be made about the manner in which motivation and cultural beliefs may affect various students' levels of engagement, but the results and analyses presented show clearly that the essence of motivational culture of schooling resides with the individual students in their interactions with the specific nature of the educational environment in which they are embedded. Motivational school culture must incorporate an understanding of the individual students' experiences in addition to knowledge about their home cultures and learning orientations. The populations represented across chapters vary in age from preschool through high school, college, and into adulthood and include a spectrum of cultural groups and socioeconomic status; therefore, the generality of these conclusions applies broadly across the student population. Research should continue to delineate these specific relationships.

Finally, who is responsible for implementing an approach tailored to each child? Facilitating a detailed and scientifically informed approach toward implementing motivational school culture responsive to individual children necessitates a coordinated effort among scientists and researchers who need to continue contributing research in this field; academic faculty involved with training educators; school personnel including administrators, teachers, school psychologists, counselors, and others; families and peers who need to be included in the process; and students who will both benefit from the coordination of these efforts and who will contribute to their solution through the development of their motivational and cultural inputs to education. With the combined efforts of all, a multidisciplinary approach can be taken to continue to refine academic motivation and the culture of schooling for the betterment of children, families, schools, and our society as a whole.

⊞ References

Bronfenbrenner, U. (1979). *The ecology of human development: Experiments by nature and design.* Cambridge, MA: Harvard University Press.

Maehr, M. L., & Fyans, L. J., Jr. (1989). School culture, motivation, and achievement. In M. L. Maehr & C. Ames (Eds.), *Advances in motivation and achievement: A research annual* (Vol. 6, pp. 215–247). Greenwich, CT: JAI Press.

14 ::

Social Competence, Sociocultural Contexts, and School Success

Kathryn R. Wentzel

The chapters in this volume provide a powerful and convincing argument that an understanding of children's social and academic successes and failures at school requires a careful and honest appraisal of the social contexts in which children are asked to learn. The authors discuss these contexts with reference to students' social relationships with teachers, peers, and parents; social aspects of learning structures; and the value and belief systems that define school culture and guide school-level decision making. One of the central messages of this work is that the nature and quality of these contexts has a profound effect on students' functioning in educational settings, often by way of students' sense of self and motivation to engage in school-based activities.

In this commentary, I discuss three general issues and themes that are reflected in these papers. The first concerns the notion that social competence is central to the task of learning and school success. Second, issues surrounding the goals that are relevant for understanding school adjustment are discussed. Indeed, if social competence is an integral part of school success, how do we identify and examine the socially valued goals that we would like students to achieve? Finally, processes of influence and theoretical issues related to social contexts and schooling are described. If sociocultural contexts are important for students' school-based competencies, how and why might this be so? I close with some general conclusions and provocations for future research in this area.

:: Perspectives on Social Competence

Much of the work described in this volume is predicated on the assumption that school success and various aspects of academic performance reflect social behavioral skills and motivation more than intellectual abilities. Implicit in these approaches is the notion that educational tasks are inherently social in nature and therefore, student success is a reflection of social competence. Indeed, many scholars have argued that the development and expression of discrete intellectual skills can be understood as a function of sociocultural contexts (e.g., Greenfield, 1997). It also is clear that school-based indicators of cognitive functioning are reflective of social-cognitive skills such as detection and interpretation of social cues in coordination with self-regulatory skills such as goal setting, evaluating levels of efficacy and self-determination, and emotion regulation (e.g., Rouse & Fantuzzo, this volume).

Beyond a recognition that learning is a social endeavor, how might this approach help scholars and educators better understand children's adjustment to school? In the social developmental literature, social competence has been described from a variety of perspectives ranging from the development of individual skills to more general adaptation within a particular setting. In these discussions, social competence frequently is associated with person-level outcomes such as effective behavioral repertoires, social problem-solving skills, positive beliefs about the self, achievement of social goals, and positive interpersonal relationships (see Rose-Krasnor, 1997). In addition, central to many definitions of social competence is the notion that social contexts are believed to play an integral role in providing opportunities for healthy development of these outcomes as well as in defining the appropriate parameters of children's social accomplishments (e.g., Bronfenbrenner, 1989). Therefore, social competence reflects a balance between the achievement of positive outcomes for the individual student as well as a student's adherence to context-specific expectations for behavior.

Support for defining social competence as person-environment fit can be found in the work of several theorists (e.g., Bronfenbrenner, 1989; Eccles & Midgley, 1989; Ford, 1992). Bronfenbrenner (1989) argues that competence can only be understood in terms of context-specific effectiveness, being a product of personal attributes such as goals, values, self-regulatory skills, and cognitive abilities, and of ways in which these attributes contribute to meeting situational requirements and demands. Bronfenbrenner further suggests that competence is facilitated by contextual supports that provide opportunities for the growth and development of these personal attributes as well as for learning what is expected by the social group. Ford (1992) expands on this notion of person-environment fit by specifying four dimensions of competence that reflect personal as well as context-specific outcomes: the achievement of personal goals; the achievement of goals that are situationally relevant; the use of appropriate means to achieve these goals; and the accomplishment of goals that result in positive developmental outcomes for the individual.

The application of ecologically based models of social competence to the realm of schooling results in a multifaceted description of children who are socially competent and well adjusted. First, socially competent students achieve goals that are personally valued as well as those that are sanctioned by others. Second, the goals they pursue result in social integration as well as in positive developmental outcomes for the student. Socially integrative outcomes are those that promote the smooth functioning of social groups at school (e.g., cooperative behavior) and are reflected in levels of social approval and social acceptance; student-related outcomes reflect healthy development of the self (e.g., perceived social competence, feelings of self-determination) and feelings of emotional well-being (Bronfenbrenner, 1989; Ford, 1992). From this description it follows that social competence is achieved to the extent that students accomplish goals that have personal as well as social value in a manner that supports continued psychological and emotional health. In addition, the ability to be socially competent is contingent on opportunities and affordances in the school context that allow students to pursue multiple goals.

Applied to the work described in this volume, an ecological perspective highlights the central importance of social contexts for promoting positive student outcomes and, in some cases, what happens when they do not adequately support the needs of children. At the broad level of school culture, Eccleston and Major describe how school culture can reflect prevailing ethnic and gender stereotypes that can result in students' less than adaptive psychological and emotional functioning, devaluing of achievement, and disengagement from the schooling process. Similarly, Irving points out the role of the dominant culture in promoting student beliefs that social discrimination is responsible for their low levels of success. Thorkildsen and her colleagues also point to the dual role of school structure and culture in the development of students' belief systems and their levels of moral engagement. Chapters by Warzon and

Ginsburg-Block and by Romo and colleagues highlight the additional importance of family and community contexts for student motivation, social-emotional functioning, and academic engagement. This work also highlights the need for home-school communication and continuity.

At the classroom and instructional level, Hudley and Daoud describe school culture in terms of a system of values, beliefs, and goals that define and organize the activities and interactions of school members. Focusing specifically on teacher support, they note that some teachers hold negative expectations for ethnic minority students' behavioral, motivational, and intellectual capabilities and that this can result in students' feelings of alienation and ultimately disengagement. In turn, Welch describes specific ways that teachers can promote engagement and increase achievement by fostering the development of a "scholar" self-concept in students. This "scholar identity" can counter the negative effects of discrimination and negative expectations. Ginsburg-Block and her colleagues describe how peer-assisted learning (e.g., collaborative and cooperative learning structures) can promote the development of students' pro-academic norms and positive social and self-concepts.

Motivational contexts are an additional theme in this volume. Rouse and Fantuzzo illustrate how a developmental-ecological framework can inform understanding of the interactive role of motivation and classroom supports in facilitating academic growth over time. Similarly, Gottfried's work demonstrates the importance of understanding motivation in context. She and her colleagues also remind us of the universality of sociocultural influences and the fact that all children are at risk for less than adaptive outcomes at school.

As a collective, these authors provide striking examples of how both distal and proximal contexts can provide excellent resources that promote the development of individual students as well as the goals of education. They also illustrate the potential damage to children's social, emotional, and intellectual well-being when a balance between the goals and needs of the student and those valued within these contexts is not achieved.

⠃⠃ Goals for Students

Social competence as discussed in this chapter reflects the importance of achieving context-specific goals that result in positive outcomes. Achieving a balanced "fit" between the needs of the individual and those of the broader educational environment requires a focused consideration of the goals that children expect to achieve as well as the goals others expect them to achieve when they are at school. Therefore, a full appreciation of how and why students thrive or fail to thrive at school requires an understanding of not only a student's goals but also those of adults in school, peers, and parents. With respect to adults, perhaps the most important task for understanding the sociocultural contexts of learning is to come to terms with fundamental questions that are central to the education of children: What are our educational goals for our children? Do we want to teach simply to the test or nurture our children in ways that will help them become productive and healthy adults and citizens? By the same token, what are the goals that children bring with them to school? Do they strive to excel in relation to their peers, satisfy their curiosities, get along with others, feel safe? Which goals result in the formation and maintenance of positive relationships with teachers and peers at school? How do children define social competence for themselves and each other?

To understand fully children's adjustment to school, it is imperative that we continue to seek answers to these questions and identify ways to coordinate the often antagonistic goals of adults and children to achieve a healthy balance of multiple objectives. A consideration of self-enhancing as well as socially integrative outcomes as dual components of social competence is important because the achievement of personal goals and social acceptance are not always compatible. Indeed, the process of achieving more adaptive levels of adjustment will always include negotiations, compromise, and coordination of the multiple and often conflicting goals of teachers, peers, students themselves, and their parents.

Although we are beginning to understand the basic goals that most adults and students wish to achieve, we know little about how and why students come to learn about and ultimately to adopt these goals as their own. For instance, how do adults communicate their expectations and goals to students and which factors predispose students to accept or reject these communications? We know that parental messages are more likely to be perceived accurately by children if they are clear and consistent, are framed in ways that are relevant and meaningful to the child, require decoding and processing by the child, are perceived by the child to be of clear importance to the parent, and are conveyed with positive intentions (Grusec & Goodnow, 1994). Do these same factors reflect effective forms of teacher-student communication and if so, can we teach teachers to communicate goals and expectations to their students in similar ways?

Also, we need to focus on understanding student characteristics that facilitate their acceptance of adults' communications. Motivational factors such as perceived autonomy, competence, and belongingness (e.g., Connell & Wellborn, 1991), and social-emotional competencies such as the ability to experience empathy and interpersonal trust (see Grusec & Goodnow, 1994) are well-documented correlates of compliance with, if not internalization of, socially valued goals. Other factors such as students' beliefs regarding the fairness, relevance, and developmental appropriateness of teachers' goals and expectations also need to be investigated in this regard (e.g., Smetana & Bitz, 1996). Social information processing skills that determine which social messages and cues are attended to, how they are interpreted, and how they are responded to are additional, critical components of socially competent behavior (Crick & Dodge, 1994). These skills have been widely researched in the area of peer relationships; extending our knowledge of their influence to the realm of teacher-student relationships and adaptation to classroom contexts is a necessary next step in research on students' competence at school.

Finally, if the achievement of socially valued goals is a critical component of students' adjustment to school, investigations of appropriate goals and expectations need to be conducted within a developmental framework. To illustrate, although children are interested in and even emotionally attached to their peers at all ages, they exhibit increased interest in their peers, spend more time with them, and exhibit a growing psychological and emotional dependence on them for support and guidance as they make the transition into adolescence (Youniss & Smollar, 1989). Therefore, efforts to understand the contributions of peer interactions to school adjustment must be sensitive to the peer relationship goals that students wish to achieve at different points in their educational careers.

Grolnick and her colleagues (Grolnick, Kurowski, & Gurland, 1999) also argue that children face normative motivational challenges as they make their way through school, with issues of social integration defining their initial transition to school, and flexible coping and adaptation to new environments marking the transitions into middle and high school. Therefore, contextual supports might be more important for goal coordination and accomplishments at different stages of schooling. Last, the role of context as it interacts with individual differences and psychological processes needs careful and systematic consideration. Models need to reflect the possible ways that children and their various social systems interact to create expectations and goals for school-based competence (see Bronfenbrenner, 1989); such social systems are the ones in which children develop, including home, peer groups, and schools. How the coordination of these systems changes as children develop and ways in which they jointly contribute to children's developing school-related goal hierarchies should be a primary target of researchers' efforts.

:: Processes of Influence

In addition to exploring issues concerning the nature of social competence at school and how to achieve a healthy balance of personal and socially valued goals, researchers also need to understand why these social and contextual supports and resources result in positive outcomes for children. At a broad level, the supports described in this volume can be viewed in terms of general mechanisms that can influence competence development. First, the structure and general features of social contexts afford opportunities and resources that can directly support or hinder competence development. Within the context of schools, structural features such as school and class size, teacher-student ratios, and funding can influence the amount and quality of social and instructional resources and opportunities available to students. Second, ongoing social interactions teach children about themselves and what they need to do to become accepted and competent members of their social worlds. Within the context of these interactions, children develop a set of goals and standards for behavior they strive to achieve (Grusec & Goodnow, 1994). Social interactions and dyadic relationships with teachers and peers at school are examples of these more proximal contexts that can influence student adjustment.

Beyond these general mechanisms, however, what are the specific ways in which social interactions and support might contribute to children's learning and development? If we improve school structures and the nature and quality of children's relationships with others, will their academic abilities and performance also improve? Understanding of the mechanisms whereby various social supports might influence school-related outcomes is fairly limited. Although somewhat speculative, we can reasonably assume that students who contribute to the positive functioning of their classes and their school are more likely to earn higher grades than those who do not, simply because they will be rewarded for doing what they are supposed to do. Rewards are likely to take the form of social acceptance and approval. Being liked and appreciated by others also is likely to result in more academic help and assistance from teachers and peers, which in turn should lead to higher grades. Engaging in socially valued behavior in the classroom also leads students to attend to and participate in instructional activities to a greater degree.

It also is feasible that social competence leads directly to academic accomplishments because it has a direct impact on cognitive development. For example, Piaget (e.g., 1983) proposed that mutual discussion, perspective taking, and conflict resolution with peers can motivate the accommodation of new and more sophisticated approaches to intellectual problem solving. Vygotsky (1978) suggested that peer relationships contribute directly to the development of academic skills when competent students teach specific learning strategies and standards for performance to peers who are less skilled. The specific processes described by Ginsburg-Block et al. also illustrate the complex pathways by which such interactions promote positive social and motivational outcomes that in turn support learning and intellectual development.

A final approach that integrates all of these perspectives to some extent argues that students who wish to achieve academically should engage in academic activities when they perceive their school and their relationships with their teachers and peers as providing specific supports that can promote healthy adjustment to school (Ford, 1992; see also Wentzel, 2004). These supports can be defined along four dimensions: clear communication of expectations for achievement; instrumental help; a safe classroom environment; and emotional nurturance and caring. These dimensions reflect essential components of social support in that (1) information is provided concerning what is expected and valued in the classroom; (2) attempts to achieve these valued outcomes are met with help and instruction; (3) attempts to achieve outcomes can be made in a safe, nonthreatening environment; and (4) students are made to feel like a valued member of the group. Moreover, these dimensions of support have utility for understanding parents' inputs and influences on their children's school success (Grusec & Goodnow, 1994). Summaries of best practices for educating minority students also include these aspects of supportive relationships as essential for effective classroom teaching (Rutherford, 1999; Scribner & Reyes, 1999).

In general, empirical evidence indicates that these various aspects of support from teachers and peers are related to students' motivation to achieve positive social and academic goals at school as well as to objective indices of academic achievement. Indeed, the various programs of research described in this volume reflect ways in which contexts provide (or fail to provide) information concerning goals and values (e.g., Eccleston & Major; Ginsburg-Block et al.; Gottfried et al.; Romo et al.; Welch; Rouse & Fantuzzo; Thorkildsen et al.), instrumental help and instruction (e.g., Ginsburg-Block et al.; Warzon & Ginsburg-Block; Rouse & Fantuzzo; Welch), a sense of safety and mutual trust, and emotional caring (Hudley & Daoud; Irving). Although still fairly limited, research also shows that students' motivation to achieve these goals serves as a mediator between opportunities afforded by these social supports and academic accomplishments (e.g., Wentzel, Filisetti, & Looney, 2007).

True, students must have some desire to achieve academically to enjoy the benefits of these supports; however, communication of expectations and values in conjunction with emotional caring can lead them to adopt these goals. When their interpersonal relationships are responsive and nurturant, children are more likely to adopt and internalize the expectations and goals that are valued by others than if their relationships are harsh and critical (Grusec & Goodnow, 1994; Ryan, 1993). As illustrated by some of the findings reported in this volume (e.g., Hudley & Daoud), positive social supports do not always result in academic gains. It is clear that supportive sociocultural contexts must also include instructional strategies and practices that result in the acquisition of knowledge and intellectual advances.

Schools can also have effects on children by their positive impact on the economic (Sederberg, 1987) and political (Reynolds, 1995) life of communities; school-to-work and service learning programs are good examples of school-based resources that can provide positive benefits to communities and families. The notion that community and family effects might mediate the impact of schools on children is intriguing but rarely studied in a systematic fashion. Therefore, a necessary next step is the development of conceptual models that consider the various social systems in which children develop, including home, peer groups, communities, and schools, and the ways these systems and children interact; such explorations could provide further clues to helping students develop school-related competence.

∷ Theory Development

Although viable mechanisms of influence have been proposed, theoretical considerations of school-based competence also must continue to focus on underlying psychological processes and skills that promote the development and display of positive student outcomes. To illustrate, researchers have clearly established significant and powerful links between prosocial and socially responsible behaviors and academic accomplishments. What have not been identified as clearly, however, are the psychological underpinnings of these behaviors.

Research on skills and strategies involved in emotion regulation, self-regulated learning, social information processing, and goal coordination might be particularly fruitful in determining the degree to which multiple aspects of school adjustment (e.g., prosocial behavior, academic performance) are supported by a core set of psychological and emotional competencies and the degree to which social behaviors themselves contribute directly to learning outcomes. The logical next step would then be to identify ways to help students develop these critical skills (e.g., see Welch, this volume). Other individual characteristics such as attachment security and family functioning (e.g., Fuligni, Eccles, Barber, & Clements, 2001), racial identity (Graham, Taylor, & Hudley, 1998), and the extent that students are oriented toward gaining social approval are also likely to influence the degree to which they are susceptible to social influence and require further study.

As noted by many of the authors in this volume, models of school-based competence also need to account for a diversity of student backgrounds and experiences. Indeed, much of what we know about these processes comes from studies of White, middle-class children. In addition to the research described herein, other researchers have found that supportive relationships with teachers might benefit minority students and girls in achieving positive behavioral and academic outcomes to a greater extent than Caucasian students and boys (e.g., Crosnoe & Needham, 2004). Adolescent peer group studies have shown that African American youth might face conflict between parental and peer values that could have a negative impact on their academic achievement (Steinberg, Brown, & Dornbusch, 1996). Hispanic adolescents are more likely than their non-Hispanic peers to be highly connected to parents and family members, with levels of family interdependence and closeness being related positively to healthy academic and social functioning

(Ceballo, 2004; Martinez, DeGarmo, & Eddy, 2004; Phinney, Kim-Jo, Osorio, & Vilhjalmsdottir, 2005). Therefore, enjoying supportive relationships at home might be a relatively strong, positive predictor of school
success for these young adolescents even when positive supports are
experienced at school.

Similarly, goal coordination skills might be more important for the
adjustment of children from minority backgrounds than for children
who come from families and communities whose expectations, educational goals, and definitions of student success are likely to vary as
a function of race, gender, neighborhood, and family background. In
short, expanding our database to include the voices of underrepresented
populations can only enrich our understanding of ways to create optimal classroom contexts within which all children can thrive socially as
well as academically.

Finally, the moderating effects of broader contextual factors requires
further study. For instance, in response to findings reported by the National Institute of Child Health and Human Development (NICHD) Child
Care Study, researchers have argued that when child care variables are
assessed in more diverse samples that include a broader range of socioeconomic statuses (SES) and ethnicity, different results are obtained (e.g.,
Sagi, Koren-Karie, Gini, Ziv, & Joels, 2002). Researchers of older children
also have found that race moderates relations between dropping out of
school and features of students' schools and families, such that the SES
of families and schools predicts dropping out for White and Hispanic
adolescents but not for African American students (Rumberger, 1995).
Some studies also have demonstrated differential teacher treatment of
students as a function of student gender, race (Irvine, 1986), and behavioral styles (Chang, 2003), with these differences sometimes attributed in
part, to teachers' own race and gender (Saft & Pianta, 2001).

∷ Conclusions

In closing, the goal of this chapter has been to provide some additional
insights into the nature of school-related competence and how it might
be supported by students' experiences within broader sociocultural contexts, including relationships with their parents, teachers, and peers; social aspects of learning structures; and the value and belief systems that
define school cultures and the communities they are in. In conjunction

with the other chapters in this volume, the hope is to provide a foundation to explore further the role of social experiences and contexts in supporting the social and intellectual accomplishments of all children.

Identifying ways in which social contexts promote the development of social and academic competencies at school requires systematic experimental research over time. However, experimental studies designed to examine processes that support social competence development in schools are rare (cf. Solomon, Schaps, Watson, & Battistich, 1992). Moreover, most school reform efforts focus on improving achievement test scores and other academic outcomes (e.g., No Child Left Behind Act of 2001) without consideration of the social and psychological consequences of these efforts. Given the strong interrelations among school success, qualities of relationships with teachers and peers, classroom climate, and school cultures, it seems essential that reform initiatives involving experimentation in schools and evaluation of student progress incorporate assessments of processes and outcomes informed by a broader sociocultural perspective.

‡‡ References

Bronfenbrenner, U. (1989). Ecological systems theory. In R. Vasta (Ed.), *Annals of child development* (Vol. 6, pp. 187–250). Greenwich, CT: JAI.

Ceballo, R. (2004). From barrios to Yale: The role of parenting strategies in Latino families. *Hispanic Journal of Behavioral Sciences, 26,* 171–186.

Chang, L. (2003). Variable effects of children's aggression, social withdrawal, and prosocial leadership as functions of teacher beliefs and behaviors. *Child Development, 74,* 535–548.

Connell, J. P., & Wellborn, J. G. (1991). Competence, autonomy, and relatedness: A motivational analysis of self-system processes. In M. R. Gunnar & L. A. Sroufe (Eds.), *Self processes and development: The Minnesota symposia on child development* (Vol. 23, pp. 43–78). Hillsdale, NJ: Erlbaum.

Crick, N., & Dodge, K. A. (1994). A review and reformulation of social information-processing mechanisms in children's social adjustment. *Psychological Bulletin, 115,* 74–101.

Crosnoe, R., & Needham, B. (2004). Holism, contextual variability, and the study of friendships in adolescent development. *Child Development, 75,* 264–279.

Eccles, J. S., & Midgley, C. (1989). Stage-environment fit: Developmentally appropriate classrooms for young adolescents. In C. Ames &

R. Ames (Eds.), *Research on motivation in education* (Vol. 3, pp. 139–186). New York: Academic Press.

Ford, M. E. (1992). *Motivating humans: Goals, emotions, and personal agency beliefs.* Newbury Park, CA: Sage.

Fuligni, A. J., Eccles, J. S., Barber, B. L., & Clements, P. (2001). Early adolescent peer orientation and adjustment during high school. *Developmental Psychology, 37,* 28–36.

Graham, S., Taylor, A., & Hudley, C. (1998). Exploring achievement values among ethnic minority early adolescents. *Journal of Educational Psychology, 90,* 606–620.

Greenfield, P. M. (1997). You can't take it with you—Why ability assessments don't cross cultures. *American Psychologist, 52,* 1115–1124.

Grolnick, W. S., Kurowski, C. O., & Gurland, S. T. (1999). Family processes and the development of children's self-regulation. *Educational Psychologist, 34,* 3–14.

Grusec, J. E., & Goodnow, J. J. (1994). Impact of parental discipline methods on the child's internalization of values: A reconceptualization of current points of view. *Developmental Psychology, 30,* 4–19.

Irvine, J. J. (1986). Teacher student interactions-Effects of student race, sex, and grade level. *Journal of Educational Psychology, 78,* 14–21.

Martinez, C. R., DeGarmo, D. S., & Eddy, J. M. (2004). Promoting academic success among Latino youths. *Hispanic Journal of Behavioral Sciences, 26,* 128–151.

Phinney, J. S., Kim-Jo, T., Osorio, S., & Vilhjalmsdottir, P. (2005). Autonomy and relatedness in adolescent-parent disagreements: Ethnic and developmental factors. *Journal of Adolescent Research, 20,* 8–39.

Piaget, J. (1983). Piaget's theory. In P. H. Mussen (Ed.), *Handbook of child psychology* (Vol. 1, pp. 103–128). New York: Wiley.

Reynolds, D. R. (1995). Rural education: Decentering the consolidation debate. In E. N. Castle (Ed.), *The changing American countryside: Rural people and places* (pp. 451–480). Lawrence: University Press of Kansas.

Rose-Krasnor, L. (1997). The nature of social competence: A theoretical review. *Social Development, 6,* 111–135.

Rumberger, R. W. (1995). Dropping out of middle school: A multilevel analysis of students and schools. *American Educational Research Journal, 32,* 583–625.

Rutherford, W. (1999). Creating student-centered classroom environments: The case of reading. In P. Reyes, J. D. Scribner, & A. P. Scribner (Eds.), *Lessons from high-performing Hispanic schools: Creating learning communities* (pp. 131–168). New York: Teachers College Press.

Ryan, R. M. (1993). Agency and organization: Intrinsic motivation, autonomy, and the self in psychological development. In J. Jacobs

(Ed.), *Nebraska symposium on motivation* (Vol. 40, pp. 1–56). Lincoln: University of Nebraska Press.

Saft, E. W., & Pianta, R. C. (2001). Teachers' perceptions of their relationships with students: Effects of child age, gender, and ethnicity of teachers and children. *School Psychology Quarterly, 16,* 125–141.

Sagi, A., Koren-Karie, N., Gini, M., Ziv, Y., & Joels, T. (2002). Shedding further light on the effects of various types and quality of early child care on infant-mother attachment relationship: The Haifa study of early child care. *Child Development, 73,* 1166–1186.

Scribner, J. D., & Reyes, P. (1999). Creating learning communities for high performing Hispanic students: A conceptual framework. In P. Reyes, J. D. Scribner, & A. P. Scribner (Eds.), *Lessons from high-performing Hispanic schools: Creating learning communities* (pp. 188–210). New York: Teachers College Press.

Sederberg, C. H. (1987). Economic role of school districts in rural communities. *Research in Rural Education, 4,* 125–130.

Smetana, J., & Bitz, B. (1996). Adolescents' conceptions of teachers' authority and their relations to rule violations in school. *Child Development, 67,* 1153–1172.

Solomon, D., Schaps, E., Watson, M., & Battistich, V. (1992). Creating caring school and classroom communities for all students. In R. Villa, J. Thousand, W. Stainback, & S. Stainback (Eds.), *Restructuring for caring and effective education: An administrative guide to creating heterogeneous schools* (pp. 41–60). Baltimore: Brookes.

Steinberg, L., Brown, B. B., & Dornbusch, S. M. (1996). *Beyond the classroom: Why school reform has failed and what parents need to do.* New York: Simon and Schuster.

Vygotsky, L. S. (1978). *Mind in society: The development of higher psychological processes.* Cambridge, MA: Harvard University Press.

Wentzel, K. R. (2004). Understanding classroom competence: The role of social-motivational and self-processes. In R. Kail (Ed.), *Advances in child development and behavior* (Vol. 32, pp. 213–241). New York: Elsevier.

Wentzel, K. R., Filisetti, L., & Looney, L. (2007). Adolescent prosocial behavior: The role of self-processes and contextual cues. *Child Development, 78,* 895–910.

Youniss, J., & Smollar, J. (1989). *Adolescents' interpersonal relationships in social context.* In T. J. Berndt & G. Ladd (Eds.), Peer relationships in child development (pp. 300–316). New York: Wiley.

Index ∷

AC. *See* Academic Controversy
academic achievement, 153
   competence motivation and, 26
   cultural mistrust and, 156
   ethnicity and, 165–66
   gender and, 165–66
   good teaching practices and, 134
   high school, 45, 49, 51
   measuring, 40
   parents influence on, 103
   student perceptions of, 242
Academic Controversy (AC), 264
academic identities, 222, 236
academic motivation inventory (AMI), 128
academic stereotypes, 177
academic underachievement, 4
ACASI. *See* audio computer-assisted
   self-interviews
achievement gap, 122, 165
   Black-White, 228
achievement goal theory, 251, 254
"acting white," 225
action readiness
   civil identities and, 91, 91*f*, 92*t*, 93*t*
   cluster analysis of, 90
   cultural identities and, 90–91
   in engagement, 88–90
   evaluation of, 90
   ideal school standards and, 92*t*, 93*t*
   internal consistency of, 89
African American Academic Outcome
   Expectations Scale, 153

allegiances, national, 77
AMI. *See* academic motivation inventory
anxiety, 55
   intrinsic motivation and, 58
   stereotypes and, 178
assigned solidarities, 76
at-risk motivation. *See* motivational risk
attachment security, 306
audio computer-assisted self-interviews
   (ACASI), 110
autonomy, 21
   intrinsic motivation and, 254

BESD. *See* binomial effect size
   display
bilingualism, 196
   limits for education in, 194
   negative reactions to, 204–6, 208
   as problem, 190
binomial effect size display (BESD), 44
birth control, 105, 108, 112
birthrates, teenage, 99
"border crossing" activities, 225

CAAI. *See* Children's Academic Anxiety
   Inventory
CAIMI. *See* Children's Academic
   Intrinsic Motivation Inventory
CCP. *See* Cultural Continuity Project
CD. *See* cultural discontinuity
cheating, 90
childbearing. *See* pregnancy, teenage

child competencies, 16
  age-salient, identifying, 26
  context, 16
  multidimensionality, 17
  person-centered empirical approaches
    to, 24
  process, 16
  time, 16
  unidimensional, 17
  unobservable, 17
child development, 16, 267
child-initiated discovery, 27
Children's Academic Anxiety Inventory
    (CAAI), 41–42
Children's Academic Intrinsic
    Motivation Inventory (CAIMI), 40,
    196
  scoring of, 42
citizenship, 75–76
civic responsibility, 85
civil identities
  action readiness and, 91, 91f, 92t, 93t
  assessing, 83t–84t
  classifications, 86t
  cluster analysis of, 85
  engagement and, 91–94
  ideal schools and, 89f, 91, 92t, 93t
  unformed, 88, 287
civil projects, commitment to, 94
civil rights movement, 150, 151
civil solidarities, 74–75
  nurturing, 94–96
civil sphere, 74
  boundaries of, 79
  capitalistic notion of, 75
  deterministic notion of, 75
  preparation for participation in, 92
civil sphere, pluralistic, 75, 76, 78,
    280, 287
CL. See learning, cooperative
classism, 148, 190
classroom functioning, 51
  measuring, 41
cluster analysis
  of action readiness, 90
  of civil identities, 85
CMI. See Revised Cultural Mistrust
    Inventory
cognitive competencies, 21–22
cognitive development, 249, 304
cognitive social learning theory, 283

cohort comparison, 44, 46t–48t, 50t
college
  attendance analyses, 55–56
  enrollment rate, 222
  graduation rate, 165
college aspirations
  parents influence on, 112, 113t
  sexual activity and, 109–14
Comer's School Development Program,
    139
communication, teacher-student, 301–2
competence perception, 55, 61
competitiveness, 258
consumerism, 189
contact theory, 212
continuation schools. See schools,
    alternative
contraceptive use, 99
Cooperative Integrated Reading and
    Comprehension, 267
coping strategies, 173
criterion-validity studies, 128
cultural awareness, 134
  teachers and, 138
  training, 138
cultural bias, 193, 289
cultural compatibility, 9
cultural continuity, 122, 291. See also
    cultural discontinuity
  behavioral aspects of, 135
  debate, 123
  families and, 125
  family satisfaction and, 129
  home and school, between, 7–8
  literature on, 136
  as measure of interpersonal relations,
    135
  needs assessments for, site-specific,
    137
  relationship satisfaction and, 125
  social contextual variables
    and, 124
  student perceptions of, 125
  teachers and, 125
  teacher satisfaction and, 129
  validating, 135
Cultural Continuity Project (CCP),
    126–39, 291
  data analysis, 130–33
  descriptive portion of, 126–27
  ethnic composition of, 127

evaluations in, 125
findings, 130–35
first steps of, 124–26
generalization of, 136
implications of, 137–39
limitations of, 135–37
measures for, 128–30
motivation and, 128
next steps in, 135–37
participants, 126–27
procedure for, 127–28
purpose of, 126
recommendations, 137
research questions, 126
cultural discontinuity (CD), 281, 291. *See
    also* cultural continuity
families and teachers, between, 125
family satisfaction and, 130
good teaching practices and, 131–32,
    132*f*
home and school, between, 6–7, 123,
    124, 134
measuring, 129
motivation and, 130–32, 133–34
reading fluency and, 130–32, 132*f*
student perceptions of, 123, 125
teacher, 129
teacher satisfaction and, 130
cultural ecological theory, 156, 211
cultural mistrust and, 157
cultural eye, seeing with, 228, 239
cultural identities, 87–88
action readiness and, 90–91
cultural mistrust, 149–51, 281, 290, 291
academic achievement and, 156
academic functioning and, 151
academic outcome expectations and,
    153–54, 155, 156
cultural ecological theory and, 157
development of, 150
examining, 151–52
gender and, 152
across geographic regions, 151
measuring, 152–53
mental health services and, 150
motivation variables and, 155
reducing, 158
research on, 150, 155
cultural paranoia, healthy, 150, 155
cultural sensitivity, 192
cultural stereotypes, 149

culture, 180
broad, 169
dominant, 299
levels of, 169
local, 169
systems view of, 188
United States, 189
culture-of-home advocates, 225

Dead Poets Society, 75
degrees, types of, 56
devaluation, 167–68
deviant behavior, 102, 115
approval of, 101
disciplining, 240–41
disengagement, 23–24, 90–91, 173–77.
    See also engagement
chronic, 174
engagement v., 89
motivation and, 174–75
peer-assisted learning and, 258
progressive, 194
of self-esteem, 173, 174
situation specific, 174
disidentification, 173–77
dropout rates, 49, 222
dysconscious racism, 193

education
bilingual, limits for, 194
ethical features of, 81
goals, 301
as independent social sphere, 74
internal consistency of, 89
poor performance in, 8
pregnancy and, 105
social, 298
understanding of, 95
emotional caring, 305
emotion regulation, 21, 306
empathy, 302
Encouraging Excellence in Children
    Extends Learning. *See* Project
    EXCEL
engagement, 81–82, 187. *See also*
    disengagement
action readiness in, 88–90
biased attitudes influencing, 193
civil identities and, 91–94
disengagement v., 89
educational policy research on, 82

identities
  academic, 222, 236
  construction of, 223
  establishment of, 235–36
  normative developmental task of
    developing, 242
  student perceptions of, 236
  unformed, 88, 287
  United States, 210
identities, civil
  action readiness and, 91, 91f, 92t, 93t
  assessing, 83t–84t
  classifications, 86t
  cluster analysis of, 85
  engagement and, 91–94
  ideal schools and, 89f, 91, 92t, 93t
  unformed, 88, 287
identities, cultural, 87–88
  action readiness and, 90–91
identities, ethnic, 85, 87t
  measure of, 158
identities, local, 85, 87t
  assignment of, 84
identities, racial, 293, 306
  measure of, 158
identity-safe environments, 177
identity threat, stigma-induced, 167
individual accountability, 261
individualism, 4, 189, 206, 258, 279
influence
  peer, 101–2
  teacher's, 205
influence, parental, 102–4
  on academic achievement, 103
  on academic success, 103
  on alternative schools, 104–5
  on college aspirations, 112, 113t
  on personal life decisions, 114
  on pregnancy, 109, 115
  on school culture, 115
intellectual conflict, 264
intellectual performance, 51–52
  measuring, 41
intelligence, fixed, 178
Intelligence Quotient (IQ)
  motivational risk and, 52, 58
  prediction of, 53, 54
interpersonal behavior problems (IBP), 23
intervention programs, 10, 15, 292
  peer-assisted learning and, 248, 253
involuntary solidarities, 77

language barriers, 125
learning. *See also* peer-assisted
    learning
  motivation for general, 256
  readiness, 288
  scaffolding, 251
  self-regulated, 306
  skills, independent, 27
  small group cooperative, 247
  social competence and, 297
  social contexts, 297
  social-emotional, 248
  as social endeavor, 298
learning behaviors, 17–18
  attention, 18, 19
  attentive regulated, 21
  attitude toward learning, 18, 19
  buffering effect and, 18
  flexibility, 18
  incorporating, intentionally, 28–29
  independent learner, 21
  persistence, 18, 19
  predictive validity of, 18
  programmatic, 18
  reinforcing, 30
  reporting mechanism, 30
  scope of, 29
  sequence of, 29
  as social enterprise, 247
  strategy, 18
learning, cooperative (CL), 261, 264
  application of, 265
  format of, 261
  group processing, 264
  interpersonal, 264
Learning Links, 29
Learning, Student Team, 265
Learning Together (LT), 264
life goals, 85, 95
The Little Brown Reader, 229, 233
local identities, 85, 87t
  assignment of, 84
LT. *See* Learning Together

marginality, 221
marginalized representation, 242
mastery goal, 251
mediation model, 53–54, 58
mental health services, 150
meta-cognitive strategies, 80
moral engagement, 7

motivation
  adverse outcomes and low, 37
  beliefs and, student, 147–48
  as cognitive engagement, 136
  community contexts for, 300
  for content area, 256
  Cultural Continuity Project and, 128
  cultural discontinuity and, 130–32, 133–34
  cultural mistrust and, 155
  determinants of, 170–77
  developmental role of, 286
  disengagement and, 174–75
  early childhood, 5–6
  ecological approach to, 292
  engagement and, 280
  enhancing, 9, 282–83
  expectancy theories of, 8–9
  expectancy value model of, 147
  expectations and, 170–71
  family contexts for, 300
  family satisfaction and, 132–33
  for general learning, 256
  low, progressive, 288
  as outcome, 294
  over time, 5, 278–80
  partial mediation of, 53f
  peer-assisted learning and, 248, 252–57, 292–94
  as point of departure, 223
  responsibility for, 63
  reward structures and, 257
  for school, 256
  school culture and, 4–5, 278–79
  school entry through early adulthood, 6
  self-reflective construct of, 279
  social, 252, 258
  sociocultural environment and, 148
  stereotypes and, 175
  stigmatization and, 174–75
  student-centered instruction and, 251
  teacher satisfaction and, 132–33
  test outcome and, 52–53
  value theories of, 8–9
motivational disadvantage. *See* motivational risk
motivational giftedness, 42
motivational research
  advancement of, 3, 4
motivational risk, 6, 56, 287

  avoidance and, 57–58
  cohort comparison v., 44, 46t–48t, 50t
  double jeopardy, 59, 63
  in gifted girls, 37
  identification of, 36, 58
  identifying, 42
  Intelligence Quotient and, 48, 52
  long-term phenomenon of, 57
  socioeconomic disadvantage and, 61
  underlying processes of, 57–58
  withdrawal and, 57–58
motivation, competence, 18
  academic achievement and, 26
  developmental importance of, 25
  learning approaches and, 19–20
  as learning readiness predictor, 288
  mathematics achievement and, 22
  nonverbal cognitive ability and, 22
  play activities and, 20–21
  practical implications of, 28–29
  preschool, 24–25
  preschool, later school success and, 24–25
  school contexts and, transactions between, 27
  school readiness and, 20–24, 26
  spatial cognitive ability and, 22
  teacher observations of, 21
  variable-centered analyses, 24, 25
  verbal assertiveness and, 21
motivation, intrinsic, 17, 191, 258, 287
  anxiety and, 58
  attribution approach to, 61–62
  autonomy and, 254
  environment and, 62
  high, 36
  increasing stability of, 38, 59, 288
  low, 36
  measuring, 40
  overjustification approach to, 61–62
  peer-assisted learning and, 251, 261, 262t–263t
  school performance and, 37
multicultural educational theory, 159

national allegiances, 77
National Assessment of Educational Progress, 165
National Education Goals Panel 2000, 16
National Institute of Child Health and Human Development (NICHD), 307

NCLB. *See* No Child Left Behind
NICHD. *See* National Institute of Child
    Health and Human Development
No Child Left Behind (NCLB),
    15, 165
    criticism of, 15, 16
    implementation of, 30
nonconventional behavior, 115
nonverbal cognitive ability, 22
numerical minority, 169
    poor performance and, 170

OLS. *See* ordinary least squares
    estimation procedure
opinions, expression of, 233–35
ordinary least squares estimation
    procedure (OLS), 42
organizational behavior theory,
    277
otherness, 221

parental influence, 102–4
    on academic success, 103
    on alternative schools, 104–5
    on college aspirations, 112, 113*t*
    on personal life decisions, 114
    on pregnancy, 109, 115
    on school culture, 115
parents
    health issues and, 112, 114
    pregnancy and perceived attitudes
        of, 105
Parent Satisfaction with Educational
    Experiences (PSEE), 128
peer-assisted learning (PAL), 10, 247,
    283, 293
    acceptability of, 268
    accessibility of, 268
    adoption of, 266
    behavioral perspectives on, 250
    cognitive restructuring and, 249
    cooperative learning approaches and,
        248
    definitions of, multiple, 248
    disengagement and, 258
    effectiveness of, 11, 247, 266
    evaluation strategies, 253–54
    evidence-based, 248, 259–66
    experimental studies on, 250
    future research on, 266–68
    implementing, 267
    interventions, 11, 248, 253

intrinsic motivation and, 261,
    262*t*–263*t*
motivation and, 248, 252–57, 292–94
observational studies of, 250
school culture and, 250
streamlining, 267
theoretical basis for, 249–52
peer contagion, 7, 101
peer influences, negative, 101
peer interaction, 283, 302
peer norms, influence of, 101–2
peer relationships, 173, 304
    problematic, 206
peer socialization, 10
    towards achievement, 258
    alternative schools and, 115
peer tutoring. *See* reciprocal peer
    tutoring (RPT)
peer tutoring, dyadic, 247
performance goal, 251
pluralism. *See* civil sphere, pluralistic
positive interdependence, 261
pregnancy, teenage, 99, 291
    consequences of, 109
    as educational issue, 116
    education level and, 105
    friends attitudes towards, 105
    as hindrance, 114
    parental attitudes and, perceived, 105
    parents influence on, 109, 115
    positive perceptions of, 108–9
    second, 102
procrastination, 58
Project EXCEL, 10, 222, 292
    academic expectations and, 229
    analyzing data in, 228–30
    categorizing students in, 229
    collecting data in, 228–30
    conclusions about, 238–39
    criterion for, 238
    designing, 224
    findings, 239
    implementation of, 226–28
    integrating, 227
    themes, 230–38
Proposition 187, 194
Proposition 227, 194, 209–10

racial discrimination, 8, 148, 150,
    190, 225
    buffers against, 155
    survival strategies, 156

Self-Description Questionnaire II, 41–42
self-determination theory, 251, 254
self-esteem
    academic outcomes and, 173
    disengagement of, 173, 174
    protecting, 174
self-handicapping behaviors, 168–69
self-management strategies, classroom-
        based, 254, 259
sexual activity, 280–81
    at alternative schools, 102
    avoiding, 100
    college aspirations and, 109–14
    delaying, 99
    early, 102
    parents influence on, 103
    peer affiliations and, 108
    risky, 100
    social gains through, 102
sexuality beliefs, 103
sexuality values, 103
Situation Self-Efficacy for Condom Use
        Scale, 111
Slavin's Success for All, 139, 257–58, 267
soccer, 207–8
social acceptance, 27, 299
social approval, 299
social cognitions, 280–82
social competence, 298–300
    dual components of, 301
    ecologically based models of, 299
    learning and, 297
    person-level outcomes and, 298
social-emotional competencies, 20–21
social groups, 73
social identity theory, 210–11
social information processing skills, 302
social learning theory, 249, 293
social psychological theory, 212
social stereotypes, 190, 284
sociocultural environment, 148–49
    motivation and, 148
socioeconomic status (SES), 8, 36, 37, 39,
        59–61, 146, 168, 196, 282, 286, 287,
        290, 294, 295
solidarities
    assigned, 76
    between/within, 78–79
    choices, 82
    comparing, 78
    distributions of, 84–85

engagement and, 82–94
    involuntary, 77
    racial, 77
    shared, 94
    voluntary, 76, 77
solidarities, civil, 74–75
    nurturing, 94–96
spatial cognitive ability, 22
specific approaches to learning (SAL), 23
STAD. See Student Teams-Achievement
        Divisions
stereotype(s), 167, 223
    academic, 177
    activating, 172
    activating group, 168
    anxiety and, 178
    challenging, 179
    cultural, 149
    eliminating negative, 177, 178
    endorsing, 171
    ethnic, 167, 299
    gender, 167, 299
    identity-safe environments and, 177
    incompetence, 156
    leadership ability, 177
    motivation and, 175
    prejudice and, 175
    racial, 77
    research on, 168
    role models and, 179
    social, 190, 284
stereotype threat, 149, 156, 168, 281, 289
    on student performance, 290
    voluntary responses to, 168
stigmatization, 166, 167, 170–77, 289
    expectations for success and, 171–72
    motivation and, 174–75
    school culture and, 8
    underrepresentation and, 170
    value and, 172–73
student(s)
    motivation, beliefs and, 147–48
    Project EXCEL categorizing by, 229
student, perceptions of
    academic achievement, 242
    cultural discontinuity, 123, 125
    identities, 236
    school culture, 6
Student Teams-Achievement Divisions
        (STAD), 265
subgroup methodology, 38, 58